GLORY TO UKR

Do a good deed today and donate to Direct Relief (directrelief.org) to help the Ukraine people during the hard times they are going through!!!!! Direct Relief is working directly with Ukraine's Ministry of Health and other on -the-ground partners. Direct Relief is providing field medics with hundreds of emergency medical backpacks as well as a wide range of urgently requested supplies such as oxygen concentrators, antibiotics, Combat Application Tourniquets, and critical-care medicines. Direct Relief has been supporting hospitals in Ukraine since before the invasion began and has shipped more than 26 million in medical aid to the country in the past six months. However more supplies are still needed for the Ukrainian people!!!!!!!!!!!!!!!!!!!!!!!!!!!!!!!!!!!! If you were in the Ukrainian people's shoes would you want all the help you can receive from anywhere it comes? I think we all answered yes to that question so do a good deed today and donate whatever you can afford to help the people of Ukraine. Even if it is only one dollar!!!! It is not the amount that you donate, it is the thought and your intentions that "MATTERS MOST".

YOU BE THE JUDGE

THE PROSECUTOR THE JUDGE
MY ATTORNEY & THE F.B.O.P

VERSUS

AMANZE ANTOINE

AMANZE ANTOINE

Dedicated to all the unspoken and unheard girls, boys, men, and women who have been treated unfairly in the Criminal Court system in the United States of America

.... Indirectly your voice is getting heard too through this book.

TABLE OF CONTENTS

Chapter 1: Who Would Have Known What Was Ahead!!   1

Chapter 2: Never Saw This Coming!!   3

Chapter 3: Where It Starts!!   7

Chapter 4: Bullpen Therapy!!   13

Chapter 5: Wednesday   15

Chapter 6: You Can't Be Serious!!   17

Chapter 7: Mind Racing!!   20

Chapter 8: Court Time!!   22

Chapter 9: Back To This Shit!!   29

Chapter 11: Visit   36

Chapter 10: Law Library Time!!   39

Chapter 12: Strip Search!!   43

Chapter 13: Sunday!!   45

Chapter 14: Monday's Visit!!   48

Chapter 15: Tuesday Morning On The Transfer!!   51

Chapter 16: Brooklyn M.D.C   54

Chapter 17: Wednesday, On The Transfer!!   58

Chapter 18: Philly F.D.C!   60

Chapter 19: Friday, Welcome To Youngstown Ohio!!   67

Chapter 20: Monday, West Virginia Here I Come!!   69

Chapter 21: North Central Regional County Jail On My Way!!   72

Chapter 22: Back To North Central Regional County Jail   85

Chapter 23: November 2018   87

Chapter 24: Treachery Season!! I See It Clearly Now!!!   90

Chapter 25: What I Told Mr. Walker Next On The Visit!   103

Chapter 26: Mr. Walker's Feedback About Everything I Asked Him To Use For My Defense At Trial!!   123

Chapter 27: Final Pre- Trial Conference   134

Chapter 28: Jury Selection The Wickedness Continues!   143

Chapter 29: It Gets More Dishonorable!!   149

Chapter 30: After Jury Selection Trial Began!   155

Chapter 31: 2nd Day Of Trial!! The Unfairness Continues!!   159

Chapter 32: 3rd Day Of Trial Same Unfairness Just A Different Day!!   161

Chapter 33: The Verdict!! You Already Know What It Was….   165

Chapter 34: You Be The Judge!! Court Is In Session…   168

Chapter 35: Guess Who Judge Irene Keeley Knew!!   177

Chapter 36: Code Of Professional Responsibility Rules   181

Chapter 37: Some More Of The Honorable Irene Keeley Dishonorable   189

Chapter 38: Baston Claim   233

Chapter 39: Today's Issue   247

Chapter 40: The Prosecutor's Prosecution!!   258

Chapter 41: How The Hell!!   272

Chapter 42: The Injustice Continues!!   278

Chapter 43: Questions For The Readers   293

Chapter 44: Ways You Can Help Me And Prevent Future Injustices To Others
Which Should Be Your Main Objective!!   307

Chapter 45: There's Still More Injustice Please Keep Reading!!   312

Chapter 46: The Injustice Kenneth Sadler Is Facing: 378

Chapter 47: The First Step Act   404

About The Author   507

Greetings to All,

I hope all is well with everyone, especially during this pandemic we are all still going through. Many of you may have seen the cover and only understood it to a certain extent, without understanding the true meaning of it. The meaning of the artwork is deeper than just seeing someone holding up an unbalanced scale. The female holding the scale is known as Lady Justice, which is in every single courtroom in the United States whether it is a state or federal courtroom. Lady Justice is supposed to have a blindfold on both of her eyes to symbolize she is blind to both sides meaning the prosecutor and the defendant. She will only base a criminal case against someone on the laws that govern that courtroom and on the evidence against the person being charged with a crime. All courtrooms throughout the United States are "obligated" to operate according to the meaning of Lady Justice! Sadly, this is not the case for millions of people who went through the court system in the United States in the past one hundred years. As you see on the cover, Lady Justice only has one eye covered with her blindfold and not on both of her eyes, the way she is supposed to. The reason for this is because many courtrooms throughout the United States do not respect or operate according to the meaning of Lady Justice in their courtroom. Lady Justice is being disrespected in so many ways in courtrooms in this country. She has one eye peeking out of her blindfold to symbolize that she really only sees, hears, and believes one person's side. That side is normally the prosecutor's and nine times out of ten, that is the side the judge is on, along with law enforcement officers and many lawyers. That is not what Lady Justice is supposed to represent. She represents Equal Justice Under Law, as you see on the cover. Lady Justice is in most courtrooms in the United States getting spit on the face daily and this book gives you one prime example of how she is not respected in a courtroom in West Virginia. There are so many untold stories, I truly do not believe there are enough numbers to count the amount of times Lady Justice has been disrespected in courtrooms throughout the United States. I know this to be a fact based on what the court system did to me, and what I have witnessed as well as what I heard it did to others. From the core of my **SOUL,** I know everything I just stated is the truth. On a different note, so many people do not know the role of judges, prosecutors, or attorneys. There is so much they are held accountable for. There are so many ethical rules they are all **"OBLIGATED"** to follow, that no one has a clue about because they did not go to law school to have any knowledge of them, or they just did not know they even existed. In this book you will learn of several ethical rules all judges, prosecutors and attorneys are obligated to follow in all levels of courtrooms in the United States of America. Let me now break down the role of a judge, a prosecutor, and a lawyer so you can familiarize yourself with that as well.

A Judge's Role:

The judge's role in criminal matters is essential for the system to work with proper dignity, fairness, and efficiency. The judge's responsibilities include safeguarding the rights of the person who has been arrested, preserving the interest of the public, avoiding both the reality and appearance of any conflict of interest or bias, respecting the role of both the prosecutor and defense attorney, preserving constitutional standards when reviewing search and arrest warrant applications and important proceedings, as well as making sure all laws and rules are followed in the courtroom and under no circumstance are they to be broken. judges are supposed to make sure Lady Justice's motto "equal justice under the law" is upheld in his or her courtroom. In a nutshell the judge's role is to make sure all proceedings in the courtroom is handled in a fair manner.

A Prosecutor's Role:

The duty of the prosecutor is to seek justice, not merely to convict. Although the prosecutor operates within the Adversary System, it is fundamental that the prosecutor's obligation is to protect the innocent as well as to convict the guilty, and to guard the rights of the accused as well to enforce the rights of the public. Therefore, the Adversarial duty of the prosecutor to pursue conviction zealously must be restrained by the superseding duty to preserve fairness and to protect innocence. The prosecutor's obligation is achieving a fair, efficient, and effective enforcement of criminal law, along with following all the ethical rules known to a prosecutor when being sworn in when taking an oath to become a prosecutor. Some of these ethical rules you will learn in this book.

A Defense Attorney's Role:

In an Adversary system that is deliberately weighted to protect the innocent, by placing the obligation on the prosecutor to prove that the person being charged with a crime is guilty. It is the role and ethical duty of the defense attorney to put the prosecutor to the test of its proof. No matter what type of crime it is, a lawyer has the obligation to represent the client zealously and courageously. It is the defense attorney who must raise issues such as illegal investigation methods, illegal search and seizures, unfair lineups, unconstitutional criminal law, improper judicial decisions and procedures, illegal incarceration, and so on. These objections often address the serious invasion of a person's right to privacy, freedom of religion or speech, the right to a fair trial, the right to freedom from cruel and unusual punishment, the right to equal protection under the laws, and other rights absolutely essential to the preservation of individual liberty and dignity. It is the defense attorney who has the duty to challenge any overreaching of police, prosecutor, judge, and system to prevent the erosion of the rights of his or her client. For this reason, the defense attorney needs to be ever vigilant and aggressive. Just like a judge and prosecutor, a defense attorney has ethical rules they are obligated to follow. In this book you too will learn about some of those ethical rules defense attorneys are obligated to follow.

Now that you know key things about the role of a judge, prosecutor, and defense attorney. I am extremely confident after reading this book you will strongly feel without a doubt that my attorney, the prosecutor in my case and the judge who presided over my case, totally disregarded the obligations they have within their roles. Hundreds of thousands of people who have been arrested and went through the court system in the United States have endured the same type of injustices I faced, that you will read in this book, by either their own attorney, the prosecutor, the judge or by all of them simultaneously.

CHAPTER 1

WHO WOULD HAVE KNOWN WHAT WAS AHEAD!!

March 20, 2018   12:40pm

OMG, I love the sound of hearing Jacky scream and moan I think to myself as I am giving her all ten inches my mom and dad blessed me with. All that is being heard is Jacky screaming and moaning and the squeaky sound of the bed going up and down up and down up and down as I have Jacky laying on her back at the edge of the bed with both her legs over my shoulders while I keep drilling in and out of her this dick she loves to receive. "Fuck me harder" she says, and I gladly picked up the speed and started pounding away making sure she felt every single stroke. After a very intense pounding session in many positions Jacky had three orgasms before I climaxed into her wet box. "I love making you cum" I said to her as I pulled out and stood on the floor looking at her laying on the bed in a relaxed state. Jacky, I have to go see my parole officer today. I am about to take a shower and get ready to go. "Ok babe go get ready" she said. I leaned over and kissed her on the lips and told her "I love you" before exiting the room then entering the bathroom to shower. I showered up, brushed my teeth then went back to the bedroom to find some clothes to put on. I threw on my white-on-white air force ones, a pair of black sweatpants, a white tee, socks, and a pair of boxer briefs. As I am putting lotion on my face Jacky is laying on the bed talking to me, "Babe dinner will be ready when you return. I am making your favorite today. Fish, rice, beans, and salad. Your dessert is always this pussy" Jacky states with a smile on her face. "I can't wait to eat when I come back, and I am not talking about the fish meal" I replied in a very seductive tone. "Oh yeah, I can't wait either for that" Jacky quickly shot back at me in a very seductive way as well. I walked over to the bed, kissed Jacky on the lips and told her "I see you when you get back, I love you." "I love you too" were the last words I heard Jacky say before leaving the front door and walking towards my car. "I hope there is no traffic on I-95" I said speaking aloud to myself while sitting in the driver's seat and starting up my car. I exited the parking lot of Jacky's building and then drove 2 blocks before jumping on the highway. From Norwalk Connecticut to New Rochelle, New York give or take would take 35-40 minutes if there is no traffic on the parkway. If traffic arises who knows how long it will take. I was hoping my drive to New York and back to Norwalk was traffic free. So far so good, no traffic for my first 25 minutes on the highway. Then out of nowhere I was in bumper to bumper traffic. While sitting in traffic all I was thinking about was Jacky's sexy ass and what position I was going to have her in when I return. Jacky was about 5'9 in height, extremely beautiful in the face with light brown eyes, a nice body with a beautiful personality to match her outer beauty. I really thought Jacky was it, my wife my soulmate and the woman I was going to spend the rest of my life with. Those thoughts of Jacky slowly started to change.

CHAPTER 2

NEVER SAW THIS COMING!!

After thirty minutes in traffic due to an accident on the highway, I finally made it to New Rochelle, New York where my parole officer's office is located. Searching for parking was something I always had to do when I had to pay her a visit. There was barely any parking where the office was located. It took about ten minutes of driving around looking for a parking spot without finding one before I decided to park in the Chase bank's parking lot which was three blocks away. I figured why not park there. I got out of the vehicle, closed the door, and hit the button on my keychain to activate the alarm on my car. I then proceeded to walk in the direction of my destination. It took about a five-minute walk for me to reach the building. I opened the door and entered the building just to be in line to go through the metal detector. After about three minutes of waiting in the line, the officer said to me "You are up next." I took my phone and keys out of my pocket and placed it on the table that was next to the metal detector before I walked through it. The metal detector did not go off when I walked through it, so I picked up my phone and keys and strolled to the glass window where the secretary awaits to take names of the parolee and the officer they are there to see.

"Good afternoon my name is Amanze Antoine, and I am here to see Parole Officer Joseph."

"Ok Antoine, have a seat she will be with you shortly." The secretary uttered.

At that time, I walked towards the waiting area. I hated waiting in this area and you could tell by the sour look on my face. This fucking area was so loud. Everyone was talking at a high pitch and the person they were speaking to was either sitting right next to them or one seat at the most apart from them. So, there was no need for them to talk so fucking loud. What really bothered me the most was all this non-stop loud talking; nobody was talking about anything. There was no substance to their entire conversation. Everybody was either talking about the best rapper out to them, counting other people's money, who got shot, how fat the female's ass they were fucking, or trying to fuck was, who got beat up, who got robbed or who was about to die. You know, the frivolous talk that goes on in mostly everybody's hood. It is like listening to a dog bark because they are saying the same shit the dog is saying, which is some shit I don't understand. It is sad the mental slavery my people do not even know they are in, but that is another book! **DAMN WHAT THE FUCK**! I am steady looking at the time on my phone thinking to myself, "I am here longer than I normally am." I've been in this loud ass waiting room for two hours now. Visiting my parole officer never took this long. The longest I ever waited was about an hour. Maybe my parole officer stepped out the office to take care of something or maybe she is out on her lunch break. Whatever the reason was, I did not appreciate waiting. I just wanted to get the fuck out of here already.

"Yooooo Amanze, what's shaking?" Blade greeted me as he took a seat next to me. "Ain't shit, same shit Blade. Just waiting to see my P. O. then get the fuck out of here." I knew Blade for years; we grew up in the same neighborhood. Sadly, we had two things in common, we both grow up without a dad and we basically grew up in jail. We were both arrested as teens and sent to prison for years. Our youthful years were all spent in prison. Not saying we did not do anything wrong to go to prison for, because we did, but the amount of time we got as teens outweighed the crimes for which we were arrested. I am also not blaming my dad for not being in my life as the reason I went to prison at the age of sixteen, because I knew right from wrong. At the same time, having a dad in my life could have played a significant role to me not going to prison. I am not the only man thinking like this. Most of the dudes I know from my hood went to prison and we all had one thing in common, we never knew our dad, or our dad was around but was not *really* around, if you catch my drift. I know I am not the only person with these thoughts. It takes a man to raise a man, not a woman even though a selected few woman can.

Blade started talking about how the police raided his house last month but did not find anything. "Yo, Amanze blue coats rushed my crib 4am, I was dead asleep. I woke up to guns in my face. They flipped my house upside down and didn't find shit!" I did not give Blade any eye contact to let him even think I was paying attention to what he was saying. I honestly did not give a fuck that the police raided his house. Yes, I knew him, but I really did not fuck with him. He was a grease ball I happen to just know because we grew up in the same hood. Nothing about Blade was genuine, you could look in his eyes and see venom. **DEADLY VENOM**!! Before Blade was able to finish his story about the police raiding his house that I really was not listening to, lil B comes in the waiting room and sits directly in front of me. I fuck with lil B because he had good energy. He was genuine and trustworthy with the heart of ten lions even though he was only 5'1. "What's good bro? Long time no see." His reply was, "Trying to stay out of jail big bro. What's good with you though, Amanze?"

"Working and staying out the way"

"Where do you work?"

"I do construction lil B." I stated.

"Are they hiring Amanze?" He asked.

"I will talk to my foreman when I go back to work, I think they are hiring. Give me your number and I'll hit you up and let you know."

"Aight, that sounds like a plan big bro."

We exchanged phone numbers and lil B continued talking; "How long you been in here Amanze?"

"Man, for almost 3 hours! I'm ready to go!"

"Damn, I hope I don't have to be here that long Amanze." I felt the sensation of my cell phone vibrating in my sweatpants pocket. I pulled it out of my pocket to see why it was vibrating. Nice! I had just received a text message from Jacky.

"I love you babe dinner is done and waiting for you to eat. What are you doing? Where are you at?" I replied, "I am still waiting to see my parole officer babe; I love you to." Her response was, "**OK** babe, let me know when you are on your way back to my place." I texted her back with just the letter "K" meaning ok.

CHAPTER 3

WHERE IT STARTS!!

Maybe two minutes after I sent Jacky my last message, Ms. Joseph opened up the door directly in front of me that led to her office and yelled out, "Mr. Antoine you are next" while she held the door open for me. Boy was I happy she called me because that meant I would soon be on my way driving back to Jacky's place to have my dessert first than dinner. Normally my parole officer's visits are short once I am inside of her office. So, I just knew I would be leaving her office after she asks me the usual questions, "Do you live at the same address? Any police contact? Are you still working?" After those questions are asked and answered, she gives me my next date to report back to her, then I am heading out the door. So again, I just knew I was going to be leaving her office soon, or so I thought! I got up from my chair and walked towards the door she held open for me to enter. "Hello, Ms. Joseph, how are you?" I stated as I went into the entrance of the door. "I am fine," she said. We both started to walk down the hall that leads to her office. At the end of the hall, you have to make a right and her office is the first one on the left. When we got to the end of the hallway, we made that right turn together. To my surprise two other male parole officers were waiting there for me.

"Face the wall and put your hands up Amanze," one of the male parole officers said to me.

Simultaneously while doing what the male parole officer just instructed me to do, Ms. Joseph stated "Amanze this has nothing to do with me or this parole office.

The feds want to question you, and they told my supervisor to have me hold you in custody when you report to me today."

"Question me about what?"

"I don't know Mr. Antoine, they just told my supervisor to have me hold you in custody when you report today, then give them a call once that happens." I just stood quietly against the wall while the male parole officer who instructed me to face the wall with my hands up was done patting me down and searching me. He then placed handcuffs on me and took me to a room where Ms. Joseph sat across from me, I guess to watch or supervise me.

Ms. Joseph and I just sat in silence. My mind was racing a million miles per second, thinking about what the fuck the feds want to question me about. All I do is work and spend time with Jacky. What could they possibly want to question me about? Within ten minutes of me being in deep thought wondering why the feds want to question me, a Spanish guy in his 50's named Mr. Perez enters the room. He is Ms. Joseph's supervisor. With a look of disgust on his face he says to me "What did you do wrong for the feds to tell me to hold you in custody today?"

"I didn't do anything wrong, and I don't know why they told you to keep me in custody."

"Yeah right, you had to do something." he said looking directly in my eyes with a smirk on his face that indicated he thought I was lying. "By the way Mr. Antoine the feds called me 5 minutes ago and said they don't want to question you, they are going to charge you with a crime." Mr. Perez stated before he walked out of the room.

Ms. Joseph gave me a look that signified I had a lot on my plate to deal with right now! The room was in total silence the entire time we were in it together. All I kept thinking to myself is that I cannot be getting charged with a crime because I did not do anything! Maybe a half an hour to forty-five minutes had passed when I heard a voice coming from the hallway through the wide-open door of the room I was in. "I am special agent Jones, and this is my partner special agent Smith, we are here to take Amanze Antoine into custody." Even though the agent was pronouncing my name wrong, I knew he was talking about me. About thirty seconds later two black men appeared in the room I was being held in alongside Mr. Perez.

One of the agents said, "Are you Amanze Antoine?"

"Yes, I am."

"Ok well I am special agent Jones, and this is my partner special agent Smith. We are taking you into federal custody. You have been indicted and charged with violating federal gun laws in the state of wild wild West Virginia. You are being charged with a federal crime and you will be extradited back to West Virginia to stand trial or take a plea deal."

"What!!!!" I stated in a shocking tone.

"You heard what I said" special agent Jones aggressively said.

"I didn't do anything! I do not even think I know anyone in West Virginia! What proof do yall have? There cannot be any because I did not violate any gun laws!!"

"Tell that to your lawyer not to me buddy, I am just here to transport you." "Sir, can you please stand up?" I complied to his order and stood. Special agent Jones started to pat search me. Ms. Joseph stated we already searched him for weapons and contraband, and he is clear. "Ok, thank you. What is your name?"

"Parole officer Joseph"

"Nice to meet you Ms. Joseph. I am Mr. Jones. Now for you Amanze Antoine, you are coming with us. You will be taken to Mount Vernon police department where you will be held until we are able to take you to court to start the extradition process. It's almost 5pm so court will be closed by the time we drive down there. Tomorrow court is closed, so I will say Thursday morning you will be in front of a judge. Umm, Ms. Joseph we are going to switch handcuffs. We are going to give you guys your handcuffs back and transport him using my handcuffs."

"Sure, whatever you want to do." Ms. Joseph stated. Ms. Joseph took off the cuffs I had on, and agent Jones placed his handcuffs on me.

To Ms. Joseph I said, "Ms. Joseph, can you get my car keys from the male parole officer who searched me? He took them along with my cell phone. Can you call my mom and ask her to come get my keys and move my car, please? I parked in Chase bank's parking lot. I know my car will get towed once someone who works there realize it does not belong to anyone who works there or to a customer. Especially if it is there overnight until the morning."

"Ok Antoine, I will contact your mother and give her your car keys. What is her number?"

I gave Ms. Joseph my mom's number and thanked her. "Come on guy" agent Jones referred to me as, we are going for a ride. Each agent held one of my arms as they escorted me out of the building to their patrol car. I was placed in the backseat of the car. Agent Jones got in the driver's seat while agent Smith jumped in the passenger seat. Agent Jones started the car and took off. The handcuffs were getting tighter and tighter during the ride due to Agent Jones not clicking the safety lock on the handcuffs, so that the handcuffs will not be able to get tighter on a person's wrist. My hands were starting to fall asleep due to the lack of blood flowing through them because the cuffs were so fucking tight. The fact that the handcuffs were cuffed towards the back of me made it even more uncomfortable.

During the ride agent Smith turned around from the passenger's seat and asked me "Where are the guns at?" "What guns? I don't have any guns I stated, and I don't know nothing about any guns." The whole ride agent Smith had to at least turn my way five times and ask me where are the guns? After I answered his question the first time, each other time he asked me I acted like I did not hear him talking and continued to look out the car's window caught up in my own thoughts the entire ride to Mount Vernon police department. The sign out front read "Mount Vernon police department" as we drove past the front entrance of the station. Agent Jones made a left turn and another quick sharp left which led to the side entrance. This is where people who have been arrested enter with their arresting officer. Agent Jones parked the car and both agents got out. Agent Smith opened the backseat door and

10

ordered me out the car. I think because he was angry I was ignoring him the ride to the police station. I did not have anything to say to him. What was the point of talking to him? He kept asking me the same questions "where the guns at? Where the guns at?" I told him I did not have any guns, nor did I know anything about any guns, the first time he asked me. So, I could not understand why he kept asking me the same fucking question. What did he think my answer was going to change? Well anyway, I got out of the car like agent Smith said. He held one of my arms like I was going to run off. His tight grip on my arm did not help the discomfort I was already feeling from the tight ass cuffs I had on. All three of us walked to the side door entrance that was about twelve feet away. Upon entering we all were greeted by a Black woman who was a Mount Vernon police officer. "Hey guys how are you doing?" she stated. "We are fine," agent Jones said as we all walked pass her.

"I'm not fine. These cuffs are too tight, and my hands feel like they are dead." I told her.

The female officer looked at both agents and said, "why is that?" "We did not know they were tight; we are going to take them off in a minute." Agent Jones stated. The female officer whose name tag spelled out the name Ross said "Oh Ok" to agent Jone's reply. Thank you, Ms. Ross I stated. "You are welcome sweetie."

I could tell Ms. Ross was not about abusing her people or on a power trip as a police officer. Special agent Jones and Smith escorted me to the holding cell area of the police station. One thing they did do though was take off the handcuffs immediately, which was a big relief to my hands. Blood started to properly circulate back into them slowly but surely. I was kept in the cell until agent Smith took me out to fingerprint me. While fingerprinting me he asked me "Are you sure you don't want to tell me where the guns are? I can get you a deal with the prosecutor in West Virginia."

You would have thought I was deaf, by how I acted like I did not hear him speaking to me. He got no response; it was like he was talking to his self. After fingerprinting me, he walked me back to the cell and I took a seat. "Can I get a phone call please?"

"No!" Agent Smith shot back at me quick.

It was like he could not wait to tell me no about anything, I can tell just by his hostile tone.

"So, you are telling me I can't get a phone call?"

"Yes, that's exactly what I am telling you!!"

"The law states any time a person is arrested or held in custody they are entitled to one phone call."

"Yes, but I do not have to respect that law Mr. Antoine, I am the law, and I can do whatever I want to do." I left it alone. I did not even bother to go back and forth with him because I saw it was a dead end. He was not going to give me a call even if Jesus his self-popped up and said give him a call. "Antoine come here; I have to take your picture" agent Jones said.

I got up, walked out of the cell and agent Jones snapped three photos of me.

CHAPTER 4

BULLPEN THERAPY!!

After my photos were taken, agent Jones told me to follow him. He placed me in another holding cell which was much smaller than the cell I just left. He pointed to what cell I was going into, waited until I entered it, then handed me a brown paper bag that had shit sandwiches for me to eat for dinner. Not shit sandwiches literally, but it damn sure looked like it and tasted like it. Agent Jones slammed and locked the cell and said, "It's time for me to go home and relax unlike you, see you Thursday." I did not even reply to that little slick ass comment, you should have seen this cell!! As you walk in there is a wooden bench on the right-hand side, I guess that is what they call giving me a mattress to sleep on. Five to seven steps from the entrance of the cell, depending on how long your legs are, is the steel toilet with a sink built above it that was connected as one unit. Two steps to the left and two steps to the right you will be touching the walls of the cell. Not to mention the A/C was on full blast, and it was not even summertime. I was not given a blanket and was forced to deal with the cold. The coldness on my body felt like I was naked in the north pole on Christmas day. My little white tee shirt and sweatpants I had on felt like I had nothing on when the strong breeze of the A/C hit me. The thin material of my clothes was not protecting me from the coldness. I laid down on the hard-wooden bench, watching the camera in front my cell watch me. Deep in thought I could not help but to think about Jacky. I knew if Ms. Joseph called my mom, my mom would have called Jacky and told her I got arrested. I knew Jacky was probably worried senseless. I should have asked Ms. Joseph at the parole building could I have made a phone call to call her before the agents came to pick me up. I was constantly thinking to myself, maybe she would have given me a call. I know Jacky was still going to be worried whether I called her or not. But not calling at all made things even worse. I was hoping Ms. Joseph called my mom so at the very least my mom and Jacky knew where I was. I had no idea what time it was because there was not a clock in sight. Wishing this whole thing were a dream I would wake up from but that did not happen. I got no sleep that night. I could not. How could I? I knew I was innocent! I could not get comfortable to be able to get some rest. Shit, if I did do something wrong to get arrested, I still would not be comfortable enough to get some rest. But even more so when you did not do anything wrong and you are arrested, it is impossible for your mind to be at ease for your body to be able to rest.

CHAPTER 5

WEDNESDAY

I can hear footsteps getting closer and closer towards me as I sat on the wooden bench. A female police officer stopped in front of the cell I was in and asked if I was hungry? "No, I do not have an appetite Miss."

"Ok, just asking because we have brown paper bags of food up front."

I replied, "I for sure do not want that Miss, even if I was hungry."

The female officer cracked a smile and walked off. I laid down on the hard ass wooden bench staring at the ceiling for **GOD** knows how long. I felt myself drifting off to sleep. I know I fell asleep because I woke up from hearing a light tap on the cell bars. Tap Tap Tap Tap Tap

"Antoine are you ok?"

I opened my eyes to see Ms. Ross standing in the front of the cell with a brown paper bag in her left hand.

"Hell no, I am not Ok Ms. Ross!!"

"What's wrong" she politely asked.

"For starters I am being arrested and I didn't do shit. Secondly, it is cold as hell back here. This damn A/C is on like we are in Costa Rica on July 4th. And thirdly, I never got a phone call to let my people know what is going on. I know they are all worried about me. I have no control over anything."

You are frustrated about what, Antoine? I am new here and I do not know who controls the A/C, but I will try to find out. As far as you not getting a phone call, I know that is wrong, because you are supposed to get one after you are arrested and in custody. My supervisor made it very clear to everyone working this shift to not give you a call your whole time here. I cannot give you a call because I will lose my Job for not obeying my supervisor's orders. As bad as I want to give you a call, I cannot sweetie. I have kids to feed. I need this money. And sweetie you being arrested is out of my hands. I had no control over that darling. I came back here to see if you wanted some food, she said as she lifted the brown paper bag in her hand.

"Hell no! I am good. What's in the bag? Shit sandwiches!?"

Ms. Ross busted out laughing because she knew those brown paper bags were full of shit sandwiches.

"This is all they have sweetie. I would give you some of my home cooked food I brought from home for my lunch today but as you can see it is a camera directly in front your cell watching everything, so that's out! I need my job and that shit could get me fired if the camera picks up me giving you my personal food from home. As much as I want to help your cute ass, I cannot because my job would depend on it."

"That is fine Ms. Ross, I understand."

Ms. Ross walked away with a seductive grin on her face. I took a piss then sat on the bench thinking about what I have been thinking about since I was arrested, **WHY AND HOW DO I HAVE CHARGES IN WEST VIRGINIA!!!**

CHAPTER 6

YOU CAN'T BE SERIOUS!!

What seemed like an hour went past when two Mount Vernon detectives came to my cell and opened it up.

"Come with us Antoine!"

I complied thinking they was going to let me go because they found out the wrong man had been arrested. I knew that was not the case after I walked out the cell and one of the detectives put a pair of handcuffs on me. They would not be placing cuffs on me if they had any plans to set me free. So, the thought of them letting me go went right out the window.

After I was handcuffed, at the same time both detectives told me to follow them. As I was walking with them, I asked where we were going?

"We want to ask you a few questions" the shorter detective said.

I kind of put together real fast what this was about. This is regular detective work in all police stations in the nation. When someone is in police custody in a police station, a detective always pull them in an office to see if that person could help them solve unsolved crimes or just see what information they can get out of them about what's going on in the streets. Some people talk and some people do not. You would never really know if someone told the police anything or not, because sometimes a person could tell detectives what they know but there is no written statement proving they told. That is what is wicked about the street, the dude that told on you could be in your face every day and you would never know. The best thing to do is stay out of the streets and just do the right thing! A lot of people do not find that out until they got two or three bids in, like me. The two detectives took me to an upstairs room that only had a desk and 3 chairs in it. "Have a seat, Mr. Antoine. Do you smoke?", the taller detective asked while pulling out a pack of cigarettes out of his top shirt pocket.

"Yeah, I smoke."

He took out one cigarette from the pack and handed it to me. I placed it in my mouth, reached for the book of matches that were already on top of the desk when I entered the room. I struck a match to light the cigarette. The taller detective started speaking, "I am detective Jackson, and this is detective Wells. We both work for the Mount Vernon police department. We would like to ask you a few questions. If you help us, we will help you. Do you know Porter" the detective asked?

"No, I don't!"

"Do you know Zimmy?"

"No, who is that?" I stated as I continued to smoke the cigarette.

"Why are you fucking lying to me Antoine those are your fucking cousins! Detective Clark knows your family very well and told us they were. Those are not your cousins huh. The question I really need you to answer is do you know anything about them. You know such as murders, drugs etc.?"

"I just told you I don't know them so why the fuck you keep asking me about them" I yelled at the detective who was asking the questions.

"This guy is saying he do not know his own family members" detective Jackson said to his partner.

"Yea that's real funny this guy does not know his own fucking family" Wells replied looking directly in my eyes with a mean ice grill.

Finally, the moment I have been waiting for, the last pull of the cigarette. "Take me back to my cell detectives we are done with you asking me questions. I have no info to give yall so can you please take me back to my cell."

They both felt my energy and seen the look in my eyes that firmly confirmed I did not want to talk to them. Detective Wells and Jackson looked at each other and laughed.

"Ok you fucken prick, follow us" Wells stated. I did not even respond to his comment. It was not worth my energy I had bigger things to worry about more than him calling me a prick. Even though it did cross my mind to tell him I will slap the shit out of you, but I did not. I kept my cool and stayed quiet. The detectives took me back to the same cell they just took me out of.

CHAPTER 7

MIND RACING!!

All I was thinking to myself was that the Mount Vernon Police department has to have something to do with me getting this charge in West Virginia. More so this thought came to my mind because of those two detectives asking me about my cousins. I personally knew the history my cousins and the Mount Vernon police department have. My cousin Porter was very close to getting a record deal a couple years back. There were a lot of haters on the streets who did not want that to happen, so they gave the police false tips about crimes they said he did that he really did not do. That made damn near the entire Mount Vernon police department harass my cousin every time they saw him. They knew his car so every time they saw him in it, they would pull it over and search it. Sometimes they even gave him bullshit charges. For example, one time they found a pocket knife the size of his pinky finger in his car and they charged him with a felony. That's not shit, one-time detectives from Mount Vernon police department obtained warrants to raid his home. They said they had probable cause to do so because of a reliable tip they received from someone saying drugs were being sold out of his home.

The swat team raided his home one night at three in the morning and claimed they found drugs, even though we all knew they planted the drugs there just to get him off the streets! Pieces of shit they are! My cousin was not a drug dealer. The most he ever did illegally was smoke weed and double park his car. My family also had a lawsuit against the Mount Vernon police department for harassment, so I knew that rubbed them the wrong way. After they got Porter off the streets, they started to harass my younger cousin Zimmy, the same way they use to harass his older brother Porter. They did the same thing to him that they did to Porter, which was they **GOT HIM OFF THE STREETS** by planting drugs on him. As I sat in the cell and reflected on the type of history the Mount Vernon police department have with my family, I was seriously asking myself did they in some way have anything to do with me getting these charges that I was 100% sure I didn't do. For hours, my mind was racing until I finally fell asleep.

"**WAKE UP! WAKE UP! WAKE UP!** time to go buddy" I heard agent Jones say to me while standing in front of my cell as I opened my eyes from a horrible night of sleep. "Time to go to court buddy" agent Smith said who was standing right next to agent Jones.

"I am not your buddy" were the words that came out my mouth as I got up from the hard ass wooden bench. I then walked over to the sink and started brushing my teeth. "Hurry up" agent Jones yelled out as I took my time brushing my teeth

"Not everybody brushes their teeth as fast as you" I shouted out while brushing my teeth with a mouth full of toothpaste. I spit the toothpaste in the sink and rinsed the remaining toothpaste out of my mouth with water then rinsed my face with cold water to fully wake up.

"You ready now" agent Jones said in a smart-ass way.

"No, I am not ready let me use your shirt to dry off my face, then I'll be ready"

Agent smith could not hold his laugh in and let out a short laugh. Agent Jones just looked at me without a comeback. I rolled up a bunch of toilet paper in my left hand and pat dried my face.

"This guy thinks he's a model, he wants to pat dry his face" agent Jones said with a smirk on his face to agent Smith

"Snap a pic of me on your phone and send it to your girl. She might agree with you that I am a model" I said being serious.

CHAPTER 8

COURT TIME!!

What the fuck! I wish I did not say anything smart to agent Jones. He put the handcuffs on me tighter than they were when he took me to Mount Vernon police department two days ago. My hands got numb within minutes after the cuffs were placed on me. The lack of blood circulation in my hands was the cause of the numbness. I kept thinking about how many slaves taken from Africa went through the same thing being shackled on their hands and feet feeling this same numbing sensation.

I was now feeling what they felt for months on the slave ship traveling from Africa to America. They survived the entire trip to America, so a half an hour ride to the court building I felt would not kill me. Even though I was uncomfortable as fuck! My mindset kept me strong through that uncomfortable ride to the courthouse to White Plains, New York.

As we pulled up in front of the courthouse you could see the sign in bold letters said "U.S Courthouse". The driver of car, agent Jones was flagged down by another law enforcement officer who was standing in front of the courthouse. The officer told agent Jones to drive around the block to the underground garage of the courthouse that was around the block. This is the part of the building where people in custody were taken to go to court that day. The garage door suddenly opened when agent Jones pulled in front of it. Agent Jones slowly drove inside of it and parked the car. Both agents got out of the car, Jones opened the back-seat door and said: "Get out Antoine time to go to court!"

I could tell he was still angry about our earlier encounter we had at the police station. I got out of the car and was taken into the building through a side door and then placed inside a holding cell. There, another agent who works inside the court building who took off the tight ass handcuffs I had on. What a relief I felt when he took off the handcuffs! It felt like my hands rose from the dead. Thank you, Jesus! I could have sworn I heard my hands say when the agents took off the handcuffs. After removing the cuffs, the agent left the cell and locked it. I started pacing back and forth in the cell thinking about what was going to happen next. I still could not believe I was arrested! I knew I did nothing wrong!

"Antoine your court appointed attorney wants to see you" the agent who took off those tight ass cuffs said as he stood in front of the cell.

He opened the cell door placed handcuffs on me and motioned for me to follow him. We walked over to the elevator and got in. I watched the agent press the tenth-floor button on the elevator. The agent guided me to a room, opens the door and tells me "this is your attorney." From the second I entered the room, the female sitting in front of me told me to have a seat which I did.

"You can leave and close the door" she said in a respectful way to the agent still standing in the doorway who brought me to the room. "Ok will do" the agent said as he stepped out and closed the door behind him.

"Hey, my name is Ms. Cooper and you are Amanze Antoine correct?"

"Yes, I am. I am your court appointed attorney for today. I will only be your attorney for today. When you get extradited to West Virginia you will be appointed a different attorney if you cannot afford one. Today you will go in front of a judge to start the extradition process. I advise you to not waive extradition to West Virginia because the sooner you get down there the sooner you can get this over with and do the time that they are going to give you. Waiving your extradition will only delay you from taking your plea and being able to put all this behind you."

She reached into a folder she had and handed me a copy of my indictment, which is a document showing a person the crime they are being charged with.

"When you get to West Virginia the prosecutor may ask you to cooperate so you can get the least amount of time possible. If that does not happen, at the very least they will offer you a plea. I advise you to take the plea and not go to trial because you will get way more time"

"First and foremost, Ms. Cooper, you are advising me to take a plea indicating you already know I am guilty of these charges. Secondly, what am I being charged with? This indictment you just gave me, I do not understand anything it is saying."

"Violating federal firearm laws," she stated in a you know what you did wrong tone.

"I am not understanding you clearly Ms. Cooper. What are you saying? I had firearms?"

"Yesssss! I do not know the details Antoine. I do not have your discovery in front of me. But, basically the prosecutor in West Virginia believes people bought firearms from a gun store legally, then gave them to you which is illegal. The prosecutor also said you transported the firearms you received from people in West Virginia to New York."

I replied, "So, you never seen my discovery, but you are telling me to take a plea? How do you know the evidence that is in my discovery does not exclude me from these charges!? You cannot be serious telling me to take a plea without even seeing my damn discovery. Are you serious!? Who the fuck are these people the prosecutor is saying they gave me firearms!? Where are these so-called firearms they are claiming I transported to New York!? I was never found in possession or caught with any firearms. Nor was I ever caught transporting firearms from West Virginia to New York. So how the fuck am I getting charged for it as if I did!? That is the question you need to find an answer to, and not tell me to take a fucking plea deal or to fucking cooperate!! As an attorney, would you not want to see evidence that proves your client committed a crime before telling him or her to take a plea deal!?"

"It really does not matter to me, it's your life not mine." Ms. Cooper stated as she rolled her eyes.

"So why the fuck are you a lawyer if you are not going to fulfill your obligation to represent me effectively according to the United States Constitution?"

Her response was "good question and I don't have an answer to that."

She got up from her chair and walked out the room slamming the door behind her. According to the U.S Constitution that response and behavior is unethical!!

Shortly after being in the room alone for what felt like 5 minutes, the door was opened by the same agent who brought me here to see this rude ass ineffective lawyer. "Antoine lets go; you are ready to be seen by the judge." I stood up and left the room then started to walk down the hallway with the agent. The agent stopped in front of a door once we got halfway down the hallway. He opened the door, and this is when I realized this was the door to the courtroom. The first thing I saw as I entered the courtroom was my beautiful mother and Jacky sitting inside the courtroom waving hello to me, with a worried look on both of their faces. Before I could say hello verbally, I was told by the agent I could not speak to them in the courtroom. So, I gave them both head nods to show I acknowledged them both. I was directed by the agent to take a sit over there, which I complied. Guess who I was told to sit next to? The same ineffective rude ass court appointed attorney who minutes ago walked out the room on me, and slammed the door shut. She sat there with a Jamaican screw face like she was born and raised in Spanish town in Jamaica. I am sitting here thinking to myself I did not do shit to this lady for her to have her faced all screwed up.

"**ALL RISE**" one court officer stated as the judge entered the courtroom from a side door. This judge looked like his grandfather's grandfather's father's father was a slave master in Texas. Which was the worst slave state to be in due to how cruel the slaves were being treated. You could see the racism in his eyes. There is a certain look you can see in the eyes of a person who is racist no matter what race they are. Racism has a certain type of look that I could pinpoint.

"You may all be seated" the judge said.

"Amanze Antoine number 2672 4- 962 on the calendar today for extradition purposes" was shouted out by the Court's Clerk.

"The government do you have anything" the judge asked the prosecutor.

"Yes, your honor I do. Today will be short and simple. Amanze Antoine the defendant has been indicted in the State of West Virginia for violating firearms laws and was taken into custody by federal agents while reporting to his parole officer in New Rochelle, New York two days ago. As far as I am concerned after speaking to his attorney before the defendant came into the courtroom, Ms. Cooper spoke to him and she said "Mr. Antoine would like to waive his right to fight extradition. He wants to go face his charges in West Virginia."

"Is that correct counsel for the defendant?" the judge asked my attorney.

"Yes, your honor the defendant waives his extradition rights and would like to face his charges in the state of West Virginia."

"I didn't tell you that" I said to Ms. Cooper.

"Your honor may I please have a moment with my client in the courtroom?"

"Sure, counsel you may" the judge replied to my attorney.

My attorney turned to me and started speaking, "Antoine your best bet is to waive your extradition rights because even if you don't today you will still be sent to West Virginia eventually to face your charge. So, it is best for you to go face the charges now rather than later. No one ever wins the fight to not get extradited! Your name is on the indictment so nine times out of ten, you will get extradited down the line! The prosecutor will be highly upset with you in West Virginia for fighting not to get extradited. When you do get extradited at a later date, which will surely happen, the prosecutor will be harder on you. So, my advice to you Mr. Antoine is to go face your charges!!"

My response was, "Why would I want to go face charges for something I did not do? Would you Ms. Cooper? If I could not go face charges in the first place, then that is what I want to do!! What are my options?"

"Well Mr. Antoine you really don't have any options because like I said sooner or later You **WILL** get extradited. So instead of fighting it, you might as well go face the charges because you will get extradited at a later date! That I can assure you!"

Me not having a full understanding of the law on the extradition process, I waived my rights to fight extradition. When in all actuality I could have fought not to get extradited and maybe I would not have ever been sent to West Virginia to face any charges at all. By being ignorant of the law and listening to this ineffective court-appointed attorney I waived my rights to fight extradition.

I was on my way to be extradited to the State of West Virginia to fight charges I had no clue about. After I agreed not to fight extradition when the judge asked me if that is what I want to do he remanded me to Westchester County Jail and told me I will be held there until the process of getting transported to West Virginia starts.

"Good luck Mr. Antoine," the judge stated before he banged his gavel and left the courtroom.

Even though I was told not to talk to my mom, and Jacky I looked back at them and said I love yall. "We love you too" they both said. The agent who brought me into the courtroom escorted me out and placed me into a holding cell.

"Mr. Antoine we will be leaving here in a little bit to bring you to the county jail." The agent uttered, as he locked the cell door and walked off.

About twenty minutes after being in the cell alone, a black and white guy were brought to the same holding cell I was in. The black male sat right down next to me on the steel bench and started talking out loud, "These motherfuckers told on me" Then looked at me as if he wanted me to respond to his comment that he just blurted out. I looked directly into his eyes with a look on my face that stated, "**NOT RIGHT NOW**"! He got the hint, so he started talking to the white dude that was in the cell with us. I had my own thoughts that I was deep into before he even came inside the cell. I did not want to be bothered by anybody! That is how I was feeling.

It was great seeing my mom and Jacky. Only if I could have left with them! I wanted to so bad! I was tired, hungry, and stressed out. You could tell by looking at my face that I was all three of them. Two agents walked over to the holding cell. One agent says "Let's go men, we are ready to take you all to Westchester County Jail. One at a time, I need you guys to walk up to me so I can handcuff you then we will be on our way men."

One at a time we walked up to him and got handcuffed. Shortly after we were brought to a van to begin our drive to the county jail. Throughout the entire ride, I sat in silence, caught up in my own thoughts while the other two men indulged in a conversation about what they were arrested for.

CHAPTER 9

BACK TO THIS SHIT!!

We just arrived at the County Jail and now I am being asked by the lady at the front desk what my name is.

"I'm Amanze Antoine miss."

"Ok you can move to the side" the young lady said. "Next up!"

"My name is Mark Jones" the Black dude behind me told her.

"Ok sweetheart you can move to the side too. And you are" she asked the white dude who was last in line.

"I am Eric Doyle."

"Ok thanks, the lady stated."

After we all gave the lady our names, a Correctional officer searched us one by one and put us in a holding cell that had a phone built into the wall. As soon as I went into the cell I got right on the phone and started dialing Jacky's phone number.

"You have a collect call from Amanze Antoine" the recording said as Jacky picked up the phone. "Press five if you would like to accept the call," the recording continued. Jacky pressed five within seconds we were connected and were able to start talking to each other.

"Babe what happened" Jacky said right away I could hear her sincere concern in her voice that she truly cared.

"I don't know babe what happened. I am getting charged for some shit I did not do. I do not know where this charge is coming from. I didn't do any of this shit they saying I did."

"Me and your mom spoke to the lawyer you had in court after you left the courtroom and she said something about people buying guns for you. She really didn't get into details."

"That's exactly what I am being charged with. I swear I didn't do that shit!!"

"I know you didn't babe because you are always with me or working."

"I know that's all I did was work and come to your place. The only thing I was doing wrong was going to your place in Connecticut. I knew I was not to leave the state of New York without asking my parole officer for permission to, but I just wanted to be with the woman who I thought was the love of my life. I want out of here Jacky!"

"I want you out of there too babe I miss you so much. I miss you too. The system is so fucked up. They charge and send you to jail without any proof of anything! I totally agree with you Amanze. The best thing for me to do is get an attorney. It is funny you said that because the next thing I was going to tell you is, your aunt told your mom her pastor from her church knows lawyers in Virginia who practices law in West Virginia. She told your mom to tell you when you get extradited out there, she will make sure you have a lawyer."

"Thank God for that Jacky!!" What a big relief that was for me to hear that. "How did yall find out when and where I was going to court?"

"Your parole officer called your mom and told her you were arrested. She also gave your mom your car keys and told her where it was parked as you requested."

"That was so nice of Ms. Joseph to do that babe."

"It was easy to find your car because it was the only car parked in Chase bank's parking lot, your mom said. After your mom told me you were arrested, I looked your name up on the internet on every federal courthouse court date calendar nearby and I saw you had a court date on March 22 in White Plains. The internet tells you everything."

"That was fast thinking Jacky, thank you for that."

"No problem babe, I will also do my best to give what I can to help you a lawyer. I will try to help your aunt with paying for a lawyer. It is something real fishy about this babe. You need a lawyer for sure."

"I know I do" I replied.

"I am going to be here till the end with you Amanze. No matter what I will stick by your side. I am not going anywhere" Jacky said in a very convincing tone of voice.

"Thank you for that Jacky, I do not want to lose you."

"Me either babe, you are going to be my husband one day! You are my husband already, but you know what I mean, making it official and walking down the aisle. Did you speak to your mom Amanze?"

"No, not yet, you are the first person I called. I am going to call her when we get off the phone."

"Yes, call her she is so worried about you! You are her only child and she hates the fact you are in jail right now. She wants you out enjoying your life! She wants grandkids from you, she wants you to be there for her, you know babe spending time with her. She was so heartbroken when she got the call that you were arrested, and she still is! I saw the hurt in her eyes when we spoke. I am a mother too so felt her pain, **EVERY DROP OF IT BABE**!! I called up the jail and found out what days you can get visits. It is on Saturdays and Mondays. Your mother and I will come to see you on Saturday."

"Thank you, I need to see yall…. "you have one-minute left on this phone call" the recording stated interrupting our conversation. "Babe there is only one-minute left."

"I know babe" Jacky said, "I love you so much and I'll call you later or tomorrow."

"Ok babe I love you too, Keep your head up."

"Ok babe I," was the only words that came out of my mouth before the phone automatically hung up without any warning that the minute was up. I did not have the chance to finish my sentence. I tried calling my mom. She did not pick up the phone the first time I called so I called again. At that time, she picked up and accepted the collect call.

"Amanze are you ok!? What is going on!?"

"Mom I don't know! This charge is bogus. I did not do any of the things they said I did. I do not know what none of this is about! They said I had people buy guns for me from West Virginia then I transported them to New York. Ma I never did that. I don't understand how they are claiming I transported firearms, but I was never caught or found in possession of any firearms."

"This shit does not make any fucking sense" my mom said in a truly angry tone.

"I need a lawyer. One that is really going to help me."

"Yes, you do son. I spoke to your aunt, and she said the pastor of her church may know a lawyer that can help you."

"I know Jacky told me when I called her."

"Your aunt said she will try her best to get you a lawyer. You know my situation Amanze, I do not have the money like I use to. I will do my best to help your aunt pay for a lawyer for you."

"I appreciate that a lot, Mom!!"

"Jacky and I are coming to see you Saturday morning. She is so sad that you are in jail Amanze. She does not know why **GOD** is making this happen to you."

I listened to my mom talk with nothing to say. I was getting even more stressed out by hearing her express the way Jacky felt. Along with the pain I heard in my mom's voice, I was lost for words. Pain is just not a physical thing. It comes in all types of forms. I felt like crying listening to my mother on the phone! For some reason, the phone lost connection and it hung up on its own. It could have happened because my mom was in a poor reception area. I was going to call back, but I decided not to because I did not want to hear that pain in my mother's voice again. It was really hurting me inside to hear my mother's pain. I put the phone down and took a seat on the bench waiting for the nurse to call my name to get a T. B shot and be asked a bunch of medical questions. I have been through this process before, so I knew what to expect. I could not be at ease no matter how hard I tried. All that deep breathing shit to calm me down did not work. I could not get over the fact I was in jail for something I did not do!

About two hours go by and the nurse finally calls me. I received a T.B shot and was asked a bunch of medical questions as I expected. "Are you healthy? Do you have any medical conditions we need to know about? Do you have this? Do you have that? Blah blah blah blah." I wanted to get away from this nurse like right now! Her breath smelled and she had the nerve to be talking directly in my face at close range. I knew she could taste the funk on her tongue and in her mouth so why was so doing this to me!! I was super tired and wanted to get some rest. I never really got a good night's sleep at the police station because the wooden bench was extremely hard and uncomfortable and all the thoughts going through my head that did not help me get any rest either. All I kept thinking about while at the police station was what is going on and why the fuck and how the fuck, I am being arrested for some shit I did not do!! My mind was still thinking this thought, but my body needed the rest it was neglected of for the past two days.

After I was done seeing the nurse with the hot mouth, I finally was given a cell on a cell block. Even though I was not comfortable because I was in jail, it was more comfortable than being in the Mount Vernon police department. At least here I have a mattress. I made up my bed with the sheets that were given to me and then sat on the bed and ate the dinner I was given. I laid down afterwards to try to get some sleep. It was nice and quiet; everyone was asleep when I made it to the cellblock, so I did not have a problem falling right to sleep.

The next morning, I woke up to the officer saying "On the chow" which means come eat right now!!

I got up quickly brushed my teeth and rinsed my face then walked out of my cell towards the direction of the eating area. I grabbed a tray of food and sat down in the first empty seat I saw. I ate my tray which consisted of cornflakes, two milks and two slices of white bread. After eating, I threw my tray in the garbage and walked to the phone, I just had to call Jacky. I picked up the phone and dialed her number. Jacky picked up on the second ring and accepted my call.

"Hey babe" Jacky said excitedly. "I was waiting for you to call. I could not sleep last night. I had you on my mind all night babe."

"I thought about you too Jacky. Are you ok?"

"No, I am not ok babe I want you home."

"This is just a stressful situation for the both of us Jacky." "Yea it is! I miss you so much Amanze, I feel so empty now that you are not around. I need you out of there and home with me where you belong."

"I feel the same way Jacky."

"Babe yesterday at work I was so mad!"

"Why, what happened?"

"This old man was so rude and disrespectful who I had as a patient. I went into his room to give him his nightly medication and this motherfucker grabbed my ass. I wanted to smack him, but I knew I would have lost my job as a nurse. I just told the head nurse who was on shift and she switched me to another patient. I could not have dealt with that a second time if I would of went into his room again to give him his medication and he did that shit again. Old man or not he needs to learn some respect and keep his damn hands to himself."

I agree with you babe. If he were not like 90 years old with serious mental health issues, I would not be able to overlook what he did."

I feel you babe.

Damn near the entire call Jacky expressed to me the way the old man who grabbed her ass made her feel which was cool because I cared how she felt. The recording I hated to hear came on, "You have one-minute left on this phone call." "Jacky, I miss and love you so much."

"I miss and love you too babe," uttered out our mouths before the minute we had left was done.

I wanted to call her back, but I did not because I was mindful of the cost of the calls. They were not cheap!! Even though as a nurse Jacky made good money, the bills and taking care of two children took most of her paychecks, I did not want to add on to deducing from her bank account. This jail shit is "**BIG BUSINESS**" for certain people. When a person is placed in jail, there is money being made off them from all different angles. The big check comes from the government paying with taxpayer's money for a person to be housed in a jail or prison, then after he or she is housed in a jail or prison they charge you to use the phone which is not cheap. Then they charge you an arm and a leg to buy food. For example, a 10-cent ramen noodle soup cost one dollar in some jails. Just imagine all the money certain people are pocketing from different angles in the prison industry!

CHAPTER 11

VISIT

Before you know it, I was awoken to my cell door being opened the next morning by a correctional officer "Antoine, you have a visit. I will give you 10 minutes to get yourself together, when you are ready come to my desk and get your pass. Ok, C.O I will be ready in ten. I got on my feet, brushed my teeth, and rinsed my face. I put on my clothes and sneakers and then walked to the officer's desk to get my pass within 10 minutes. After receiving my pass, the officer opens the housing unit door for me to leave. I quickly walked to the visiting room door and tried to push it open, but it was locked. I knocked several times, shortly after a guard came an opened the door, "your name is?" The officer asked. "Amanze Antoine" I stated as I handed him my pass. Ok, go through the next door and enjoy your visit Antoine. I walked to and through the next door which was the entrance to the actual visit room itself. There was a bunch of people coming to see their loved ones who were incarcerated. "Do you see your visitors?" the officer asked who was sitting at a desk on the left of the door's entrance. Yes, they are both walking this way right now. First my mom opened her arms to give me a strong warm hug, then right after Jacky jumped into my arms and gave me a bear hug along with a nice sloppy kiss with lots of tongue, which I gladly took. Then we all went to our assigned seats and began our hour-long visit. Son, how are you? My mom asked. I am stressed out!! I want out of here!! I want you out of here too son! You need a lawyer! I know, I do! The feds do not play fair Ma! Someone in here told me their cousin got 20 years when he was arrested by the feds for selling drugs, and they did not even have any evidence against him. The feds said he was selling drugs but never caught him in possession of any drugs, never saw him selling drugs, and never found any drugs on the people he allegedly sold the drugs to. All they had were people testifying at his trial saying his cousin sold them drugs. That was the only evidence the feds had at trial, and he lost the trial and got 20 years. That is crazy, was what the look on my mom's face stated.

You were doing so good, Amanze. You were working and staying out of trouble. This whole situation just came out of nowhere! I know Ma, this whole situation is crazy.

Speaking of working, can you please call my job and tell them what happened please, so they do not think I just quit without any notice. Ok son, I will when I leave here. Thank you, Ma. I appreciate that.

Babe, you know I've been saving money to get my body done. But if needed, I'll give it to your aunt to help pay for a lawyer for you. It's not much but it's something babe, Jacky stated. Thank you, babe I appreciate that. No problem, I'll do what I can to help you Amanze. I have a friend who went to college in West Virginia, and she said it's super racist out there. So, babe I think you really need a lawyer when you get out there, so you don't get lost in the system. I for sure need a lawyer, because I will be going to trial without a doubt if these charges are not dropped against me when I get to West Virginia. I agree, Amanze you need a lawyer my mom said. Your aunt will see what she can do lawyer-wise for you. She said she will come to visit you on Monday with Jacky. I look forward to seeing her on Monday, and to hear what she has to say about getting me a lawyer, I stated. For the entire visit we all spoke about how unfair it was for me to get charged with a crime that the evidence did not support. Towards the end of the visit Jacky and I could not help but look at each other seductively even though this was not a good situation for me. From the looks in our eyes you could tell we both were thinking hardcore porno thoughts! "Antoine you have 5 minutes left" the guard shouted out. Damn, that was a fast visit! My mom said as we all were still indulging in conversation, "Amanze be safe and keep your head up son, remember they can imprison your body but not your mind." "You are right ma. I will try my best to keep my head up, it is easier said than done!!" "I know it is son but try your best to." "Yeah babes try your best to" Jacky said repeating what my mom just said. "I will babe" I told Jacky as I looked into her eyes. "Ok Antoine, time is up" the officer shouted. "That was not 5 minutes" my mom said just as I stood up from the chair I was sitting in. My mom got up from her chair and we hugged each other goodbye. "I love You Ma!" "I love you too Son." Jacky quickly rushed into my arms for a hug as soon as my mother and I released each other from our hug, we gave each other the tightest hug ever then looked each other in the eyes and said "I love you," along with another sloppy kiss like the one she greeted me with. "Amanze I am going to stick by your side no matter what, I truly love you" Jacky stated. "See you on Monday babe, when I come back up here with your aunt" Jacky said. My mother and Jacky started walking towards the door of freedom as they were leaving the jail. For some strange reason when Jacky just told me she was "going to stick by my side no matter what," I did not believe it. I cannot explain it. It was just a gut feeling I felt. Staying and watching my mom and Jacky leave was the worst feeling ever. I wanted to leave with them so bad, but I knew that would not be happening today!

CHAPTER 10

LAW LIBRARY TIME!!

I walked over to the correctional officer's desk and asked him what times I can go to the law library? He told me at ten a.m. you can. Ok thank you sir, I stated "You have about 2 more hours until you can go. Just come back up here when that clock over there says ten. What is your name?"

"Amanze Antoine." I told him.

"I'll have a pass written up for you by 10 so you can go." "Ok thanks a lot, sir I appreciate it" I said before walking off.

I had to go to the law library to research the charge I was being charged with. I had two hours to burn before I could go so, I worked out for forty-five minutes and then got into the shower. After showering I stayed in my cell looking at the clock that was directly in front of my cell wishing 10 am was already here. I had about 45 minutes left before I could go. I was in my cell caught up thinking the worst. I have seen innocent people "spend years on top of years in prison for something they did not do." I was hoping not to be one of those people! I knew how foul the court system is/was and how unfair it can be.

If I was already indicted and arrested for a crime I know I did not do, I knew it was a possibility I may be one of those innocent people in jail who gets prison time for a crime they didn't commit. Having a past criminal record that did not help. Even though I had a past criminal record did not make me guilty of the crime I was being charged with! What makes me guilty of a crime is the evidence showing I committed the crime. The fact I have a criminal record does not make me guilty. Some people's first thought is, **WELL** he committed crimes in the past, so he had to commit this new crime he is being charged with. **THAT IS NOT A FACT**!! Why is it not a fact? It is not a fact because people do change after going to prison. It may take some one time going to prison to change who they are. For some, it may take them going to prison two or three times before they change who they are as an individual by "changing the way they think" which is requisite to do to truly change who you are as a person. I was for sure one of those people who changed who they were as a person!!! Sitting in my cell waiting to go to the law library. I wondered to myself what if my case was to go to trial and one of the jurors googled my name and my criminal record popped up? Would they reach a verdict based on the evidence seen at my trial or based on them thinking I was guilty because I had a past criminal record, I contemplated that question until I heard the officer say "Antoine you still want to go to the law library? It's 10 am." As I stuck my head out of the cell I said, "yes I still will like to go sir." "Ok come to my desk and pick up your pass that I have already written out. I'll be there in a second." I put on my sneakers and walked to the officer's desk, I picked up my pass and then walked quickly to the door that leads to the law library. I had to wait for another correctional officer to open it up because it was locked. A female officer came within 2 minutes and opened the door. I handed her my pass and went to the nearest computer. I searched for cases that had people charged with the same exact crime I was being charged with. All the cases I looked up all had one thing in common!! All the people who were charged with the same crime I was being charged with "all got caught with the firearms" the prosecutor said someone bought for them or the firearms were either found in their homes, cars or on their person. I could not put together why am I being charged with this charge if I was never caught or found in possession of any firearms. It did not make any fucking sense to me!! To get another point of view I asked the person sitting next to me was he good at law? "I understand a lot of it" the brown skin brother said. Aight cool, can I ask you a question?

"Sure, what is it bro?" "What does this charge right here say a person did? I said while pointing at the computer screen showing him the charge, I wanted him to clarify for me. "Move your finger please, let me see. He said as he leaned over towards the computer squinting his eyes. "Ummm that's saying you conspired with two or more people to buy firearms for you illegally. It's saying they went into a gun store and purchased firearms legally, but since they were really purchased for you, therefore making it illegal." I do not get what you said. All this is saying is that people went into a gun store and bought firearms as if they were buying them for themselves. Then they gave the firearms to you after they legally purchased them. I do not understand how I could be charged with this, when I never received any firearms from anyone nor was, I ever found in possession of any firearms. "So, you're telling me you never were caught with any firearms?" No, I was not! If you never were caught with any firearm, I can't see how the hell you are being charged with this crime bro!" Wait let me ask you this, were you ever caught receiving any firearms from anyone? No, that is impossible!! I never received any firearms from anyone so how could I ever be seen receiving any firearms!!" Taking off his glasses the brother I was speaking to continued, "One thing I know bro is that the feds don't play fair! They are convicting people with no evidence at trial. My cousin years ago had a federal case. The feds charged him for selling drugs and he was never found in possession of any drugs nor was he ever caught selling any drugs. They gave him 20 years after he lost the trial. The feds had people lie on the stand at his trial saying he sold drugs to them. Even though they had no drugs to prove he did. My cousin still lost the trial. Tell me that's not some bullshit! Yeah, that's crazy" I stated! Little did I know, I would soon be under the same circumstance his cousin got 20 years for. "Thanks, bro, for your help and insight." "No problem, anytime" the good brother said. I got up from my chair and left the law library in shock still thinking about how unfair the feds were to his cousin. I was praying in my head I hope this gets cleared up once I get extradited to West Virginia, and this charge gets dropped against me. I knew I was innocent. I went back to my cell and laid in bed thinking about what the guy in the law library said about his cousin for hours, even after leaving the law library. I was so fucking stressed. All I wanted to do was go to sleep, which I ended up doing until dinner time. "On the chow" the officer yelled out, you know what that means. I get out of bed, ate my tray, and went right back to bed trying to sleep this day away so I can get my early morning visit from Jacky and my mom.

CHAPTER 12

STRIP SEARCH!!

Now was the part I had to go through I hated most about getting a visit, getting strip-searched by another man. Seeing your loved ones on a visit was great but this was the worst part of the visit! "Take your clothes off, lift your balls, show me the bottom of your feet, turn around, squat and cough". Those were the words that came out of the officer's mouth who was searching me. "What a job officer! You did not blink when you searched me, you don't feel funny searching another man like this," I said with a disgusted look on my face. "Don't come to jail if you don't like getting searched this way the officer said!" I did not come to jail by choice! Your fellow law enforcement officer locked me up for some shit I did not do! "Yeah, that's what you all say" he said with a smirk on his face. I did not even entertain the officer anymore, because it was pointless. I had more important battles to fight.

I was hoping my aunt gets me a lawyer like she said she would. I knew going to court with a legal aid or court-appointed attorney was like going to court with the prosecutor representing you as your attorney. One thing is for sure, a loss on your end will be taken when a legal aid or court-appointed attorney is representing you. Either they trick or scare you into taking a plea or if you go to trial, they make sure you lose. That is just the unwritten rule in all courtrooms throughout the United States. BIG FACTS!!!!!!!!!!!!!! I also know from experience you are guilty as soon as you step foot in the courtroom. You know the saying you are innocent until proven guilty? THAT'S BULLSHIT!!!!!!!! You are guilty until you prove your innocence. A lot of times even if you do prove your innocence, you still get lots of prison time.

This happens because your legal aid or court-appointed attorney did not raise the proper defense they knew they could have raised for you to win at trial, making the end result you losing a trial. Even some paid attorneys sell you out the same way a legal aid or court-appointed attorney does. That is the story of thousands of thousands of people currently incarcerated in the United States!! Therefore, it is critical to have an "effective attorney" that does his or her job to the best of their ability. I knew I needed a lawyer.

After leaving the visiting room search area I went to my housing unit and went straight to bed. That visit made me even more stressed because I wanted to leave with my mom and Jacky. Just the fact of knowing I did not do anything wrong and could not leave the jail made the stress level in my body reach its boiling point, the more I thought about it.

I got back out of bed when dinner was getting served. As I look at my tray, I saw mashed potatoes, carrots, two slices of bread and some type of meat. I did not know what type of meat it was. It did not taste or look like chicken, beef, or pork. Whatever it was, I ate it and enjoyed it! That is what you call being so hungry that anything you eat tastes like a five-star meal.

After I ate, I worked out in my cell a little bit, took a shower, and went back to sleep until the next morning.

CHAPTER 13

SUNDAY!!

The next morning, I went to the law library and started looking up more cases of people who were charged with the same charges I was being charged with. Out of the 20 cases I looked up, I kept noticing the same thing! They all were caught with the firearms they were accused of having someone buy for them, or the guns were recovered in the state they supposedly transported them to. "How the fuck could I get charged with this shit?" I said out loud talking to myself. I just could not see how, when there is no evidence against me supporting this charge. I was convinced the prosecutor in West Virginia did some underhanded shit to get me indicted on these charges at the grand jury!! A person is not supposed to get indicted by a grand jury if the evidence does not support the charge or charges. I knew the evidence presented to the grand jury by the prosecutor had to have been false for the prosecutor to get me indicted. I knew I was innocent. I firmly believed the prosecutor did some grimy unethical shit to get me indicted by the grand jury he or she was in full control over. In the back of my mind I foresaw it was not going to be fair when I get to West Virginia and face this charge. If the prosecutor could get me indicted and charged with a crime that evidence did not support, only time would tell what else the prosecutor had in store for me. At this stage in my journey I did not know what to expect, and to what degree the prosecutor, the judge and my lawyer would go to make sure I got convicted. I sat at the computer a little bit longer looking up cases then I left. I called Jacky and she said she was going through her purse to find a piece of chewing gum and came across the business card the court-appointed attorney gave to her the day her and my mom came to court. "Babe, I decided to call her to ask her when will you get transported to West Virginia? Babe, she said there is a good chance on Tuesday you will be transferred from the jail you are in now to Brooklyn MDC, then from there you will be transferred to Philadelphia F.D.C. She said after that she does not know the exact jail you will be going to but from F.D.C it should be within a few days when you are taken to a County Jail in West Virginia." Ok babe, thanks for calling her to find that out for me. No babe, you know I got your back, I will do everything I can to help you, Jacky said.

Babe do not get mad, but my sister told me to leave you. I told her you were arrested, and she said I deserve someone better than you, because you were in jail. She also told my mother you got locked up. My mom called me and told me the same thing. She said you are in jail and you cannot do anything for me so why stay with you. She said I need to find a man who will give me money and pay my bills. Amanze, my mother knows I do not care about no man's money. I make my own money, and I do not need any man to take care of me or my kids!

Babe, I promise I will never leave you!! I love you Amanze, I am not going to listen to them.

Why did you tell your sister I was locked up? I knew if she found out I was arrested she would put in her two cents on what you should and should not do. You talk too much! I wish you would have never told her. I know, I wish I would have not either, Amanze. She tried to hook me up with someone at her job, but I told her I was good. Jacky, she doesn't have any respect for me doing that shit! I do not like your sister, she violated!! You have nothing to worry about Amanze. I am never leaving you in life! What my mom and sister say does not affect me whatsoever. I am not ever going to leave you! On my kids, I am not!!

You have one-minute remaining on this phone call this recording just fucking said!!

Ok Jacky, I love you and I hope you mean what you say. I hope you are a woman of your word and stick by my side." "I love you too babe, I'm a woman of my word, you will see!!" Click, the phone hung up!

After hanging up the phone with Jacky I just went back to my cell, because I was so angry about what Jacky's mom and sister told her to do. I did not want to take my anger out on anyone. Any little thing someone said or did would have set me on fire!

I locked in my cell did 1,000 push-ups, took a birdbath, and laid in bed in deep thought, like I have been doing since the first day I was arrested. I kept falling asleep and waking up, falling asleep and waking up throughout the entire night. I could not sleep for anything!!

Eventually, I did fall asleep. I slept through breakfast the next morning and got up to eat lunch.

CHAPTER 14

MONDAY'S VISIT!!

While eating my lunch, the correctional officer screamed out my name and said I had a visit. I was already dressed and ready, so I just left my lunch in my cell and went to the officer's desk to get my pass for the visit. The officer wrote up my pass, opened the door, and said have a good one! "Ok, thank you," I said as I exited the door and walked down the hall to the visiting room entrance door. I knocked on the door like most people have to do. Because even though an officer was always assigned to be at the door, there was never an officer there. A guard finally came to the door after me giving the door about 50 knocks. I handed the officer my pass and walked to the other door directly in front of me, to get to the actual visit room as I did on my last visit. As soon as the other officer opened that door Jacky and my aunt saw me come into the visiting room and walked toward me to greet me. Warm hugs were received from both of them, along with that nice sloppy kiss from Jacky that was always very welcomed. We sat down in our seats and began to talk. "Well Amanze, how are you" my aunt asked. My facial expression read how does it look like I am doing. "Not so good" I said in a low tone. "As you may already know my pastor from my church said he knows a few lawyers in Virginia who practice law in West Virginia. As soon as you get to West Virginia, I will make sure you have an attorney Amanze." I was convinced I was going to have a lawyer when I got to West Virginia, by how confident my aunt sounded. At least I will have a lawyer when I get down there! So, I thought!! "Ok thank you for that," I replied to my aunt after she told me I will for sure have a lawyer once I get to West Virginia. No problem Amanze, you know your aunty loves you. Jacky just sat there super quiet listening and staring in my eyes while my aunt and I spoke about her getting a lawyer for me. Jacky was always respectful and just a good person in general. That was the main reason why I fell in love with her. She did not have a bad bone in her body. She had a good soul. She only had one downfall in my eyes. She was too naive to certain things and I always use to tell her to open her eyes because it is a cold world!! Once people see how naive you are Jacky, they will run you over than spin around the block and run you over again. I always tried to make her a better and stronger person, as I should. That was something her mom and sister did not know.

I was telling my aunt how the Mount Vernon police department detectives were asking me about her sons. "What did they ask you about them Amanze? Did I know them or anything about them I stated." She gave me the look like they still focus on my sons!! I did not want to waste any more time talking about that, so I shifted the conversation to Jacky.

"What's up babe talk to me" I said to Jacky with a very seductive look in my eyes. Even though I was locked up for something I did not do, the thought of bending Jacky over the table came through my mind while looking at her. I could not help but think about the wonderful sex we use to have every day when I was free!!

I am not doing well, babe. I would be doing much better if you were home with me. My job is stressing me out, I am working longer hours than expected and I am missing you like crazy Amanze. "I want you home" was the last sentence that came out of her mouth before she started crying. I sat there and I let Jacky vent about all that was bothering her throughout the entire visit. I listened to her giving her all my attention!! I could see it and hear it in her voice she was really hurt by this situation. You never really know how you affect someone until something occurs and you see how much that person is affected by it!

"You have five minutes left Antoine" the guard sounded off. Damn, the visit went by fast. It seemed like we just sat down a minute ago.

49

I love yall and thank yall so much for coming to see me. "Anytime," Jacky said. You know your aunty will always find time to come check on you. I appreciate that, and please tell your pastor thank you too for his help trying to find me a lawyer. "Ok, I will.

You take care of yourself and stay prayed up, God is real, and **GOD** can help you Amanze, my aunt said in a very sincere tone.

Jacky, I love you so much. I wish I was home. I know this is hard on you babe. Please hang in there. "I will try my best to Amanze. It's just so hard without you being home with me. I know babe but please try to.

"Time is up Antoine," the officer with the tight ass pants said. I got up hugged and kissed Jacky goodbye then hugged my aunt goodbye. I love yall. "We love you too" were the last words all three of us exchanged during the visit.

Like the first visit after I left being strip-searched, I went straight to my cell and laid down forcing myself to sleep by just lying in bed with my eyes closed. That shit hurts not being able to leave with your loved ones. I am locked up for some shit I did not do, was the repeated thought that went through my head.

Everyone thinks once the feds arrest you, they have serious evidence on you, and you had to commit a crime! That is the stigma the feds have on the streets. I see that stigma is not a fact, because I know I did not do the shit they charged me with!!

CHAPTER 15

TUESDAY MORNING ON THE TRANSFER!!

"Pack up Antoine they need you down at bookings." For what? I asked the officer. "You are getting transferred to Brooklyn M.D.C today by the feds."

The lawyer was right about what she told Jacky I was leaving on Tuesday.

Officer, can I take a shower before I leave? Sure, hurry up through Antoine. Ok, cool I stated. After showering I got dressed and left.

The officer escorted me and others to bookings. Bookings is the part of the jail where inmates are received into the jail, released from the jail, or transferred out of the jail.

Upon arriving at bookings, I saw three federal agents. You could tell they were agents because they have a different type of look about them, more than any other law enforcement branch. They look sophisticated. "Have a seat right here Mr. Antoine," one of the agents said to me as the officer escorting me and the other men were walking toward the agents' direction.

I am thinking to myself, how the fuck does this mother fucker know I am Antoine? Out of all the people the officer was escorting, the agent looked directly at me and knew who I was out of the entire group. **CRAZY**! "Date of birth Mr. Antoine?" "12-17-1980" I retorted back to the agent.

Ok Antoine, I have to search you and the rest of the men real fast. Then we will be on our way to Brooklyn MDC. Please follow me Antoine." I followed the agent to a back room, and he searched me and then handcuffed me. You can have a sit over there the agent said while pointing to a row of seats. We will be leaving real soon Mr. Antoine, the agent said. I took a seat and watched the agent search three more people. He handcuffed them and told them to be seated in one of the seats in the row of seats I was sitting in. "Excuse me sir, I said stopping one of the agents. How long do you think it's going to take me to get to West Virginia?" "I'll say by Monday" the agent said. "Ok, thank you Mr. agent."

The last guy that was searched by the agent and told to have a seat looked really familiar. I did not want to stare at him, so I took several glimpses his way trying to put together in my head where I knew him from. Oh yeah, that's Ronald the light bulb in my head went off. "Ronald what's good my brother?" He looked at me and squinted his eyes at me. I guess he did that because he had bad eyes and that helped him see more clearly. "Amanze, what's going on my youth" he said in a Jamaican accent "long time don't see my youth. Blood clot ya old now my youth. You have grey hair now last time mi see ya was 15 years ago. You look young back then but now you look old to blood clot," he said in a joking manner. I just busted out laughing. Ronald was an older guy I knew from being in prison with him. We did about two years together in the same prison years ago. He was a cool dude, so we got close. "What happened why you locked up Ronald?" "Mi get deported back to yard five years ago and mi come back to the United States, and Mr. Charlie lock mi up because mi na supposed to be back in the United States but me come back to foreign to work and feed mi family. Dam lock mi up! Mi do not do no crime my youth, mi just a work work work. The man dem give mi 7 blood clot years because mi come back to blood clot United States of American. Crazy my youth!! Right?" "That is crazy Ronald. They gave you seven years because you got deported back to Jamaica and you come back to the United States to work without committing no crime. I understand you were not supposed to come back to the United States, but seven years for that is fucking crazy!! That is fucked up, the feds locked me up because they said I had people buy guns out of a gun store for me then I transported them to New York from West Virginia." "Ya a gunman my youth?" "Hell no" I am not no gunman! I did not do that shit! The feds never found me with any guns, but I am still being charged even though they have no evidence against me. That shit

52

crazy too Ronald!" "America crazy my youth" Ronald said. "I know! They charged me in West Virginia so now I am being extradited to West Virginia." "Blood clot, white man crazy out there my youth!! **KKK** land that, Ronald stated!! Make sure ya have a lawyer ya trust my youth before dem hang ya blood clot." "I know Ronald, I got to get a good lawyer. My aunt said she got me when I get down there. I hope she keeps her word and gets me a lawyer." "Amanze make sure ya get all ya discovery from ya lawyer dem so you can know what dem ras clot prosecutor intend to use pon ya if ya go to trial my youth." "They can't have anything because I didn't do this shit Ronald." Dem prosecutor them crafty my youth them, might have everything fake pon ya my youth!" "Ok, men come on. We are going to get on the van, and we will be in Brooklyn by 12 pm. Please, no talking in the van. Gentlemen you may stand and please follow me the agent stated." We all got up and proceeded to the van one by one, each man got in. Every man sat in silence for the entire ride caught up in their own thoughts.

CHAPTER 16

BROOKLYN M.D.C

The bus pulled up in front of M.D.C Brooklyn around the same time the agent said we will arrive. "Fellows it's 11:57" the agent said out loud. One by one the agent let us out of the van to go inside so we can be processed in. I was the first to go inside.

"Name and date of birth please," the female nurse asked me. My name is Amanze Antoine, and I was born on 12-17-1980, miss. Ok, thank you sir.

Do you have any medical issues? No, I do not. Do you take any medication sir? "Nah." Are you pretty much healthy? Yes, I am ok.

Well sick call is from Monday through Friday. If you feel sick or something does not feel right, please fill out a sick call slip and give it to the officer in your housing unit.

You will be seen by either myself or by another nurse on duty. Did you get that? Yes, I did miss. "Ok sir, please take a seat in the cell over there," the nurse said as she looked towards the cell, she wanted me to sit in.

I went into the cell and took a seat and waited for everyone else who took the ride on the van with me to be seen by the nurse. The nurse was pretty fast with speaking to everyone that rode in the van with me. Shortly after we were seen by the nurse, we all were being escorted to a housing unit by a correctional officer.

While being escorted to the housing unit I saw a dude named Fraizer from Yonkers, New York. I have known him since my teen years, he was in the hallway mopping the floor. Fraizer was a fighter at heart and well respected in Yonkers. Some people did not like him, but one thing was for sure they respected him.

Fraizer, what's good? I said. Oh shit, what's good Amanze? Damn bro long time no see. I know, he said. How long have you been here, Fraizer? I have been here like nine months. I blew trial on two counts of the indictment and now I am waiting to get sentenced. I beat the top count, but lost trial to the rest of the counts.

What's going on with you Amanze? I'm about to get extradited to West Virginia to face some charges. The feds got me on false charges. "They are good for doing that Amanze!" They said I was getting firearms from West Virginia and transporting them to N.Y. They charged me with some shit I did not do. I am not going to be here for long, I should be out of here in a few days. I think I will be going to F.D.C in Philly from here.

Fraizer and I could not really talk for long because the officer who was escorting me told me I had to keep it moving. Fraizer, it was good seeing your bro, unfortunately under these circumstances. "It's alright my nigga, we going to see each other in the streets and turn up in the club or something" he said as I shook his hand and hugged him. "Fraizer keep your head up boy!" "You too Amanze!" "One love bro," I said as I walked towards the housing unit I was going to be housed at. "I see what unit you're going into Amanze. I am going to send you over some food depending on who is working tomorrow. I got you bro, Fraizer shouted out, just before I walked into the housing unit.

Everyone who drove in the van with me were all going to the same housing unit. We all had to stop at the officer's office when we entered the housing unit to get the cell number we were going to.

I was hoping Ronald was my cellmate since I knew him, but he was not. I got this dude named Wildout from New Jersey. He was cool, quiet, and laid back.

I am glad he was, because I could not have put up with someone loud in my cell. I was a little relieved to get a cellmate that was on the same type of time I was on, who was laid back, quiet, and really did not like talking a lot.

M. D. C Brooklyn was an actual federal jail for federal inmates. Unlike Westchester County Jail where I just came from, which only holds federal prisoners in its jail due to a contract it has with the federal government. Things were a lot different at M.D.C than it was at Westchester County Jail.

At M.D.C., federal inmates only receive 300 minutes per month to communicate with their families, which is fucking insane!! Each call is 15 minutes long. On average, there is 30 days in a month. If you wanted to make a 15-minute call per day to your loved ones everyday out of the month you could not, because that takes you over the 300-minute limit per month.

If you wanted to use the phone everyday out of the month you would have to literally time yourself and make sure you stay "exactly" 10 minutes on the phone each day out of the month which equals 300 minutes if the month has 30 days in it. 10 minutes daily is not enough time to talk to your mom, dad, children, the love of your life, etc.!! There is only but so much a person can say in 10 minutes on the phone.

I found out all federal prisons are like this. When I got to M.D.C. this was my first time in a federal jail, so all this shit was new to me.

Thank God, there were other means to communicate with your family. Communicating through emails was another way to communicate with your peoples.

The thing about communicating through email, is it takes a long time for your people to receive your message after you send it to them. And, the time it takes for you to receive the message they send to you.

It takes 90 minutes for your people to receive the message you send them and another 90 minutes for you to receive the message they send to you.

"What's the hold up on the messages?" Jacky asked me on the phone. Babe, I don't know why it takes so long for us to get each other messages.

I sent you a message at 10am and you got it at 11:30am Jacky. "The federal prison system is crazy Amanze." I know Jacky, I got to get the fuck out of here.

The good part about it Amanze is at least we get to communicate with each other even though it takes a long time to receive each other's messages. Yeah, you are right babe. I said in agreement.

So how is everything going with you, the kids and work?" The kids are doing well. Their dad is always a big help, even though we are not together he is still a good dad to them. He helps me out a lot with our son and daughter. He is a good dad Amanze. I have seen personally how he was with his kids when I was out. The kids were very lucky to have a dad like him. He made sure they were always taken care of. Where I grew up a dad who was always around taking care of his child or children was hard to come by. So, I def respected the kids' dad for really being a dad. A lot of times where I am from dudes just make babies and leave the responsibility on the mother to raise the child or children.

Trust me, I know. I saw my grandmother, mom and aunt raise children on their own not to mention most of the people I grew up with mothers.

Amanze, how long do you think you will be in that jail in Brooklyn before you get transferred? I'm not sure, they didn't say, it could be any day.

Jacky went on talking about how the kids were doing in school and how work was stressing her out.

You have one-minute left on this phone call the recording said. One thing this jail and Westchester County Jail had in common was this fucking phone recording stating I had one-minute left on my call.

Jacky, I love you and try to enjoy the rest of your day.

I can't fully enjoy it because you are not home with me Amanze. My life has changed since you left Amanze.

Click the phone hung up. Damn, Jacky's last words were felt. I knew what she meant because I felt the same way. I got off the phone, talked to Ronald a little bit, worked out, showered, and went to bed.

CHAPTER 17

WEDNESDAY, ON THE TRANSFER!!

The next morning to my surprise I was getting transferred to Philadelphia F.D.C. "Antoine pack up and hurry, you are moving" were the words that came out of the female officer's mouth who was working in the housing unit.

Ok, miss, let me use the bathroom quickly and I'll be right down. I said from the door of my cell that was on the second floor.

"Ok, hurry up. Antoine, they are waiting for you."

I put up the towel on my cell's window so my cellmate knew I was using the bathroom, so he would not enter it. After using the bathroom, I washed my hands and started to walk toward the officer's desk.

Before getting to the officer's desk I told Ronald and my cellmate I was leaving and shook both of their hands goodbye.

Antoine, look, you see that officer down the hall? The female officer working the housing unit said as she held open the door for me to leave the unit.

Yes, I see him miss. Ok, he is waiting for you, just walk down the hall to him. Ok miss, I said as I walked towards the officer.

Damn, it's about time. The officer said to me when I got to him. "I had to take a shit man." Ok, that's understandable, the male officer stated.

He took me to a huge cell where everyone in the cell was going to F.D.C. Philly. One by one we were called out the cell to be searched, handcuffed, and then placed on the bus.

In total, there were 30 of us on the bus. Unlike my quiet van ride from Westchester County Jail to M.D.C. this bus ride was loud as fuck!!

This shit reminded me of waiting in the waiting area in the parole building. I hated it!

I just stared out the window the entire ride looking at cars that drove past and still in deep thought like I always been since the day I got arrested.

CHAPTER 18

PHILLY F.D.C!

"What is your name?" The officer asked.

"Amanze Antoine" is my name, I stated.

"Ok, please have a seat over there and a nurse will see you soon sir." said the officer.

"Can I ask you a question officer? Sure, what is it?"

"How long will I be in Philly?" I asked.

"Maybe, for two days Antoine."

"From here you will go to Youngstown Ohio County Jail," he answered.

"And after I go there, how long will it take for me to get to West Virginia?"

"Uhhhh, I will say may be Monday. That is when inmates are transferred in Youngstown."

After looking through some paperwork, the officer said, "your court date in West Virginia is on Monday. So, you will be in court Monday, Antoine."

"Thank you, officer. I appreciate that."

Forty-five minutes later everyone who was on the bus was seen by the nurse, and we were on our way to a housing unit to get an assigned bed, for however long we were going to be here for.

We were escorted to the housing unit by a Black female guard. She told everyone she was escorting to "do not talk about your case to no one!" She continued; this is not Philadelphia this is "telladelphia." I said, "damn it's like that?" She said, "yeah, it's like that, you can't trust nobody in here child."

I thought to myself, damn this is coming from an officer who works here, so that shit get to be real. Everyone being escorted by her was looking like they were in shock by what the female officer just said.

I was looking at them like you might be one of them niggas she is talking about, who telling. I knew the female officer did not literally mean the whole Philadelphia was telling, it was just a figure of speech she used.

Niggas was telling in my hood too. Just like they are telling in everybody hood.

I did not have to tell nothing to nobody about my case, because I did not do this shit. So, I was not worried about what the female officer was saying. What the female officer had said was just another reminder why it is best to leave the streets alone and do the right thing.

I got to my cell door and opened it up to see someone laying on the bottom bunk bed. As soon as walked in the cell he sat up on the bed.

"What's good bro, the police told me this is going to be my cell, this is cell twenty-nine, right?" I asked him. Yeah, it is.

My name is Murda, he said as he extended his hand to me to shake it. I am Amanze. Where you from? He asked.

"I am from Mount Vernon, New York."

"Money earning" Mount Vernon, he shot back to me.

"I am from Newark, New Jersey."

"You got soap and shit?" He asked.

"Nah, I don't have shit. I am fresh off the bus."

He went over to his locker and pulled out two bars of soap, one toothpaste and six ramen noodle soups. This the best I can do for you bro, I am fucked up myself right now.

Thanks, I appreciate that brother. I might only be here for a day, so one bar of soap should be good enough. I stated as I handed him back one bar of soap. He took the soap and put it back into his locker.

Out of nowhere he started talking about what he was in jail for. Yo, Amanze, I got booked for some drug sales. I was locked up in a New Jersey state prison and I had a cell phone helping direct traffic to my brother, who was selling kilos in the town.

One night the correctional officer found the cell phone in my cell and saw what I was doing, because of the text messages and shit. The prison gave the cell phone to the feds and the feds booked us all.

I copped out to 12 years. I am waiting to get sentenced right now. My brother got 20 years. He is in U.S.P Canon.

My cellmate was cool, but he kept talking the whole fucking night! You would have thought he knew me for years', because of all the shit he was telling me.

"Murda, I'm going to catch up with you in the A.M." I told him trying to give him a hint that I am about to go to bed after I jumped up on the top bunk bed. I had a long day, and I need some rest.

"Ok, I respect that homie," Murda said.

I laid in the bed with the blanket over my head, you know what I was doing. I was in deep thought about how I could have gotten arrested for this charge, and praying things goes well once I got to West Virginia.

I know God might not have been hearing my prayers, because the only time I pray like a preacher's son is when something goes wrong. I eventually went to sleep and woke up the next morning.

As always, the first thing I did was brush my teeth and rinse my face. I got on the phone and called Jacky to let her know where I was at. I could not call her yesterday when I arrived because at F.D.C it takes 24 hours for you to be processed into their phone system to you are able to use the phone.

Jacky and I conversation on the phone was like the rest of phone calls we had since I been arrested. We spoke about the kids, her job, how much we loved each other, and hopes of me getting a lawyer once I reached West Virginia.

The only thing different about this conversation was me telling her I was at F. D. C and me having a court date for Monday.

"Monday, babe!!! I am taking off work and driving to West Virginia to go to your court date babe. I'm going to text your mom right now while we are on the phone to see if she can take off work so we can drive down there together."

"Ok Jacky, thank you!"

"No problem Amanze, I got your back."

Minutes later Jacky stated, babe, your mom just answered my text I sent her. She said she will drive down there with me. That day we went to court for you, the attorney you had told your mom and I, you would be going to court in Clarksburg, West Virginia.

Once you are in West Virginia, I'll google the federal courthouse in Clarksburg, and find out exactly where the court is located babe.

"Thanks again, Jacky." These phone calls seem to go by fast. It felt like we just got on the phone and the 15 minutes was already up.

I hung up the phone and walked over to the food area to get my breakfast tray. Cold cereal, 2 milks, 2 slices of wheat bread and some fruit. I ate the shit out of that breakfast!! I was so hungry, and the cereal was fruit loops. Yummy!

"Anybody want another breakfast tray?" This dude shouted out, while holding his tray in his hands. Before anybody could answer, "yeah, right here" I said, as I raised my right arm while sitting down eating my last spoon full of cereal.

The dude walked right over to me, sat the tray down on the table, and then took a seat right across from me.

"Thanks, I'm hungry like a motherfucker."

"No problem bro, you can have it. I don't really eat that shit, that shit got too much sugar in it for me. So, where you from?"

"I'm from Mount Vernon, New York."

"OK, OK, OK, he said. I'm from Philly, born and raised."

"Where did you get locked up at in Philly?"

I did not get locked up in Philly. I am getting extradited to West Virginia to face a firearm charge. I might be leaving here tomorrow or Friday. My stay here will not be long.

"Oh, aight," he continued.

I heard West Virginia is super racist, that is what my brother told me. He was out there getting money and they gave him 30 years for selling drugs. He did not even get caught selling that much either. His past criminal record put him in a certain category on the sentence guideline chart and the judge even though she did not have to sentenced him in a certain guideline range and she still did. They do not play fair!!! They do what they want.

In West Virginia, my brother said "ain't nothing black out there but the sky at night."

I wish I would have never told the brother I wanted the extra breakfast tray. The statements he just stated just fucked my entire mood up.

I knew if it was nothing black in West Virginia, the chances of me getting a fair chance in court was slim to none.

Even in places where there are black faces, the chances of getting a fair chance in court was still slim to none. So I knew, West Virginia was not going to be fair to me at all.

Throughout that entire day, all that was going through my head was what I might be going through when I got into the West Virginia courtroom. There was not one good thought that went through my head!!! At All!!!

I got I back on the phone and called my mom and Jacky, expressing these negative thoughts I was having about West Virginia. Phone calls cost $3.15 per call so I did not call a lot. $3.15 is a lot of money for a 15-minute call.

"REMEMBER, I TOLD YOU THIS JAIL SHIT IS BIG BUSINESS!!"

First, they take your money to make phone calls, charge you an arm and a leg, because they know you have to use the phone to communicate. Then "they know" you have to spend money buying food at commissary. So they "**JACKUP**" the prices on food, knowing you have to eat and will pay the price they set on the food.

Commissary itself, like the phone system is a separate entity that brings in millions of dollars yearly for "certain people".

Then the federal government uses taxpayer's money to pay each warden or superintendent of every prison $30K- $60K per year to house each inmate there. Most of that money never gets spent on the inmate, and it goes to "certain people's pockets as profit!"

"Modern day slavery" is the best term to use for the mass incarceration, that has been going on in this country for years.

The United States federal government spends almost 81 billion dollars each year on incarceration, according to the Bureau of Justice Statistics.

That number does not reflect the cost to individuals, families, or the communities disproportionately affected by the criminal justice system.

Yet, this costly system is often ineffective at protecting safety, preparing people for reentry, and reducing recidivism. The prison industry is truly legalized slavery.

It is about who can the government make money off of thing. That is the outlook of the U.S government, and this is why the United States has the largest number of incarcerated people in the world.

Yes, black people and Latinos are targeted more to be incarcerated. Because according to the Bureau of Justice Statistics there are 2.336 million Black and 1.054 million Latinos incarcerated throughout the entire United States. Whereas whites there are only 397,000 incarcerated throughout the entire United States.

Even though whites take up 72.4% of the United States population of 331,883,986. Whereas blacks take up 12.6% and Latinos take up 16.3% of the United States population.

So that lets you know right there who is targeted more to bring to prison. However, there's still some white people in here with us that goes through the same shit we go through daily. We are all on the same boat!! And the name of that boat is called **HUMAN WAREHOUSE A.K.A THE PRISON INDUSTRY!!!!!!!!!!!**

After that short conversation with the brother from Philly, I went straight to my cell and laid down. That is my favorite thing to do when I get stressed out. The only time I would leave the cell was if my cellmate had to use the bathroom, or if I were going to call Jacky or message her on the computer. But overall that whole day I stayed in bed not wanting to do nothing! I just laid in bed thinking and thinking and thinking.

CHAPTER 19

FRIDAY, WELCOME TO YOUNGSTOWN OHIO!!

"Amanze, Amanze," my cellmate Murda said as he tapped me on the leg trying to wake me up from a deep sleep. "Yeah," I said in a just waking up tone.

"Police just told me to tell you to pack up all your things, because you are getting transferred."

"Aight, thanks Murda."

I laid in the bed for a few minutes allowing my body to wake up a little more before I got up brushed my teeth and took a quick shower.

"Aight Murda, I am out of here. Keep your head up bro."

"You do the same Amanze," were the words Murda and I exchanged before I went to the officer's desk and told him I was ready.

Me and three other men got to the Youngstown County Jail fast. Since there were only four of us in total, we were seen by the nurse and sent to a housing unit rapidly. This time my cellmate was a dude from down south. I forget his name.

The first thing I noticed when I entered the cell was how high my cellmate was.

"You good man? What you high on homie?" were my first two sentences to him.

"I'm high off k2," he said with a smirk on his face.

"You smoke?"

"Hell, no I don't smoke that shit!" I stated in a loud tone.

"Bro listen, I am your new cellmate. I do not care how high you get, just leave me alone, and we will be good. I am only here for two days. I am out of here Monday."

He just looked at me and started smiling. I just let him be, he was harmless, and he was higher than a helicopter. He could barely walk when he stood up. I was thankful I only had to put up with this dude getting high all day for only 2 days. Because come Monday, I would be going to West Virginia. Was that really a good thing though? Only GOD knew my fate!

"What the fuck is this?" I said out loud while looking at the food on my tray. The food at this jail tastes like animal shit. The food tasted like everyone from this town had their dogs and cats' shit in one big pot, stirred it up and served it for breakfast, lunch, and dinner at this jail.

I knew what I wish I were eating, and it was not food. The thoughts of what I would be doing to Jacky if I were home quickly went through my head.

This jail was a little different than M.D.C and F.D.C. I could not message Jacky through a computer system. Phone calls were our only way to communicate with each other. I was calling Jacky more than I normally would since the phone calls were cheaper than $3.15 for a 15-minute call.

Monday could not get here any sooner. I could not wait to get into court to see what the fuck was going on and praying for it to be a huge misunderstanding.

The entire 2 days I was in Youngstown County Jail, I did the same thing every day. Which was stay to myself, lay in bed damn near all day, call Jacky, my mom, watch my cellmate go to mars every day when he smoked his K2, and fast. No way, I was not going to eat all the cats and dogs' shit of this town.

CHAPTER 20

MONDAY, WEST VIRGINIA HERE I COME!!

Monday was now here, and I was on my way to West Virginia. The ride was about 4 hours long. The longest four hours in my life! As soon as we pulled up in front of the courthouse two federal agents were waiting for my arrival.

The officer who was in the passenger seat of the car got out of the car and gave a folder to one of the agents waiting in front of the courthouse. They spoke for a few minutes, but I could not hear what was being said.

The officer then walked back to the vehicle after he was done talking, opened the backseat door, and told me to get out of the car in a nasty tone. The 2 agents then took me in their custody. I was taken inside the court building and placed in a cell with shackles on my feet.

About an hour and a half later, I was taken out that cell and brought to a small room to talk to my court appointed attorney. Ms. H was her name. A white woman about 5'5 with a southern accent.

"How do you pronounce your first name was her first question?" "**A-MA-ZAY** is how you pronounce it miss."

"Ok, now Amanze, do you know what you are being charged with?"

"I know what I am being charged with, but what I don't know is how it is even possible for me to get this charge? Because, I didn't do this shit."

"Amanze, I took a look at your rap sheet and I saw that every time you been arrested you took a plea deal."

"And your point is?" I asked her.

You may want to do the same thing for this case and get this all behind you!

"Are you serious!? You cannot be!! You are telling me to take a fucking plea for some shit I did not do! I know there is no proof of me doing what they said I did, because I really did not do this shit. But here you go, telling me to take a plea!!"

"I really don't know what proof they have against you Amanze because I did not receive your discovery from the prosecutor yet."

"So you are telling me to take a plea and you have not even seen my discovery yet! What type of lawyer are you!? You are just like the lawyer I had in New York! You are not a lawyer, you're a fucking prosecutor!!"

"I see your damn rap sheet Amanze!! You have a gun charge that you are still on parole for!! You like guns!! It does not take a rocket scientist to know that you are guilty of this charge Amanze, you can go to trial if you want!! You will get more time! So, my advice to you and always will be my advice to you is to take a plea deal!!"

"Kiss my ass Ms. H" I said before getting up off my seat. I started calling for an agent to get me the fuck out of that room, which happened quickly.

About 20 minutes after the agent took me out of the room where I was speaking to the court appointed attorney, I was brought into the courtroom to see the judge for what is called an arraignment.

The judge asked me how do I plea? I told him not guilty!!

As I expected, my mom and Jacky were within the courtroom along with my "gangsta grandmother." I turned to their direction and said, I need a lawyer. This one right here, pointing to Ms. H, is no good!!

As I turned back and looked at the court-appointed attorney who was seated next to me, I could see the deceitfulness written all over her eyes. I felt in my soul this lady was not going to help me.

"You are remanded to the North Central Regional County Jail" the judge said. As he stared at me like he was a hungry lion in the jungle, who just saw his prey he was about to kill.

"Bond hearing will be held on Thursday. Court is adjourned" the judge said before walking out of the courtroom.

"I love yall," I stated as I looked back at my mom, grandmother, and Jacky as the federal court officer was escorting me out of the courtroom.

"We love you too" was all I heard from all three of them before my last footstep left that courtroom. The agent then placed me in the same holding cell I was in when I first arrived at the court building.

CHAPTER 21

NORTH CENTRAL REGIONAL COUNTY JAIL ON MY WAY!!

About an hour later I was on my way to the North County Regional County Jail. The ride took about 45 minutes to get there.

"Yes, how can I help you?" a voice said through an intercom in front of the jail as the driver of the car had his window rolled down.

"We have one for you from Clarksburg's federal court sir" the agent driving the car said.

"Ok sir, thank you" the voice said through the intercom.

Moments later, the front gate to the entrance of the jail started to slowly open. The agent drove in and parked the car. The 2 agents did not get out of the car until the gate was closed and secured.

They both smoked a cigarette, before letting me out of the back seat to take me inside of the jail. Just like every other jail in the United States that receives a person in their prison or jail, you must see a nurse which I did, minutes after I was brought inside the jail.

Afterwards, a white correctional officer told me to take a seat and he would be back to put me in a cell.

"Can I get a phone call officer before you put me in a cell?"

"No, not yet we have to process you first," the officer stated.

I sat there and took observation of my surroundings. The first thing I noticed was I was the only black dude in sight. The second thing I noticed was the tattoo of the white boy sitting next to me on his neck that said, "white power." I was waiting for him to say anything slick so I can take off on him, but he did not, he just sat there in his own zone caught up in his own thoughts.

The officer came minutes later and took me to the cell he said he was going to take me minutes ago. "What the fuck is this" I said out loud, when I took my first step into that cell. This fucking cell was jam packed. It had at least 30 people in the cell that was only meant to hold 10 people.

People were sleeping on the floor, some were standing, and some were sitting down. There were about 8 mattresses on the floor with people laying on them. The cell smelled like a fucking zoo!! "Officer, how long am I going to be in here for?" I asked before his key locked the cell.

"I don't know guy, I'll try to speed things up, but I am not making any promises."

I looked at the officer like for real! Are you fucking serious? "Excuse me," I said to a dude laying on the floor two feet from the cell's entrance. I did not want to be rude and just step over him without saying excuse me.

I think I said excuse me like 30 times while making my way to a seat, stepping over the people laying on the floor. There was all type of garbage on the floor! You call smell that the toilet was not cleaned in God only knows how long. All you could smell is the scent of piss along with funk in the air. The sink was so fucking dirty!! It looked like if you drank or touched any water from that sink you would die on the spot!!

I could tell most of the dudes in the cell were drug addicts, just by the way they looked. Some were moaning from the pain of being dope sick, some were still high on whatever drug they were high on when they got arrested, and some were just catching up on the sleep their body was in desperate need of, due to them neglecting their daily needed sleep by running the streets all day and night.

I really did not try to talk to anyone. A couple of people did ask me where I was from and I told them, but that is as far as the conversation went. I was not trying to get familiar with nobody, I felt so out of place!!!! I was the only black dude in the cell. I was waiting for someone to come out their mouth the wrong way so I can set an example real quick!

I was in that damn cell for two days before I was sent to a housing unit. Unfucking believable!! Just imagine not taking a shower or brushing your teeth for two days! Not just me though, but everyone in the cell with you! How do you think that cell smelled? It smelled like every zoo in America put together. I was the only dude during those 2 days trying to get every correctional officer's attention that walked by to get me a toothbrush and toothpaste. It seems like nobody in the cell cared. Nasty! Nasty! Nasty!

Cellblock F-1 was the housing unit I was sent to. This unit had 8 cells total. Four of the cells had double bunks and the other 4 cells had only one bed in it making it at max a 12-man housing unit. However, it was not a 12-man housing unit, it was a 21-man unit. This meant some cells had 3 to 4 people in them when the cell was only meant to hold one or two people. This shit got to be illegal!!

In some of these 10 x 8 cells you stepped in there were 3 mattresses on the floor. Some people were sleeping with their heads right next to the toilet in their cell, that is how close their mattress was to the toilet. I never saw no shit like this before. It was different out here.

New York state was not like this. There was one man to a cell in New York. Not down here though!!

Wait, that is not it!! When you go into a housing unit you are not assigned a cell like most jails in the United States. In this West Virginia County Jail, you had to find a cell to live in once you enter a housing unit. If no one invites you in to be their cellmate, guess what? You are out of luck chuck! You just do not have anywhere to sleep unless you are ready to fight for a cell.

As I entered housing unit F-1, I had fire in my eyes. My body language was saying I ain't with nothing and yall going to respect me or we out of here.

Luckily, I did not have to go through trying to find a cell to sleep in. A black dude from Detroit came up to me as soon as I walked into the housing unit, and said you can move into my cell bro. I think I knew why he did that. I was the only other black dude in the housing unit.

His name was Eddie. He was 22 years old, heavy set and brown skinned. He told me he was locked up for drugs and already sentenced to five years. He said he would be getting transferred from this jail soon to finish up the remainder of his time in another jail. Which was common to do once someone is sentenced, he explained. I told him what I was locked up for as well.

"That's crazy," was the only thing he said after I broke down my entire situation to him. I cut the conversation short to call my mother and Jacky who I have not called in two days, because I knew they are worried.

I called my mom first and explained to her I was not able to call because I was stuck in a cell for 2 days without any access to a phone. "Son be safe out there" she kept telling me. She started speaking about my aunt getting a lawyer for me.

"Amanze, call me back in an hour, I'm going to call your aunt and get an update about getting you a lawyer, when you call back I should have an answer for you."

"Ok, ma, will do. I love you and I'll call you back soon."

"Ok, I love you son.

I hung up the phone and called Jacky next. Hi babe, she said happy to hear my voice as much I was to hear hers. Sorry I did not call you sooner, I was unable to. I was forced to be locked in a cell for two days without any access to a phone.

"That is fine Amanze, as long as you are good that is all that matters."

"How are you though Jacky?" "Same shit babe, just wanting you home by my side!

How about you? I'm waiting to hear what my aunt has to say about getting me a lawyer, because I am in West Virginia now. I just spoke to my mom and she told me to call her back in an hour, to give her time to contact my aunt to get an update about her getting me a lawyer.

The lawyer I have now is no good. She wanted me to plead guilty to this shit when I went to court, "She is crazy!!"

Amanze, you need a lawyer! Who you telling I know I do!

Babe, I just wanted to call you real fast, so you know I was good, because you did not hear from me in days. I am about to shower and take care of my hygiene. I feel so dirty!!

I could hear it in Jacky's voice she wanted to continue talking to me so I told her we can talk until the phone call is over.

"Ok, babe are you sure that's what you want to do?"

"Yes, babe I'll be ok, let's talk babe."

We spoke about the norms, the kids and how stressful her job was at times. A few minutes before the phone was about to hang up, Jacky told me how her mom and sister keep telling her to leave me.

"Jacky, if you want you can go. I do not want to hold your life up. I love you but at the same time I love you enough to not hold your life up and let you go so you can live your life. This jail shit is not for a lot of women and I understand that."

"No, I am not going nowhere Amanze, I love you. You are a great man. I am not letting you go Amanze so another female can enjoy you for a lifetime. My mom and sister do not know how much of a good man you are, but I do. I'm telling you like I told them both I am sticking by your side and that's what I'm going to do!!"

Moments later you know what we heard right? "You have one-minute remaining on this phone call." Damn, that same recording is even in West Virginia I said to myself.

"Ok, Jacky I love you and I'm going to hold you to your word. I hope you have a good day."

"I love you too Amanze. I hope you have a good day too even though you are in jail and babe you can hold me to my word. I am not going nowhere!! I'm never leaving you" she said just before the phone hung up.

After I hung up the phone, I jumped my stink ass in the shower. OMG was I thankful my cellmate let me use his shower slippers to take a shower. I for sure was not taking a shower without any shower slippers. My feet might have had fell off by the looking at the shower floor.

While showering I brushed my teeth about three times. My cellmate had looked out before I got in the shower and gave me a brand-new toothbrush and toothpaste.

I noticed on the shower wall the words white power was written on it and right next to it was a drawing of a **NAZI** sign symbol. I knew what that meant! There were some racist motherfuckers in here or there used to be racist motherfuckers in here who wrote all of that on the shower wall in the past.

Whether it was written on the wall by someone who was currently housed in this cellblock or not, I still felt uncomfortable being in this jail.

Not saying that I was comfortable in any jail, but you get my point right!

I jumped out of the shower after about 30 minutes in it to call my mom back. My mom said my aunt's pastor is still working on getting in contact with a couple of lawyers he knew.

I was expecting better news than that, but I guess things were in the making. My mom also said she will be coming back to West Virginia to show support for my bond hearing which was tomorrow.

To my surprise Jacky was going to ride down here with her. Jacky did not bring this up when I was on the phone with her. I guess she wanted to surprise me.

"Son I also called the jail you are in and I found out your visit days. One of your visit days is on Friday so Jacky and I will be coming to see you before we drive back to New York if the judge does not let you out on bond."

"I would love that if I am not able to get out on bond."

"Son, I have to go right now, I am at work and I think I hear my boss coming this way. I love you Amanze, keep your head up baby."

"I love you too Ma." Muah was the sound of this kiss I gave my mom through the phone. I got one back from her before she hung up the phone.

That night in the cell I could tell my cellmate was happy to see another black face, shit so was I! That night we stayed up all night talking even though I had to get up super early to go back to court for my bond hearing. I was so hoping I got out on bond but for some reason a little voice in my head was telling me I was **NOT**.

Long story short, I went to court the next morning and was denied getting out on bond. Like the judge did the last time I went to court, I was remanded back to the North Central Regional County Jail.

The best and worst part of my week was being able to see my mom and Jacky. The best part of the week was seeing them on the visit. The worst part was when my mother told me my aunt will not be able to get me an attorney. Because all the lawyers her pastor knew wanted 100,000 and better to represent me and nobody in the family had that type of money on hand. Once my mom told me that my heart dropped on my lap.

"Me and your aunty looked online for lawyers around here because it might be cheaper to get a lawyer who lives and works in West Virginia, but we didn't come across no one of interest. All lawyers say they are great lawyers when you go to their websites, but there is no proof if they really are or not. We are not from around here, so we do not know which lawyers are good or not. When you go back to your housing unit Amanze, ask people who live in West Virginia do they know any good lawyers? I will trust their word before I trust what I read on a lawyer's website" my mom said.

"Ok ma, I will ask when I go back."

I knew I could not go to trial (which I intended to do) with this court appointed attorney I had. She was no good for me!! I don't think she was any good for any of her clients!!"

After leaving the visit I went back to the cell block and asked everyone in the unit did they know a good lawyer who was reasonable? No one could think of one. Everyone in there had a court appointed attorney. That is all they ever knew when they went to court.

That following Monday I got an attorney visit from that no-good court appointed attorney, rather the devil in a skirt and high heels. Before I even got the chance to take a seat in the visit room this snake for a lawyer began to talk.

"Hey Amanze, I have something important to tell you bud. The prosecutor Ms. Wesley told me if you do not take a plea for this charge, the prosecution team will seek a superseding indictment. Which means in legal terms your ass will be getting more charges!!"

"Well, since you want to be a messenger, tell the prosecution team they might as well start superseding. Because I am not taking a plea for something I did not do."

"I think it's best for you to take a plea Antoine. We won't get a lot of time if we take a plea."

Ms. H you are saying "we" won't get a lot of time if "we" take a plea, like you going to be doing the time with me or something, "We" not doing the time, I'm going to be the one doing the time. Ms. H what evidence do they have against me? Nothing!!!! Because I did not do this shit.

You come up here to see me on a visit still talking some plea shit. You told me I was being charged for having some people purchase firearms for me in West Virginia, then I transported the firearms back to New York is what you told me Ms. H.

I was never ever caught transporting any firearms from West Virginia to New York or caught receiving firearms from any one in West Virginia ever! So, I am trying to understand why the fuck you are telling me to take a plea like I am guilty, when there is no evidence to support that I committed this crime. Would you take a plea if you were in my shoes? Huh!

Ms. H did not answer that question but said, "this is the feds", they do what they want to do. Even if there is no evidence against you, they will still charge you. It is on you to get the charges up off you. That is what you are dealing with here, and I will not go against them for you! They want a conviction and my job is to give them one.

So, you as my attorney you are telling me you not going to fight for me? It is my Constitutional right to have an "effective lawyer" who will fight for me in court. Ms. H you took an oath when you became a lawyer to follow the United States Constitution and here you go, going against your oath you took by not protecting my right to have an effective attorney!

I said what I said Antoine, and I will repeat it again. My advice to you is to take a plea deal and that is my final decision! Antoine, I can't help that the prosecutor is charging you with this because of who you may know.

Who am I supposedly supposed to know Ms. H? Ms. H looked at me but did not give me an answer. What does someone I may know have to do with me receiving a charge for a crime I didn't do? I asked her even though she did not answer my first question.

Being charged with a crime should be based on the evidence proving the person committed a crime, not be based on who the prosecutor says I know. So, you just not going to answer my question Ms. H? I asked you about who the prosecutor is saying I know? That's irrelevant Antoine.

Sometimes the people you may know get in a jam or a little bit of trouble with the law, and plant your identification card at a traffic stop or accidentally leave it there and that's how your name gets caught up in the mix of things.

Stories are then made up by special agents and police officers and you get the shit end of the stick. Unfortunately, you do not have a lot going good for you. For one you are black and an out of towner going to court in West Virginia, Where your kind is not welcomed and there's never a good outcome.

For two you have a criminal record, so it will be so easy for us to get you convicted at trial. I have seen many trials in this state so trust me, I know what I am talking about. Listen to me, if you decide to go to trial I can promise you the judge will find a way to tell the jury of your trial that you have a criminal record, even though the judge is not supposed to.

Once the jury knows you have a criminal record, your chances of losing trial increases enormously. This is West Virginia, they do what they want out here Antoine! Take what I just told you for what you think it is worth, I still stand by my advice. Take a plea deal!! I tell that to all my clients. You are not the first and you will not be the last client I tell that to! Antoine, take the plea!

Speaking to this lawyer was like talking to a brick wall. There was nothing I could have said to her to make her do her job and help me. I ended our visit by saying I do not feel well, and I would like to go back to my cell and sleep it off. Before getting up to leave, she still had the nerve to ask me again "are you going to take a plea deal the next time I go to court?" I just looked at her like she had 3 heads and walked out of the room.

Unlike Westchester County Jail, I didn't have to get stripped search after leaving the visit. I saw an officer in the hallway as I stepped out the room and asked him can he please take me back to cellblock F-1. The officer respectfully said, "sure, no problem" and took me back to my housing unit.

I called both my mom and Jacky when I got back in the housing unit. They both were displeased about what the lawyer said on the visit.

My next move after brainstorming was to write a letter to the judge telling him I wanted to fire my attorney, because she did not have my best interest at heart. That I did **ASAP**! I wrote the letter and asked my cellmate for a stamp, envelope, and then placed the letter in the mailbox.

That following week I was taken to court and assigned a new court appointed attorney by the judge. I was also given three new charges. One charge for selling crack cocaine, the second charge was for transporting three more firearms to New York and the third charge was for being in possession of three firearms.

What is this? I said to my new attorney as he handed me the indictment showing I had three new charges. "Those are your new charges Antoine," that's what it is!

I am being charge for selling drugs and I never sold drugs in my life. And for this gun charge, how am I being charged with transporting guns to New York? I was never caught transporting these guns to New York. No guns were ever found in my possession. So how am I being charged with being in possession of three firearms!!!

Things just got worse in two ways, I received new charges and I was just assigned the rudest lawyer in the United States. I was convinced the new lawyer was a part of the **KKK!** I saw hate in his eyes. He never gave me a chance to speak. He always spoke over me whenever I tried to express myself to him about my case.

Just like my first court appointed attorney, he was telling me to take a plea without him even seeing my discovery, which is insane!

Discovery is all the evidence the prosecutor has against a person. Until a lawyer sees a client's discovery, he or she is not supposed to tell his or her client to take a plea. Because there could be evidence in his or her client's discovery, that shows his or her client is not guilty of a crime, and trial will be the better option than taking a plea.

The mention of me telling my new attorney Mr. R, I wanted to go to trial made him extremely mad and very hostile vocally.

"Why the hell would you want to go to trial Antoine? For what!"

"Because I can" I replied. I want to exercise my "Constitutional right" to a trial Mr. R," I also yelled at him.

This entire conversation between my new attorney and I happened on the first day we met, which was the same day the judge assigned him to me. I knew I had to fire him the same way I fired my last attorney Ms. H. That was exactly what I did.

I wrote another letter to the judge complaining about him. I told the judge in the letter I felt he was a racist. Two weeks later I was brought back to court. The judge said he acknowledged my Letter about my attorney, and he assigned me a new court appointed attorney that same day.

This new attorney I was given was black. Just because he was black did not mean shit to me!! All I wanted him to do is represent me to the best of his ability like I wanted my last 2 court appointed attorneys to do.

I was not concerned about the color of his skin!!

"Hello, I'm Mr. Walker your new attorney," he said to me while we both sat in a small room in the court building.

"What are you trying to do Antoine? You want to take a plea or go to trial?"

"I want to go to trial I said in a confident tone."

"Ok, good because I just received your discovery from the prosecutor and the prosecutor really has nothing on you whatsoever, so I feel trial is the best thing for you to do Antoine."

For some reason, my gut told me not to trust him. Maybe because when he was talking to me, he was not looking at me in my eyes!

"Ok so when will we start trial" I asked.

"In a few months Antoine."

"A few months! I want to trial faster than a few months. I want to get this over with ASAP. I want you to put me in for a speedy trial so I can get this trial over with."

"Speedy trial Antoine, there's no need for me to put in a motion asking for a speedy trial. By the time that motion gets heard by the judge you would have already started trial. Trust me Antoine you will get a trial very soon! I will have my secretary make copies of all your discovery when I head back to the office today and mail it to you, I will come visit you before trial Mr. Antoine so we can discuss the things we are going to use for trial as your defense."

"Ok sounds good Mr. Walker."

"Antoine I am here to help you" he said in a fake sincere way.

After he left the room, I just felt he was a snake. I cannot explain why I felt that way, but I did. The feeling in my gut was telling me I could not trust him. It seemed like all the court appointed attorneys the judge was assigning me left a bad taste in my mouth. I thought if I complained about this lawyer so soon the judge would think I am the issue, and not the attorneys he was assigning to me.

I felt complaining about this lawyer would have not made a difference in terms of getting an attorney that was going to really be for me. It seems like all the attorneys the judge was assigning to my case were not on my side. So why complain about getting assigned a new lawyer, when the probability of me getting assigned a lawyer who was not on my side or one who did not have my best interest at heart was very high?

I asked myself that question and decided to just deal with this attorney. Because it seemed like even if the judge gave me a new attorney, he or she would have been just like the rest of my court appointed attorneys I had.

That was my mindset at that time. My gut did not trust Mr. Walker. I left the room after speaking to him thinking to myself it is going to be a battle ahead of me and **BOY WAS I CORRECT!!**

CHAPTER 22

BACK TO NORTH CENTRAL REGIONAL COUNTY JAIL

After returning to the housing unit from court, I called my mom and Jacky. I told them I was assigned a new lawyer by the judge and how I already did not trust him. I am still going to trial I told them because I did not do this crap!! In so many words they both indirectly told me to take a plea deal. Not because I was guilty but because they were afraid of me going to trial with this court appointed attorney and end up losing. They thought the end result would not be in my favor.

Eddie told me when I was in court the officer told him tomorrow he will be getting transferred to another jail to finish up the remaining of his time. That night we stayed up talking all night in the cell because we both knew he was out of here in the morning. Morning time came and went, and Eddie was no longer in the Jail. That meant I was the only black dude in the housing unit now.

I thought without a doubt I was going to bump heads with one of the white boys who were in the cellblock with me, sooner or later. Reason being is a few of them had white power and confederate flag tattoos on them. I knew what that meant.

As soon as one of them come out the mouth to me, it is lit! I am going to the hole for however long. I was cool with that because I was going to be respected one way or another.

To my surprise we never bumped heads, the entire time I was there.

They all showed me respect and I showed them the same respect back.

I got super cool with a white boy name Fetty, who was a part of the Aryan brotherhood. This dude showed me a lot of love!

One day we were talking after we were on the cell block a couple of months together. He told me the brotherhood he was in, was not supposed to hate different races.

"Amanze, the only thing we are supposed to do is be for our people, not hate other races. We do have ignorant people in the brotherhood who do hateful shit to different races but that's not what were supposed to stand for."

I believed him because not once did he act funny in any type of way towards me, nor did I feel any type of bad vibes when I was around him. Believe you me, I always had one eye open in case he was trying to rock me to sleep, then try to do some grimy shit to me. But my gut always accepted him, so I knew he was good!

The Aryan brotherhood had their numbers up in the housing unit, and I was the only black guy in the cell block. They could had easily jumped me and got me out of the housing unit they were in. Even though I would have fought back, it is obvious who would had won. It would have been 15 dudes on one.

But instead they all showed me respect, and never not once came out their mouth to me. Going through that whole experience and being around some of the Aryan brotherhood dudes made me look at them differently. Even though most may say and think they are all racist, I cannot say the same! At least about the ones I was around.

CHAPTER 23

NOVEMBER 2018

Damn, it took long enough but I finally received my discovery in the mail.

Again, for those of you who do not know what discovery is, it is the evidence the prosecutor feels makes a person guilty of the charge or charges he or she is charged with. Discovery is all the evidence a prosecutor can or may use against a person at trial if that person chooses to go to trial.

And lastly, discovery is also the evidence a person charged with a crime could use at his or her trial as part of their defense to prove their innocence by poking holes through the prosecutor's case.

My discovery was so much paperwork! It took me three weeks to read through it all. I seriously took my time reading it for hours out the day because I really wanted to fully understand the evidence the prosecutor claims made me guilty of these charges, I knew I was not guilty of.

As I was reading through my discovery, on a separate piece of paper I would write down all the things that did not make any sense to me, and all the things I wanted my attorney to use as part of my defense at trial to prove I was innocent of these charges.

Mr. Walker also had his secretary send with my discovery "the exact story the prosecution team intended to tell the jury of my trial, what they thought I did, that made me guilty of all the charges I was going to trial for.

I found lots and lots of evidence in my discovery that made the prosecutor's story not add up!! Whatsoever!!!!

THIS IS THE PROSECUTOR'S STORY OF WHAT I SUPPOSEDLY DID:

The prosecutor claims on June 9, 2017 the star city police of West Virginia conducted a traffic stop on a Ford F-250 pickup truck for a defective taillight. The driver of the vehicle was Mr. Tommy along with a passenger (the prosecutor claims was me) in the right rear seat.

Tommy admitted to the officer he had smoked crack cocaine a few hours before the stop. The officer stated that he had asked Tommy to exit the truck to speak with him back between his cruiser and Tommy's truck. The officer asked Tommy for his consent to search the vehicle, which Tommy granted. The officer noticed that Tommy seemed to be nervous.

Prior to the searching of the vehicle, the officer asked the passenger (who the prosecutor claims were me) to step out of the vehicle. The passenger repeatedly stated that he needed to use the bathroom and asked the officer if he could go to the gas station across the street, to use the bathroom. The officer said no and a few moments later, a second police cruiser arrived to back up the officer. When the passenger observed the second police cruiser arrive, he fled on foot into a nearby wooded area, while leaving behind his state identification and his Cellular phone.

The officer searched Tommy's vehicle and found a suitcase containing three firearms. Two of the firearms found were purchased legally by Tommy earlier that day, and one firearm was allegedly stolen.

Tommy allegedly confessed to purchasing those firearms for the passenger earlier that evening.

The passenger was in route to transporting those firearms out of state before the traffic stop occurred.

Another person named Parker (who was not an occupant in the truck the night of this alleged traffic stop on June 19, 2017.) purchased firearms in her name legally from a gun store for the fleeing passenger (again who the prosecutor claims was me) of the June 19, 2017 traffic stop of Tommy's pickup truck a month prior to that traffic stop.

Weeks after the traffic stop, Tommy and Parker claims the passenger who fled from the traffic stop on June 19, 2017 gave them both crack cocaine, to purchase firearm for him in local gun stores. After the passenger received these firearms from Tommy and Parker, he trafficked them to New York, and sold it to individuals in the New York City area.

The fleeing passenger trafficked crack cocaine to West Virginia and distributed it in the Northern district of West Virginia. The prosecutor then claims the fleeing passenger had Chris Anderson sell crack cocaine for him, and after Chris was done selling the drugs he received, he would send the money to the fleeing passenger, Amanze Antoine, to New York using "Western Union." Amanze Antoine after fleeing from officers the night of the traffic stop on June 19, 2017 also called Chris Anderson moments after he got away according to Chris Anderson.

Above is the story the prosecutor intended to tell the jury of my trial. After reading that story, I dissected my entire discovery like a scientist dissecting a frog. Paying very close attention to every detail. Again, and again, and again, I went over my discovery, I knew I was not guilty of these charges. So, I found in my discovery all the things that did not add up or make sense so I could bring it to my attorney's attention, so that it can be utilized for my defense at trial. I needed my chances of winning to be high! Trust and believe I found every single hole in the prosecutor's made-up story to prove my innocence!!!! Wouldn't you have done the same thing!

CHAPTER 24

TREACHERY SEASON!! I SEE IT CLEARLY NOW!!!

3 weeks later.

I knew Mr. Walker was coming to visit me because when I called his office last week, his secretary said he was. It was getting late, so I decided to call his office to make sure he was still coming.

"What do you want?" were the first words that came out my attorney's rude ass secretary's mouth, after she accepted my call.

Not you! Then I continued, "miss I was just calling to make sure Mr. Walker is still coming to visit me today. It's getting late and he is not here yet, so I was just seeing if he is still coming." Sucking her teeth, she said "what the hell did I tell you last week! He is coming right!!"

"Yes," I replied and all I heard was the dial tone right after. This rude ass chick really hung up the phone on me. Un-fucking real I thought to myself! I did not let that break me though.

I went to my cell and made sure I had all of what I wanted to show Mr. Walker. I had all the paperwork in order that I found in my discovery I wanted Mr. Walker to see and use for my trial as part of my defense to increase my chances of winning at trial.

30 minutes later

"Antoine, Antoine, you have an attorney visit, the correctional officer said as she opened the door to the housing unit."

"Ok, miss let me grab my paperwork from my cell and I'll be ready to go." I ran to my cell, grabbed my paperwork and was out the door to see my attorney.

"What's going on Mr. Walker?" I said when I entered the visit room before I took a seat. "Hey," he stated back as if it hurts his mouth to say that 3 letter word!

I quickly thought to myself this does not look or sound like the Mr. Walker who told me he thought trial was the best thing for me to do when we first met.

"Ok Walker, when you had my discovery mailed to me, I went through it and read all of it thoroughly. I would like to bring some things to your attention, that I feel are vital to my case. All these things I would like for you to use as part of my defense for trial, please. Because they are things of substance.

I truly feel in my heart once the jury of my trial hears and sees this evidence I'm about to show you, will increase my chances of victory at trial. Mr. Walker, you follow me? Mr. Walker looked at me and shook his head yes. I asked you that because you are over there looking through your phone while I am talking to you, and you are not even paying attention to me.

"Yes, I am following you Antoine. You don't have to look at someone to be paying attention to them, he said in a super smart tone. I'm listening, I will give you a chance to tell me all of what you wish for me to present to the jury of your trial.

Then after you are done speaking, I will give you my opinion on those things you are requesting me to use as your defense," Mr. Walker said with a demonic look on his face. His energy was throwing me off!!

Below are all the things I said, showed, and brought to my attorney Mr. Walker's attention the day he came to visit me. Which was give or take 2 weeks before my trial was actually going to start. The documents you will see and read are the actual documents itself, that I showed Mr. Walker during his visit with me.

Some of the documents are circled, underlined, or both. The reason for that is while I was talking to Mr. Walker, and explaining to him what I wanted him to use as part of my defense at trial.

I simultaneously was circling and underlining things I was pointing out to him while I was speaking to him bringing certain things to his attention that I wanted him to take heed to.

You will be viewing many written reports done by special agent Matt Bassett and other documents that was in my discovery that the prosecutor gave my attorney. Special agent Bassett was the head lead investigator for my case. He was the person in charge of investigating my entire case.

This included him interviewing many people and making written reports about their entire conversation. **HEADS UP,** all of special agent Bassett written reports has the word "Redacted" used to cover up certain information on his reports to hide it. I just want it to be known that I didn't do that, and I had no control over that, **THE PROSECUTOR DID**. When the prosecutor received all special agent Bassett reports from him, she was the one that put the word "Redacted" on certain information to keep it hidden.

BACK TO THE VISIT ROOM WITH MR. WALKER AND I

First and foremost, Mr. Walker, I was never at that traffic stop in West Virginia on June 19, 2017. I have people willing to testify at my trial to where I was at the night of this traffic stop. Here are their names and numbers I said as I handed a pre-written piece of paper to Mr. Walker with the names and numbers of the people who was willing to testify on my behalf at trial to contest where I was at the night of this traffic stop on June 19, 2017.

The second thing I said to Mr. Walker was I don't understand how the hell I'm being charged for receiving firearms from people, trafficking firearms, selling firearms, for trafficking, and distributing drugs if for **ONE**, I was never caught or seen receiving any firearms from these allege people the prosecutor claims gave me firearms.

For **TWO,** I was never caught trafficking or selling firearms. And for **THREE,** I was never caught trafficking or distributing crack cocaine ever in my life so how the hell am I being charged with these crimes as if I were caught doing all the above.

At trial that is the first thing I need you to bring to the jury's attention during your opening arguments Mr. Walker please I said in a very very very very frustrating tone. Mr. Walker just looked at me like I was an alien from Mars, so I looked at him like he was too.

Anyway, I went on to talk about Chris Anderson to Mr. Walker. Chris Anderson was the person the prosecutor stated will testify against me at trial and tell the jury I called him on the phone after this alleged traffic stop, the prosecutor states I fled from on June 19, 2017.

According to the prosecutor Chris is going to testify that he sold drugs for me in West Virginia in the past and after he was done selling the drugs I allegedly gave to him, he would send me the money to New York through Western Union. Mr. Walker, here are some things I want you to bring to the jury's attention when Chris takes the stand at my trial.

I took out page 1 of 4 of report #28 that I have also included in this book on **page 99** written by special agent Bassett. Mr. Walker, the first thing I noticed about the written report agent Bassett did about Chris was during agent Bassett interview with Chris, Chris keeps on referring to a person by the named Shawn who he did all the illegal things for that the prosecutor is charging me for, and my name is clearly not Shawn Mr. Walker! I do not know what type of games the prosecutor is playing, because I am pretty sure the prosecutor knows my name is not Shawn as well!!

But anyway, Mr. Walker right here in the first paragraph on page 1 of 4 of report #28 Chris states he was helping me distribute crack cocaine. You also told me during our phone call last month that the prosecutor told you Chris will be testifying at my trial that after he was done allegedly helping me distribute drugs he would send me the money to New York, using Western Union.

Mr. Walker, I need you to contact whomever you have to contact that works at the Western Union Headquarters and give them my name, and tell them to look at their records to see if money have ever been sent to me through Western Union.

Mr. Walker I never used Western Union in my life, so I am 1,000% sure they will not have a record of me receiving money from anyone through Western Union. Chris is lying, he never sent me no money through Western Union. When you contact Western Union please ask the person who is assisting you are they willing to come to my trial and testify on my behalf, to tell the jury of my trial they do not have any record of me receiving any money through Western Union or at the very least have them put it in writing so you can show it to the jury.

Mr. Walker, this is important for you to follow up on and get done. The jury needs to know all of this when Chris Anderson gets on the stand and starts lying about sending me money through Western Union. You follow me Mr. Walker?

"Carry on Antoine, I'll give you my thoughts on everything after I hear everything you have to say," Mr. Walker said in a brushing me off kind of way.

"Really," I said in an agitated manner.

Even though I was bothered by the energy I was receiving from Mr. Walker, I still went on to tell him about the state identification card of me that the prosecutor claims I left behind at the traffic stop, I allegedly fled from on June 19, 2017.

After reading my discovery weeks ago I saw what Ms. H meant when she told me maybe someone I may have known planted or accidentally left my identification card somewhere when they got caught up in a jam.

Maybe it was someone I did not know, who knows! Mr. Walker, that identification card that was allegedly left behind at this traffic stop could have been found and used by anyone!!

Mr. Walker "months" before this traffic stop occurred on June 19, 2017. I personally reported that same identification that was found or supposedly found at the June 19, 2017 traffic stop missing, lost, or stolen to the Department of Motor Vehicles in New York.

I am pretty sure the Department of Motor Vehicles still has records of me reporting this to them. Mr. Walker, I need you to contact the Department of Motor Vehicle in New York please also. I need you to please do the same thing you are going to do when you talk to the person who is going to be assisting you when you call Western Union, please ask them are they willing to come to my trial and testify on my behalf that I did in fact report the same identification card found at this traffic stop on June 19, 2017 missing, lost or stolen, once they verify that I did. If they are not willing to testify at the very least can they put it in writing so we can show it to the jury of my trial. Mr. Walker, this is vital to my defense and I need you to please get this done.

Moving right along, Mr. Walker, take a look at this. This is Page 2 of 4 of report # 28 written by special agent Bassett which I have also included in this section on **page 100** and right here in paragraph # 10 Chris told special agent Bassett he remembers a person named Shawn calling him right after the traffic stop with Tommy happened.

He told special agent Bassett that Shawn was the person who fled from police officers at that June 19, 2017 traffic stop of Tommy's truck. Mr. Walker my name is not Shawn!! My name is Amanze, so it is fucking clear I was not that person at that traffic stop on June 19, 2017. I am pretty sure the prosecutor knows that too, but she still wants to charge me with this shit.

Let me show you something else **Mr.** Walker in paragraph 10 on page 2 of 4 report # 28 Chris said someone named Shawn called him after the traffic stop that occurred on June 19, 2017 that the prosecutor is saying now it was not Shawn, it was me.

Now look at this Mr. Walker, this is Chris Anderson cell phone records from the night of this traffic stop which I have also included in this section of the book on **page 101**.

It shows Chris having no incoming calls that night from 10:00 pm on June 19, 2017 to June 20, 2017 until 2:53pm. The prosecutor said this traffic stop happened at 10:00pm on June 19, 2017, that I allegedly fled from and I called him the night of the traffic stop which Chris's phone records shows he had no incoming calls in the timeframe the prosecutor is stating I called him.

As you read on page 2 of 4 of report # 28 Chris stated to special agent Bassett, a dude a named Shawn called him after this traffic stop. The prosecutor is now saying it was me who called him and hide at his house. Chris's phone records clearly show no one called him during the duration of this traffic stop, Mr. Walker Chris's phone records show he is a fucking liar!!! And the prosecutor is still charging me with this shit.

I know the prosecutor saw these phone records showing no one called Chris during the duration of this traffic stop on June 19, 2017 because she was the one that gave it to you in my discovery. She has to know Chris is lying because his phone records were right in her fucking face. The person at the traffic stop name was Shawn not fucking Amanze, Mr. Walker!! I need Chris's phone records shown to the jury of my trial when he testifies stating I called him after the traffic stop to show the jury, he is a fucking liar.

Also, I need you to show report # 28 to the jury and point out to them Chris was referring to someone as Shawn who fled from the traffic stop on June 19, 2017 not **AMANZE ANTOINE**!! Are you paying attention to what I am saying to you Mr. Walker? He gave me a look that stated to me why you just asked me that. Mr. Walker, I am asking you this because you are going through your phone while I am talking to you.

"I can chew bubble gum and walk Antoine," I am listening to you.

Even though I felt disrespected by Mr. Walker doing whatever he was doing on his phone while I was explaining to him valuable things I wanted him to use as part of my defense for trial I still continued to talk. I really felt like slapping the shit out of him, but I kept my cool.

Mr. Walker, on page 1 of 4 of report # 28 Chris made a statement to special agent Bassett but I could not get the details of what he told agent Bassett due to the word "redacted" covering up certain words as you can see Mr. Walker I said as I showed him what I was talking about on report # 28 that I have again included on **page 99** in this book.

You see right here Mr. Walker, in the 3rd paragraph Chris told special agent Bassett he was diagnosed with something and was taking multiple prescriptions including injected treatment and oral medication. As you can see Mr. Walker the prosecutor used the word "redacted" to cover up certain information on this report so I could not tell what Chris told special agent Bassett he was diagnosed with.

I could not help but to think the prosecutor was hiding something vital, and she did not want me to know and that is why the prosecutor used the word "redacted" on special agent Bassett's reports covering up certain information.

So out of curiosity I had my friend find out what Chris was diagnosed with. My friend goggled Chris's name and what popped up was the details of a plea Chris took in a federal court for a pending criminal case he has.

Look right here Mr. Walker, I said as I pulled out paperwork my friend sent me showing the details of what Chris told the judge when he took a plea agreement in federal court. Mr. Walker, Chris Anderson informed the court he was undergoing mental health treatment for schizophrenia. Please look at this as I pointed to the spot on the paper where Chris informed the Court of this.

"Readers," I have also included the paperwork in this section that show what Chris informed the court he was undergoing mental health treatment for schizophrenia on **page 102** in this book.

I requested Mr. Walker to bring up what Chris was undergoing mental health treatment for to the jury of my trial's attention. The jury needed to know it is very possible whatever Chris comes on the stand and states he saw, did, heard, or what someone else did is very questionable due to his mental health condition.

I continued by telling Mr. Walker that schizophrenia is a psychotic mental illness that is characterized by distorted view of the real world, by greatly reduced ability to carry out one's daily task, by abnormal ways of thinking, feeling, perceiving, and behaving.

After I gave Mr. Walker a description of what schizophrenia was, I told him it is extremely vital for the jury of my trial to know about Chris's mental health condition when he gets on the stand to testify against me.

Reason being was to give the jury of my trial a reasonable explanation on why Chris thought he sent me money through Western Union, and why he thought either me or Shawn called him the night the traffic stop took place.

Along with Chris referring to me as Shawn when my name is **AMANZE ANTOINE**!! Mr. Walker the jury needs to know Chris's mental health condition may make him at any given time think something happened that really did not happen.

It can make him perceive things as happening when in all actuality it did not happen. His mental condition could also make him formulate in his mind a false account of what he thinks he observed or is observing.

Mr. Walker, I think this is very important to tell the jury because I feel it will make the jury view his testimony differently when he comes on the stand and testify.

Mr. Walker it is imperative that the jury of my trial knows Chris's mental health condition in order to weight his testimony differently."

U.S. Department of Justice
Bureau of Alcohol, Tobacco, Firearms and Explosives

Report of Investigation

Title of Investigation: PARKER, Margaret et al	Investigation Number: 775075-17-0051	Report Number: 28

SUMMARY OF EVENT:

INTERVIEW & CONFESSION OF [Redacted] On August 10, 2017, Bureau of Alcohol, Tobacco, Firearms and Explosives (ATF) Special Agents (SAs) Matthew Bassett and Matthew Kocher interviewed [Redacted] at his residence in Morgantown, WV. [Redacted] confessed to helping Amanze ANTOINE distribute crack cocaine, conspiring with him to straw-purchase firearms, sheltering ANTOINE after he fled from police, and helping ANTOINE find straw purchsers.

NARRATIVE:

1. On August 10, 2017, ATF SAs Bassett and Kocher went to [Redacted], the residence of [Redacted] [Redacted] agreed to speak with SAs and invited them into his apartment.

2. [Redacted] stated that he had lived in [Redacted] for a month or two, and had met a black male he knew as "Shawn" at the bus depot in Morgantown. [Redacted] said Shawn had asked [Redacted] to help him meet people and sell crack cocaine in the Morgantown area, and [Redacted] had agreed to do so. [Redacted] said he had been clean of hard drugs for a while until he met Shawn, at which point he began using about a half-gram of crack cocaine per day.

3. [Redacted] said Shawn had lived with him, first at the Morgantown Motel, and then in [Redacted]. [Redacted] said he had paid for the motel room with his father's credit card, and [Redacted] now paid his rent for the apartment. [Redacted] noted that he had been diagnosed with [Redacted], which is why [Redacted] paid his rent, and that he took multiple prescriptions. [Redacted] told SAs he received regular treatment for his [Redacted] and was compliant with his medications. [Redacted] appeared to SAs to be coherent, rational and unimpaired throughout the course of the interview.)

4. [Redacted] described taking oral and injected treatments for [Redacted] as well as [Redacted] to help with his [Redacted]. [Redacted] claimed that since Shawn left, he had been getting off hard drugs and could "piss clean, except for THC." SA Bassett observed what appeared to be a glass smoking pipe beside [Redacted] bed. [Redacted] said he had been on [Redacted] "for years," taking it since approximately the beginning of 2016.

5. [Redacted] said that Shawn had sold heroin at some point, but primarily supplied crack cocaine, which [Redacted] referred to as "work." [Redacted] said that he helped Shawn by giving him a place to stay and

Prepared by: Matthew H. Bassett	Title: Special Agent, Clarksburg Field Office	Signature:	Date: 8/14/17
Authorized by: Gregory R. Perry	Title: Acting Resident Agent in Charge, Clarksburg Field Office	Signature:	Date: 7-14-17
Second level reviewer (optional): Stuart L. Lowrey	Title: Special Agent in Charge, Louisville Field Division	Signature:	Date: 8/28/17

Page 1 of 4

ATF EF 3120.2(10-2004)
For Official Use Only

Title of Investigation PARKER, Margaret et al	Invest n Number 7750 7-0051	Report Number 28

finding rides for him, and in return, Shawn gave him crack cocaine. [Redacted] said Shawn "always talked about guns" and he wanted them so that he could sell them back home in the New York City area.

6. [Redacted] said Shawn only wanted handguns, specifically .40 caliber and .45 caliber handguns. [Redacted] recalled Shawn began asking him for help getting firearms immediately, when they first met. [Redacted] saw Shawn offer crack cocaine to people, as an enticement for them to buy Shawn firearms. [Redacted] said Shawn carried around crack cocaine in pill bottles, and he would dump out the crack and show it to people in order to convince them he could pay.

7. [Redacted] said he had gone with Shawn to the "sportsman's store" on two occasions; [Redacted] said this was a big box store out by the highway. [Redacted] recalled that on both occasions, a "fat girl" named [Redacted] had purchased firearms at Shawn's behest. [Redacted] said Shawn had taken the firearms and paid the girl in crack cocaine. [Redacted] believed that Shawn got a .22 caliber handgun from [Redacted] at one point.

8. [Redacted] said that [Redacted] knew which firearms to buy because Shawn showed [Redacted] "an ad" that depicted the firearms he wanted. [Redacted] remembered that Shawn wanted "40s, 45s, and 9mms." [Redacted] said [Redacted] had gone directly into the store, bought the firearms, come back out, and given the weapons to Shawn. [Redacted] said Shawn left for New York City shortly thereafter. [Redacted] said that after acquiring firearms, Shawn would usually leave town, bringing the weapons to New York either that night or the very next day. [Redacted] said Shawn would pay people in crack cocaine for rides to Pittsburgh, whereupon he would board a Greyhound bus to New York.

9. [Redacted] said he had also gone with Shawn to a pawn shop in Westover, WV, with a guy named "Tom." [Redacted] said he and Shawn had first gone into the pawn shop, and Shawn had picked out "two 9mm pistols, I think." [Redacted] said he and Shawn came back out of the pawn shop, told Tom which weapons to buy, and Tom had gone in to get them. [Redacted] remembered Tom coming back out and saying that his transaction might be delayed for up to three days, and asking Shawn for direction. [Redacted] remembered that Shawn had told Tom to just give it a try and see what happens, and Tom had, in fact, been able to buy the weapons.

10. [Redacted] said that Tom was supposed to drive Shawn to Pittsburgh that same night, but Tom got pulled over in Star City, WV, and Shawn ran from the police. [Redacted] remembered Shawn calling him after the traffic stop, and coming to hide out at [Redacted] apartment. [Redacted] said Shawn arrived covered in trash, because after fleeing the police, he had hidden in a dumpster for eight or nine hours. [Redacted] said Shawn had urinated on himself twice, trying to avoid any movement that might lead police to him, and had hidden for so long, in an uncomfortable position, that Shawn was limping. [Redacted] said the police took Shawn's ID card during the traffic stop, which led Shawn to believe he was about to be arrested, and so he fled. [Redacted] said that on the night of the traffic stop, Shawn had a suitcase with guns and clothes in it.

11. [Redacted] said he had helped Shawn by giving him some clean clothes. [Redacted] also remembered calling Shawn's parole officer, because Shawn "was on paper" in New York. [Redacted] said he had pretended to be an employee of a hospital in New York, and told the parole officer that Shawn had injured himself in an accident on a job site and would be out of touch for a few days. [Redacted] remembered that the parole officer "had bought the story." [Redacted] said this was when he learned that Shawn's real name was "Amanza or Amanze," because [Redacted] had had to use Shawn's real name when he spoke to the parole officer.

12. ANDERSON also let Shawn call his girlfriend, whom Shawn called his wife even though [Redacted] thought they were not yet actually married. [Redacted] said Shawn had also used his phone to call Shawn's mother.

ATF EF 3120.2 (10-2004) For Official Use Only

CHRISTOPHER ANDERSON PHONE RECORDS FROM JUNE 19, 2017 WITHIN THE DURATION OF THE TRAFFIC STOP

CALLING_NBR	CALLED_NBR	DIALED_DIGITS	MOBILE ROLE	START_DATE	END_DATE	DURATION (SEC)	Call Type	NEID
(304) 901-9236	(304) 279-1984	(304) 279-1984	Outbound	06/19/2017 21:05:10	06/19/2017 21:05:52	42	Voice	45
(304) 901-9236	(304) 441-1542		Outbound	06/19/2017 21:09:50	06/19/2017 21:09:50	0	Text Detail	197
(304) 901-9236	(304) 906-5348		Outbound	06/19/2017 22:18:31	06/19/2017 22:18:31	0	Text Detail	196
(304) 901-9236	(304) 906-5348		Inbound	06/19/2017 22:19:44	06/19/2017 22:19:44	0	Text Detail	229
(304) 901-9236	(304) 906-5348		Outbound	06/19/2017 22:20:26	06/19/2017 22:20:26	0	Text Detail	195
(304) 906-5348	(304) 901-9236		Inbound	06/19/2017 22:21:56	06/19/2017 22:21:56	0	Text Detail	195
(304) 901-9236	(304) 906-5348		Outbound	06/19/2017 22:22:31	06/19/2017 22:22:31	0	Text Detail	196
(304) 906-5348	(304) 901-9236		Inbound	06/19/2017 22:22:55	06/19/2017 22:22:55	0	Text Detail	196
(304) 901-9236	(681) 212-0148	(681) 212-0148	Outbound	06/19/2017 22:24:13	06/19/2017 22:25:58	105	Voice	45
(681) 212-0148	(304) 419-8831	(304) 419-8831	Routed_Call	06/19/2017 22:28:31	06/19/2017 22:32:55	265	Voice	63
(681) 212-0148	(304) 901-9236	(304) 901-9236	Inbound	06/19/2017 22:28:34	06/19/2017 22:32:55	281	Voice	45
(304) 906-5348	(304) 901-9236		Inbound	06/19/2017 22:54:34	06/19/2017 22:54:34	0	Text Detail	193
(304) 906-5348	(304) 901-9236		Outbound	06/19/2017 22:55:00	06/19/2017 22:55:00	0	Text Detail	198
(304) 906-5348	(304) 901-9236		Inbound	06/19/2017 22:55:45	06/19/2017 22:55:45	0	Text Detail	194
(304) 901-9236	(681) 212-0148		Outbound	06/19/2017 22:58:16	06/19/2017 22:58:16	0	Text Detail	195
(304) 901-9236	(681) 212-0148		Outbound	06/19/2017 23:01:54	06/19/2017 23:01:54	0	Text Detail	196
(304) 901-9236	(681) 212-0148	(681) 212-0148	Outbound	06/19/2017 23:03:42	06/19/2017 23:04:32	50	Voice	45
(304) 901-9236	(681) 212-0148		Outbound	06/19/2017 23:05:13	06/19/2017 23:05:13	0	Text Detail	195
(304) 901-9236	(681) 212-0148		Outbound	06/19/2017 23:10:18	06/19/2017 23:10:18	0	Text Detail	197
(304) 901-9236	(681) 212-0148	(681) 212-0148	Outbound	08/19/2017 23:56:28	06/19/2017 23:57:27	59	Voice	45
(304) 901-9236	(681) 212-0148	(681) 212-0148	Outbound	06/19/2017 23:59:19	06/19/2017 23:59:52	33	Voice	45
(304) 901-9236	(681) 212-0148	(681) 212-0148	Outbound	06/19/2017 23:59:57	06/20/2017 00:00:31	34	Voice	45
(304) 901-9236	(681) 212-0148	(681) 212-0148	Outbound	06/20/2017 00:01:11	06/20/2017 00:01:32	22	Voice	45
(304) 901-9236	(681) 212-0148	(681) 212-0148	Outbound	06/20/2017 00:04:09	06/20/2017 00:04:43	34	Voice	45
(681) 212-0148	(304) 419-8619	(304) 419-8619	Routed_Call	06/20/2017 00:14:51	06/20/2017 00:32:19	1048	Voice	63
(681) 212-0148	(304) 901-9236	(304) 901-9236	Inbound	06/20/2017 00:14:53	06/20/2017 00:32:20	1047	Voice	45
(304) 906-5348	(304) 901-9236		Inbound	06/20/2017 00:26:56	06/20/2017 00:26:56	0	Text Detail	194
(304) 901-9236	(1304) 685-5325	(1304) 685-5325	Outbound	06/20/2017 00:32:44	06/20/2017 00:33:17	33	Voice	45
(681) 212-0148	(304) 419-8684	(304) 419-8684	Routed_Call	06/20/2017 00:35:34	06/20/2017 00:36:02	28	Voice	63
(681) 212-0148	(304) 901-9236	(304) 901-9236	Inbound	06/20/2017 00:35:37	06/20/2017 00:36:02	25	Voice	45
(304) 901-9236	(914) 649-0893	(914) 649-0893	Outbound	06/20/2017 00:36:10	06/20/2017 00:38:02	112	Voice	45
-3333	(304) 901-9236		Inbound	06/20/2017 02:18:25	06/20/2017 02:18:25	0	Text Detail	226
-3333	(304) 901-9236		Inbound	06/20/2017 02:22:17	06/20/2017 02:22:17	0	Text Detail	226
-3333	(304) 901-9236		Inbound	06/20/2017 02:22:18	06/20/2017 02:22:18	0	Text Detail	226
-3333	(304) 901-9236		Inbound	06/20/2017 02:22:54	06/20/2017 02:22:54	0	Text Detail	226
-3333	(304) 901-9236		Inbound	06/20/2017 02:22:55	06/20/2017 02:22:55	0	Text Detail	226
-3333	(304) 901-9236		Inbound	06/20/2017 03:02:17	06/20/2017 03:02:17	0	Text Detail	226
-3333	(304) 901-9236		Inbound	06/20/2017 03:03:04	06/20/2017 03:03:04	0	Text Detail	226
-3333	(304) 901-9236		Inbound	06/20/2017 03:03:05	06/20/2017 03:03:05	0	Text Detail	226

(handwritten annotations: "calls with" and "Texts" bracketed next to the (681) 212-0148 entries; "calling of" and "Texts →" noted in the margin)

SPRINT CORPORATION

Count One of the Indictment; Defendant understood the consequences of his plea of guilty, in particular the maximum statutory penalty to which he would be exposed for Count One; Defendant made a knowing and voluntary plea of guilty to Count One of the Indictment; and Defendant's plea is independently supported by Special Agent Matt Bassett's testimony which provides, beyond a reasonable doubt, proof of each of the essential elements of the charges to which Defendant has plea guilty.

The undersigned Magistrate Judge therefore recommends Defendant's plea of guilty to Count One of the Indictment herein be accepted conditioned upon the Court's receipt and review of this Report and Recommendation.

The undersigned magistrate judge released Defendant on the terms of the Order Setting Conditions of Release{2018 U.S. Dist. LEXIS 13} (ECF No. 27) filed on July 5, 2018,

Any party may, within fourteen (14) days after being served with a copy of this Report and Recommendation, file with the Clerk of the Court written objections identifying the portions of the Report and Recommendation to which objection is made, and the basis for such objection. A copy of such objections should also be submitted to the Honorable Irene M. Keeley, United States District Judge. Failure to timely file objections to the Report and Recommendation set forth above will result in waiver of the right to appeal from a judgment of this Court based upon such report and recommendation. 28 U.S.C. § 636(b)(1); United States v. Schronce, 727 F.2d 91 (4th Cir. 1984), cert. denied, 467 U.S. 1208, 104 S. Ct. 2395, 81 L. Ed. 2d 352 (1984); Wright v. Collins, 766 F.2d 841 (4th Cir. 1985); Thomas v. Arn, 474 U.S. 140, 106 S. Ct. 466, 88 L. Ed. 2d 435 (1985).

The Clerk of the Court is directed to send a copy of this Report and Recommendation to counsel of record.

Respectfully submitted on August 23, 2018

/s/ Michael John Aloi

MICHAEL JOHN ALOI

UNITED STATES MAGISTRATE JUDGE

Footnotes

1

Defendant, Mr. Anderson, informed the Court he was currently undergoing mental health treatment for schizophrenia at Chestnut Ridge Hospital in Morgantown, W.Va. The Defendant further informed the Court he was currently taking the medication clozaril (clozapine) for his condition. Defendant stated that the medication has been helpful and that he has not been hospitalized for several months since beginning treatment with clozaril. The Defendant confirmed with the Court that he understands the nature of the proceedings against him and confirmed he is competent to enter a guilty plea to Count One. Counsel for the Defendant, Mr. Berry, confirmed the same, stating he fully believes the Defendant is competent and understands the charges and proceedings against him as well as the consequences of pleading guilty.

1ydcases   5

CHAPTER 25

WHAT I TOLD MR. WALKER NEXT ON THE VISIT!

The next thing I brought to Mr. Walker's attention was reports # 1 and 3 written by special agent Bassett which I have also included at the end of this section on **pages 116- 119** in this book.

I pointed out to Mr. Walker according to report # 1 written by special agent Bassett it states that Parker (which is one of the people the prosecutor claims allegedly bought firearms for me) went into a gun store name Cashland pawn on June 6, 2017.

While Parker was in that gun store, she made the manager of the store suspicious of her committing a criminal act because the manager thought Parker was trying to buy firearms that day for the person who she came into the store with. Not for herself, like she was pretending to be.

According to report # 1 because the manager felt that way, he then called special agent Bassett to report a suspicious interaction at the gun store that just took place, involving Parker and the companion she was with.

Mr. Walker look right here in the second paragraph of report # 1, the manager stated to special agent Bassett when he called him that Parker and a "skinny, dirty white guy with short hair" came into the gun store to look at firearms.

During this interaction he said to special agent Bassett he observed **PARKER'S** companion just kind of wandering around like knows the game!

What the manager meant by "like he knows the game," meaning parker's companion knew the game of straw purchasing which is when one person buys a firearm legally in their name at a gun store, but the firearm is really for someone else, usually for the person the purchaser of the firearm is with.

See right here Mr. Walker in report # 1 the manager then told special agent Bassett parker's companion (the skinny dirty white boy as described by the gun store manager in report # 1) seemed to be trying to avoid the appearance of involvement in Parker's gun purchase. The manager said parker appeared to be in a hurry and tried to negotiate a deal where she would pay $400.00 dollars for two Hi-Point pistols. The manager told special agent Bassett he told parker he could not give such a low price because both firearms were new.

Now right here Mr. Walker in report # 1 the manager then said Parker and her companion then left the store after he rebuffed that offer, but then returned after a few minutes and said parker selected one Hi-point pistol to purchase. The manager said that all these behaviors made him suspicious of a straw purchase.

So as Parker began filling out **ATF** form 4473, which is a form a person fills out who is purchasing a firearm that includes that person getting a background check done after he or she completes filling out the **ATF** 4473 form.

Mr. Walker look at this, according to report # 1 written by special agent Bassett the manager told him while Parker was filling out the form the manager mentioned to Parker that background checks were sometimes delayed. The manager then said, "Parker became visibly concerned, asking him am I going to leave with this gun?"

The manager of the store told Parker he could not guarantee that, and it would depend on the background check results. The manager said Parker then stopped filling out the **ATF** 4473 form and choose not to buy the Hi-point pistol.

The manager told special agent Bassett according to report # 1 Mr. Walker that Parker's companion had then "slipped up". After the manager's above noted statement about background checks, the manager clearly heard Parker's companion tell Parker "Somebody's waiting for us" and Parker and her companion then left the gun store.

"Readers," I pointed all that out to my attorney in report # 1 because it was going to be connected to what I was going to bring to his attention next. I then pulled out report # 3 written by special agent Bassett, again which is also included at the end of this section on **pages 118 and 119.**

I pointed out to my attorney where it stated in report # 3 that Parker went into another gun shop called Sportsman's Warehouse on June 5, 2017 a day before she went into Cashland Pawn gun store where the manager called special agent Bassett to report a suspicious interaction relating to him thinking parker was buying firearms for the white male companion she was with on June 6, 2017 which I have explained in great detail above.

Mr. Walker look, I stated as I pointed to where I wanted Mr. Walker to look at in report # 3. It states right here on June 5, 2017 Parker went into Sportsman's warehouse gun store and bought 2 firearms that day the prosecutor claims were bought and given to me after she purchased them.

Also Mr. Walker, it states in report # 3 special agent Bassett says the video surveillance footage from Parker's 2 firearms purchased on June 5, 2017 at Sportsman's warehouse gun store, shows parker with the same white companion she was with in Cashland Pawn gun store the very next day on June 6, 2017 where the store manager called special agent Bassett because he thought Parker was trying to purchase firearms for the white male she was with.

The manager of that gun store called special agent Bassett to report a suspicious interaction he had with Parker and her companion, (the same companion Parker was with in Sportsman's Warehouse gun store where Parker purchased 2 firearms the prosecutor claims were bought and given to me right after Parker purchased them) relating to the manager thinking Parker was really buying the firearms she wanted to purchase that day for her companion she was with and not for herself due to the suspicious interaction the manager had with them that day in the gun store he manages according to report #1 written by special agent Bassett that I have included in this book on **pages 116 and 117.**

"Readers" how do we know this was the same companion Parker was with on both days the day Parker bought firearms from Sportsman's Warehouse gun store on June 5, 2017? That again the prosecutor claims were bought and given to me on June 6, 2017 when Parker went into Cashland pawn gun store with a companion, when again the manager of that gun store called special agent Bassett to report a suspicious interaction the manager had with Parker and Parker's companion relating again to the manager thinking the firearms Parker wanted to purchase that day from that gun store was really for the male companion she was with? **GREAT QUESTION RIGHT!** The answer is because it says so in paragraph 5 page 1 of 2 of report # 3 that is also included at the end of this section on **pages 118 and 119**.

Mr. Walker, right here in report # 3 it states special agent Bassett provided the manager of Cashland pawn gun shop with video footage from Sportsman's Warehouse gun store showing Parker's previous purchases of 2 firearms on June 5, 2017 who had called special agent Bassett on June 6, 2017 to report the suspicious interaction he had with Parker and Parker's companion.

When special agent Bassett showed this video footage to the gun store's manager of Cashland Pawn on June 15, 2017, according to report # 3, special agent Bassett states once the manager looked at the surveillance video footage from Sportsman's Warehouse gun store showing parker's 2 firearms purchases on June 5, 2017, the manager told Special agent Bassett he recognized the male companion in the video Parker was with the day Parker purchased 2 firearms from Sportsman's Warehouse (that again the prosecutor claims were bought and given to me right after parker purchased them) as " Parker's buddy" from Parker's June 6, 2017 visit to the gun shop he manages Cashland Pawn when he called special agent Bassett to report a suspicious relating to him thinking Parker was really buying the firearms she wanted to purchase that day for the companion she was with and not for herself. I also had brought to Mr. Walker's attention the first 2 sentencing on page 2 of 2 of report # 3 that states after special agent Bassett reviewed the same video he had shown to the manager of Cashland Pawn he noticed Parker's companion was fidgeting, pacing and making exaggerated movements suggesting nervousness or agitation. And because of that someone that worked in the gun store said the erratic behavior of Parker's companion on June 5, 2017 had attracted the attention of loss prevention who began monitoring surveillance video cameras in real time.

After all the above was mentioned to my attorney, I told him as a part of defense for trial I wanted him to inform the Jury of my trial that there is a great possibility the 2 firearms Parker purchased from Sportman's Warehouse gun store on June 5, 2017, that the prosecutor claims and will tell the jury of my trial were bought and given to me by Parker minutes after she purchased them, then trafficked to New York and sold were possibly bought and given to Parker's companion who she was with while she purchased those 2 firearms, which happens to be the same companion Parker was with the very next day on June 6, 2017 in Cashland Pawn gun store where the manager called special agent Bassett to report suspicious interaction he had with Parker and the same companion Parker was with when she purchased the 2 firearms in Sportsman's Warehouse gun store on June 5, 2017 relating to the manager thinking Parker was really purchasing the firearm she wanted to buy that day for the companion she was with and not for herself like she was pretending it to be for, according to the manager.

Mr. Walker it is very essential you bring all of this up to the jury of my trial, because it will create a logical reasonable doubt in the minds of the jury of my trial and make them think "that's possibly what may have happened." Mr. Walker that is a very valid thing to tell the jury of my trial for many reasons.

For one Mr. Walker, I was never seen with or caught receiving any firearms from Parker. Nor was I ever found in possession of any of the firearms the prosecutor is claiming Parker bought and gave to me, and I never was caught trafficking any firearms or selling any firearms in New York or anywhere for that matter. So honestly, there is no proof to what the prosecutor is claiming happened.

Mr. Walker not once in the report # 3 special agent Bassett wrote it states I was seen receiving firearms from Parker, caught in possession of any firearms parker bought, or caught trafficking firearms to New York, nor caught selling them.

I do not understand how I am getting charged with this shit Mr. Walker!!!! Not one fucking time in any of special agent Bassett reports does it state any of what I just told you.

This is why you have to bring up the fact to the jury of my trial, there is an extremely good possibility Parker bought those firearms on June 5, 2017 (the prosecutor is claiming that was bought and given to me) for the male companion she was with that day she bought them in Sportsman's Warehouse gun store.

The reason why this is a logical thing to say Mr. Walker, is because the very next day after she purchased the 2 firearms, she went into Cashland Pawn gun shop with this same male companion she was with when she bought the 2 firearms (that prosecutor claims was bought by Parker and given to me) and the manager of that gun shop reported his encounter with them to special agent Bassett. The manager seriously suspected something off for him to tell him call special agent Bassett, to parker was attempting to purchase guns she wanted to buy that day for the male companion she was with and not for herself.

Mr. Walker, you have to call the manager of Cashland Pawn gun shop as a witness on my behalf for trial so that he can tell the jury about the encounter he had with Parker and Parker's companion on June 6, 2017 in the gun shop he works in.

Mr. Walker by the manager testifying at my trial it would give the jury more reason to believe it's very possible the firearms Parker bought from Sportsman's Warehouse gun store on June 5, 2017 were bought and given to the companion Parker was with that day she purchased those 2 firearms which was the same companion in Cashland Pawn gun shop parker was with the next day on June 6, 2017 where the manager called special agent Bassett to report to agent Bassett he felt parker was attempting to purchase firearms for the companion she was with.

I know once you explain it to the jury of my trial the way I just explained it to you, some of the jurors will think to themselves that could of very well possibly happened and find me not guilty based on that!!

Mr. Walker just looked at me with a silly ass smirk on his face that I wanted to smack off his face! I kept my composer though and kept talking about things I felt was important for him to use as my defense for trial.

Mr. Walker report # 3 also states in paragraph 3 on May 27, 2017 Parker bought 3 firearms from Sportsman's Warehouse gun store. The prosecutor is also claiming those firearms, were purchased, and given to me, then trafficked to New York, and sold to different people.

Mr. Walker please look at this in report # 3, special agent Bassett stated the video surveillance footage of Parker's 3 firearms purchase on May 27, 2017 at Sportsman's Warehouse gun store depicts an unidentified black male arriving at the gun store with Parker. Mr. Walker in special agent Bassett # 3 written report or in any of the reports he wrote does it state the unidentified man who was with Parker on May 27, 2017 when she purchased 3 firearms was me!!

Mr. Walker I need you to please use the same defense strategy I asked you to use with Parker's 2 firearms purchase on June 5, 2017 at the same Sportsman's Warehouse gun store she purchased 3 firearms from on May 27, 2017.

I need you to tell the jury of my trial that there is a strong possibility the 3 firearms Parker purchased on May 27, 2017 were given to the unidentified black male Parker arrived and entered Sportsman's Warehouse gun store (according to report #3 written by special agent Bassett) with that day she bought those 3 firearms.

Mr. Walker this could have very possibly happened, and I feel it is a very reasonable thing to tell the jury of my trial because I was never caught with or seen receiving any of those firearms Parker bought on May 27, 2017. Nor was I ever found in possession of any of the firearms Parker purchased on May 27, 2017. I was also never caught trafficking any of the firearms Parker bought on May 27, 2017 from Sportsman's Warehouse.

Mr. Walker, the prosecutor has no proof that I did any of the things she is saying I did.

Mr. Walker, I need you to tell the jury of my trial exactly what I just told you, please. Bringing up all the things I just said to the jury at my trial's attention will increase my chances of winning because it will create a **"LOGICAL REASONABLE DOUBT"** which is all that is needed to win at trial!!

Another thing I wanted to tell you Mr. Walker, you do not have to find out the names of the white companion and unidentified black male Parker was with when she purchased the firearms on June 5, 2017 and on May 27, 2017. I am not here to try to get anyone in trouble if Parker did purchase those firearms for them.

I am not here to do the police's job for them. I live by certain morals and principles. Helping police is not one of them, even if I am being charged with a crime I did not do!!

The only sole purpose and reason I want you to bring up what I said to the jury of my trial is to create a logical reasonable doubt that I was not the person who received the firearms Parker purchased on May 27, 2017 and June 6, 2017 and it is a good possibility those firearms were given to the people Parker was with when she purchased them. That is the only reason why Mr. Walker I want you to bring up what I am saying to the jury of my trial it is not to get anyone in trouble.

Now Mr. Walker this is report # 5, (which I have also included in the back of this section readers on **page 120.**) it states one of the firearms (Walther pistol) was stolen back in "2015" from Fairmont, West Virginia, that the prosecutor claims I was in possession of and left behind in a suitcase that was found in Tommy's truck at this alleged traffic stop I allegedly fled from on June 19, 2017.

In paragraph 8 on page 2 of 2 of report # 5 it states the person who was a charged with stealing that Walther pistol and who was found in possession of that pistol "back in 2015" is currently serving time from charges stemming from the theft of that same pistol I am being charged for being in possession of on June 19, 2017 at this alleged traffic stop I supposedly fled from according to the prosecutor's story.

Again Mr. Walker the prosecutor states I left this same Walther pistol (that someone was found in possession of in "2015" and charged for the theft of it) behind in a suitcase found in Tommy's truck after I allegedly fled from this traffic stop on June 19, 2017.

Mr. Walker I have never worked in a police department in my life nor am I a detective or police officer. But from my understanding after reading a law book in this County Jail's law library when a person is found in possession of a firearm and charged for the theft of that firearm, (like the person found in possession of and charged for the theft of the Walther pistol back in "2015" that I am charged for being in possession of in 2017). The law book I read states that a person found with a firearm that was reported stolen which lead to that person getting criminal charges, that stolen firearm is supposed to be kept secured in the police department evidence room. Because it is evidence of a crime, the crime for the theft of that firearm, and is not supposed to leave that evidence room in the police department under no circumstance.

And in my case Mr. Walker someone was found in possession of a Walther pistol and charged with the theft of that pistol back in "2015". This is the same pistol the prosecutor is claiming I was in possession of 2 years later in "2017" at this June 19, 2017 traffic stop I allegedly fled and got away from.

Am I correct, Mr. Walker? When a person is found in possession of a stolen firearm and charged for the theft of that firearm, that firearm is then placed in the police department's evidence room and under no circumstance is that firearm supposed to leave that evidence room, because it's the evidence of a crime?

Mr. Walker just shook his head in agreement to my question. So, if that is correct Mr. Walker "how the fuck am I being charged with being in possession of a firearm in "2018" that was not supposed to leave the Fairmont Police Department evidence room since 2015?"

That Walther pistol I was charged with in "2018" was supposed to be kept secured in the Fairmont, West Virginia Police Department evidence room and not supposed to leave that room under no circumstance because it's evidence of a crime!!

So how can the same Walther pistol that was supposed to be kept secured at Fairmont's Police Department evidence room since 2015 be found in Tommy's truck on June 19, 2017 after a police officer searched his truck according to the prosecutor.

The only way that gun could have left the police department's evidence is if a police officer took it out of the evidence room and put it back on the streets!! Police officers are the only ones who has access to the evidence rooms in police station, correct Mr. Walker?

Again Mr. Walker shook his head in agreement. Ok so not only am I being charged with being in possession of a firearm that was not supposed to leave the police department's evidence room, but it's also dirty fucking police officers stealing guns from the police evidence room and putting it back on the streets.

This needs to all be brought to my jury's attention at trial Mr. Walker. There is a lot of under handed shit going on in my case and the jury of my trial needs to know about it all!!

I have an important question for you Mr. Walker that I just thought of, I said looking at him dead in his eyes.

Mr. Walker, if this gun I'm being charged with being in possession of on June 19, 2017 was supposed to be secured in the Fairmont's Police Department evidence room back in "2015" when it was found on the person who was charged for the theft of it, and was not supposed to leave Fairmont's Police Department evidence room under no circumstance.

Are you sure that pistol really made its way out of that police evidence room by it being taken out of it by an officer?

I ask this because it could be possible that gun is sitting in the Fairmont's Police Department evidence room as we speak, and the prosecutor is just doing some under handed shit charging me with it, Mr. Walker.

I do not put anything past the prosecutor, because I see her work!! She charged me with receiving guns from people, trafficking drugs, and firearms and I was never caught doing none of that shit. So that shows the prosecutor did underhanded shit to get me charged with a crime in the first place.

I feel the prosecutor is liable to do anything to get anyone charged with a crime, she charged me with these crimes without having any evidence against me to support them.

One of two things happened here Mr. Walker, either someone who works in the police department took that gun out of the Fairmont's Police Department evidence room which they were not supposed to do and put that gun back on the streets by either giving it to someone or sold it to someone. Or the prosecutor is straight up fucking lying about the officer finding that gun in particular on June 19, 2017 in Tommy's truck, after it was allegedly searched by a police officer, and found in a suitcase the prosecutor claims I left behind after I allegedly fled from this traffic stop.

Mr. Walker I need you to please do an investigation to see which option I am correct about. The option of a dirty cop putting that gun back on the street somehow, or the option of the prosecutor just fucking lying about that gun in particular being found at this traffic stop on June 19, 2017 but is still charging me with it.

After saying all of this to Mr. Walker I gave him the look and body language as if I wanted his feedback, but he gave me the look back as if he did not have anything to say.

So, I just continued, I was very furious inside because I felt Mr. Walker did not give a fuck about anything I was talking about!! I could tell by his body language that he did not!!!

Lastly Mr. Walker I want to bring this to your attention. The phones the prosecutor is alleging belongs to me and is claiming I left behind in Tommy's truck and dropped on the ground after I supposedly fled from this traffic stop on June 19, 2017 do not belong to me nor were they registered under my name!!

Mr. Walker so I clearly do not understand how the prosecutor came up with the fucking conclusion that those phones belonged to me. I know the prosecutor also saw this in my discovery she gave to you Mr. Walker, I said as I pulled out Motown Taxi Cab Company's records, (that I have also included in the back of this section on **pages 121 and 122**) and placed them on the table.

I pointed out specific things to Mr. Walker, like I did with all the other documents and reports I placed on the table.

Mr. Walker look, this is Motown Taxicab Company's log of each phone number and person's name who calls for a taxicab. Motown Taxicab company's log shows the phone number of one of the phones the prosecutor claims I left behind at this June 19, 2017 traffic stop belongs to a person named Chris!!

Look right here I said as I pointed to a certain section of the taxi cab's log. Motown Taxicab company makes it mandatory for a person who calls for a taxi to leave their name or a taxi will not be provided to them.

You see right here Mr. Walker the same cell phone number the prosecutor is claiming was the phone number of the phone I allegedly left behind in Tommy's truck after I supposedly fled from this traffic stop on June 19, 2017, shows a person named Chris called and order cabs from Motown Taxicab Company many times using this same phone the prosecutor is claiming is my phone!!

My name is not fucking Chris!! My name is Amanze!! Not once in Motown Taxicab records does it show a person calling and ordering a taxi used the name Amanze Antoine. They used the name Chris, not my name as you can see in the Motown Taxicab Company log, I have on the table.

Mr. Walker, it's common sense the person who owns that phone that the prosecutor claims belonged to me belongs to a person named Chris. That phone

114

does not belong to me! I don't understand how the prosecutor is saying this phone belongs to me after the Taxicab Company's log I know she saw in my discovery, clearly tells you the person who owns that phone name is Chris based on the name the person is giving the taxicab company when ordering a taxicab!!

Mr. Walker, I need this also brought to the jury of my trial's attention please. It is a lot of shady shit going on and the jury needs to know about it!! It's urgent you bring this up about the phone to the jury of my trial Mr. Walker, because my last court date the prosecutor said she will be using text messages found in that phone and show the jury them, to proof I engaged in wrongdoing.

That phone does not belong to me. The person who was engaging in wrongdoing was the person who owns that phone, not me!!! The prosecutor knows the person who owns that phone name is Chris and whatever was found in that phone in terms of text messages was Chris's wrongdoing not mine!

But the prosecutor still insists on using text messages from that phone at my trial, as if I was the one who texted certain messages to people. That shit is crazy and so fucking unfair!!

U.S. Department of Justice
Bureau of Alcohol, Tobacco, Firearms and Explosives

Report of Investigation

Title of Investigation: PARKER, Margaret et al	Investigation Number: 775075-17-0051	Report Number: 1

SUMMARY OF EVENT:

ALLEGATION OF FEDERAL FIREARMS VIOLATIONS BY MARGARET PARKER: On June 6, 2017, Bureau of Alcohol, Tobacco, Firearms and Explosives (ATF) Special Agent (SA) Matthew Bassett received information from Rob Summers, a Federal Firearms Licensee (FFL), regarding ▮▮▮▮ suspicions that Margaret PARKER was attempting to straw-purchase firearms at his business. Following a review of ATF Reports of Multiple Handgun Sales, SA Bassett initiated an investigation into federal firearms violations by Margaret PARKER et al.

NARRATIVE:

1. On June 6, 2017, ATF SA Bassett received a phone call from ▮▮▮▮▮ manager at Cashland Pawn, a Federal Firearms Licensee (FFL) located at 530 Brockway Avenue, Morgantown, WV. ▮▮▮▮ informed SA Bassett that he was calling to report a suspicious interaction at that business that had just taken place, involving Margaret PARKER (W/F, DOB: ▮▮▮ 1984, SSN # ▮▮▮▮-9962, cell phone 304-319-6200, 170 Durham Lane, Morgantown, WV) and an unknown other male.

2. ▮▮▮▮ stated that PARKER and a "skinny, dirty white guy with short hair" had come into the store to look at firearms. During this interaction, ▮▮▮▮ said he observed PARKER's companion "just kinda wandering around...like he knows the game." ▮▮▮▮ stated that PARKER's companion seemed to be trying to avoid the appearance of involvement in her purchase, ▮▮▮▮ said that PARKER appeared to be in a hurry, and had tried to negotiate a deal where she would pay $400 for two Hi-Point pistols. ▮▮▮▮ told SA Bassett that he told PARKER he could not give her such a low price, because both firearms were new.

3. ▮▮▮▮ said PARKER and her companion then left the store after he rebuffed that offer, but then returned after a few minutes. PARKER then selected one Hi-Point pistol, which ▮▮▮▮ described as "the cheapest one."

4. ▮▮▮▮ said that all of this behavior had made him suspicious, and so as PARKER began filling out the ATF Form 4473, Firearms Transaction Record, he mentioned to PARKER that background checks were sometimes delayed. ▮▮▮▮ said PARKER became visibly concerned, asking him, "Am I going to leave with this gun?" ▮▮▮▮ said he could not guarantee that, and it would depend on the background results. ▮▮▮▮ said PARKER then stopped filling out the ATF F 4473 and chose not to buy the Hi-Point pistol.

5. ▮▮▮▮ told SA Bassett that PARKER's unidentified male companion had then "slipped up." After Summers'

Prepared by: Matthew H. Bassett	Title: Special Agent, Clarksburg Field Office	Signature:	Date: 6/16/17
Authorized by: Dewayne P. Haddix	Title: Resident Agent in Charge, Clarksburg Field Office	Signature:	Date: 6/16/17
Second level reviewer (optional): Stuart L. Lowrey	Title: Special Agent in Charge, Louisville Field Division	Signature:	Date:

Page 1 of 2

ATF EF 3120.2 (10-2004)
For Official Use Only

Title of Investigation: PARKER, Margaret et al		Investigation Number: 77507-17-0051	Report Number: 1

above-noted statement about background checks, Redacted clearly heard PARKER's companion tell PARKER, "Somebody's waiting for us." PARKER and her companion then left the store.

Attachments: NCIC / Driver's Check for Margaret PARKER.
ATF Multiple Sale Report #M20170202452
ATF Multiple Sale Report #M20170194476.

ATF EF 3120.2 (10-2004)
For Official Use Only

.S. Department of Justice
Bureau of Alcohol, Tobacco, Firearms and Exṗ ̇ves

Report of Ḭ ̇estigation

Title of Investigation: PARKER, Margaret et al	Investigation Number: 775075-17-0051	Report Number: 3

SUMMARY OF EVENT:

RETRIEVAL AND REVIEW OF SURVEILLANCE VIDEO INVOLVING PARKER: On June 15, 2017, Bureau of Alcohol, Tobacco, Firearms and Explosives (ATF) Special Agent (SA) Matthew Bassett went to Sportsman's Warehouse in Morgantown, WV. SA Bassett met with store ████ Redacted ████ provided SA Bassett with a DVD containing store surveillance video of Margaret PARKER's two recent multiple handgun purchases from that business. SA Bassett reviewed the video and determined that Margaret PARKER appeared to be married to Ellis Parker, a convicted felon.

NARRATIVE:

1. On June 15, 2017, ATF SA Bassett went to Sportsman's Warehouse, a Federal Firearms Licensee (FFL) located at 5200 Gateway Drive, Morgantown, WV. SA Bassett met with store ████ Redacted ████ provided SA Bassett with copies of the ATF Form 4473s, Firearm Transaction Record, completed by Margaret PARKER on May 27, 2017 and June 5, 2017. ████ also provided SA Bassett with a DVD containing store surveillance video of both of those purchases.

2. SA Bassett then reviewed the store surveillance video, and noticed that a tattoo visible in PARKER's driver's license photograph, appeared consistent with one visible on PARKER's person. SA Bassett noted that on May 27, 2017, PARKER arrived in the company of an unidentified black male, with whom she spoke for a few minutes outside Sportsman's Warehouse before entering. PARKER could also be seen talking on a cell phone.

3. During the May 27, 2017 visit, PARKER's black male companion could be seen handling firearms, leaning over the counter to look at firearms, and talking to store employees. However, despite the fact that they arrived and entered the store together, PARKER and the black male did not appear to communicate during their time in Sportsman's Warehouse, and PARKER waited alone in the check-out line to pay.

4. During the June 5, 2017 visit, SA Bassett noticed that PARKER had arrived in the company of a young female child. Prior to PARKER entering the store with the child, a thin white male left PARKER's vehicle and entered the store alone. However, once inside the store, the thin white male met PARKER at the firearms counter.

5. SA Bassett provided ████ Redacted ████ of Cashland Pawn with an image of PARKER's white male companion; ████ Redacted ████ stated that he recognized the male as PARKER's "buddy" from her June 6, 2017 visit to his store. In

Prepared by: Matthew H. Bassett	Title: Special Agent, Clarksburg Field Office	Signature:	Date: 6/16/17
Authorized by: Dewayne P. Haddix	Title: Resident Agent in Charge, Clarksburg Field Office	Signature:	Date: 6/16/17
Second level reviewer (optional): Stuart L. Lowry	Title: Special Agent in Charge, Louisville Field Division	(Signature):	Date:

ATF EF 3120.2 (10-2004)
For Official Use Only

Investigation: ,ER, Margaret et al	Investigation Number: 77507 17-0051	Report Number: 3

reviewing the video, SA Bassett noticed the male subject fidgeting, pacing, and making exaggerated upper body movements suggesting nervousness or agitation.

6. Store ███ Redacted ███ told SA Bassett that the erratic behavior of PARKER's companion on June 5th had attracted the attention of loss prevention staff, who began monitoring surveillance video cameras in real time. SA Bassett also observed PARKER counting out a large quantity of cash at the check-out counter. PARKER then left the store, walked to a blue Jeep Grand Cherokee, whereupon a black male could be seen opening the rear left door from the inside of the vehicle and taking the plastic bags containing the firearms from PARKER.

REPORT #5 WRITTEN BY Special Agent Bassett

6. Officer Junkins told SA Bassett that he had subsequently conducted a consent search of the pickup truck. Officer Junkins stated that when he searched the left rear seat, next to where AMANZE had been sitting, he found a suitcase containing three firearms, specifically:

    a. A Walther pistol, model PK380, .380 caliber, serial number WB020112. Officer Junkins noted that this pistol was recovered loaded. Junkins also noted that an NCIC query showed this pistol to be stolen from Fairmont, WV.

    b. A Taurus pistol, model PT 709 Slim, 9mm caliber, serial number TJZ01115, and

    c. A Smith & Wesson pistol, model M&P 9, 9mm caliber, serial number HBA6241.

7. Officer Junkins told SA Bassett that he had impounded the Ford F-250, and another officer had given CALHOUN a ride home. Officer Junkins stated that he received information from the other officer that CALHOUN had confessed to purchasing both firearms at a pawn shop in Westover, WV previously that evening. According to Officer Junkins' information, CALHOUN had claimed to have bought the firearms under duress by AMANZE. Officer Junkins provided SA Bassett with copies of computer-assisted dispatch (CAD) reports from the traffic stop, and advised that he was still writing his full police report from this stop.

8. SA Bassett subsequently contacted Fairmont Police Department (FPD) Detective Adrian Hayhurst. Det. Hayhurst confirmed that he had investigated the theft of that same Walther PK380 pistol from a victim in the Fairmont, WV area, in or around June 2015. Det. Hayhurst noted that the suspect in that theft was currently serving a prison sentence stemming from his theft of the Walther pistol, as well as other crimes.

9. Prior to speaking with Officer Junkins, SA Bassett had contacted Dawn Tatar, proprietor of West Virginia Jewelry & Loan. Tatar confirmed that Tommy CALHOUN had purchased two pistols from her business on June 19, 2017. Tatar provided SA Bassett with copies of the ATF Form 4473 that CALHOUN had completed on June 19, 2017.

Attachments: NCIC Criminal History Check of Tommy CALHOUN.
                NCIC Criminal History Check of Antoine AMANZE.
                NCIC Stolen Firearm Checks for Recovered Firearms.
                Copy of Star City PD Dispatch Summary for Call #C17-0002278.
                Photograph of AMANZE Identification Card.
                Copy of ATF Form 4473, Dated 6/19/17, Completed by Tommy CALHOUN.

120

Conf Num	Passenger	Place	City	State	Destination/Pickup Date	Cab	Fare	Cab Type	Dest Grp Status
956805	christopher - 3049019236	379 baldwin st	Morgantown	WV	MOTN 8/21/2017 21:40	5509	Any	MOTN, Same	C - thomasr
956924	christopher - 3049019236	379 Baldwin St	Morgantown	WV	1448 Van Voorhis Rd, MOTN 8/21/2017 21:38		$8.00 Any	MOTN, Same	CN - ramij
931373	christopher - 3049019236	Sheetz , 1012 University Ave	Morgantown	WV	1448 Van Voorhis Rd, MOTN 8/17/2017 21:22	5508	$12.00 Any	MOTN, Same	C - nickm
929981	christopher - 3049019236	1448 Van Voorhis Rd	Morgantown	WV	185 Garrett St, MOTN 8/17/2017 15:39	5507	$12.00 Any	MOTN, Same	C - murtaza
926364	christopher - 3049019236	Sheetz , 1012 University Ave	Morgantown	WV	1448 Van Voorhis Rd, MOTN 8/16/2017 20:31	5509	$12.00 Any	MOTN, Same	C - thomasr
923517	christopher - 3049019236	1448 Van Voorhis Rd	Morgantown	WV	1212 Vanvoorhis Rd, MOTN 8/16/2017 12:52	5509	$5.00 Any	MOTN, Same	C - Amian
923069	christopher - 3049019236	1448 Van Voorhis Rd	Morgantown	WV	1212 Vanvoorhis Rd, MOTN 8/16/2017 11:36	5506	$5.00 Any	MOTN, Same	NL - Amian
911251	christopher - 3049019236	1448 Van Voorhis Rd	Morgantown	WV	1235 Parkway Dr, MOTN 8/14/2017 19:34	5509	$8.00 Any	MOTN, Same	NL - hamil
906634	christopher - 3049019236	379 Baldwin St	Morgantown	WV	1448 Van Voorhis Rd, MOTN 8/13/2017 23:57	5509	$7.00 Any	MOTN, Same	C - waseem
905807	christopher - 3049019236	Animal House , 379 High St	Morgantown	WV	1448 Van Voorhis Rd, MOTN 8/13/2017 21:25	5506	$12.00 Any	MOTN, Same	C - waseem
902850	christopher - 3049019236	1448 Van Voorhis Rd	Morgantown	WV	MOTN 8/13/2017 11:59	5506	Any	MOTN, Same	C - usmanj
859366	christopher - 3049019236	978 dorsey ave	Morgantown	WV	Van Voorhis Rd, MOTN 8/3/2017 1:00	5506	$14.00 Any	MOTN, Same	C - nicolew
838632	christopher - 3049019236	Bus Garage , 185 Garrett St	Morgantown	WV	MOTN 8/2/2017 21:47	5506	Any	MOTN, Same	C - thomasr
837388	christopher - 3049019236	Bus Garage , 185 Garrett St	Morgantown	WV	t and s vanvorhis, MOTN 8/2/2017 18:13		$12.00 Any	MOTN, Same	CN - nickm
835202	christopher - 3049019236	1448 Van Voorhis Rd	Morgantown	WV	MOTN 8/2/2017 14:28	5507	Any	MOTN, Same	C - usmanj

Conf Num	Passenger	Place	City	State	Destination/Pickup Date	Cab	Fare	Cab Type	Dest Grp Status
587964	christopher - 3049019236	Towers , 360 Evansdale Drive	Morgantown	WV	2151 University Ave , MOTN 4/22/2017 17:12	5506	$8.00 Any	MOTN, Same	C - oakfini
537252	rental - 3049019236	Morgantown Motel 2 , Smithtown Rd	Morgantown	WV	76 Brookhaven Road, MOTN 4/13/2017 22:17	5506	$14.00 Any	MOTN, Same	C - thomasr

121

Conf Num	Tag Name	Place	City	ST	Destination	Pickup Date	Cab	Rate	Cab Type	Dest Group	Status
956805	christopher - 3049019236	379 baldwin st	Morganto wn	WV	MOTN	6/21/2017 21:40	5509		Any	MOTN, Same	C - thomasr
956924	christopher - 3049019236	379 Baldwin St	Morganto wn	WV	1448 Van Voorhis Rd, MOTN	6/21/2017 21:38		$8.00	Any	MOTN, Same	CN - ramil
931373	christopher - 3049019236	Sheetz , 1012 University Ave	Morganto wn	WV	1448 Van Voorhis Rd, MOTN	6/17/2017 21:22	5508	$12.00	Any	MOTN, Same	C - nickm
929981	christopher - 3049019236	1448 Van Voorhis Rd	Morganto wn	WV	185 Garrett St, MOTN	6/17/2017 15:39	5507	$12.00	Any	MOTN, Same	C - murtaza
926364	christopher - 3049019236	Sheetz , 1012 University Ave	Morganto wn	WV	1448 Van Voorhis Rd, MOTN	6/16/2017 20:31	5509	$12.00	Any	MOTN, Same	C - thomasr
923517	christopher - 3049019236	1448 Van Voorhis Rd	Morganto wn	WV	1212 Vanvoorhi s Rd, MOTN	6/16/2017 12:52	5509	$5.00	Any	MOTN, Same	C - Amian
922069	christopher - 3049019236	1448 Van Voorhis Rd	Morganto wn	WV	1212 Vanvoorhi s Rd, MOTN	6/16/2017 11:36	5506	$5.00	Any	MOTN, Same	NL - Amian
921251	christopher - 3049019236	1448 Van Voorhis Rd	Morganto wn	WV	1235 Parkview Dr, MOTN	6/14/2017 19:34	5509	$8.00	Any	MOTN, Same	NL - ramil
906624	christopher - 3049019236	379 Baldwin St	Morganto wn	WV	1448 Van Voorhis Rd, MOTN	6/13/2017 23:57	5509	$7.00	Any	MOTN, Same	C - waseem
905807	christopher - 3049019236	Animal House , 379 High St	Morganto wn	WV	1448 Van Voorhis Rd, MOTN	6/13/2017 21:25	5506	$12.00	Any	MOTN, Same	C - waseem
902850	christopher - 3049019236	1448 Van Voorhis Rd	Morganto wn	WV	MOTN	6/13/2017 11:59	5508		Any	MOTN, Same	C - usmanj
839366	christopher - 3049019236	975 dorsey ave	Morganto wn	WV	Van Voorhis Rd, MOTN	6/3/2017 1:00	5506	$14.00	Any	MOTN, Same	C - nicolew
838632	christopher - 3049019236	Bus Garage , 185 Garrett St	Morganto wn	WV	MOTN	6/2/2017 21:47	5508		Any	MOTN, Same	C - thomasr
837388	christopher - 3049019236	Bus Garage , 185 Garrett St	Morganto wn	WV	t and s vanvors, MOTN	6/2/2017 18:13		$12.00	Any	MOTN, Same	CN - nickm
835902	christopher - 3049019236	1448 Van Voorhis Rd	Morganto wn	WV	MOTN	6/2/2017 14:28	5507		Any	MOTN, Same	C - usmanj
Conf Num	Tag Name	Place	City	ST	Destination	Pickup Date	Cab	Rate	Cab Type	Dest Group	Status
587064	christopher - 3049019236	Towers , 350 Evansdale Drive	Morganto wn	WV	2151 University Ave , MOTN	4/22/2017 17:12	5508	$8.00	Any	MOTN, Same	C - caitlini
537252	denise - 3049019236	Morganto wn Motel 2 Smithtown Rd	Morganto wn	WV	75 Brookehav en Road, MOTN	4/13/2017 22:17	5506	$14.00	Any	MOTN, Same	C - thomasr

MR. WALKER'S FEEDBACK ABOUT EVERYTHING I ASKED HIM TO USE FOR MY DEFENSE AT TRIAL!!

"I'm done Mr. Walker, that is everything I would like for you to use as part of my defense at trial. Now what is your feedback on everything I just said?"

Mr. Walker took one more glimpse at his cell phone before placing it in the inside of his blue suit jacket. He looked me in my eyes with the energy of hate pouring out of his pupils and said, Antoine everything you brought to my attention is valid and things that **"COULD"** be used as your defense, Antoine. The question is whether I am going to use it or not for your defense. Do you think my job is to really help you Antoine?

Before I could answer he continued. Do you really think I would bring up all the things you want me to use as your defense at trial to the jury's attention, to make the prosecutor I've known for years look like she arrested the wrong person, and does not know how to do her job correctly? Do you!

"Is it not your fucking job to help me Mr. Walker?"

"Yes, it **"CAN"** be my job to help you, but am I is the question. I am going to be upfront with you Antoine, if I were you, I will take a plea deal because I am not going against the prosecutor for you!! Sorry, I cannot help you! In my eyes you do not have a defense for trial!! The prosecutor and judge want you convicted and that is exactly what I am going to give them one way or another!

Either through getting you to take a plea or if you go to trial make sure you lose. I will not raise one objection at trial if you do decide to go to trial. I will make sure the prosecutor has her way with you, that I can promise you! One way or another Antoine you will get convicted.

The judge told me personally she will get a conviction out of you by "any means necessary." judge Keeley will not let you win in her courtroom she assured me of that more than once. No one "**EVER**" wins in her courtroom as far back as I can remember, your best bet is to take a plea Mr. Antoine. "

Fuck you and a plea deal Frank, I said calling Mr. Walker by his first name. Fuck a plea deal, I am going to trial!!

Ok, tough guy if you go to trial you will get more time when you lose, and I am "**TELLING**" you that you are going to lose! I am trying to help you out by getting you to plead guilty so that you can do less time. Right now, I have negotiated a plea deal with the prosecutor for you. The plea deal is you get sentenced anywhere from 57-71 months in a federal prison. Nothing more than 71 months! That is a great deal Antoine, you can do that easily.

I have seen in your rap sheet you, have already served 8 years in the past so another 57-71 months you can do standing on your head. When or if you go to trial you will lose. I am telling you right now you will get nothing less than 10 years. You can bet your last dollar on that Antoine. Do not count on **GOD**! What you can definitely count on is getting nothing less than 10 years if you decide to go to trial.

Antoine you have a girl who I know wants you home sooner than later. I know your mother and grandmother wants you home sooner than later but most importantly you do too.

Do not be a dumb ass or a wise guy, just take the fucking plea deal! I have your best interest at heart, Antoine. I am telling you that is the best thing for you to do. Do not be a dick, Antoine. Take the plea is my advice to you as your attorney.

You are not my fucking attorney Mr. Walker you are my fucking prosecutor, just like the rest of the court appointed attorneys the judge assigned to me. What I don't get about you Mr. Walker is that I just showed you evidence that can convince a jury at trial that I am innocent of these charges, and you still are telling me to take a fucking plea deal.

I felt in my heart you were a snake the very first day I met your black ass!! I knew my gut feeling was right about your black ass!

Why the fuck you choose to even take my case as my lawyer if you were not going to represent me the proper way you are supposed to according to the United States Constitution. You are supposed to be an effective attorney and fight for me, not against me like you are doing right now.

You really looked me in my eyes the first day we met and told me trial was the best thing for me to do, because the prosecutor had nothing on me. Now you are fucking telling me to take a fucking plea deal. You really deceived me!!! "You are a fucking bitch Mr. Walker!!!!!" I said looking him dead in his creep ass eyes. I could tell by the look in his eyes when I called him a bitch, I hit a nerve, and he was really upset because I could see the anger in his eyes.

Out of anger he started to tell me what was really going on and why I was really being charged with these crimes!!!!!!!!!!!!!! I just sat back quietly and listened in shock until he was done talking.

"No, I am not a bitch, Antoine! You are the real bitch! You are everybody bitch, my bitch, the prosecutor's bitch, the judge's bitch, Parker's bitch, Tommy's bitch, Chris's bitch, special agent Bassett's bitch and police officer Junkin's bitch!!!!"

The only reason why you were charged with these crimes in the first place was because police officer Junkins who conducted the traffic stop on tommy's pickup truck on June 19, 2017 lied on you, and said you were the suspect who fled from the traffic stop, that we all know you were not present at.

Officer Junkins told one of his fellow officers who I know very well, and his fellow officer told me exactly what happened that night of the traffic stop.

Officer Junkins found your state identification card in tommy's truck on the floor when he searched his vehicle and made up the whole story about you giving him your identification card before you fled on foot into a wooden area.

Officer Junkins said when he found your identification card on the floor of tommy's truck and he looked at the photo on it, he knew right away it was not the suspect who fled from the traffic stop.

After he ran a background check on the name on the identification card he found in Tommy's truck, he found out you had many prior convictions and because of that you fit the description of a person who fit the charge you are facing now!! It all started when police officer Junkins found 3 firearms in Tommy's truck in a bag or suitcase, after Tommy gave him consent to search his vehicle.

He asked Tommy who the firearms belonged to, and Tommy said he did not know. The officer then radioed into another police officer at the police station he works in and gave the officer the serial numbers of each firearm, for the officer to do a background check on all 3 firearms found in Tommy's truck.

Minutes later officer Junkins received the results of the background check of the firearms. The results showed 2 out of the 3 firearms belonged to Tommy legally, it showed he bought them earlier that day from a local gun store. And the last firearm, the Walther pistol you spoke about Mr. Antoine popped up as stolen from Jarrod Hamrick and was supposed to be in the Fairmont police department's evidence room since 2015 due to it being found on a person unlawfully, making that the result of that person being charged with the theft of that gun.

After police officer Junkins told Tommy the results of the background check on the firearms found in his truck, Tommy confessed to the officer that he knew a police officer who worked at the Fairmont Police Department, and that is how he got the stolen Walther pistol that was supposed to be in the police station's evidence room, Tommy said the officer he knew who worked in the Fairmount Police Department gave him the Walther pistol you are being charged with for $100.00 several months ago, and he decided to sell it to the guy who fled from the traffic stop he knew as Shawn, for some crack cocaine. Tommy also confessed to the officer that he purchased the 2 firearms earlier that day also for the guy who fled from the traffic stop for some crack as well.

Officer Junkins then told Tommy he had to charge him for being in possession of the stolen firearm that was found in his truck, because he was the driver of the registered vehicle. He told Tommy he had to report to the **ATF** that he went into a gun store and bought firearms under his name that were really not for him.

Officer Junkins told his fellow officer who told me all of this and that, Tommy began pleading to him not to arrest him, because he never been to jail and was afraid of going.

Officer Junkins then started to feel bad for him because Tommy was old enough to be his father, and thought to himself what if this were my dad what would I want another police officer to do for me?

Officer Junkins then told Tommy the only way he would not go to jail that night was if he gave a statement saying the stolen pistol found in his truck belonged to the fleeing suspect, and that's all it would take to pin the charges on him. Since all 3 firearms were found in the same bag or suitcase.

Officer Junkins told Tommy he had to also say all 3 firearms belonged to the fleeing suspect and that he threated his life to buy him the 2 pistols he bought earlier that day to make the story sound more believable, including giving him crack cocaine as Tommy's reward for buying him the pistols.

Tommy agreed to do so to avoid going to jail that night. Officer Junkins then asked Tommy for the suspect's full name who had fled from the traffic stop in order to bring up charges on him and issue a warrant for his arrest, but Tommy only knew the fleeing perpetrator as Shawn from New York and did not know his last name.

Which did not help Tommy or officer Junkins to complete their plan to pin charges on the fleeing subject, because a last name was needed in order to do so.

So Mr. Junkins came up with another marvelous idea and told Tommy the only way he will not go to jail that night was if he made a statement saying the guy who fled from the traffic stop was the guy on the identification card he found in Tommy's truck.

Since he had the guy's I.D showing his first and last name due to the identification card he found having his first and last name on it, and especially after the background check on the name on the identification card found in Tommy's truck showed up that this guy had many prior felonies, including firearm charges, making him a perfect candidate to receive the firearm charges for the firearms found in Tommy's truck.

Tommy had no problem doing that because he did not want to go to jail that night. The officer just out of curiosity asked Tommy, "how did the identification card found in your truck get there?" Tommy told him the guy who fled had it in the front of his jean pants pocket. When he leaned the front seat back in his truck earlier that day to lay down because he was tired, it fell out of his pocket along with pocket change he also had in his pocket.

Tommy said he did not want to wake him and tell him because he seemed really tired. But was going to tell him when he awoke, but he forgot to because there was so much going on that day.

Antoine, normally when a stolen gun is found in a person's vehicle the driver of the car goes to jail no matter if the driver says the gun did not belong to him, and it belonged to someone else.

Tommy did not go to jail that night for the stolen gun even though he was supposed to, because the gun was found in the vehicle he was driving.

Officer Junkins made sure he did not go to jail that night after Tommy gave a statement saying you were the guy who fled from the traffic stop, and you were the person who the stolen gun belonged to. Along with him saying he bought the 2 firearms for you earlier that day out of fear, and after he bought and gave them to you, he was rewarded by you with crack cocaine.

So, that makes you Tommy's and officer Junkin's bitch!!

Antoine, do you remember the letter I mailed to you I believe back in October ("Readers" I have included the letter Mr. Walker is referring to in the back of this section on **page 133.**) where I stated that I received a copy of the police officer's dashcam footage from his patrol car the night of the traffic stop, after you kept requesting for me to get it? And I also stated in the letter I will bring the dashcam footage down to you so you can view it, remember that Antoine? Mr. Walker said in a pissed off way.

Well, I "was" going to bring it down for your viewing but as you can see, I never did and not planning to. The dashcam footage was going to be used by me as part of your defense for trial until the prosecutor told me she wants a conviction out of you, and to make sure the dashcam footage gets lost somehow which it already has. "I think my dog ate it."

I personally looked at the dashcam video before "my dog ate it," Mr. Walker said with a look on his face like he was the devil himself. The dashcam footage clearly shows you were not the person who fled from the traffic stop on June 19, 2017. But that will never be shown to the jury of your trial!!!

So, "that makes you my bitch and the prosecutor's bitch."

Antoine, there is more!! Before officer Junkins let Tommy go that night he gave Junkins plenty of helpful information and this is how Parker and Chris Anderson got into the picture and got involved in all of this.

Tommy told officer Junkins he met Shawn the guy who actually fled from the traffic stop on June 19, 2017 through Christopher Anderson. Tommy said he met Shawn when Chris introduced them, when Chris asked does he want to make some extra money and get some free crack cocaine if he went into a gun store and bought firearms for Shawn.

At first Tommy was hesitated to do it but when Chris told Tommy that Tommy's friend Parker did it twice for Shawn a month ago and there were no issues made Tommy feel more confident to do it, so he agreed to. Especially after Chris told Tommy how easy it was for Parker to make the extra money and receive a lot of crack cocaine for doing so.

Officer Junkins reported all the information he found out from Tommy to special agent Bassett of the **ATF,** because it had to do with firearms. This is when special agent Bassett looked up Parker's name on his work computer and found out she purchased 5 firearms from Sportsman's Warehouse gun store within days apart. After finding that out special agent Bassett went to her home and told Parker he needed to see the five firearms she purchased from Sportsman's Warehouse gun store, because there was a rumor going on around town that she did not buy the firearms for herself but really bought them for a guy named Shawn. Parker could not produce the firearms she bought from Sportsman's Warehouse because they were already long gone.

That is when Parker confessed to special agent Bassett that she bought the firearms for this guy name Shawn from your neck of the woods "Antoine, she met Shawn through Chris Anderson." Special agent Bassett asked Parker did she know Shawn's last name and she said she did not. All she knew was he was from New York which was not enough to bring charges on him, a first and last name was needed to do that.

Special agent Bassett then got Chris's phone number and address from Parker and was going to pay him a visit next. Before agent Bassett left Parker's home he asked her when the last time was she saw Shawn and she said not in weeks. He told her if Shawn was to contact her again, to give him a call and let him know, which Parker agreed to do. But Shawn never contacted her again.

When special agent Bassett went to Chris's home, he told him Tommy and Parker said he introduced them to a guy name Shawn from New York, who they both bought firearms for that he helped orchestrate. Chris confessed to agent Bassett that he did and cosigned exactly what Tommy and Parker said. Chris also confessed to selling crack cocaine for Shawn. Agent Bassett asked Chris did he know Shawn's last name and like Tommy and Parker he did not. All he knew about Shawn was he is from New York. Agent Bassett asked him when the last time he has seen or heard from Shawn, and he said not for weeks. Special agent Bassett told Parker the same thing he told Chris if he sees or hears from him to contact him to let him know, which Chris agreed to. A month later special agent Bassett made his way back to Parker's home and asked her did she hear from Shawn, and Parker said no she has not.

Special agent Bassett came up with a clever idea just like police officer Junkins did. He told Parker if any of the guns she bought and gave to Shawn pop up in a murder in New York or anywhere for that matter she will get charged for murder, and never see a day in the streets again, and will be taken away from her children. And to save her ass she needed to come up with a story.

After police officer Junkins spoke to special agent Bassett and told him the real story about what happened the night of the June 19, 2017 traffic stop, special agent Bassett made an executive decision to follow suit. He went back to Parker's home and suggested that Parker use your name as the scapegoat incase those guns she bought ever pop up in a murder or other crimes. Parker willingly agreed because she was scared and wanted to save her ass.

Then he went to Chris's home and told Chris the same thing. He told Chris if those firearms he helped Parker buy for Shawn pop up in a murder than he will be charged with accessory to murder so he needed to save his ass as well and suggested he use your name as the person he introduced to Parker and Tommy who he assisted with having them buy guns for "Shawn," which was you Antoine, "the real bitch" not me like you said a few minutes ago. Agent Bassett told Chris everything he did for Shawn he needed to say he did for you to really cover his ass. And what do you the think Chris did, he covered his ass. I would of did the same thing too if I were him. This is how and why you got a distributing crack cocaine charge, receiving firearms from Parker and Tommy and charged you with possession of firearms charges, and trafficking guns charges. This all happened based on what Tommy, Parker, and Chris said you did even though there is no real proof against you. Chris was coerced to say he assisted you with getting Tommy and Parker to buy firearms for you. Tommy and Parker were also coerced to agree to that along with them agreeing to you rewarding them with crack cocaine after they purchased the guns for you. Because Chris lied and said he saw you sell crack cocaine before and assisted you by selling it for you, this is how and why you were charged with distributing crack cocaine even though you did not get caught with any drugs.

"This is the feds," Antoine. You don't need no evidence to charge someone with a crime for the feds, all you need is a person saying you did something, or they did something for you, and you are going down hard and fast like you have, LOL! You are everybody's bitch!!! Well, I am done here. "I have to go home and fuck my old lady," Mr. Walker said as he got up and walked out of the visit room and proceeded to walk towards the exit door to leave the jail. I hurried and got up then walked out the visit room myself and yelled at the top of my lungs to Mr. Walker **"YOU ARE A PIECE OF SHIT!!!"** I swear to **GOD** if I had a gun, I would have walk behind him and blow his head clean off then did every day of my time for murder with no regrets. **FACTS**!!! I no longer feel that way anymore but at that moment I did and really would of did it if I had a gun! I went back to my cell to channel my anger and I filed an ethic complaint against my attorney to the State of West Virginia office of Lawyer Disciplinary Counsel.

THE LETTER FROM MY ATTORNEY MR. WALKER TELLING ME HE RECEIVED THE DASHCAM VIDEO AND WILL BRING IT DOWN FOR ME TO REVIEW IT

FRANK WALKER
L A W

October 4, 2018

Attorney-Client Privileged

Amanze Antoine #3628016
North Central Regional Jail
#1 Lois Lane
Greenwood, WV 26415

Re: *US v. Antoine – 18-17*

Amanze:

   I have received your recent letters asking for a speedy trial. The trial will remain set in December. I again ask for a list of your witnesses for trial and any pre-trial motions you wish to file.

   I have just received a copy of the dashcam from the stop and will bring down for your viewing.

Sincerely,

/s/ Frank C. Walker II

Frank C. Walker II

www.FrankWalkerLaw.com
Pennsylvania Office – 3000 N. Lewis Run Road, Clairton, Pennsylvania 15025
Morgantown, West Virginia Office – The Monongahela Building, 235 High Street, Suite 418, Morgantown, West Virginia 26505
Office 1.800.496.4143 (Toll-Free) – 412.405.8556 (Local) | Cell 412.532.6805 | Fax 412.202.9193 | frank@frankwalkerlaw.com

CRIMINAL DEFENSE · PERSONAL INJURY - MEDICAL MALPRACTICE - WRONGFUL DEATH

CHAPTER 27

FINAL PRE- TRIAL CONFERENCE

December 3, 2018

Today I went to court for my final pre-trial conference. A final pre-trial conference permits the judge to meet with the opposing parties (prosecutor and my attorney) to ensure an efficient and fair processing of the case, encourage plea negotiations, hear motions or schedule them for hearings, narrow the issues to be tried at trial, and set the trial date if not already done. The final pre-trial conference is often the last serious opportunity for resolving the case before trial.

Almost immediately after I arrived in the federal court building after being transported there by 2 agents from the County Jail, I was told by one of the agents my attorney wanted to see me before we went in front of the judge. I was taken to an attorney/client room where lawyers can talk to their clients in private. This attorney client room was a non- contact room meaning there is a glass in between Mr. Walker and I that prevents us from being able to touch one another, but we can hear each other very very clearly.

When I entered this small room, I saw Mr. Walker was already seated. This motherfucker is still telling me his advice to me is to take a plea deal. I really wanted to choke the shit out of him when he told me that again. I looked at him and told him "you can't be fucking serious Mr.

Walker"!! I really did not do this shit and your bitch ass is telling me to take a fucking plea! After all the slime ball shit you told me the officer, the prosecutor, agent Bassett, Chris, Tommy, and Parker did to me when you came to visit me last week and you are still fucking telling me to take a fucking plea. I do not want to talk about a fucking plea, "I want to talk about my fucking defense for trial." Mr. Walker simply stated in a very calm manner "I don't have a defense to use for you at trial Antoine," and he refused to even entertain a conversation about a defense for my trial. Every time I attempted to talk about a defense for trial, he would cut me off and speak over me saying **"I DON'T HAVE A DEFENSE FOR YOU!"**

After about 10 minutes of me attempting to talk to Mr.

Walker about my defense for trial while the whole time I was talking to him he was playing with his phone paying me no mind, he finally just got up without warning and walked out of the room, and cut off the lights leaving me in total darkness. I could not turn the lights back on, because the light switch was on his side of the room that I did not have access to because of the glass that separated us, and prevented me from having access to the side he was on totally. I sat in total darkness for about 10 minutes before one of the bald-headed U.S Marshalls came to the room and opened the door up to let me out so that I could be taken into the courtroom to start my final pre-trial conference.

When I got into the courtroom to begin my final pre-trial conference the first thing, I told the judge was I no longer wanted Mr. Walker to be my attorney because I know he is not on my side. "Your honor, I no longer want Mr. Walker as my attorney because he is not helping me at all. He works for you and the prosecutor not for me." The judge looked at me in a monstrous way and said in a stern voice "He went to law school, not you Antoine!! I am not giving you a new attorney!! You must deal with Mr. Walker and start listening to him. You might not like what you hear but you must start listening to Mr. Walker. Mr. Walker is a fine attorney and he is doing his job to the best of his ability."

"Your honor no he is not, he is not helping me at all!! I tried explaining to him certain things I wanted him to use as part of my defense for trial that will help prove I am not guilty of these charges, and after showing him these things he tells me "I don't have a defense." He did this minutes ago and he did this when he came to visit me in the County Jail last week. I don't trust him, and I want a new attorney your honor, I do not want to go to trial with Mr. Walker, he is not on my side!!"

"Mr. Antoine, the judge said your attorney is not being removed from your case. He will be your trial lawyer!! I am not giving you a new attorney!! It will not happen in this courtroom so stop complaining. He's going to be your trial attorney whether you like it or not!!"

I knew I was not going to receive a fair trial and the fight was rigged for me to lose, but I was still going to trial because I did not do this shit. I definitely see what Mr.

Walker meant when he said, "the judge would make sure I get convicted by any means necessary."

Days ahead I would see more vividly what by any means necessary really meant. I felt in my mind, body, and soul there was nothing I could do but to accept the fact Mr.

Walker was going to be my attorney for trial. No matter how much I complained about him, the judge did not give a fuck, and would not change my lawyer for nothing. I knew everyone in the courtroom was against me. I knew I was not going to receive a fair trial, but I still was going because I am innocent.

I just sat through my final pre-trial conference listening to my lawyer, the prosecutor and judge talk in legal terms that I did not understand. "Most" people who get arrested and go through the court system can relate to that as well.

Attorneys, prosecutors, and judges all know the average person who gets arrested does not know or understand the law or legal terms used in a courtroom. They know it sounds like a foreign language to most of us. By them knowing that they take advantage of our ignorance to the law and do as they please with us legally but it's really not legit. They get away with it because we don't know what's going on but they do because they understand the law, something most of us don't understand.

Because many of us who enter the courtroom as the defendant are ignorant to the law you are scared or get tricked into taking a plea deal. Court-appointed attorneys are best known for this. By the judge, prosecutor, and your attorney knowing that you are ignorant to the law and don't really understand anything that is being said or done in the courtroom they use strategic tactics to get a conviction out of you, normally by the way of a plea deal that you were scared or tricked into taking by your attorney! They can say what they want to say after reading this book, but I know what is really going on!

A lot of people who get arrested may be guilty of a crime but not the crime they are initially charged with, a lot of times people get over charged by the prosecutor with higher crimes with more severe penalties than the crime they are actually guilty of. They do not know because they are ignorant to the law. The court appointed attorney that most of us get who cannot afford a paid lawyer 9 times out of 10 he or she is in it with the prosecutor and judge to get a conviction out of you. Again, normally by your attorney convincing you somehow to take a plea! Some court appointed attorneys go as low as getting your loved ones involved into convincing you to take a plea. What they do is play on your mom, dad, girl, etc. who are ignorant to the law as well and tell them the best thing for you to do is take a plea deal, because if you do not and you go to trial you will get double the time. These court appointed attorneys know our loved ones wants us home sooner than later so 9 times out of 10 after the lawyer tells them that our loved ones will try to convince us to take a plea because they don't want you to take the chance at trial and get more time if you lose. The court appointed attorneys knows your loved ones want you home sooner than later and by them telling them you will get more time if you go to trial and lose they indirectly know your loved ones will try to convince to take a plea.

These court appointed attorneys are very very crafty and use different tricky tactics to get you to take a plea to satisfy their goal to get a conviction out of you. As I said above, they can say what they want to say after reading this book. I been going through the court system since I was 16 years old, **TRUST ME I KNOW WHAT I AM TALKING ABOUT**! A person getting over charged does not happen all the time. Some people get charged for the exact crime they are guilty of. The point I want you to clearly understand is everybody works against you in the courtroom and in a lot of cases even your own attorney. The goal is to get a conviction and your attorney, prosecutor and judge all work together to make that happen. Yes, I said the judge is in that equation as well, yes, the person who is supposed to be the fair person in the courtroom a lot of times is the ringleader securing a conviction.

The court system in the United States is designed for anyone who enters it will take a loss in some way shape or form. Especially if you do not have any money for a paid lawyer and you are forced to deal with a court-appointed attorney. I got three words for you: **YOU ARE FUCKED!!!!!** At times even if you do have money to hire an attorney you still get fucked over because that attorney works against you like a court appointed attorney and helps get you convicted by any means necessary. There are not a lot of attorneys left like Nialena Carvavaos from Philadelphia, Sunny Hostin from the view, Elizabeth Franklin-Best and Ranee Saunders, both from Columbia, South Carolina and their great paralegal LaDonna Falvey, Joey Jackson from New York who works for the HLN T.V channel, Emily Compagno from Fox news, Eboni K. Williams from the revolt tv show called state of the culture. Those attorneys I named above go the extra mile for their clients and will defend them with their all!! That is rare to find!! There are not too many lawyers like them breathing.

Sitting in my pre-trial conference I was wishing I had one of those attorneys I just named above. Because I know things would have turned out way differently if I had one of those attorneys, but I knew I could not afford them. Lawyers like them cost because lawyers like them know that they are rare, so their value goes up.

The conclusion of the final pretrial conference was my trial was set to start on December 11, 2018, 8 days from today. The entire ride being transported back to the county jail by two agents I thought about writing the judge a letter telling her in writing I did not want Mr. Walker as my attorney and my reasons why I did not. Even though the judge made it very clear today in her courtroom that she was not going to give me a new attorney, I still thought it was a good idea for me to still write her a letter in order for me to keep a track record of my complaints about me not wanting Mr. Walker as my attorney and the reasons why I did not want him as my attorney. If at a later date I needed to bring up the issue of ineffective assistant of counsel to the Court of Appeal, which is a higher court that hears appeals from lower court's decisions like the lower court I was currently about to go to trial in. The Court of Appeal is known for sometimes granting a person a new trial, or letting someone go free, because his or her lawyer did not do their job effectively during a trial.

For some reason I knew I was going to lose trial so I was thinking ahead of the game, I thought if I wrote a letter to the judge about the things my attorney had done to me and why I didn't want him as my attorney the Court of Appeals would see the track record of me always complaining about my attorney in both open court and in writing. I felt the letter would help me in the long run so as soon as I went back to the County Jail I went into my cell and wrote a letter to the judge. In this letter I included everything my attorney did to me in the attorney client room when I went to court that day along with the other things. I have included at the end of this section on **pages 140-142** is the "exact" letter I wrote to the judge on 12-04-2018 so please read it.

THIS IS THE LETTER I WROTE TO THE JUDGE ON 12-3-2018 TELLING HER I NO LONGER WANTED MR. WALKER AS MY ATTORNEY

12-4-2018

Dear Honorable Keeley

I'm writing because after I left court on December 3, 2018 my attorney Mr. Walker came downstairs to speak to me. While in the attorney/client room my attorney Mr. Walker told me he does not have a defense for me at all and my trial starts on December 11, 2018. This was said to me after I asked Mr. Walker lets talk about my defense for trial. He simply stated there is no defense and refuse to even talk about one. After about 10 minutes of me talking to Mr. Walker which he was paying me no mind he then got up turned off the lights in the room and walked out the room closed the door and left me in the dark until the bald U.S Marshal came and took me to the holding cell. Also when I came back to the Regional Jail from court I received legal mail that Mr. Walker sent to me. In the legal mail it was a list of the witness and Exhibit list Mr. Walker put in on my behalf on November 19, 2018. Mr. Walker didn't put in all the Exhibit or witnesses I requested for him to put in on my behalf which I have an email sent to him about all the Exhibits and witnesses I wanted him to put on my behalf which Mr. Walker replied to that email my girl sent him the morning

of November 19, 2018 saying that he
will add all the Exhibits and witnesses
I requested. My girlfriend will print out
the email sent with his reply to it.
Mr. Walker clearly lied to me again
and I need new Counsel. A lawyer
is not suppose to deceive or mislead his
client. I feel my attorney is angry because
I wrote him up for lying to me and
because of that he will not represent
me to the best of his ability. You told
me Honorable Keeley that my attorney will
fight for me at trial and you felt
he is fit for the Job however I disagree
because Mr. Walker told me to my face after
I left your courtroom on 12-3-18 that
he does not have a defense for me. He
was also very rude while we were talking
by playing with his phone while I'm asking
him about a defense. Honorable Keeley I
need a new attorney. I understand you feel
Mr. Walker is a good attorney but I don't
think he is in this case for me because
of the things he do and say to me. I
don't feel comfortable with Mr. Walker
and I don't want to move forward with
an attorney that states to ~~me~~ does not
have a defense for his client a week
before trial or an attorney that did not
place Exhibits or witnesses to the Courts
that his client requested him to and he
agreed to do but lied and didn't do it.

141

Honorable Keeley I need a new attorney,
I feel Mr. Walker will on purpose be
ineffective at trial because I wrote
him up to the BAR and displinary for
counsel. I'M entitled by the Consitution
to have an effective attorney and I
don't feel I'M receiving right now,
I will show you the exhibit and
witness list I sent Mr Walker along
with him stating he will add it on
for my behalf then I will show
you the witness list and Exhibit list
Mr. Walker put in on November 19, 2018,
Mr. Walker did not put about 75% of
the Exhibits or witnesses I requested
which he agreed to do by the email he
sent back to my girlfriend. And on
the Exhibit list he put in on my behalf
he put the dashcam, I thought it was
not a dashcam. I don't trust nothing
he tells me and can you please give me
a new attorney..

                            Sincerly

                         AMANZE Antoine
                         # 36d8016.

142

CHAPTER 28

JURY SELECTION THE WICKEDNESS CONTINUES!

DECEMBER 11, 2018

For those of you who do not understand the process of the jury selection proceedings let me break it down for you before I move forward:

Jury selection consists of potential jurors to be selected for a trial. They are supposed to be randomly selected and placed on a list called a "venire" which is a legal term meaning a list of persons from which jurors are summoned to court for duty. The venire must be a fair cross-section of the community under the Sixth Amendment Right to an impartial jury. All persons who are on the venire list must show up to court and are all subject to something called "voir dire."

Voir Dire is a legal term that means the people who were selected to be potential jurors for a trial must speak the truth when being questioned by the judge, prosecutor, or attorney about any bias they may have or other reasons for them not to be able to serve as a juror for a trial in terms of them being an impartial juror. In a nutshell the voir dire is the process of the potential jurors for a trial being asked questions they are not supposed to lie about.

Ok, now back to what happened in the courtroom the day my jury selection began. I entered the courtroom with 2 federal agents escorting me. To my surprise upon entering the courtroom I saw about 45 people sitting in the back of the courtroom who were all selected to be a potential juror for my trial. It caught me off guard to see so many people in the courtroom because no one gave me any warning about what to expect when I entered the courtroom that day. The 2 agents escorted me to a seat right next to my attorney Mr. Walker, trust me I was seated next to him by force not by choice.

"All rise" the court officer said out loud as the judge entered the courtroom. Everyone stood up as if there was something honorable about this judge to stand up for. You may now be seated said the judge to everyone in the courtroom as she took a seat herself. The entire room sat down. "Hello ladies and gentlemen, my name is judge Irene Keeley, and I am the judge presiding over this trial. Some of you will be chosen today to be a juror in the trial of the defendant, Amanze Antoine."

"Amanze Antoine has been convicted on or about November 30,1999 for Robbery in the first degree, and he was also convicted on February 24,2010 for criminal possession of a firearm ladies and gentlemen." This is what the judge told all the potential jurors for my trial. The look on some of the potential jurors faces after the judge told them about my prior convictions, said shame on you!! I could tell by how they looked at me what they were thinking!

After the judge said what she said to the potential jurors of my trial, I looked at my attorney sitting right next to me and his non-verbal communication stated, "I told you to take a plea deal".

According to the law, the judge was not supposed to tell the potential jurors about any of my prior convictions,

Because by doing so it put me at a disadvantage because it puts bad thoughts in the potential juror heads about me. The judge knew this and still did it. The judge disregarded the law and did what she wanted to do. **SMFH** is all I could do.

I knew there was a possibility some people would find me guilty at trial just based on them knowing I had a criminal record. Even though they were not supposed to and base their verdict on the evidence. I knew that was still a possibility. Things were already starting off bad for me!! I could not help but think to myself how very unfair it was for the judge to do that, never mind the law that stated she could not do it, but because my past convictions was no longer who I was as a person.

Yes, I have made poor decisions in the past but that is not the man who I have become!! That is what should matter, the man I have become not the man I used to be!! People make poor decisions in life all the time, and people also change and do not make those same poor decisions they made 10 years ago, a year ago, or even the poor decision they made yesterday ever in life again. So I really found it to be extremely unfair for the judge to tell the potential jurors of my trial I had a past criminal record, because I truly have changed who I am as a person by rewiring my mind and changing how I think which ultimately changed my actions and my lifestyle. It took me many times to go to jail to change, but I got it together and truly became a better person. The potential jurors in the courtroom did not know that about me. All they knew about me was my past criminal history the judge just told them about me which hindered me tremendously from the very start.

By the judge doing that it showed how much of an unfair person she was and how dirty she would play to make sure my chances of getting convicted at trial were very high. Again "by law" the judge was not supposed to tell the potential jurors of my trial about any of my past convictions to prevent them from having any bias thoughts about me in order to keep the trial fair. The judge did not care about that law, I quickly learned. That was just the beginning of all the unfairness that was about to occur throughout my entire trial. I have included at the end of this section page 6 lines 13-20 of my jury selection transcripts on **page 148** showing the judge telling all the potential jurors about my past criminal convictions at the beginning of jury selection.

Luckily, the judge did follow one law which was asking all the potential jurors in her courtroom did anyone know her before jury selection actually started. Two potential jurors raised their hands when the judge asked this question and said they went to the same church as the judge, and another stated the judge was an acquaintance with his family!

Red flags went off in my head immediately after hearing that! My first thought was the judge had to have some type of say so about the people who were chosen to come into her courtroom to be potential jurors for my trial. There is no way in hell with the population in West Virginia being 1.792 million 2 people from the judge's church and 1 person whom the judge is an acquaintance with his family just randomly were chosen to be a potential juror for my trial. The probability of that happening is extremely low. I felt in the inner core of my heart this entire jury selection proceedings were rigged. I knew the judge had some type of say so about was chosen to come in her courtroom to be a potential juror. The judge had a better chance of hitting the lottery back-to-back in the same month than to have 3 randomly chosen people to be potential jurors in her courtroom who she knew very well. All I kept thinking about was my attorney telling me the judge told him she would do get a conviction out of me by any means necessary.

I knew that statement was not a myth based on what I was seeing in Judge Irene Keeley courtroom today. I started thinking to myself how many other potential jurors knew the judge but kept it to themselves when the judge asked did anyone know her. My inner self told me there were others who knew the judge but kept quiet when asked.

I know I am right! Your gut never lies to you!! **GUESS WHAT?** One of the potential jurors who stated they knew the judge was selected to be a juror for my trial. How unfair is that? **I THINK VERY UNFAIR!!** How about you? I damn sure did not like the fact of the person who knew the judge very well was selected to be a juror for my trial. I looked at my attorney Mr. Walker when the person who knew the judge was selected to be a juror for my trial, and he winked his fucking eye at me.

The proper thing the judge should have done to all the potential jurors who stated they knew her was to disqualify them all from becoming actual jurors in my trial. Which the judge could have easily done using a legal term called "challenge for cause". "Challenge for cause" broken down in a language the average person understands means disqualifying a potential juror from being selected as a juror for a trial because of a bias or other reasons that are reasonable that may make a person feel this potential juror will not be an impartial juror, if chosen to become a juror for a trial?

A reasonable judge would have disqualified all the potential jurors who knew him or her without any parties even asking him or her to do so. Reason being is so no parties (myself or the prosecutor) will feel any type of bias if this potential juror is chosen to be a juror in the trial. **COME ON,** who would not feel a person who personally knows the judge, would not be fair to them if that person was selected to be a juror in his or her trial.

I knew based on the character the judge has already shown me of herself and how unfairly she has already treated me in her courtroom thus far, I knew it was very very possible the judge would tell the jurors she knew who was selected to be jurors in my trial to find me guilty, even though the evidence would not support a conviction. I know that is what happened.

THIS IS PAGE 6 LINES 13-20 OF MY JURY SELECTION TRANSCRIPTS SHOW THE JUDGE TOLD THE POTENTIAL JURORS ABOUT MY PRIOR CRIMINAL RECORD

```
 1   Amanze Antoine, not being a licensed importer, manufacturer,
 2   dealer, and collector of firearms, within the meaning of
 3   Chapter 44, Title 18, United States Code, willfully did
 4   transport into the state of New York where he then resided, a
 5   Kal-TEC model PF-9, 9mm pistol, serial number SYP49, and a
 6   Ruger model LCP .380 caliber pistol, said firearms having been
 7   acquired by the defendant outside the state of New York and in
 8   the Northern District of West Virginia, in violation of Title
 9   18, United States Code, Sections 922(a)(3) and 924 (a)(1)(D).
10          Count Four, which is the final count, charges unlawful
11   possession of a firearm and states on June 19, 2017, in or near
12   Morgantown, Monongalia County, within the Northern District of
13   West Virginia, defendant, Amanze Antoine, having been convicted
14   in a court of crime -- of a crime punishable by imprisonment
15   for a term exceeding one year, that is on or about November 30,
16   1999, was convicted in the Supreme Court in the state of New
17   York in case number 3624-98, of robbery in the first degree,
18   and on or about February 24, 2010, was convicted in the state
19   of New York, County Court, County of Westchester, in case
20   number 00261-2009, of criminal possession of a firearm, did
21   knowingly possess in and affecting commerce, firearms, that is
22   a Walther pistol model PK380 .380 caliber, serial number
23   WB020112, a Taurus pistol, model PT709 Slim, 9mm caliber,
24   serial number TJZ01115, and a Smith & Wesson pistol, model P --
25   or M and P 9, 9mm caliber, serial number HBA6241, in violation
```

Stacy Harlow, CVR-M/CM/RVR-M/RCP/RBC
Post Office Box 969 Clarksburg, WV 26302-0969 (304)623-7154 .

148

CHAPTER 29

IT GETS MORE DISHONORABLE!!

The judge gave the prosecutor extra " peremptory challenges" than the law permits. The legal term " peremptory challenges" means when the judge gives the prosecutor and my attorney a chance to disqualify a potential juror from becoming a juror for a trial without having to express any reason for it. The only exception to a use of a peremptory challenge is it cannot be used to exclude a person from becoming a juror for a trial based on a person's race, religion age, disability, or any other discriminating factors. Now that you know what a peremptory challenge lets continue.

By law according to Rule 24 of the Federal Rules of Criminal Procedures the prosecutor is only allowed 6 peremptory challenges during jury selection and my attorney and I get 10 peremptory challenges. The judge gave the prosecutor 10 peremptory challenges and not the 6 that the law only allows the prosecutor to receive. Why was this so important some may ask? It puts me more at of a disadvantage and made my jury selection proceedings more unfair than it has already been, by decreasing my chances of winning at trial even more!! Why? Because some of the extra peremptory challenges given to the prosecutor she was not supposed to receive according to the law, these extra peremptory challenges the prosecutor received were used to exclude people from becoming jurors in my trial who I wanted to be chosen to become jurors for my trial because I felt for whatever reason after hearing them talk during "voir dire" that they would be fair jurors to me and base their verdict solely on the evidence being shown at my trial and not just find me guilty just because. Just because what? Just because they could.

In the part of this book called "**YOU BE THE JUDGE**" which is in a few pages, I will get in more detail about each thing I just said occurred during my jury selection proceedings by showing you the actual jury selection transcripts so you can read it for yourself and see the things I said happened truly happened.

The **YOU BE THE JUDGE**" section will also include different things that happened to put me throughout my entire court proceedings that was unfair, unethical, unprofessional, or straight up the devil's work.

The purpose of the "**YOU BE THE JUDGE**" section of this book is for you to **BE THE JUDGE** and make a decision on whether or not you feel I was treated unfairly by the judge, the prosecutor, and my attorney after you finish reading what took place, how it took place, and what ethical rules and laws were broken by all of them in the courtroom.

THIS IS THE LETTER I WROTE TO THE JUDGE ON 12-3-2018 TELLING HER I NO LONGER WANTED MR. WALKER AS MY ATTORNEY

12-4-2018

Dear Honorable Keeley

I'm writing because after I left court on December 3, 2018 my attorney Mr. Walker came downstairs to speak to me. While in the attorney/client room my attorney Mr. Walker told me he does not have a defense for me at all and my trial starts on December 11, 2018. This was said to me after I asked Mr. Walker lets talk about my defense for trial. He simply stated there is no defense and refuse to even talk about one. After about 10 minutes of me talking to Mr. Walker which he was paying me no mind he then got up turned off the lights in the room and walked out the room closed the door and left me in the dark until the bald U.S Marshal came and took me to the holding cell. Also when I came back to the Regional Jail from court I received legal mail that Mr. Walker seat to me. In the legal mail it was a list of the witness and Exhibit list Mr. Walker put in on my behalf on November 19, 2018. Mr. Walker didn't put in all the Exhibit or witnesses I requested for him to put in on my behalf which I have an email sent to him about all the Exhibits and witnesses I wanted him to put on my behalf which Mr. Walker replied to that email my girl sent him the morning

151

of November 19, 2018 saying that he
will add all the Exhibts and witnesses
I requested. My girlfriend will print out
the email sent with his reply to it.
Mr. WAlker clearly lied to me again
and I need new counsel. A lawyer
is not suppose to deceive of mislead his
client. I feel my attorney is angry because
I wrote him up for lying to me and
because of that he will not represent
me to the best of his ability. You told
me Honorable keeley that my attorney will
fight for me at trial and you felt
he is fit for the Job however I disagree
because Mr. WAlker told me to my face after
I left your courtroom on 12-3-18 that
he does not have a defense for me. He
was also very rude while we were talking
by playing with his phone while I'm asking
him about a defense. Honorable keeley I
need a new attorney. I understand you feel
Mr. WAlker is a good attorney but I don't
think he is in this case for me because
of the things he do and say to me. I
don't feel comfortable with Mr. WAlker
and I don't want to move forward with
an attorney that states he ~~he~~ does not
have a defense for his client a week
before trial or an attorney that did not
place Exhibits or witnesses to the courts
that his client requested him to and he
agreed to do but lied and didn't do it.

Honorable Keeley I need a new attorney,
I feel Mr. Walker will on purpose be
ineffective at trial because I wrote
him up to the BAR and displinary for
counsel. I'm entitled by the Consitution
to have an effective attorney and I
don't feel I'm receiving right now,
I will show you the exhibit and
witness list I sent Mr Walker along
with him stating he will add it on
for my behalf then I will show
you the witness list and Exhibit list
Mr. Walker put in on November 19, 2018.
Mr. Walker did not put about 75% of
the Exhibits or witnesses I requested
which he agreed to do by the email he
sent back to my girlfriend. And on
the Exhibit list he put in on my behalf
he put the dashcam. I thought it was
not a dashcam. I don't trust nothing
he tells me and can you please give me
a new attorney.

Sincerly
AMANZE Antoine
362806.

THIS IS PAGE 6 lines 13-20 OF MY JURY SELECTION TRANSCRIPTS SHOW THE JUDGE TOLD THE POTENTIAL JURORS ABOUT MY PRIOR CRIMINAL RECORD

```
 1   Amanze Antoine, not being a licensed importer, manufacturer,
 2   dealer, and collector of firearms, within the meaning of
 3   Chapter 44, Title 18, United States Code, willfully did
 4   transport into the state of New York where he then resided, a
 5   Kal-TEC model PF-9, 9mm pistol, serial number SYP49, and a
 6   Ruger model LCP .380 caliber pistol, said firearms having been
 7   acquired by the defendant outside the state of New York and in
 8   the Northern District of West Virginia, in violation of Title
 9   18, United States Code, Sections 922(a)(3) and 924 (a)(1)(D).
10        Count Four, which is the final count, charges unlawful
11   possession of a firearm and states on June 19, 2017, in or near
12   Morgantown, Monongalia County, within the Northern District of
13   West Virginia, defendant, Amanze Antoine, having been convicted
14   in a court of crime -- of a crime punishable by imprisonment
15   for a term exceeding one year, that is on or about November 30,
16   1999, was convicted in the Supreme Court in the state of New
17   York in case number 3624-98, of robbery in the first degree,
18   and on or about February 24, 2010, was convicted in the state
19   of New York, County Court, County of Westchester, in case
20   number 00261-2009, of criminal possession of a firearm, did
21   knowingly possess in and affecting commerce, firearms, that is
22   a Walther pistol model PK380 .380 caliber, serial number
23   WB020112, a Taurus pistol, model PT709 Slim, 9mm caliber,
24   serial number TJZ01115, and a Smith & Wesson pistol, model P --
25   or M and P 9, 9mm caliber, serial number HBA6241, in violation
```

CHAPTER 30

AFTER JURY SELECTION TRIAL BEGAN!

December 11, 2018 12:00 pm

"May the jurors selected for this trial and the prosecutor please leave the courtroom for a few minutes please. An important issue has come up that I must discuss with Mr. Antoine and his attorney" the judge said.

After the jury and prosecutor left the courtroom the judge began to chat. "Mr. Walker your client Mr. Antoine wrote a letter to me dated 12-4-2018 that I received yesterday. Readers I have included a copy of this letter on **pages 151 –153** In the letter it states he does not want you as his attorney anymore and he reported you to the Bar." "Readers" the Bar is a place where clients send complaints about their attorney they may have about him or her. "Ok, Mr. Walker in this letter Mr. Antoine gives detailed reasons why he does not want you as his attorney. I am just going to cut to the chase here Mr. Antoine, we already went over this issue last week in the final pre-trial conference. I am not going to give you a new attorney!! It is either you represent yourself or Mr. Walker represents you!!! You need to starting listening to Mr. Walker, he's a great attorney!!"

Two years later after doing some research on some ethical rules all lawyers, judges and prosecutors are obligated to follow. I found out the judge was not supposed to force me to keep Mr. Walker as my attorney after I expressed to her, I wanted to discharge him as my attorney.

I also found out that this same ethical rule states Mr. Walker was mandated to withdraw himself from representing me once it was clear to him, I no longer wanted him as my attorney. The judge did not enforce that ethical rule which was her job to do so. Instead, the judge did what she wanted to do like she always does and forced me to proceed to trial with an attorney I expressed to her many times in her courtroom I wanted discharged from representing me.

My attorney is on the same boat the judge is in because he knew what that ethical rule stated he was supposed to do when a client wants to discharge his or her attorney, but he did not enforce that rule upon himself and withdraw his self from representing me. Instead he did what he wanted to do and still represented me as my attorney. "Readers" when you get to the **YOU BE THE JUDGE** section of this book I will also show you the ethical rule above copied out of the ethical rulebook itself, along with the trial transcripts showing you everything the judge stated after telling the prosecutor and jury to leave the courtroom, so she could privately discuss the letter I wrote to her with my attorney and I .

After the judge made it clear that she was not going to give me a new attorney after bringing the letter I wrote her to my attorney's attention, she told the court officer to go call the jury and prosecutor back into the courtroom so my trial can begin which the court officer did.

Before the prosecutor called her first witness to the stand the judge asked all witnesses who were in the courtroom to leave the courtroom, this only happened after I begged my attorney to place an oral motion in the court requesting the judge to do so. The only witness who was in the courtroom when the judge asked all witnesses to leave the courtroom was special agent Bassett, who was sitting with the prosecutor at the prosecutor's table. I noticed special agent Bassett did not budge from his chair when the judge told all witnesses to leave the courtroom. He knew he was going to be a witness in my trial, so I do not know why his ass did not get out of the courtroom. I think I know why he did not move because he knew he could do whatever the fuck he wanted to do and nobody was going to say shit about it, and he was correct. It did not surprise me at all when the judge allowed special agent Bassett to remain in the courtroom after she instructed all witnesses to leave the courtroom, despite the fact the judge was very aware of special agent Bassett being a witness that would be called to the stand by the prosecutor to testify against me. SMFH!! How did this put me at a huge disadvantage?

Please, continue to read to find out. In the **"YOU BE THE JUDGE"** section of this book you will read my actual trial transcripts showing you this took place, and also to get a very clear understanding how this puts me at a huge disadvantage at trial.

The first witness the prosecutor called to the stand was Victor Perez, my parole officer's supervisor in New York. Why the fuck is he a witness in my trial was the thoughts my head formulated. Mr. Perez comes on the stand just to tell the jury I was on parole in the state of New York for criminal possession of a firearm. How unfair was that?! Very unfair!! I am on trial for firearm charges and here goes Mr. Perez telling the jury of my trial I was on parole for a firearm charge in the state of New York! This cannot be really happening I thought to myself, but it really was. What does a charge I am on parole for have to do with the charges I am going to trial for? **NOTHING!!**

The prosecutor's only purpose for calling Mr. Perez to the stand as a witness was to tell the jury I was on parole for a gun in New York State, just so the jury can have a more of a bad taste in their mouth about me in order to decrease my chances of winning at trial. "By federal law" the prosecutor was not supposed to call a witness to the stand just to expose the criminal record of the person going to be trial. That was prejudicial like a motherfucker!! The prosecutor's goal was definitely met, because my chances of winning at trial once the jury heard what Mr. Perez said on the stand for sure decreased my chances of winning at trial. The faces on some of the jurors hearing what Mr. Perez said on the stand told me so!! The prosecutor knew having Mr. Perez testify at my trial stating what he stated on the stand against me was against the law but just like my lawyer and judge **SHE DID NOT GIVE A FLYING FUCK!!**

My attorney did not object to what Mr. Perez was saying on the stand nor did the judge stop his testimony, so that is how I concluded they did not give a flying fuck either.

My attorney Mr. Walker had that silly ass smirk on his face I wanted to slap off him when I glanced over at him, when Mr. Perez said what he said about me when he was on the stand.

Day one of trial was very depressing but I still held my head up like a real general do!! I knew the judge, prosecutor, and my own attorney were all working against me as a team, but I did not let that break my spirits. I stood tall on all 10 toes! I still felt trial was the best thing for me to do because I was not guilty of these charges!!

CHAPTER 31

2nd DAY OF TRIAL!!
THE UNFAIRNESS CONTINUES!!

Upon entering the courtroom to begin day 2 of the trial and sitting next to my attorney, the first thing the snake I had for an attorney said to me was, "the plea deal is still on the table, I advise you to take it Antoine, because you will get more time than the plea deal after you lose trial"

"I'm not taking a plea deal Mr. Walker! I did not do this shit!! Stop talking to me about a plea deal!! I'm going to trial and that's that!!"

The second day of trial I watched Parker and Chris get on the stand and lie the same way that Bill Clinton came on national television and lied about Monica not sucking his dick. Everything Parker and Chris were coerced to say they said on the stand along with them adding some extra lies like saying I lived with Chris and I sold the drugs for months, despite no drugs ever being found in my case. "Ms. Parker did you buy firearms and give them to Mr. Antoine? Did Antoine give you crack cocaine after you gave him the firearms you bought for him?" Parker answered yes to the questions she was asked by the prosecutor.

"Chris Anderson did you sell crack cocaine for Amanze Antoine? Did you help him find people to buy firearms for him? Did the finding of people include Parker and Tommy? Did he transport those firearms back to New York once he received them from Parker? Mr. Anderson, did you send Antoine money through Western Union after you were done selling all the crack cocaine, he gave you to sell for him?"

Chris, who was lying through his fucking teeth answered yes to all the prosecutor's questions, like parker did.

I could not believe this shit!! They really were coming on the stand fucking lying!! Pieces of shits!! Most people think just because a person is arrested for a crime, he or her did it and that is not a fact! Law enforcement at times make shit up and coerce people to come on the stand and lie just to "secure a conviction" on their prey at trial. I saw this with my own eyes today. They had people testify against me at trial today who acted as if they really knew me. The game law enforcement officers, prosecutors, judges, and lawyers play to get someone convicted is a dirty dirty dirty game with no rules included, and that is what makes them extremely dangerous and deadly like a king cobra snake.

Scratch that, a cobra snake's venom has nothing on them! The venom they spit out makes people suffer for years on top of years in a prison cell. And when the cobra snake injects his or her venom in a person that person dies within minutes and not suffer for years. So, who's venom is worse theirs or the venom of a king cobra snake? I say theirs are and that's the God's honest truth!!

During the entire first and second day of trial guess who was sitting next to the prosecutor from start to finish each day, even though he was not supposed to be in the courtroom because the judge asked all witnesses to leave the courtroom at the very beginning of my trial? Special agent Bassett was, and some of you got that answer correct.

CHAPTER 32

3RD DAY OF TRIAL SAME UNFAIRNESS JUST A DIFFERENT DAY!!

Today Tommy took the stand and said everything he was coerced to say. Police officer Junkins the officer who was the officer at this alleged traffic stop I allegedly fled from gave his false testimony today as well. These 2 motherfuckers with a straight face lied on the stand and said I was the fleeing person that fled from the traffic stop on June 19, 2017. Tommy could not even look into my face when he pointed to me and said, "Yes, I bought the firearms for Antoine." I could see the shame in his eyes knowing he knew he was lying when he was testifying against me on the stand. That did not stop him though because he still followed through and said everything he was coerced to say once he got on the stand.

Tommy and officer Junkins are both fucking cowards, straight up and down they both fucking placed me at the traffic stop by simply verbally stating I was there to the jury of my trial. Unexpectedly the prosecutor played video footage from this alleged traffic stop that occurred on June 19, 2017 that was captured by a nearby store's surveillance camera and told the jury I was the fleeing person in the video footage even though the video did not depict me, it showed an "unclear picture" of a person fleeing from the traffic stop. You could tell by the height of the person in the video footage who fled that I was not him!! I am 6'4, the person in the video footage who fled was waaaayyy shorter!! But that did not stop the prosecutor from saying it was me!!

Stinking bitch, I do not ever call females bitches because that's total disrespect to me, but me calling the prosecutor one is an exception to that rule I live by.

My fucking attorney did not use anything I asked him to use as part of my defense for my trial to dispute the fact that certain things did not add up, and it was very possible for me to be innocent of these charges.

You have no idea how I felt when my attorney did not use none of the things I brought to his attention to use as part of my defense the day he came to visit me in the county jail!! I wanted to kill him! Just being honest.

My snake for an attorney Mr. Walker did some trifling and devilish shit to me before getting up from his chair to question police officer Junkins. He turns to me and says to me in a low tone "I bet you when I ask police officer Junkins did he find guns or drugs on you he will say no, but you will still lose trial. If I win the bet your girl sucks my dick, deal Antoine?" I was going to spit in his face! It took a lot of control not to! A lot!!! When he got up from his chair and asked officer Junkins those 2 exact questions officer Junkins said no to both questions.

Please take a quick look at page 215 lines 1-10 of my trial transcripts I have included at the end of this section on **page 164** to show you Mr. Walker's questioning officer Junkins and his response to the questions I just stated above my attorney asked him. My attorney Mr. Walker is another one. Another one what? "**A COWARD!!**" Do you agree?

I always knew the court system was not fair, but I never knew to what extent of unfairness it was until now. This whole experience going to trial showed me how far some prosecutors, lawyers, judges, and law enforcement officers will go to make sure they get a conviction out of someone.

Just imagine the total number of people they did the same thing to who's story is untold and unheard. I could not help but to think that to myself after I sat back at my trial and saw what they all did to me.

Special agent bastard I mean Bassett was the last witness called to the witness stand by the prosecutor. I know I said earlier I was going to explain in the **YOU**

162

BE THE JUDGE SECTION OF THE BOOK why my trial was unfair by special agent Bassett staying in the courtroom after judge Keeley instructed all witnesses to leave the courtroom before trial was going to actually start. However, I will let you know right now why my trial was unfair but still get into detail later in the book about this issue.

What made my trial unfair and put me at a disadvantage when special agent Bassett did not leave the courtroom when the judge told all witnesses to leave the courtroom before trial actually started and sat right next to the prosecutor in the courtroom for the entire 3 days my trial lasted and was the last witness called to the witness stand at my trial by the prosecutor, because this allowed him to hear all the testimonies of every single witness of my trial before he was called to the stand himself to testify against me. That gave him an opportunity to get his story together and base his testimony on what he heard all the witnesses say who took the stand before him. That gave him the advantage and me the disadvantage. His testimony basically cosigned with what all the other witnesses said who testified before him. Not very shocking because he heard all their testimonies before he was called to the witness stand to testify!! Do you agree?

After special agent Bassett was done on the stand my life was in the jury's hands to choose a verdict, guilty or not guilty.

You would have thought I was **T.D** Jakes the way I was praying in my head for the jury to find me not guilty. As I prayed my heart was telling me praying is not going to help you because the fight was fixed. So, I stopped praying, and waited for the verdict I knew I was going to get, rather than what my heart was telling me I was going to get!!

PAGE 215 LINES 1-10 OF MY TRIAL TRANSCRIPTS SHOWING MR. WALKER ASKING POLICE OFFERICE JUNKINS ON THE STAND WAS I EVER CAUGHT WITH ANY DRUGS AND GUNS AND HIS RESPOND TO THOSE QUESTIONS WERE NO!!

```
 1          THE COURT:  Cross-examination.
 2          MR. WALKER:  Thank you.
 3                      CROSS-EXAMINATION
 4   BY MR. WALKER:
 5   Q.   Officer, you didn't find a gun on the person of Mr.
 6   Antoine, did you?
 7   A.   No, sir, I did not.
 8   Q.   You didn't find crack cocaine on the person of Mr.
 9   Antoine, did you?
10   A.   I did not.
11   Q.   To your knowledge, were the guns submitted for fingerprint
12   analysis?
13   A.   Not to my knowledge.
14   Q.   To your knowledge, were the guns submitted for DNA
15   analysis?
16   A.   Not to my knowledge.
17   Q.   You performed a field sobriety test on Mr. Calhoun, did
18   you not?
19   A.   I did.
20   Q.   And your finding was that he was under the influence?
21   A.   I believe that he was under the influence; however, he
22   passed my field sobriety test so I did not have enough to
23   arrest him on that reason.
24   Q.   But he was taken into custody?
25   A.   He was taken up to the Star City Police Department for
```

Stacy Harlow, CVR-M/CM/RVR-M/RCP/RBC
Post Office Box 969 Clarksburg, WV 26302-0969 (304)623-7154

CHAPTER 33

THE VERDICT!!
YOU ALREADY KNOW WHAT IT WAS....

As the guilty verdict was read off the judge, prosecutor, my attorney, and special agent Bassett sat back in their seats smiling as if they already knew what the verdict was going to be. I wish somebody snapped a picture of all their faces so it could have been put in this book. That picture would have said more than a thousand words.

The jury found me guilty of the firearm charges and distributing crack cocaine in the Northern district of West Virginia. I was never seen or caught with firearms or distributing crack cocaine in the Northern District of West Virginia. One of the jurors after the verdict was read looked at me and shook his head. I sensed what he was indirectly telling me was some under handed shit happened to you in this courtroom. To this day I wonder what he was thinking and what was the reason he shook his head at me. I should have asked him. After the verdict was read in open court the judge remanded me back to North Central regional county jail until my sentencing date.

March 27, 2019 was my sentencing date. What a birthday gift to my mother!!!!!

The devil for a judge sentenced me to 120 months to be served in a federal prison. As of November 15, 2021, I am currently incarcerated at F.C.I. Raybrook in the state of New York.

In 2019, I appealed my sentence of 120 months to a higher Court called the 4th Circuit Court of Appeals. The sole purpose of the Court of Appeals is to correct any unethical errors the district or lower court did to someone who was convicted in it. The Court of Appeals is to make sure all laws and rules that were not followed be enforced and followed. However, some Courts like the 4th Circuit Court of Appeals do not follow the law themselves and ignore what a district or lower Court did to someone that was unethical and unlawful. I say this because I am living off experience.

In the next section called **YOU BE THE JUDGE** you will see some unethical conduct I brought to the 4th Circuit Court of Appeal's attention that judge Keeley, my attorney, and the prosecutor did to me and that did not stop the Court of Appeals denying my appeal appealing my sentence of 120 months that judge Keeley sentenced me to.

On December 2, 2021 the 4th circuit Court of Appeals denied my appeal using frivolous reasons and only some of the issues I brought to their attention, they said they were not obligated to hear them because I was the one who raised the issues, and not my Court appointed attorney which is totally wrong. "Most" court appointed attorneys don't help their clients, so they don't raise issues on their clients appeals that are likely to overturn their client's conviction, and that was the reason why I raised my own issues to the Court of Appeals. I wanted them to hear how my Court appointed appeal's attorney who was assigned to do my appeals refused to put the issues in my appeal that I asked him to, because he knew my case would get overturned if he did raise the issues I wanted him to raise on my appeal to the Court of Appeals.

The 4th Circuit Court of Appeals are to blame for still allowing the unethical conduct judge Keeley, my attorney, and prosecutor did to me because after it was brought to the Court of Appeals attention all the unethical things that was done to me in judge Keeley's courtroom the Court of Appeals did nothing about it and condoned that shit. This entire court system from the lower to higher courts are corrupted and needs to be reformed or remade to become a fair system. You can help change this unfair court system. Please keep reading to find out how.

WHATEVER HAPPENED TO JACKY?

Good question. After 2 weeks of me being sentenced to 120 months Jacky left me and moved on with her life. I guess her mom and sister finally got to her or 120 months was too much for her to bare. Some women can bare it and some woman just cannot. Whatever the reason was for her leaving I still wish her the best in life!! I have no malice in my heart towards her whatsoever. **LIFE GOES ON**!!!

CHAPTER 34

YOU BE THE JUDGE!! COURT IS IN SESSION...

This section of this book is called **"YOU BE THE JUDGE!!"** In this section of the book I will give you several things that happened to me throughout my entire court proceedings that I feel were unfair, unprofessional, unethical, or the devil's work that the judge, the prosecutor, and my attorney did to me.

Some of these things I have already mentioned in the book in previous pages and some things I have not. After I am done explaining in detail to you how and why I was treated unfairly I would like **"YOU TO BE THE JUDGE"** yourself after you evaluate all the information I give you about each unfair thing that happened to me and make a decision on whether or not I was treated unfairly in your eyes.

In this section I will also break down what certain legal terms mean that are used in court rooms throughout the United States, because I know the average Joe did not go to law school to understand the meaning of these legal terms. After reading this entire book, and you feel I was treated unfairly I will show you ways how you can help me get the justice I deserve. You will also learn ways you can help change this unfair court system and help prevent future injustices from happening in all courtrooms throughout the United States of America which **IS VERY MUCH NEEDED!!!** Let me say that again **"WHICH IS VERY MUCH NEEDED!!!"**

ATTENTION READER!!

In this entire section I will be referencing you to different pages of my trial transcripts or other documents pertaining to my case, that I have included in this section to prove my point of me being treated unfairly. To make it easier for you to quickly recognize where I am directing you to read on these trial transcripts or other documents, I have either circled or underlined where I am wanting you to read. Now Let's Get to It!

The Sixth Amendment of the United States Constitution which I have included at the end of this section on **page 172** in this book.

In all criminal prosecutions, the accused shall enjoy the right to speedy and public trial by an "Impartial Jury" of the state and district wherein the crime shall have been committed.

The Sixth Amendment of the Constitution also promises me an impartial jury which means an "unbiased and just" jury.

With that being said, the prosecutor Zelda Wesley called Victor Perez to the witness stand at my trial to testify against me who was my parole officer's supervisor in New York. When Mr. Perez was on the witness stand the prosecutor asked him was I on parole? Mr. Perez answered "yes, he is on parole for criminal possession of a weapon, and also told the jury of my trial that I served eight years in prison."

I have included at the end of this Section Pages 63-65 of my trial transcripts on **pages 173- 175** which is part of victor Perez's testimony showing what he stated at my trial which is exactly what I stated above. My Constitutional Right under the sixth Amendment as you have read above grants me a trial with an "impartial jury". An impartial jury includes a jury not influenced in no way by external influence. By the prosecutor calling a witness to the witness stand asking that witness a question that she knows will expose to the jury my past criminal record about me being on parole for a firearm and serving 8 years in prison in the past I feel created jurors in my trial un-impartial jurors due to the fact they were exposed to my past criminal record which is an external influence and not permitted according to the Sixth Amendment. The prosecutor knew "by law" she was not supposed to have any witness come on the witness stand to expose my past criminal history because such exposer can make jurors of my trial bias towards me, but the prosecutor disregarded that law and did what the hell she wanted.

By Mr. Victor Perez telling the jury of my trial about my past criminal record this for sure had a negative influence on the jury of my trial which made them not impartial. My past criminal record had nothing to do with the charges I was going to trial for and should have never been mentioned to the jury of my trial, point blank period.

"Within Constitutional Provision" an impartial jury is one which is of impartial frame of mind, is influenced only by legal, competent evidence produced during trial, and base its verdict upon evidence connecting the defendant with the commission of the crime charged, external influence such as the prosecutor calling a witness to the stand just to expose to the jury of my trial my past criminal record infected my trial with unfairness as to make the result a denial of an "impartial jury/juror" that my sixth amendment states I am morally obligated too. In other words, this is what my sixth Amendment grants me under law!

QUESTIONS FOR THE READERS:

1. Do you think I had an impartial jury after the prosecutor called a witness to the stand just to have that witness expose to the jury my past criminal record?

2. Let us rewind a little bit. Do you remember in the part of the book when I showed you page 6 of my jury selection transcripts showing you that the judge also exposed to all the potential jurors of my start that I had a past criminal record before jury selection actually started! If you do not remember I have included page 6 of my jury selection transcripts at the end of this section on **page 176** to remind you what was said by the judge to all the potential jurors of my trial before jury selection started. After reading

page 6 of my jury selection transcripts do you think I had an impartial jury after the judge exposed my criminal history to all the potential jurors of my trial, some of which was selected to be juror in my trial?

YOU BE THE JUDGE!!

Court Is in Session......

Legal terms you may need to understand when reading my trial transcripts:

1. The legal term "the court" used in my trial transcripts is another way of saying the judge in all courtrooms in the United States.

TRANSCRIPTS OR OTHER DOCUMENTS I REFFERRED TO YOU TO IN THIS SECTION

This is the Sixth Amendment of the United States Constitution showing you I have a Constitutional Right to an impartial jury.

Amendment VI [1791]

In all criminal prosecutions, the accused shall enjoy the right to a speedy and public trial, by an impartial jury of the State and district wherein the crime shall have been committed, which district shall have been previously ascertained by law, and to be informed of the nature and cause of the accusation; to be confronted with the witnesses against him; to have compulsory process for obtaining witnesses in his favor; and to have the Assistance of Counsel for his defence.

These are pages 63-65 of my trial transcripts which is part of
Victor Perez's testimony showing exactly what he said to the
Jury at my trial about me.

Page 63:

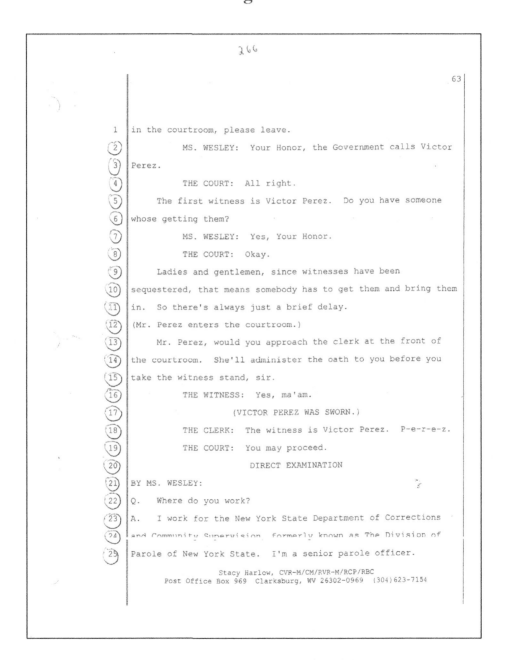

266

63

1   in the courtroom, please leave.

2   MS. WESLEY: Your Honor, the Government calls Victor

3   Perez.

4   THE COURT: All right.

5   The first witness is Victor Perez. Do you have someone

6   whose getting them?

7   MS. WESLEY: Yes, Your Honor.

8   THE COURT: Okay.

9   Ladies and gentlemen, since witnesses have been

10 sequestered, that means somebody has to get them and bring them

11 in. So there's always just a brief delay.

12 (Mr. Perez enters the courtroom.)

13   Mr. Perez, would you approach the clerk at the front of

14 the courtroom. She'll administer the oath to you before you

15 take the witness stand, sir.

16   THE WITNESS: Yes, ma'am.

17   (VICTOR PEREZ WAS SWORN.)

18   THE CLERK: The witness is Victor Perez. P-e-r-e-z.

19   THE COURT: You may proceed.

20   DIRECT EXAMINATION

21 BY MS. WESLEY:

22 Q.   Where do you work?

23 A.   I work for the New York State Department of Corrections

24 and Community Supervision, formerly known as The Division of

25 Parole of New York State. I'm a senior parole officer.

```
                                                              64

1   Q.   Okay.  And how long have you worked in that capacity?
2   A.   I've worked as a senior parole officer for the last four
3   years.  I've worked as a parole officer for the last 26 years.
4   Q.   And what are your duties as a parole officer?
5   A.   As a parole officer your duties are to make sure that the
6   persons who are released from incarceration for the New York
7   State prison abide by the conditions of parole, which are
8   basically twelve, or any other special conditions, depending on
9   what they were incarcerated for.
10  Q.   Okay.  Do you know Amanze Antoine?
11  A.   Yes, I do.
12  Q.   And is your knowledge of Mr. Antoine connected through
13  your employment?
14  A.   Yes, it is.
15  Q.   Okay.  Is Mr. Antoine on supervision with the New York
16  State parole?
17  A.   Yes, he is.
18  Q.   And when did his supervision begin?
19  A.   Mr. Antoine was released to parole supervision on August
20  3rd of 2016 and made his arrival report -- actually, he went to
21  a residential drug program, Christopher's. He was -- did not
22  stay there.  Made his arrival report to us on August 16th of
23  2016.
24  Q.   And why is Mr. Antoine on parole?
25  A.   He was convicted of criminal possession of a weapon in the
```

65

1 second degree. Served eight years, with five years post-

2 release supervision.

3 Q.   Is that a felony conviction?

4 A.   Yes, it is.

5 Q.   And that conviction is from what county and state?

6 A.   It is from Westchester County of New York State.

7 Q.   Okay. And what year is that conviction from, sir?

8 A.   That conviction was 2010. Actually the conviction was

9 2009. He was convicted on October 29th of 2009. He was

10 sentenced on -- in 2010. February 24th, I believe, of 2010.

11 Q.   Okay. And when is his parole scheduled to conclude?

12 A.   He will max out, what we call max out, maximum expiration

13 date of his parole supervision is August 3rd of 2021.

14 Q.   Okay. And so, obviously, Mr. Antoine was on parole in

15 June of 2017; is that correct, sir?

16 A.   That is correct.

17 Q.   Okay. What state is Mr. Antoine a resident of?

18 A.   He is a resident of New York State.

19 Q.   Sir, do you see the person you know as Mr. Antoine in the

20 courtroom today?

21 A.   He's hidden, I believe, behind the computer over there.

22 So it's difficult to see from here.

23   THE COURT: You may stand up.

24   THE WITNESS: Yes, I do.

25 BY MS. WESLEY:

This is page 6 lines 10-20 of my jury selection transcripts showing judge Irene Keeley telling the potential jurors of my trial about my past criminal convictions.

1   Amanze Antoine, not being a licensed importer, manufacturer,

2   dealer, and collector of firearms, within the meaning of

3   Chapter 44, Title 18, United States Code, willfully did

4   transport into the state of New York where he then resided, a

5   Kal-TEC model PF-9, 9mm pistol, serial number SYP49, and a

6   Ruger model LCP .380 caliber pistol, said firearms having been

7   acquired by the defendant outside the state of New York and in

8   the Northern District of West Virginia, in violation of Title

9   18, United States Code, Sections 922(a)(3) and 924 (a)(1)(D).

10   Count Four, which is the final count, charges unlawful

11   possession of a firearm and states on June 19, 2017, in or near

12   Morgantown, Monongalia County, within the Northern District of

13   West Virginia, defendant, Amanze Antoine, having been convicted

14   in a court of crime -- of a crime punishable by imprisonment

15   for a term exceeding one year, that is on or about November 30,

16   1999, was convicted in the Supreme Court in the state of New

17   York in case number 3624-98, of robbery in the first degree,

18   and on or about February 24, 2010, was convicted in the state

19   of New York, County Court, County of Westchester, in case

20   number 00261-2009, of criminal possession of a firearm, did

21   knowingly possess in and affecting commerce, firearms, that is

22   a Walther pistol model PK380 .380.caliber, serial number

23   WB020112, a Taurus pistol, model PT709 Slim, 9mm caliber,

24   serial number TJZ01115, and a Smith & Wesson pistol, model P --

25   or M and P 9, 9mm caliber, serial number HBA6241, in violation

CHAPTER 35

GUESS WHO JUDGE IRENE KEELEY KNEW!!

During jury selection the judge asked all the potential jurors of my trial did anyone know her (the judge) which is what the laws requires a judge to do before jury selection actually starts. "One potential juror name James Allen raised his hand and said yes he knew the judge, because the judge was an acquaintance of his family. And two other potential jurors Anastasia Shaffer and Dennis Burnworth both raised their hands and said they knew the judge because they both go to the same church as the judge" **ONE OUT OF THE THREE POTENTIAL JURORS WHO KNEW THE JUDGE WERE SELECTED TO BE A JUROR IN MY TRIAL**.

THE PROOF:

I have included page 11 lines 1-25 and page 12 lines 1-11 of my jury selection transcripts on **pages 179 and 180** in this book showing you how all three people I named above knew the judge. Again, one of which who was chosen to become a juror for my trial.

QUESTIONS FOR THE READERS:

1. Do you think I had a fair trial?

2. Do you think it was fair to me for a person who went to the same church as the judge be selected to be a juror in my trial? If so, why?

3. Do you think the judge helped make the list for all the potential jurors who came into her courtroom (which is illegal) that day to partake in jury selection? With the population in West Virginia being 1.792 million, what a coincidence the list of

people to come into the judge's courtroom to be potential jurors for my trial consisted of 3 people who knew the judge very well. Do you agree?

YOU BE THE JUDGE!!

Court Is in Session...

Legal terms you will see you in my jury selection transcripts I will give you the meaning too.

1. The Court - means the judge. It is just another name for the judge of the court used in all courtrooms throughout the United States.

2. Prospective Juror - means potential juror for a trial.

TRANSCRIPTS OR OTHER DOCUMENTS I REFFERRED YOU TO IN THIS SECTION

These are pages 11 lines 1-25 and page 12 lines 1-11 of my jury selection transcripts showing you the judge knew 3 potential jurors for my trial very well. One of whom was chosen to be a juror for my trial.

11

1   THE COURT: Yes, sir. Would you please stand and
2 tell us your name?
3   PROSPECTIVE JUROR: James Allen.
4   THE COURT: And, Mr. Allen, how do you know me?
5   PROSPECTIVE JUROR: Acquaintance of our family.
6   THE COURT: All right. Would that that acquaintance,
7 in any way, affect your ability to serve as a juror in this
8 case and to be fair to both sides and make your decision based
9 solely on the evidence presented and the law as I will give it
10 in my charge?
11   PROSPECTIVE JUROR: No.
12   THE COURT: No. Thank you. You can be seated.
13   PROSPECTIVE JUROR: (Raising hand.)
14   THE COURT: Yes, ma'am. Your name? I'm sorry; I
15 didn't see your hand.
16   PROSPECTIVE JUROR: Anastasia Shaffer.
17   THE COURT: And, Ms. Shaffer, how do you know me?
18   PROSPECTIVE JUROR: We attend the same Parrish.
19   THE COURT: All right. Does the fact that we attend
20 the same Parrish church in any way affect your ability to serve
21 as a juror in this case and to be fair to both sides?
22   PROSPECTIVE JUROR: No, it would not.
23   THE COURT: Thank you.
24   PROSPECTIVE JUROR: (Raising hand.)
25   THE COURT: Yes, sir. Your name?

Stacy Harlow, CVR-M/CM/RVR-M/RCP/RBC
Post Office Box 969 Clarksburg, WV 26302-0969 (304)623-7154

179

```
                                                              . 12
                                                                 |
 1            PROSPECTIVE JUROR:  Dennis Burnworth.

 2            THE COURT:  And how do you know me?

 3            PROSPECTIVE JUROR:  You're acquainted with my wife

 4   and her family, Jean Ann Lynch.

 5            THE COURT:  All right.  Would --

 6            PROSPECTIVE JUROR:  We attend the same church.

 7            THE COURT:  Would the church and family acquaintance

 8   in any way affect your ability to serve as a juror in this case

 9   and to be fair to both sides?

10            PROSPECTIVE JUROR:  No, it would not.

11            THE COURT:  Thank you.

12       Anyone else?

13            PROSPECTIVE JURORS:  (No verbal response.)

14            THE COURT:  Thank you.  Now, in this case, the

15   defendant, as you've heard, is Amanze Antoine.  Mr. Antoine is

16   represented by his attorney, Mr. Frank Carle Walker, II.  I'm

17   going to ask Mr. Walter to please stand to introduce himself to

18   you and to introduce his client.

19            MR. WALKER:  Good morning.  My name is Frank Walker

20   and I represent Mr. Antoine.

21            THE COURT:  And, Mr. Antoine, if you'll please stand.

22            THE DEFENDANT:  (Complies.)

23            THE COURT:  Okay.  Thank you.  You can both be

24   seated.

25            THE DEFENDANT:  (Complies.)
```

CHAPTER 36

CODE OF PROFESSIONAL RESPONSIBILITY RULES

Today on our court's calendar is for you to decide whether my attorney Frank Walker is guilty of breaking any of the "CODE OF PROFESSIONAL RESPONSIBILITY" rules that all attorneys in the United States are "obligated" to follow.

As I have previously explained in this book the Code of Professional Responsibility Rules are rules all lawyers are "obligated" to follow. These rules are the fundamental ethical principles to guide a lawyer so he or she knows what conduct is expected as an attorney. "The Code of Professional Responsibility Rules are the minimum standards for all lawyers in the United States."

Now that you understand the importance of the Code of Professional Responsibility Rules and why they were made, I will now give you three of the rules (which I have included in the back of this section on **pages 184 and 185** in this book that was copied out of the Code of Professional Responsibility rule book itself) that were violated by my attorney Frank Walker and the honorable judge Irene Keeley:

The Code of Professional Responsibility rules

1. DR 6-101 Failing to Act Competently

A. A lawyer shall not:

(1) Handle a legal matter which he knows or should know that he is competent to handle without associating with him a lawyer who is competent to handle it.

(2) Handle a legal matter without preparation adequate in the circumstance.

(3) Neglect a legal matter entrusted in him.

2. Canon's 7th rule of the Code of Professional Responsibility which states:

A lawyer should represent a client zealously within the Bounds of the law.

3. And lastly the Code of Professional Responsibility Rule:

DR 2-110 Withdrawal from Employment.

A. Mandatory Withdrawal.

A lawyer representing a client before a tribunal with its permission if required by its rules, shall withdraw from employment if:

1. He knows or it is obvious that his client is bringing the legal action, conducting the defense or asserting a position in litigation, or is otherwise having steps taken for him, merely for the purpose of harassing or maliciously injuring any person.

2. He knows or it is obvious that his continued employment will result in violation of a Disciplinary Rule.

3. His mental or physical condition renders it unreasonably difficult for him to carry out the employment effectively.

4. "He is discharged by his client."

After reading all the above code of Professional Responsibility Rules I would like you to ask yourself the following questions:

1. After reading in this book about what my attorney did and said to me when he came to visit me at the North Central Regional County Jail after I brought to his attention all the things I wanted him to use as part of my defense for trial, do you think my attorney handled this legal matter with adequate preparation and represented me zealously as the Code of Professional Responsibility Rules above states he was "obligated" to do? If not, why?

2. As you read previously in this book I wrote the judge a letter (which I have again included at the end of this section on **pages 186-188.**) dated 12-4-2018 expressing to the judge that I wanted a new attorney and Mr. Walker discharged from representing me as my attorney along with the detailed reasons why as you can see when you read the letter. I also made this request to judge Keeley in open court. The judge disregarded all my requests to discharge Mr. Walker as my attorney and forced me to go to trial with him.

    After reading the Code of Profession Responsibility DR 2-110 withdrawal from Employment (B) (4) above that mandates an attorney to withdraw his or her self from representing a client once his or her client wants his attorney discharged from representing him or her, do you feel it was unfair for my attorney to not enforce this code of Professional Responsibility Rule on his self and withdraw his self from representing as my attorney once I made it clear to him and the judge in open court and in writing that I wanted him discharged from representing me as my attorney?

3. Do you think it was unfair of the judge to not make sure the code of Professional Responsibility Rule was enforced that mandates an attorney to withdraw his or herself from representing a client once a client wants to discharge his or her attorney? What do you think the judge should have done in my situation?

YOU BE THE JUDGE!!

Court Is in Session....

Legal terms you may need to understand in this section:

1. Tribunal- means a courtroom.

TRANSCRIPTS OR OTHER DOCUMENTS I REFFERRED YOU TO IN THIS SECTION.

This is a copy of rule DR 6-101 titled Failing to Act Competently and Canon 7 rule copied out of the Code of professional Responsibility Rule book that all attorneys in the United States are "obligated" to follow.

of his client properly should not be permitted to do so. A lawyer who is a stockholder in or is associated with a professional legal corporation may, however, limit his liability for malpractice of his associates in the corporation, but only to the extent permitted by law.[5]

DISCIPLINARY RULES

DR 6-101   Failing to Act Competently.

(A) A lawyer shall not:

(1) Handle a legal matter which he knows or should know that he is not competent to handle, without associating with him a lawyer who is competent to handle it.

(2) Handle a legal matter without preparation adequate in the circumstances.

(3) Neglect a legal matter entrusted to him.[6]

DR 6-102   Limiting Liability to Client.

(A) A lawyer shall not attempt to exonerate himself from or limit his liability to his client for his personal malpractice.

CANON 7

A Lawyer Should Represent a Client Zealously Within the Bounds of the Law

ETHICAL CONSIDERATIONS

EC 7-1   The duty of a lawyer, both to his client [1] and to the legal system, is to represent his client zealously [2] within the bounds of the law,[3] which

---

[5] See ABA Opinion 303 (1961); cf. Code of Professional Responsibility, EC 2-11.

[6] The annual report for 1967-1968 of the Committee on Grievances of the Association of the Bar of the City of New York showed a receipt of 2,232 complaints; of the 828 offenses against clients, 76 involved conversion, 49 involved "overreaching," and 452, or more than half of all such offenses, involved neglect. Annual Report of the Committee on Grievances of the Association of the Bar of the City of New York, N.Y.L.J., Sept. 12, 1968, at 4, col. 5.

[1] "The right to be heard would be, in many cases, of little avail if it did not comprehend the right to be heard by counsel. Even the intelligent and educated layman has small and sometimes no skill in the science of law." Powell v. Alabama, 287 U.S. 45, 68-69, 77 L.Ed. 158, 170, 53 S.Ct. 55, 64 (1932).

[2] Cf. ABA Canon 4.
"At times . . . [the tax lawyer] will be wise to discard some arguments and he should exercise discretion to emphasize the arguments which in his judgment are most likely to be persuasive. But this process involves legal judgment rather than moral attitudes. The tax lawyer should put aside private disagreements with Congressional and Treasury policies. His own notions of policy, and his personal view of what the law should be, are irrelevant. The job entrusted to him by his client is to use all his learning and ability to protect his client's rights, not to

Black's Law Dictionary 4th Ed. Rev—d   XLIX

---

is equally entitled to performance unfettered by his attorney's economic and social predilections." Paul, The Lawyer as a Tax Adviser, 25 Rocky Mt. L. Rev. 412, 418 (1953).

[3] See ABA Canons 15 and 32.
ABA Canon 5, although only speaking of one accused of crime, imposes a similar obligation on the lawyer: "[T]he lawyer is bound, by all fair and honorable means, to present every defense that the law of the land permits, to the end that no person may be deprived of life or liberty, but by due process of law."

"Any persuasion or pressure on the advocate which deters him from planning and carrying out the litigation on the basis of 'what, within the framework of the law, is best for my client's interest?' interferes with the obligation to represent the client fully within the law.

"This obligation, in its fullest sense, is the heart of the adversary process. Each attorney, as an advocate, acts for and seeks that which in his judgment is best for his client, within the bounds authoritatively established. The advocate does not decide what is just in this case— he would be usurping the function of the judge and jury— he acts for and seeks for his client that which he is entitled to under the law. He can do no less and properly represent the client." Thode, The Ethical Standard for the Advocate, 39 Texas L.Rev. 575, 584 (1961).

"The [Texas public opinion] survey indicates that distrust of the lawyer can be traced directly to certain factors. Foremost of these is a basic misunderstanding of the function of the lawyer as an advocate in an adversary system.

"Lawyers are accused of taking advantage of 'loopholes' and 'technicalities' to win. Persons who make this charge are unaware, or do not understand, that the lawyer is hired to win, and if he does not exercise every legitimate effort in his client's behalf, then he is betraying a sacred trust." Rochelle & Payne, The Struggle for Public Understanding, 25 Texas B.J. 109, 159 (1962).

"The importance of the attorney's undivided allegiance and faithful service to one accused of crime, irrespective of the attorney's personal opinion as to the guilt of his client, lies in Canon 5 of the American Bar Association Canon of Ethics.

"The difficulty lies, of course, in ascertaining whether the attorney has been guilty of an error of judgment, such as an election with respect to trial tactics, or has otherwise been actuated by his conscience or belief that his client should be convicted in any event. All too frequently courts are called upon to review actions of defense counsel which are, at the most, errors of judgment, not properly reviewable on habeas corpus unless the trial is a farce and a mockery of justice which requires the court to intervene. . . . But when defense counsel, in a truly adverse proceeding, admits that his conscience would not permit him to adopt certain customary trial procedures, this extends beyond the realm of judgment and strongly suggests an invasion of constitutional rights." Johns v. Smyth, 176 F.Supp. 949, 952 (E.D.Va.1959), modified, United States ex rel. Wilkins v. Banmiller, 205 F.Supp. 123, 128, n. 5 (E.D.Pa.1962), aff'd, 325 F.2d 514 (3d Cir. 1963), cert. denied, 379 U.S. 847, 13 L.Ed.2d 51, 85 S.Ct. 87 (1964).

"The adversary system in law administration bears a striking resemblance to the competitive economic system. In each we assume that the individual through partisanship or through self-interest will strive mightily for his side, and that kind of striving we must have. But neither system would be tolerable without restraints and modi-

This is a copy of rule DR 2-110 titled Withdrawal from Employment copied out of the code of Professional Responsibility Rule book that all attorneys in the United States are "obligated" to follow.

(B) This Disciplinary Rule does not prohibit payment to a former partner or associate pursuant to a separation or retirement agreement.

DR 2-108 Agreements Restricting the Practice of a Lawyer.

(A) A lawyer shall not be a party to or participate in a partnership or employment agreement with another lawyer that restricts the right of a lawyer to practice law after the termination of a relationship created by the agreement, except as a condition to payment of retirement benefits.[142]

(B) In connection with the settlement of a controversy or suit, a lawyer shall not enter into an agreement that restricts his right to practice law.

DR 2-109 Acceptance of Employment.

(A) A lawyer shall not accept employment on behalf of a person if he knows or it is obvious that such person wishes to:

    (1) Bring a legal action, conduct a defense, or assert a position in litigation, or otherwise have steps taken for him, merely for the purpose of harassing or maliciously injuring any person.[143]

    (2) Present a claim or defense in litigation that is not warranted under existing law, unless it can be supported by good faith argument for an extension, modification, or reversal of existing law.

DR 2-110 Withdrawal from Employment.[144]

(A) In General.

    (1) If permission for withdrawal from employment is required by the rules of a tribunal, a lawyer shall not withdraw from employment in a proceeding before that tribunal without its permission.

    (2) In any event, a lawyer shall not withdraw from employment until he has

taken reasonable steps to avoid foreseeable prejudice to the rights of his client, including giving due notice to his client, allowing time for employment of other counsel, delivering to the client all papers and property to which the client is entitled, and complying with applicable laws and rules.

    (3) A lawyer who withdraws from employment shall refund promptly any part of a fee paid in advance that has not been earned.

(B) Mandatory withdrawal.

    A lawyer representing a client before a tribunal, with its permission if required by its rules, shall withdraw from employment, and a lawyer representing a client in other matters shall withdraw from employment, if:

    (1) He knows or it is obvious that his client is bringing the legal action, conducting the defense, or asserting a position in the litigation, or is otherwise having steps taken for him, merely for the purpose of harassing or maliciously injuring any person.

    (2) He knows or it is obvious that his continued employment will result in violation of a Disciplinary Rule.[145]

    (3) His mental or physical condition renders it unreasonably difficult for him to carry out the employment effectively.

    (4) He is discharged by his client.

(C) Permissive withdrawal.[146]

    If DR 2-110(B) is not applicable, a lawyer may not request permission to withdraw in matters pending before a tribunal, and may not withdraw in other matters, unless such request or such withdrawal is because:

    (1) His client:

        (a) Insists upon presenting a claim or defense that is not warranted under existing law and cannot be supported by good faith argument for an extension, modification, or reversal of existing law.[147]

        (b) Personally seeks to pursue an illegal course of conduct.

        (c) Insists that the lawyer pursue a course of conduct that is illegal or that is prohibited under the Disciplinary Rules.

        (d) By other conduct renders it unreasonably difficult for the law-

---

[142] "[A] general covenant restricting an employed lawyer, after leaving the employment, from practicing in the community for a stated period, appears to this Committee to be an unwarranted restriction on the right of a lawyer to choose where he will practice and inconsistent with our professional status. Accordingly, the Committee is of the opinion it would be improper for the employing lawyer to require the covenant and likewise for the employed lawyer to agree to it." ABA Opinion 300 (1961).

[143] *See* ABA Canon 30.
"*Rule 13.* . . . A member of the State Bar shall not accept employment to prosecute or defend a case solely out of spite, or solely for the purpose of harassing or delaying another . . . ." Cal. Business and Professions Code § 6067 (West 1962).

[144] *Cf.* ABA Canon 44.

[145] *See also* Code of Professional Responsibility, DR 5-102 and DR 5-105.

[146] *Cf.* ABA Canon 4.

[147] *Cf.* Anders v. California, 386 U.S. 738, 18 L.Ed.2d 493, 87 S.Ct. 1396 (1967), *rehearing denied*, 388 U.S. 924, 18 L.Ed.2d 1377, 87 S.Ct. 2094 (1967).

XXXV

185

This is a copy of the letter I wrote to judge Irene Keeley dated 1 12-4-2018 expressing to her I wanted to discharge Mr. Walker as my attorney along with giving detailed reasons why.

12-4-2018

Dear Honorable Keeley

I'm writing because after I left court on December 3, 2018 my attorney Mr. Walker came downstairs to speak to me. While in the attorney/client room my attorney Mr. Walker told me he does not have a defense for me at all and my trial starts on December 11, 2018. This was said to me after I asked Mr. Walker lets talk about my defense for trial. He simply stated there is no defense and refuse to even talk about one. After about 10 minutes of me talking to Mr. Walker which he was paying me no mind he then got up turned off the lights in the room and walked out the room closed the door and left me in the dark until the bald U.S Marshal came and took me to the holding cell. Also when I came back to the Regional Jail from court I received legal mail that Mr. Walker sent to me. In the legal mail it was a list of the witness and Exhibit list Mr. Walker put in on my behalf on November 19, 2018. Mr. Walker didn't put in all the Exhibit or witnesses I requested for him to put in on my behalf which I have an email sent to him about all the Exhibits and witnesses I wanted him to put on my behalf which Mr. Walker replied to that email my girl sent him the morning

186

of November 19, 2018 saying that he
will add all the Exhibts and witnesses
I requested. My girlfriend will print out
the email sent with his reply to it.
Mr. WALker clearly lied to me again
and I need new counsel. A lawyer
is not suppose to deceive or mislead his
client. I feel my attorney is angry because
I wrote him up for lying to me and
because of that he will not represent
me to the best of his ability. You told
me Honorable Keeley that my attorney will
fight for me at trial and you felt
he is fit for the job however I disagree
because Mr. WALker told me to my face after
I left your courtroom on 12-3-18 that
he does not have a defense for me. He
was also very rude while we were talking
by playing with his phone while I'm asking
him about a defense. Honorable Keeley I
need a new attorney. I understand you feel
Mr. WALker is a good attorney but I don't
think he is in this case for me because
of the things he do and say to me. I
don't feel comfortable with Mr. WALker
and I don't want to move forward with
an attorney that states he ~~he~~ does not
have a defense for his client a week
before trial or an attorney that did not
place Exhibits or witnesses to the courts
that his client requested him to and he
agreed to do but lied and didn't do it.

Honorable Keeley I need a new attorney.
I feel Mr. Walker will on purpose be
ineffective at trial because I wrote
him up to the BAR and displinary for
counsel. I'm entitled by the Consitution
to have an effective attorney and I
don't feel I'm receiving right now,
I will show you the exhibit and
witness list I sent Mr Walker along
with him stating he will add it on
for my behalf then I will show
you the witness list and Exhibit list
Mr. Walker put in on November 19, 2018.
Mr. Walker did not put about 75% of
the Exhibits or witnesses I requested
which he agreed to do by the email he
sent back to my girlfriend. And on
the Exhibit list he put in on my behalf
he put the dashcam. I thought it was
not a dashcam. I don't trust nothing
he tells me and can you please give me
a new attorney.

Sincerly
AMANZE Antoine
3628016.

188

CHAPTER 37

SOME MORE OF THE HONORABLE IRENE KEELEY DISHONORABLE CONDUCT

Ajudge's role in a criminal matter is essential for the criminal justice system to work with proper dignity, fairness, and efficiency. In order to make sure this happens the American Bar Association whose job is to set the standards for the conduct of all judges, prosecutors, and lawyers in all courtrooms in the United States of America adopted 36 Judicial Ethic rules that all judges in every courtroom in the United States whether state or federal court are "obligated to follow.

These rules are called **CANON OF JUDICIAL ETHIC RULES**. Most people in the United States do not even know they exist! I have included all 36 of this Judicial Ethic Rules all judges in the United States are "obligated" to follow at the end of this section on **pages 191 - 195** in this book. However, I will only speak about 3 of those 36 Judicial Ethic Rules the judge Irene Keeley violated which are as followed:

1. The 3rd Canon Judicial Ethic rule which is titled "Constitutional Obligations" states:

   "It is the duty of all judges in the United States to support the Federal Constitution and that of the State whose laws they administer; in so doing, they should fearlessly observe and apply fundamental limitation and guarantees."

2. The 4th Canon Judicial Ethic Rule is titled: "Avoidance of Impropriety" which states:

   "A judge's official conduct should be free from impropriety and the appearance of impropriety; he should avoid infractions of law; and his personal behavior not only upon the bench and in the performance of judicial duties, but also in his everyday life, should be beyond reproach."

3. And lastly the 5th Judicial Ethic Rule is titled "Essential Conduct" that states:

   "A judge should be temperate, attentive, patient, impartial, and, since he is to administer the law and apply it to the facts, he should be studious of the principles of the law and diligent in endeavoring to ascertain the facts."

TRANSCRIPTS OR OTHER DOCUMENTS I REFFERRED YOU TO IN THIS SECTION.

This is a copy of all 36 CANON Judicial Ethic rules copied out of the CANON Judicial Ethic rule book that all judges in every courtroom whether in a state or federal court are "obligated" to follow in the United States.

CANONS OF JUDICIAL ETHICS *
With Amendments to January 1, 1968

Ancient Precedents.

"And I charged your judges at that time, saying Hear the causes between your brethren. and judge righteously between every man and his brother, and the stranger that is with him.

"Ye shall not respect persons in judgment; but ye shall hear the small as well as the great; ye shall not be afraid of the face of man; for the judgment is God's; and the cause that is too hard for you, bring it unto me, and I wil hear it."—*Deuteronomy*, I, 16–17.

"Thou shalt not wrest judgment; thou sha't not respect persons, neither take a gift; for a gift doth blind the eyes of the wise, and pervert the words of the righteous."—*Deuteronomy*, XVI, 19.

"We will not make any justiciaries, constables. sheriffs or bailiffs, but from those who understand the law of the realm and are well disposed to observe it."—*Magna Charta*, XLV.

"Judges ought to remember that their office is *jus dicere* not *jus dare;* to interpret law, and not to make law, or give law." . . .

"Judges ought to be more learned than witty; more reverend than plausible; and more advised than confident. Above all things, integrity is their portion and proper virtue." . . .

"Patience and gravity of hearing is an essential part of justice; and an over speaking judge is no well-tuned cymbal. It is no grace to a judge first to find that which he might have heard in due time from the Bar, or to show quickness of conceit in cutting off evidence or counsel too short; or to prevent information by questions though pertinent."

"The place of justice is a hallowed place; and therefore not only the Bench, but the foot pace and precincts and purprise thereof ought to be preserved without scandal and corruption." . . . —*Bacon's Essay "Of Judicature."*

Preamble.

In addition to the Canons for Professional Conduct of Lawyers which it has formulated and adopted, the American Bar Association, mindful

* These Canons, to and including Canon 34, were adopted by the American Bar Association at its Forty-Seventh Annual Meeting, at Philadelphia, Pennsylvania, on July 9, 1924. The Committee of the Association which prepared the Canons was appointed in 1922, and composed of the following: William H. Taft, District of Columbia, Chairman; Leslie C. Cornish, Maine; Robert von Moschzisker, Pennsylvania; Charles A. Boston, New York; and Garret W. McEnerney, California. George Sutherland, of Utah, originally a member of the Committee, retired and was succeeded by Mr. McEnerney. In 1923 Frank M. Angellotti, of California, took the place of Mr. McEnerney.

Canons 28 and 30 were amended at the Fifty-Sixth Annual Meeting, Grand Rapids, Michigan, August 30-September 1, 1933. Canon 28 was further amended at the Seventy-Third Annual Meeting, Washington, D. C., September 29, 1950. Canons 35 and 36 were adopted at the Sixtieth Annual Meeting, at Kansas City, Missouri, September 30, 1937. Canon 35 was amended at San Francisco, Calif., Sept. 1952.

Black's Law Dictionary 4th Ed. Rev.   LXIX

that the character and conduct of a judge should never be objects of indifference, and that declared ethical standards tend to become habits of life, deems it desirable to set forth its views respecting those principles which should govern the personal practice of members of the judiciary in the administration of their office. The Association accordingly adopts the following Canons, the spirit of which it suggests as a proper guide and reminder for judges, and as indicating what the people have a right to expect from them.

1. Relations of the Judiciary.

The assumption of the office of judge casts upon the incumbent duties in respect to his personal conduct which concern his relation to the state and its inhabitants, the litigants before him, the principles of law, the practitioners of law in his court, and the witnesses, jurors and attendants who aid him in the administration of its functions.

2. The Public Interest.

Courts exist to promote justice, and thus to serve the public interest. Their administration should be speedy and careful. Every judge should at all times be alert in his rulings and in the conduct of the business of the court, so far as he can, to make it useful to litigants and to the community. He should avoid unconsciously falling into the attitude of mind that the litigants are made for the courts instead of the courts for the litigants.

3. Constitutional Obligations.

It is the duty of all judges in the United States to support the federal Constitution and that of the state whose laws they administer; in so doing, they should fearlessly observe and apply fundamental limitations and guarantees.

4. Avoidance of Impropriety.

A judge's official conduct should be free from impropriety and the appearance of impropriety; he should avoid infractions of law; and his personal behavior, not only upon the Bench and in the performance of judicial duties, but also in his everyday life, should be beyond reproach.

5. Essential Conduct.

A judge should be temperate, attentive, patient, impartial, and, since he is to administer the law and apply it to the facts, he should be studious of the principles of the law and diligent in endeavoring to ascertain the facts.

6. Industry.

A judge should exhibit an industry and application commensurate with the duties imposed upon him.

191

7. Promptness.

A judge should be prompt in the performance of his judicial duties, recognizing that the time of litigants, jurors and attorneys is of value and that habitual lack of punctuality on his part justifies dissatisfaction with the administration of the business of the court.

8. Court Organization.

A judge should organize the court with a view to the prompt and convenient dispatch of its business and he should not tolerate abuses and neglect by clerks, and other assistants who are sometimes prone to presume too much upon his good natured acquiescence by reason of friendly association with him.

It is desirable too, where the judicial system permits, that he should cooperate with other judges of the same court, and in other courts, as members of a single judicial system, to promote the more satisfactory administration of justice.

9. Consideration for Jurors and Others.

A judge should be considerate of jurors, witnesses and others in attendance upon the court.

10. Courtesy and Civility.

A judge should be courteous to counsel, especially to those who are young and inexperienced, and also to all others appearing or concerned in the administration of justice in the court.

He should also require, and so far as his power extends, enforce on the part of clerks, court officers and counsel civility and courtesy to the court and to jurors, witnesses, litigants and others having business in the court.

11. Unprofessional Conduct of Attorneys and Counsel.

A judge should utilize his opportunities to criticise and correct unprofessional conduct of attorneys and counsellors, brought to his attention; and, if adverse comment is not a sufficient corrective, should send the matter at once to the proper investigating and disciplinary authorities.

12. Appointees of the Judiciary and Their Compensation.

Trustees, receivers, masters, referees, guardians and other persons appointed by a judge to aid in the administration of justice should have the strictest probity and impartiality and should be selected with a view solely to their character and fitness. The power of making such appointments should not be exercised by him for personal or partisan advantage. He should not permit his appointments to be controlled by others than himself. He should also avoid nepotism and undue favoritism in his appointments.

While not hesitating to fix or approve just amounts, he should be most scrupulous in granting or approving compensation for the services or charges of such appointees to avoid excessive allowances, whether or not excepted to or complained of. He cannot rid himself of this responsibility by the consent of counsel.

13. Kinship or Influence.

A judge should not act in a controversy where a near relative is a party; he should not suffer his conduct to justify the impression that any person can improperly influence him or unduly enjoy his favor, or that he is affected by the kinship, rank, position or influence of any party or other person.

14. Independence.

A judge should not be swayed by partisan demands, public clamor or considerations of personal popularity or notoriety, nor be apprehensive of unjust criticism.

15. Interference in Conduct of Trial.

A judge may properly intervene in a trial of a case to promote expedition, and prevent unnecessary waste of time, or to clear up some obscurity, but he should bear in mind that his undue interference, impatience, or participation in the examination of witnesses, or a severe attitude on his part toward witnesses, especially those who are excited or terrified by the unusual circumstances of a trial, may tend to prevent the proper presentation of the cause, or the ascertainment of the truth in respect thereto.

Conversation between the judge and counsel in court is often necessary, but the judge should be studious to avoid controversies which are apt to obscure the merits of the dispute between litigants and lead to its unjust disposition. In addressing counsel, litigants, or witnesses, he should avoid a controversial manner or tone.

He should avoid interruptions of counsel in their arguments except to clarify his mind as to their positions, and he should not be tempted to the unnecessary display of learning or a premature judgment.

16. Ex parte Applications.

A judge should discourage ex parte hearings of applications for injunctions and receiverships where the order may work detriment to absent parties; he should act upon such ex parte applications only where the necessity for quick action is clearly shown; if this be demonstrated, then he should endeavor to counteract the effect of the absence of opposing counsel by a scrupulous cross-examination and investigation as to the facts and the principles of law on which the application is based, granting relief only when fully satisfied that the law permits it and the emergency demands it. He should remember that an injunction is a limitation upon the freedom of action of defendants and should not be granted lightly or inadvisedly. One applying for such relief must sustain the burden of showing clearly its necessity and this burden is increased in the absence of the party whose freedom of action is sought to be restrained even though only temporarily.

17. Ex parte Communications.

A judge should not permit private interviews, arguments or communications designed to influence his judicial action, where interests to

192

be affected thereby are not represented before him, except in cases where provision is made by law for *ex parte* application.

While the conditions under which briefs of argument are to be received are largely matters of local rule or practice, he should not permit the contents of such brief presented to him to be concealed from opposing counsel. Ordinarily all communications of counsel to the judge intended or calculated to influence action should be made known to opposing counsel.

18. Continuances.

Delay in the administration of justice is a common cause of complaint; counsel are frequently responsible for this delay. A judge, without being arbitrary or forcing cases unreasonably or unjustly to trial when unprepared, to the detriment of parties, may well endeavor to hold counsel to a proper appreciation of their duties to the public interest, to their own clients, and to the adverse party and his counsel, so as to enforce due diligence in the dispatch of business before the court.

19. Judicial Opinions.

In disposing of controverted cases, a judge should indicate the reasons for his action in an opinion showing that he has not disregarded or overlooked serious arguments of counsel. He thus shows his full understanding of the case, avoids the suspicion of arbitrary conclusion, promotes confidence in his intellectual integrity and may contribute useful precedent to the growth of the law.

It is desirable that Courts of Appeals in reversing cases and granting new trials should so indicate their views on questions of law argued before them and necessarily arising in the controversy that upon the new trial counsel may be aided to avoid the repetition of erroneous positions of law and shall not be left in doubt by the failure of the court to decide such questions.

But the volume of reported decisions is such and is so rapidly increasing that in writing opinions which are to be published judges may well take this fact into consideration, and curtail them accordingly, without substantially departing from the principles stated above.

It is of high importance that judges constituting a court of last resort should use effort and self-restraint to promote solidarity of conclusion and the consequent influence of judicial decision. A judge should not yield to pride of opinion or value more highly his individual reputation than that of the court to which he should be loyal. Except in case of conscientious difference of opinion on fundamental principle, dissenting opinions should be discouraged in courts of last resort.

20. Influence of Decisions Upon the Development of the Law.

A judge should be mindful that his duty is the application of general law to particular instances, that ours is a government of law and not of men, and that he violates his duty as a minister of justice under such a system if he seeks to do what he may personally consider substantial justice in a particular case and disregards the general law as he knows it to be binding on him. Such action may become a precedent unsettling accepted principles and may have detrimental consequences beyond the immediate controversy. He should administer his office with a due regard to the integrity of the system of the law itself, remembering that he is not a depository of arbitrary power, but a judge under the sanction of law.

21. Idiosyncrasies and Inconsistencies.

Justice should not be moulded by the individual idiosyncrasies of those who administer it. A judge should adopt the usual and expected method of doing justice, and not seek to be extreme or peculiar in his judgments, or spectacular or sensational in the conduct of the court. Though vested with discretion in the imposition of mild or severe sentences he should not compel persons brought before him to submit to some humiliating act or discipline of his own devising, without authority of law, because he thinks it will have a beneficial corrective influence.

In imposing sentence he should endeavor to conform to a reasonable standard of punishment and should not seek popularity or publicity either by exceptional severity or undue leniency.

22. Review.

In order that a litigant may secure the full benefit of the right of review accorded to him by law, a trial judge should scrupulously grant to the defeated party opportunity to present the questions arising upon the trial exactly as they arose, were presented, and decided, by full and fair bill of exceptions or otherwise; any failure in this regard on the part of the judge is peculiarly worthy of condemnation because the wrong done may be irremediable.

23. Legislation.

A judge has exceptional opportunity to observe the operation of statutes, especially those relating to practice, and to ascertain whether they tend to impede the just disposition of controversies; and he may well contribute to the public interest by advising those having authority to remedy defects of procedure, of the result of his observation and experience.

24. Inconsistent Obligations.

A judge should not accept inconsistent duties; nor incur obligations, pecuniary or otherwise, which will in any way interfere or appear to interfere with his devotion to the expeditious and proper administration of his official functions.

25. Business Promotions and Solicitations for Charity.

A judge should avoid giving ground for any reasonable suspicion that he is utilizing the power or prestige of his office to persuade or coerce others to patronize or contribute, either to the success of private business ventures, or to charitable enterprises. He should, therefore, not enter into such private business, or pursue such a course of conduct, as would justify such suspicion, nor use the power of his office or the influence of his name to promote the business interests of others; he should not solicit for charities, nor should he enter into any business relation which, in the normal course of events reasonably to be expected, might bring his personal interest into conflict with the impartial performance of his official duties.

LXXI

193

CANONS OF JUDICIAL ETHICS

26. **Personal Investments and Relations.**

A judge should abstain from making personal investments in enterprises which are apt to be involved in litigation in the court; and, after his accession to the Bench, he should not retain such investments previously made, longer than a period sufficient to enable him to dispose of them without serious loss. It is desirable that he should, so far as reasonably possible, refrain from all relations which would normally tend to arouse the suspicion that such relations warp or bias his judgment, or prevent his impartial attitude of mind in the administration of his judicial duties.

He should not utilize information coming to him in a judicial capacity for purposes of speculation; and it detracts from the public confidence in his integrity and the soundness of his judicial judgment for him at any time to become a speculative investor upon the hazard of a margin.

27. **Executorships and Trusteeships.**

While a judge is not disqualified from holding executorships or trusteeships, he should not accept or continue to hold any fiduciary or other position if the holding of it would interfere or seem to interfere with the proper performance of his judicial duties, or if the business interests of those represented require investments in enterprises that are apt to come before him judicially, or to be involved in questions of law to be determined by him.

28. **Partisan Politics.***

While entitled to entertain his personal views of political questions, and while not required to surrender his rights or opinions as a citizen, it is inevitable that suspicion of being warped by political bias will attach to a judge who becomes the active promoter of the interests of one political party as against another. He should avoid making political speeches, making or soliciting payment of assessments or contributions to party funds, the public endorsement of candidates for political office and participation in party conventions.

He should neither accept nor retain a place on any party committee nor act as party leader, nor engage generally in partisan activities.

Where, however, it is necessary for judges to be nominated and elected as candidates of a political party, nothing herein contained shall prevent the judge from attending or speaking at political gatherings, or from making contributions to the campaign funds of the party that has nominated him and seeks his election or re-election.

29. **Self-Interest.**

A judge should abstain from performing or taking part in any judicial act in which his personal interests are involved. If he has personal litigation in the court of which he is judge, he need not resign his judgeship on that account, but he should, of course, refrain from any judicial act in such a controversy.

30. **Candidacy for Office.****

A candidate for judicial position should not make or suffer others to make for him, promises of conduct in office which appeal to the cupidity or prejudices of the appointing or electing power; he should not announce in advance his conclusions of law on disputed issues to secure class support, and he should do nothing while a candidate to create

---

* As amended August 31, 1933 and September 20, 1950.
** As amended August 31, 1933.

the impression that if chosen, he will administer his office with bias, partiality or improper discrimination.

While holding a judicial position he should not become an active candidate either at a party primary or at a general election for any office other than a judicial office. If a judge should decide to become a candidate for any office not judicial, he should resign in order that it cannot be said that he is using the power or prestige of his judicial position to promote his own candidacy or the success of his party.

If a judge becomes a candidate for any judicial office, he should refrain from all conduct which might tend to arouse reasonable suspicion that he is using the power or prestige of his judicial position to promote his candidacy or the success of his party.

He should not permit others to do anything in behalf of his candidacy which would reasonably lead to such suspicion.

31. **Private Law Practice.**

In many states the practice of law by one holding judicial position is forbidden. In superior courts of general jurisdiction, it should never be permitted. In inferior courts in some states, it is permitted because the county or municipality is not able to pay adequate living compensation for a competent judge. In such cases one who practises law is in a position of great delicacy and must be scrupulously careful to avoid conduct in his practice whereby he utilizes or seems to utilize his judicial position to further his professional success.

He should not practise in the court in which he is a judge, even when presided over by another judge, or appear therein for himself in any controversy.

If forbidden to practise law, he should refrain from accepting any professional employment while in office.

He may properly act as arbitrator or lecture upon or instruct in law, or write upon the subject, and accept compensation therefor, if such course does not interfere with the due performance of his judicial duties, and is not forbidden by some positive provision of law.

32. **Gifts and Favors.**

A judge should not accept any presents or favors from litigants, or from lawyers practising before him or from others whose interests are likely to be submitted to him for judgment.

33. **Social Relations.**

It is not necessary to the proper performance of judicial duty that a judge should live in retirement or seclusion; it is desirable that, so far as reasonable attention to the completion of his work will permit, he continue to mingle in social intercourse and that he should not discontinue his interest in or appearance at meetings of members of the Bar. He should, however, in pending or prospective litigation before him be particularly careful to avoid such action as may reasonably tend to awaken the suspicion that his social or business relations or friendships constitute an element in influencing his judicial conduct.

34. **A Summary of Judicial Obligation.**

In every particular his conduct should be above reproach. He should be conscientious, studious, thorough, courteous, patient, punctual, just, impartial, fearless of public clamor, regardless of

CANONS OF JUDICIAL ETHICS

public praise, and indifferent to private political or partisan influences; he should administer justice according to law, and deal with his appointments as a public trust; he should not allow other affairs or his private interests to interfere with the prompt and proper performance of his judicial duties, nor should he administer the office for the purpose of advancing his personal ambitions or increasing his popularity.

35. Improper Publicizing of Court Proceedings.*

Proceedings in court should be conducted with fitting dignity and decorum. The taking of photographs in the court room, during sessions of the court or recesses between sessions, and the broadcasting or televising of court proceedings detract from the essential dignity of the proceedings, distract participants and witnesses in giving testimony, and create misconceptions with respect thereto in the mind of the public and should not be permitted.

* Adopted September 30, 1937; amended September 15, 1952 and February 5, 1963.

Provided that this restriction shall not apply to the broadcasting or televising, under the supervision of the court, of such portions of naturalization proceedings (other than the interrogation of applicants) as are designed and carried out exclusively as a ceremony for the purpose of publicly demonstrating in an impressive manner the essential dignity and the serious nature of naturalization.

36. Conduct of Court Proceedings.*

Proceedings in court should be so conducted as to reflect the importance and seriousness of the inquiry to ascertain the truth.

The oath should be administered to witnesses in a manner calculated to impress them with the importance and solemnity of their promise to adhere to the truth. Each witness should be sworn separately and impressively at the bar or the court, and the clerk should be required to make a formal record of the administration of the oath, including the name of the witness.

* Adopted September 30, 1937.

LXXIII

Rule 24 (b) (2) of the Federal Rules of Criminal Procedures is one out of the many rules all judges, prosecutors, and attorneys are "obligated" to follow in all federal courtrooms throughout the entire United States. I have included in this book a copy of Rule 24 that was copies out of the Federal Rules of Criminal Procedures book itself on **page 199** in this book.

Rule 24 states:

"The government (the prosecutor) has 6 peremptory challenges and (I) the defendant has 10 peremptory challenges," during the Jury selection proceedings.

Rule 24 states nothing about allowing an ATF special agent (agent Matt Bassett) is allowed to assist the prosecutor in the process of peremptory challenges or in the Jury selection process. Special agent Matt Bassett was the head investigator "in charge" of investigating these charges I was falsely charged with. He was also the special agent who testified in the grand Jury proceeding as the prosecutor's main witness in order to falsely secure these criminal charges that were falsely brought up against me. And he also was going to be a witness that was going to testify against me at trial on the prosecutor's behalf. However, he was still allowed to assist prosecutor Zelda Wesley with selecting all the Jurors for my trial that include him assisting Zelda Wesley with the peremptory challenge process.

Special agent Matt Bassett should not have been allowed to partake in the jury selection proceedings by judge Irene Keeley. For one he is not the defendant, (the person being charged with a crime) a prosecutor or an attorney. According to Rule 24 and all of the other rules in the Federal Rules of Criminal Procedures law book those are the only people who can participate in the Jury selection process, which includes the process of peremptory challenges. Nowhere does it state in the Federal Rules of Criminal Procedures law book an ATF special agent is allowed to assist the prosecutor with the Jury selection proceedings.

Matt Bassett is an ATF federal special agent whose job description and duties consist of investigating crime and arresting people. His job description does not consist of assisting a prosecutor in selecting a Jury for a trial he is a witness of. Only an attorney, prosecutor, and a defendant who is going to trial fighting for his or her life is qualified to partake in the Jury selection process not a special agent, according to the Federal Rules of Criminal Procedures.

Please take a look at page 13 lines 22-25 of my jury selection transcripts that I have included at the end of this section on this issue on **page 209** in this book that shows prosecutor Zelda Wesley introduced Special Agent Matt Bassett (who was seated at the same table as she was in the courtroom) to the potential jurors of my trial within minutes of jury selection starting. As you can clearly see on page 13 of my jury selection transcripts prosecutor Zelda Wesley clearly stated on the record, "I'm Zelda Wesley and seated at counsel table with me is Timothy Helman who's also an attorney for the government and this is Matt Bassett who is a Special Agent with the Bureau of Alcohol, Tobacco and Firearms." This clearly proves special agent Matt Bassett was seated side by side with prosecutor Zelda Wesley partaking in the jury selection process which is not fair for many reasons.

As I stated above his job description does not consist of selecting a jury and by special agent Bassett helping to select a juror in a trial he investigated, and was going to be a witness for denied me my "SUBSTANTIAL AND CONSTITUTIONAL" right to a fair trial, because I feel special agent Bassett tailored a jury of "his liking" who he thought was going to return a guilty verdict which they did. Judge Keeley allowed this to happen in her courtroom and this shows how unethical and shady she is because under he was supposed to help the prosecutor with Jury selection.

Please look at page 76 lines 20-25 of my jury selection transcripts on **page 210** in this book when judge Keeley asked all the potential jurors for my trial did any of them know Special Agent Bassett because he was going to be a witness in my trial. I have shown you this page of my jury selection transcripts just to show you how unfair judge Keeley was/is. Judge Keeley knew special agent Bassett was the head investigator of my case and knew he was going to be called to the witness stand as a witness against me at my trial by prosecutor Zelda Wesley. But she still made the conscious decision to not tell Special Agent Matt Bassett he could not assist prosecutor Zelda Wesley with selecting the jury for my trial, not only because it was not his job description but because in general that would be the fair thing to do when considering he was the head lead investigator for my case and who was going to be a witness for my trial as well. It's a judge's duty to safeguard a person has been charged with a crime right to fairness in a courtroom, and judge Keeley failed to do so by allowing special agent Bassett to participate in the selecting of jurors for my trial.

This is a copy of rule 24 (b) (2) copied out of the Federal Rules of Criminal Procedures Rule Book that all judges and lawyers are "obligated" to follow in all criminal proceedings.

(Next Page)

Rule 24. Trial Jurors

(a) Examination.

 (1) *In General.* The court may examine prospective jurors or may permit the attorneys for the parties to do so.

 (2) *Court Examination.* If the court examines the jurors, it must permit the attorneys for the parties to:

  (A) ask further questions that the court considers proper; or

  (B) submit further questions that the court may ask if it considers them proper.

(b) Peremptory Challenges. Each side is entitled to the number of peremptory challenges to prospective jurors specified below. The court may allow additional peremptory challenges to multiple defendants, and may allow the defendants to exercise those challenges separately or jointly.

 (1) *Capital Case.* Each side has 20 peremptory challenges when the government seeks the death penalty.

 (2) *Other Felony Case.* The government has 6 peremptory challenges and the defendant or defendants jointly have 10 peremptory challenges when the defendant is charged with a crime punishable by imprisonment of more than one year.

 (3) *Misdemeanor Case.* Each side has 3 peremptory challenges when the defendant is charged with a crime punishable by fine, imprisonment of one year or less, or both.

JUDGE IRENE KEELEY'S CONDUCT THAT SHOWS SHE IS NOT TRUSTWORTHY, EXTREMELY DECEITFUL, DISHONEST, A CHEAT, INSINCERE, ARTFUL, CORRUPT, UNPRINCIPLED, SHADY, DISHONORARLE, and UNPROFESSIONAL:

JUDGE KEELEY ALREADY KNEW
THE VERDICT!!

Please look at page 19 lines 18-25 of my trial transcripts I have included at the end of this section on **page 211** in this book. This page of my trial transcripts shows the prejudicial statement made by judge Keeley to me that proves the guilty verdict for my trial was premeditated to be a guilty verdict. When you read page 19 lines 18 - 25 of my trial transcripts you will read the judge stated, "okay I don't know how many times, I don't mean to interrupt you again Mr. Antoine, but I told you at the final pre-trial conference the ruling on the motion to suppress involving your phone (a phone she claims was mine) is over and done as this trial is in just a moment. If you want to take that up on appeal because you do not like it, fine." The statement made by the judge "If you want to take that up on appeal because you don't like it, fine" was made by the judge "before" trial even started which indicates the judge already knew what the outcome of my trial was going to be which was going to be a guilty verdict. The judge told me to take my issue up on appeal an appeal can "only" be done after a person gets sentenced after losing trial or by taking a plea. So for the judge to tell me to take an issue up on appeal before trial even started insinuates the judge knew the result of my trial was going to be a guilty verdict, and the only way to raise an issue I had about her ruling on my motion to suppress was on an appeal.

How could judge Keeley give an option to raise an issue on appeal if my trial did not even start yet, and the jury of my trial did not hear any evidence in my case to determine their verdict on my trial. The only way judge Keeley could make a statement stating "take it up on appeal" is if and only if the judge knew I was going to lose trial before hand because the trial was already rigged and set up for me to lose.

SHAME ON YOU JUDGE KEELEY!!

As I already mentioned in this book judge Irene Keeley allowed special agent Bassett who was a witness in my trial to stay inside of the courtroom from start to finish of all 3 days of my trial after she instructed all witnesses to leave the courtroom before trial was going to actually begin. I will now show you the trial transcripts proving to you judge Keeley knew special agent Bassett was going to be a witness in my trial but still willfully and knowingly allowed him to stay inside the courtroom for all 3 days of my trial despite her instructing all witnesses to leave the courtroom on the first day trial was going to actually start. As I have previously explained in the book, this put me at a more of a disadvantage than I was already in. It was very important for special agent Bassett to not be in the courtroom from start to finish of my trial to prevent his future testimony on the witness stand from getting influenced by what he was going to hear from all the other witnesses testimonies who took the witness stand on day 1, day 2, and day 3 of my trial.

That was very possible to be done by special agent Bassett because he was the "very last" witness to be called to the witness stand by the prosecutor at my trial. In other words to prevent special agent Bassett from "let me get my story straight before I go on the witness stand" syndrome. Special agent Bassett had the opportunity to tailor his witness testimony before he was called to the witness stand based on all of the other witnesses testimonies he heard before he was called to the witness stand which was not fair and clearly put me at a disadvantage.

Please take a look at page 62 lines 22-25 and page 63 line 1 of my trial transcripts on **pages 212 and 213** in this book where the record reflects my attorney Mr. Walker puts in an oral motion of sequester that I "pleaded" for him to do, and moments after judge Keeley stating "All right motion to sequester granted" then judge Keeley stated, "if there are any witnesses in the courtroom please leave!" The legal term "oral motion of sequester" that you see in my trial transcripts means my attorney Mr. Walker orally asked the judge to remove all witness from the courtroom before trial started.

As you read these trial transcripts in this section I will refer you to, you will see the following legal terms I feel you will need the meaning of:

1. Government – means the prosecutor in all federal courtrooms in the United States.

2. U.S Attorney - means the prosecutor as well.

3. Prospective Juror - means potential juror for a trial.

   To prove to you that special agent Bassett stayed seated inside the courtroom after judge Keeley instructed all witness to leave the courtroom before trial actually started and he sat side by side next to prosecutor Zelda Wesley from the start to the end of my trial, even though judge Keeley knew he was going to be a witness in my trial please examine the following trial transcripts have included in the back of this section I am going to reference you to. Thank you!

4. Please look at page 57 lines 13-16 of my trial transcripts on **page 214** in this book which is the introduction of the prosecutor's opening statements. The legal term opening statements means a presentation made to the jury of a trial giving an overview of the case and the evidence to be presented. Opening statements are "only" made at the actual beginning of a trial. On page 57 lines 13-16 of my trial transcripts as you read it you can see before prosecutor Zelda Wesley actually went on with her opening statements she introduced everyone who was seated at the same table with her which you can see as you read page 57 lines 13-16 it includes special agent Bassett sitting at the same table with prosecutor Zelda Wesley minutes before Ms. Wesley started her opening statements which was minutes before the trial actually begun.

5. Now please again look at page 62 lines 22-25 and page 63 line 1 of my trial transcripts on **page 212 and 213** in this book where the record reflects my attorney put in an oral motion to sequester that was granted by the judge then moments after it was granted by the judge the judge stated "if there are any witnesses in the courtroom, please leave." As you can see by reading those pages of my trial transcripts the Court Reporter whose job is to put on the record "everything" that occurs in the courtroom never made a record of "anyone" exiting the courtroom after judge Keeley instructed all be witnesses to leave the courtroom which is the court reporter's job to do if anyone was to exit the courtroom. Special agent Matt Bassett never respected the judge's instruction for all witnesses to leave the courtroom even though he knew he was going to be a witness in my trial. And what makes it worse is Judge Keeley also knew he was going to be a witness in my trial but still allowed him to stay inside the courtroom after she ordered all witnesses who was in the courtroom to leave the courtroom.

6. "To prove that judge Keeley knew special agent Bassett was going to be a witness in my trial" but still allowed him to stay inside of the courtroom after she instructed all witnesses to leave the courtroom, lets rewind back to my jury selection proceedings which was prior to my attorney putting an oral motion to sequester the judge to have all witnesses who were in the courtroom to leave the courtroom.

   Please take a look at page 76 lines 20-25 of my jury selection transcripts on **page 210** in this book where the record reflects judge Keeley asked all then potential jurors of my trial did any of them know special Matt Bassett and the reason why judge Keeley asked them that is because he was going to be a witness in my trial and by law she has to ask all the potential jurors do they know "any" of the witnesses who is scheduled to testify against me at my trial. Page 76 lines 20-21 of my jury selection transcripts clearly proves judge

Keeley knew special agent Bassett was going to be a witness in my trial because the only purpose for judge Keeley asking all the potential jurors did anyone know him was because she knew he was a witness in my trial along with all the other names she asked the potential jurors did they know when she asked them did they know special agent Matt Bassett. Therefore, the judge clearly knew special agent Bassett was going to be a witness called to the witness stand by the prosecutor to testify against me at my trial, but did the unethical thing and allowed him to stay inside the courtroom after she instructed all witnesses to leave the courtroom after she granted my attorney's oral motion to sequester all witnesses out of the courtroom before the prosecutor called her first witness to the witness stand to actually start my trial!

7. To further prove what I am saying about special agent Bassett is a fact please take a look at pages 63 line 12, 67 line 2, 73 line 7, 75 line 25, 96 line 19, 126 line 6, 149 line 25, 161 line 19, 195 line 6, 184 line 3, 188 line 14 and 217 line 25 of my trial transcripts on **pages 215- 226** in this book where the record reflects all 12 witnesses who were called to the witness stand to testify against me by the prosecutor Zelda Wesley the court reporter put in the record when "the witness entered the courtroom". The only witness that the record did not reflect enters the courtroom by the court reporter when he was called to the witness stand by prosecutor Zelda Wesley to testify against me was **special agent Bassett**. Check it out, please go to page 232 line 25 and page 233 line 1 of my trial transcripts on **pages 227 and 228** where the record reflects when prosecutor Zelda Wesley called special agent Bassett to the witness stand in order for him to testify against me. If you notice there is no record made by the court reporter stating special agent Bassett "enters" the courtroom as the court reporter did for every other single witness who was called to the witness stand by prosecutor Zelda Wesley to testify against

me at trial. And the reason for that is because Special agent Bassett was already in the courtroom sitting at the same table as prosecutor Zelda Wesley when he was called to the witness stand to testify against me, so there was no need for him to "enter the courtroom" like all the other witnesses who were called to the witness stand to testify against me by prosecutor Zelda Wesley.

8. Please take a look at page 275 lines 11-16 of my trial transcripts on **page 230** in this book where the record reflects judge Keeley asking prosecutor Zelda Wesley at the ending of Ms. Wesley questioning special agent Bassett on the witness stand, "Is there anything further for witness special agent Bassett" and Ms. Wesley stated "no your honor," then Judge Keeley said to Special agent Bassett "you may return to your seat," which was the seat right next to prosecutor Zelda Wesley where he was seated at for the entire 3 days of my trial at the prosecutor's table. The fact that judge Keeley told special agent Bassett to return to his seat after he was done testifying against me on the witness stand without a doubt proves special agent Bassett was called to the witness stand from inside of the courtroom not from outside of the courtroom like all the rest of the witnesses were called to the witness stand at my trial by the prosecutor. And when all the other witnesses were called to the witness stand by the prosecutor, the record reflects the court reporter stating when they entered the courtroom except for when special agent Bassett was called to the witness stand by the prosecutor. **NEED I SAY MORE!!** I think I do!

9. Lastly take a look at page 271 lines 14-16 of my trial transcripts on **page 231** in this book where it shows you my attorney Mr. Walker questioning Special agent Bassett when he was on the witness stand. My attorney asked Mr. Bassett "was he in the courtroom when Ms. Parker testified" and Special agent Bassett replied, "I was." Special agent Bassett indirectly even admitted he was in the courtroom when he was not supposed to be inside the

courtroom by stating he was in the courtroom when Ms. Parker testified. Reason being is because judge Keeley instructed all witnesses of my trial to leave the courtroom before prosecutor Zelda Wesley called her first witness to the witness stand at my trial. Therefore, special agent Bassett was not supposed to be inside the courtroom, to hear "any witness testimony".

I have clearly proven above that special agent Bassett stayed inside of the courtroom after judge Keeley ordered all witnesses of my trial to leave the courtroom, and he was able to hear "every witness testimony of my trial before being the last witness called to the witness stand by prosecutor Zelda Wesley." This gave special agent Bassett the opportunity to tailor his testimony before he was called to the witness stand by the prosecutor to fit the stories of all the other witness's testimony he heard before he was called to the witness stand which I feel was extremely unfair. Do you agree?

A. Do any of you feel judge Irene Keeley should have told Special agent Bassett to leave the courtroom after she told all witnesses to leave the courtroom and agent Bassett did not?

B. Do you think prosecutor Zelda Wesley should have told special agent Bassett who was sitting right next to her to leave the courtroom when the judge instructed all witnesses of my trial to leave the courtroom? Do you think my attorney should have said something once he saw special agent Bassett still seated in the courtroom after judge Keeley instructed all witnesses to leave the courtroom? Why?

After reading what the judge did to me above do you feel judge Irene Keeley violated the three ethical rules I stated in previous pages which as a reminder are as follows:

1.) "Constitutional Obligations" that states:

"It's the duty of all judges in the United States to support the Federal Constitution and that of the state whose laws they administer; in doing so they should fearlessly observe and apply fundamental limitation and guarantee."

2.) "Avoidance of Impropriety" which states:

"A judge's official conduct should be free from impropriety and the appearance of impropriety; he should avoid infractions of law; and his personal behavior, not only upon the bench and in the performance of judicial duties but also in his everyday life should be beyond reproach."

3.) "Essential Conduct" states:

" A judge should be temperate, attentive, patient, impartial and since he is an administer of the law and apply it to the facts he should be studious of the principles of law and diligent in endeavoring to ascertain the facts."

Now that you were reminded of those 3 ethical rules do you feel judge Irene Keeley violated any of them? If yes, how?

Not to get off topic but something came to my mind as I was writing the above ethical rules. Why when those ethical rules are referring to a judge it is using the word "he" and not "she" or rather both terms he and she because there are female judges in the United States as well, **SO FUCKING BIAS!!** Do you agree?

4.) The Fifth Amendment of the United States Constitution (which I have also included in the back of this section on **page 232**) states:

"No person shall be deprived of life, liberty or property without due process of law."

The term "due process of law" you see in the Fifth Amendment of the United States Constitution comes in two different forms. These two forms of due process of law are "substantive due process" which is a restraint on government prohibiting laws that are too vague, overbroad, unreasonable, arbitrary or capricious and you have "procedural due process" which requires the steps in a criminal proceeding to be fundamentally fair, assuring to some degree of certitude that justification exists for arrest, prosecution, and punishment. Now that you know what "due process of law" means, do you think my substantive or procedural due process rights were violated after reading throughout this book what my lawyer, the prosecutor, and the judge did to me? Please explain?

YOU BE THE JUDGE!!

Court Is in Session....

TRANSCRIPTS OR OTHER DOCUMENTS I REFFERRED YOU TO IN THIS SECTION

This is page 13 lines 22-25 of my jury selection transcripts showing prosecutor Zelda Wesley introducing Special Agent Matt Bassett to all the potential jurors of my trial who were seated at the same table as prosecutor Zelda Wesley at the very beginning of jury selection.

```
                                                                    13

 1              MR. WALKER:  (Complies.)
 2              THE COURT:  Now, do any of the jurors know Mr.
 3   Walker?
 4              PROSPECTIVE JURORS:  (No verbal response.)
 5              THE COURT:  Are you related to Mr. Walker?
 6              PROSPECTIVE JURORS:  (No verbal response.)
 7              THE COURT:  Have you had any professional dealings
 8   with Mr. Walker, who is an attorney in Morgantown, West
 9   Virginia?
10              PROSPECTIVE JURORS:  (No verbal response.)
11              THE COURT:  All right.  Are any of you familiar, are
12   you related to or know Mr. -- familiar with, related to, or
13   know Mr. Antoine, the defendant in this case?
14              PROSPECTIVE JURORS:  (No verbal response.)
15              THE COURT:  Thank you.
16         Now, the government is represented by Assistant United
17   States Attorney Zelda Wesley and Assistant United States
18   Attorney Timothy Helman.  I'm going to ask Ms. Wesley to stand,
19   introduce herself to you, and your fellow attorney, and also I
20   believe it's the Government representative or agent at the
21   table.
22              MS. WESLEY:  Good morning.  I'm Zelda Wesley and
23   seated at counsel table with me is Timothy Helman, who's also
24   an attorney for the Government.  And this is Matt Bassett, who
25   is a Special Agent with the Bureau of Alcohol, Tobacco, and

                    Stacy Harlow, CVR-M/CM/RVR-M/RCP/RBC
          Post Office Box 969  Clarksburg, WV 26302-0969  (304)623-7154
```

This is page 76 lines 20-25 of my jury selection transcript showing you judge Keeley asking all the potential Jurors of my trial did anyone know special agent Bassett because he was going to be a witness in my trial. The point of this page transcript is to show you judge Irene Keeley knew special agent Bassett was going to be a witness in my trial.

```
                                                            ← 76

1          PROSPECTIVE JUROR:  Michelle Muckleroy, and he has
2    been at our facility to work with some of our staff.
3          THE COURT:  All right.  Is there anything about that
4    relationship with your employer and the staff of your company
5    that would affect your ability to serve as a juror in this case
6    and to be fair to both sides?
7          PROSPECTIVE JUROR:  No.
8          THE COURT:  You'll weigh his testimony just as you
9    would, for credibility, as you would any other witness?
10         PROSPECTIVE JUROR:  Yes, I would.
11         THE COURT:  Thank you.
12      Ruth Hunt.
13      No?  Ms. Hunt is not being called.
14      Victor Propst, who is the chief of the Star City Police
15   Department.
16      Not called.  Donald Fries.
17      No?
18      Shonda Joseph.
19         PROSPECTIVE JURORS:  (No verbal response.)
20         THE COURT:  Matthew Bassett is the case agent and
21   you-all have been introduced to Mr. Bassett.
22         PROSPECTIVE JURORS:  (No verbal response.)
23         THE COURT:  And as I understand it, none of you knows
24   Mr. Bassett. correct?
25         PROSPECTIVE JURORS:  (No verbal response.)

            Stacy Harlow, CVR-M/CM/RVR-M/RCP/RBC
      Post Office Box 969  Clarksburg, WV 26302-0969  (304)623-7154
```

This is Page 19 lines 18-25 of my trial transcripts showing the prejudicial statement made by judge Irene Keeley to me that proves the guilty verdict of my trial was premeditated by her.

```
 1   need to change attorneys, because the facts aren't changing.
 2   We're not changing attorneys.  Okay?  And this case is going to
 3   be tried.
 4            THE DEFENDANT:  So, Your Honor, so was you like aware
 5   that Mr. Walker told my mom and that -- that the prosecutor
 6   does -- she does have the rest of the case?  I mean the tape
 7   that they just saying that they don't have.
 8            THE COURT:  If the prosecutor has anymore tape than
 9   we saw at the final pretrial conference, you'll get to play it
10   at this trial.  Okay?  I told you that.
11            THE DEFENDANT:  No, Your Honor.  All right.  Then on
12   the top of that, yesterday I told Mr. Walker that certain
13   things are not in my discovery that should be that the
14   Government should have gave over.  So --
15            THE COURT:  Like what?
16            THE DEFENDANT:  My -- the -- the court ordered for
17   the phones.  And there's only certain things that's --
18            THE COURT:  Okay.  I don't how many times -- I don't
19   mean to interrupt you again, Mr. Antoine, but I told you at the
20   final pretrial conference, the ruling on the motion to suppress
21   involving your phone is over and done as far as this trial is -
22   -- just a moment.
23            THE DEFENDANT:  All right, Your Honor.
24            THE COURT:  If you want to take that up on appeal
25   because you don't like it, fine.  That is not any evidence that
```

Stacy Harlow, CVR-M/CM/RVR-M/RCP/RBC
Post Office Box 969 Clarksburg, WV 26302-0969 (304) 623-7154

This is page 62 lines 22-25 and page 63 line 1 of my trial transcripts showing the judge grant my attorney's oral motion to have all witnesses to leave the courtroom and also showing you judge Irene Keeley telling all witnesses to leave the courtroom.

```
 1  expect.  Why?  We're not going to hear about DNA evidence.
 2  We're not going to hear about fingerprints.  All we're going to
 3  hear is from individuals who are co-conspirators and have an
 4  interest in the outcome, based on their testimony.
 5        Now, as you're well aware, the defendant sits in this
 6  chair clothed in the presumption of innocence, and he shall
 7  remain clothed in that presumption unless and until the
 8  Government, through Ms. Wesley, can prove him guilty beyond a
 9  reasonable doubt.  I don't believe they'll be able to do it.
10  Why?  No DNA evidence, no fingerprint evidence, testimony from
11  co-defendants who are supremely interested in the outcome of
12  the case.
13        So at the conclusion of this case, I'll stand right here
14  before you and I'll ask you to return a verdict worthy of the
15  evidence you've heard, but also worthy of the evidence you
16  expected to hear and didn't hear.  And I'm confident at the
17  conclusion, your verdict will be not guilty.  Thank you.
18              THE COURT:  All right.
19        Ladies and gentlemen, that concludes the opening
20  statements.  The Government bears the burden of proof and may
21  begin its case-in-chief.
22              MR. WALKER:  Your Honor, I move to sequester all
23  witnesses, if it hasn't been done.
24              THE COURT:  All right.
25        Motion to sequester granted.  If there are any witnesses
```

Stacy Harlow, CVR-M/CM/RVR-M/RCP/RBC
Post Office Box 969 Clarksburg, WV 26302-0969 (304) 623-7154

Page 63 line 1:

1   in the courtroom, please leave.

2   MS. WESLEY: Your Honor, the Government calls Victor

3   Perez.

4   THE COURT: All right.

5   The first witness is Victor Perez. Do you have someone

6   whose getting them?

7   MS. WESLEY: Yes, Your Honor.

8   THE COURT: Okay.

9   Ladies and gentlemen, since witnesses have been

10   sequestered, that means somebody has to get them and bring them

11   in. So there's always just a brief delay.

12   (Mr. Perez enters the courtroom.)

13   Mr. Perez, would you approach the clerk at the front of

14   the courtroom. She'll administer the oath to you before you

15   take the witness stand, sir.

16   THE WITNESS: Yes, ma'am.

17   (VICTOR PEREZ WAS SWORN.)

18   THE CLERK: The witness is Victor Perez. P-e-r-e-z.

19   THE COURT: You may proceed.

20   DIRECT EXAMINATION

21   BY MS. WESLEY:

22   Q.   Where do you work?

23   A.   I work for the New York State Department of Corrections

24   and Community Supervision, formerly known as The Division of

25   Parole of New York State. I'm a senior parole officer.

The is page 57 lines 13-16 of my trial transcripts which is the introduction of the prosecutor's opening statements. This page of my trial transcripts shows you moments before prosecutor actually went on with her opening statements she introduced everyone who was seated at her table to the Jury which included special agent Bassett sitting at the same table as she when trial actually begun, and minutes later the first witness was called to the witness stand by prosecutor Wesley.

```
 1   beyond a reasonable doubt.
 2        Don't discuss the case with anyone and keep an open mind
 3   until all the evidence has been received.  At that time, I will
 4   give you your complete and final instructions, both orally and
 5   in writing, and then and only then will you be fully prepared
 6   to begin your deliberations and reach your verdict.
 7        That concludes the preliminary instructions of the Court,
 8   ladies and gentlemen.  We'll now hear from the attorneys in
 9   opening statement.  The Government will begin.
10        Ms. Wesley.
11          MS. WESLEY:  Thank you.
12               GOVERNMENT'S OPENING STATEMENT
13        May please the Court, and ladies and gentlemen of the
14   jury.  Again, my name is Zelda Wesley and I'm the Assistant
15   United States Attorney.  Seated at counsel table with me is
16   Special Agent Matt Bassett from the ATF, Tim Helman, who is an
17   AUSA from our Martinsburg's office, and Laurel Jones, who's a
18   paralegal in our office, and we're here today on behalf of the
19   Government.
20        Now, the Court has already advised you that this portion
21   of the trial is called opening statements, and it's an
22   opportunity for the parties to give you a preview of what we
23   expect the evidence in this case to be, and also to give you an
24   expectation of what we think the evidence in this case will
25   show.
              Stacy Harlow, CVR-M/CM/RVR-M/RCP/RBC
         Post Office Box 969  Clarksburg, WV 26302-0969  (304) 623-7154
```

These are pages 63 line 12, 67 line 21, 73 line 7, 75 line 25, 96 line 19, 126 line 6, 149 line 25, 161 line 19, 195 line 6, 184 line 3, 188 line 14, and 217 line 25 of my trial transcripts all showing when all 12 witnesses were called to the witness stand to testify against me by prosecutor Zelda Wesley the court reporter put it on the record " When the witness entered the courtroom." Page 63 line 12:

```
                                                              63

 1   in the courtroom, please leave.
 2           MS. WESLEY:  Your Honor, the Government calls Victor
 3   Perez.
 4           THE COURT:  All right.
 5       The first witness is Victor Perez.  Do you have someone
 6   whose getting them?
 7           MS. WESLEY:  Yes, Your Honor.
 8           THE COURT:  Okay.
 9       Ladies and gentlemen, since witnesses have been
10   sequestered, that means somebody has to get them and bring them
11   in.  So there's always just a brief delay.
12   (Mr. Perez enters the courtroom.)
13       Mr. Perez, would you approach the clerk at the front of
14   the courtroom.  She'll administer the oath to you before you
15   take the witness stand, sir.
16           THE WITNESS:  Yes, ma'am.
17               (VICTOR PEREZ WAS SWORN.)
18           THE CLERK:  The witness is Victor Perez.  P-e-r-e-z.
19           THE COURT:  You may proceed.
20                   DIRECT EXAMINATION
21   BY MS. WESLEY:
22   Q.  Where do you work?
23   A.  I work for the New York State Department of Corrections
24   and Community Supervision, formerly known as The Division of
25   Parole of New York State.  I'm a senior parole officer.
             Stacy Harlow, CVR-M/CM/RVR-M/RCP/RBC
         Post Office Box 969  Clarksburg, WV 26302-0969  (304)623-7154
```

Page 67 line 21:

```
 1   Q.   Okay.
 2            MS. WESLEY:  I have no further questions of this
 3   witness, Your Honor.
 4            THE COURT:  All right.
 5        Cross-examination.
 6            MR. WALKER:  A moment, Your Honor?
 7            THE COURT:  Yes.
 8            MR. WALKER:  No questions, Your Honor.
 9            THE COURT:  All right.  Thank you.
10        The witness may step down.
11        Is Mr. Perez excused?
12            MS. WESLEY:  He is, Your Honor.
13            THE COURT:  Not subject to recall.
14        Okay.  Thank you, Mr. Perez.  You're excused and free to
15   go.
16            THE WITNESS:  Thank you, ma'am.
17            THE COURT:  The Government may call its next witness.
18            MS. WESLEY:  Your Honor, the Government calls
19   Detective Dennine Smiddy.
20            THE COURT:  Detective Dennine Smiddy.
21   (Ms. Smiddy enters the courtroom.)
22        Ms. Smiddy, good afternoon.  Would you please approach the
23   clerk standing in the front of the courtroom in the black
24   jacket and she will administer the oath to you before you take
25   the witness stand.
```

Stacy Harlow, CVR-M/CM/RVR-M/RCP/RBC
Post Office Box 969 Clarksburg, WV 26302-0969 (304)623-7154

```
                                                                    73

   1        Before the witness leaves, she's got the envelope in which

   2   the exhibit was contained.  Is there any reason to hold that?

   3   It was not admitted into evidence.  I just want to make sure

   4   before she leaves that she can take that with her.

   5             MR. WALKER:  Oh, no.

   6             THE COURT:  Okay.  Thank you.

  (7)  (Mr. Mahdavi enters the courtroom.)

   8        Mr. Mahdavi, good afternoon, sir.  Would you please

   9   approach the clerk standing at the front of the courtroom in

  10   the black jack and she'll administer the oath to you before you

  11   take the witness stand.

  12             (ANTHONY MAHDAVI WAS SWORN.)

  13             THE CLERK:  The witness is Anthony Mahdavi.  M-a-h-d-

  14   a-v-i.

  15             THE COURT:  All right.  Mr. Mahdavi, please speak in

  16   a loud, clear voice into the microphone so that all the jurors

  17   may hear you.

  18        You may proceed.

  19                        DIRECT EXAMINATION

  20   BY MS. WESLEY:

  21   Q.   Where do you work?

  22   A.   Tony's Street Dreamz.

  23   Q.   And how long have you worked there?

  24   A.   My dad owns it, I've been here forever.

  25   Q.   Okay.  And in what capacity are you employed there?
```

Page 75 line 25 :

                                                              75
```

1  Special Agent Matt Bassett of the ATF and provide him with a

2  recording of the surveillance footage that was captured on June

3  the 19th of 2017?

4  A.  Yes, ma'am.

5  Q.  And the surveillance recording that you provided to Mr.

6  Bassett, it was an accurate depiction of what was captured on

7  those video recordings?

8  A.  Yes.

9  Q.  Okay.

10       MS. WESLEY:  I have nothing further to this witness,

11  Your Honor.

12       THE COURT:  All right.  Thank you.

13  Is there any cross-examination, Mr. Walker?

14       MR. WALKER:  None, Your Honor.

15       THE COURT:  All right.

16  Is the witness subject to recall?

17       MS. WESLEY:  Not from the Government, Your Honor.

18       MR. WALKER:  No, Your Honor.

19       THE COURT:  All right.  Thank you.

20  You may step down, Mr. Mahdavi, and you're free to go.

21       THE WITNESS:  Thank you.

22       THE COURT:  The Government may call its next witness.

23       MS. WESLEY:  Will Jackson.

24       THE COURT:  Will Jackson.

25  (Mr. Jackson enters the courtroom.)
```

96

```
 1          MR. WALKER:  Yes, Your Honor.

 2          THE COURT:  All right.  Thank you very much.  And the

 3   same with the exhibits, right.

 4          MS. WESLEY:  Yes, Your Honor.

 5          THE COURT:  Okay.  Thank you.  You may call your next

 6   witness.

 7       Oh, sorry.  We need to bring the jury in.  I apologize for

 8   that.  I was trying to track the -- this is your fifth witness,

 9   right?

10          MS. WESLEY:  Chris Anderson, Your Honor.

11          THE COURT:  Yeah, fifth witness is

12   Chris Anderson.  Thank you.

13   (Jurors entering courtroom.)

14          THE COURT:  Welcome back, ladies and gentlemen.  The

15   Government's case-in-chief will continue.

16       Ms. Wesley, you may call your next witness.

17          MS. WESLEY:  Your Honor, we call Chris Anderson.

18          THE COURT:  Chris Anderson.

19   (Mr. Anderson enters the courtroom.)

20          THE COURT:  All right.  Mr. Anderson, would you

21   please approach the front of the courtroom.  Do you see the

22   lady standing here in the black jacket with the blonde hair?

23   She's going to administer the oath to you before you take the

24   witness stand.

25               (CHRIS ANDERSON WAS SWORN.)
```

126

```
 1      You may step down, Mr. Anderson.  You're excused as a
 2   witness and free to go.
 3        The Government may call its next witness.
 4            MS. WESLEY:  Margaret Parker.
 5            THE COURT:  All right.
 6   (Ms. Parkers enters the courtroom.)
 7            THE COURT: Good afternoon, Ms. Parker.  Would you
 8   please approach the clerk here in the front of the courtroom?
 9   She's standing in the black jacket.  Please approach.  She will
10   administer the oath to you, if you come forward.  Please raise
11   your right hand.
12                 (MARGARET PARKER WAS SWORN.)
13            THE CLERK:  The witness is Margaret Parker.  P-a-r-k-
14   e-r.
15            THE COURT:  Ms. Parker, I'm going to ask that you
16   speak in a loud, clear voice.
17        Ms. Parker, I'm over here.  Would you speak in a loud,
18   clear voice into the microphone so that all jurors may hear
19   you, please?
20            THE WITNESS:  Yes.
21            THE COURT:  Thank you.
22                 DIRECT EXAMINATION
23   BY MS. WESLEY:
24   Q.   Would you tell us how old you are?
25   A.   34.
```

```
                                                                    149

    1   Q.   Okay.

    2           MR. WALKER:  No further questions, Your Honor.

    3           THE COURT:  All right.

    4   Is there any redirect?

    5           MS. WESLEY:  No, Your Honor.

    6           THE COURT:  Is the witness subject to recall?

    7           MR. WALKER:  No, Your Honor.

    8           THE COURT:  All right.

    9   Ms. Parker, you may step down.  You're excused as a

   10   witness.  You may leave.

   11           THE WITNESS:  Thanks.

   12           THE COURT:  You're free to go.

   13           THE WITNESS:  Thank you.

   14           THE COURT:  Ms. Wesley, I don't if -- how long your

   15   next witness will be, but it's 20 till 5:00.

   16           MS. WESLEY:  We have an interstate nexus witness.

   17   That should be short.

   18           THE COURT:  Okay.  We'll call one more witness, then.

   19           MS. WESLEY:  We call Special Agent Matt Kocher.  And

   20   he's already getting the agent.

   21           THE COURT:  All right.  Fine.

   22   Ladies and gentlemen, I'm aware this has been a long day

   23   for you.  This will be the last witness for the day.  Thank you

   24   for your patience.

   25   (Special Agent Kocher enters the courtroom.)
```

221

```
                                                                    161

 1                        P R O C E E D I N G S
 2              (12-12-18 at 9:08 A.M., defendant present)
 3                  THE COURT:  Good morning.  All jurors are now here.
 4    The computer on the bench is fixed; we're ready to proceed
 5    unless there is any -- there are any matters that the parties
 6    would like to take up before I bring the jury in.
 7                  MS. WESLEY:  Not from the Government, Your Honor.
 8                  MR. WALKER:  Not from the defense.
 9                  THE COURT:  All right.  Thank you.
10        We can bring the jury in.
11    (Jurors entering courtroom.)
12                  THE COURT:  Good morning, ladies and gentlemen.
13    Welcome back.  Thank you for being here on a timely basis this
14    morning.  We're ready to resume the Government's case-in-chief.
15        Ms. Wesley, your next witness.
16                  MS. WESLEY:  Your Honor, the Government calls Tommy
17    Calhoun.
18                  THE COURT:  Tommy Calhoun.
19    (Mr. Calhoun enters the courtroom.)
20                  THE COURT:  Mr. Calhoun.
21                  THE WITNESS:  Yes.
22                  THE COURT:  Good morning.  Would you please come
23    forward to the front of the courtroom where the clerk is
24    standing?  If you'll raise your right hand, she'll administer
25    the oath to you before you take the witness stand.
```

1 (Jurors entering the courtroom.)

2   THE COURT: Welcome back, ladies and gentlemen. We

3 are ready to resume the Government's case-in-chief.

4   MS. WESLEY: We call Officer Nick Junkins.

5   THE COURT: Officer Nick Junkins.

6 (Officer Junkins enters the courtroom.)

7   THE COURT: Good morning, Officer Junkins. Please

8 approach the clerk in the front of the courtroom, who will

9 administer the oath to you before you take the witness stand.

10   (NICK JUNKINS WAS SWORN.)

11   THE CLERK: The witness is Officer Nick Junkins. J-

12 u-n-k-i-n-s.

13   THE COURT: Officer Junkins, will you please speak in

14 a loud, clear voice into the microphone so that all jurors may

15 hear you.

16   You may proceed.

17   MS. WESLEY: Okay.

18   DIRECT EXAMINATION

19 BY MS. WESLEY:

20 Q.   Where do you presently work?

21 A.   The Marion County Sheriff's Office.

22 Q.   And how long have you held that employment?

23 A.   Approximately eight months.

24 Q.   Okay. And at some point in time did you work for Star

25 City Police Department?

Page 184 line 3:

```
 1  retrieve the exhibit?
 2          THE COURT:  You may retrieve the exhibit.
 3  (Ms. Tatar enters the courtroom.)
 4          THE COURT:  Good morning, Ms. Tatar.  Would you
 5  please approach the clerk?  She will administer the oath to you
 6  before you take the witness stand.
 7                  (DAWN TATAR WAS SWORN.)
 8          THE CLERK:  The witness is Dawn Tatar.  T-a-t-a-r.
 9          THE COURT:  All right.  Ms. Tatar, if you'll please
10  speak in a loud, clear voice into the microphone.
11      You may proceed.
12                  DIRECT EXAMINATION
13  BY MS. WESLEY:
14  Q.   Where do you work?
15  A.   WV Jewelry and Loan, LLC.
16  Q.   And in what capacity are you involved in that business?
17  A.   I am the owner/member.
18  Q.   Okay.  And how long have you owned that business?
19  A.   Eleven years.
20  Q.   And where is the business located?
21  A.   188 Highland Avenue, Westover, West Virginia.
22  Q.   And is that a business that will sell firearms?
23  A.   Yes.
24  Q.   And are you a federal firearms licensee?
25  A.   I am.
```

Stacy Harlow, CVR-M/CM/RVR-M/RCP/RBC
Post Office Box 969 Clarksburg, WV 26302-0969 (304) 623-7154

1   MR. WALKER: No.

2   THE COURT: You're excused as a witness and free to

3 go.

4   THE WITNESS: Thank you.

5   THE COURT: Thank you.

6   MS. WESLEY: Your Honor, we would call Maria Lopez.

7 And may I retrieve the exhibits?

8   THE COURT: You may call -- you may retrieve the

9 exhibits and Ms. Lopez is the next witness.

10   Ms. Tatar, you are free -- it's a little congested in here

11 this morning, but you're free to go if you can wind your way

12 through there.

13   THE WITNESS: Thank you.

14 (Ms. Lopez enters the courtroom.)

15   THE COURT: Good morning, Ms. Lopez. Please approach

16 to the front of the courtroom. The clerk is standing there and

17 will administer the oath before you take the witness stand.

18   (MARIA LOPEZ WAS SWORN.)

19   THE CLERK: The witness is Maria Lopez. L-o-p-e-z.

20   THE COURT: Ms. Lopez.

21   THE WITNESS: Yes.

22   THE COURT: I'm here to your left. This -- I'm Judge

23 Keeley. I just wanted to instruct you to please speak in a

24 loud, clear voice into the microphone. You can move it down

25 closer to your mouth. I want to make sure all the jurors can

Stacy Harlow, CVR-M/CM/RVR-M/RCP/RBC
Post Office Box 969 Clarksburg, WV 26302-0969 (304)623-7154

1 Q.   Okay. Did you try to --- attempt to reconcile this

2 discrepancy with Mr. Calhoun?

3 A.   I did not.

4 Q.   Now, were any pictures taken of the suitcase and the

5 contents?

6 A.   No, I don't believe so.

7 Q.   Was a citation issued for the broken taillight?

8 A.   No.

9   MR. WALKER: Thank you, Your Honor. No further

10 questions.

11   THE COURT: All right.

12   Is there redirect?

13   MS. WESLEY: No, Your Honor.

14   THE COURT: Is the witness subject to recall?

15   MR. WALKER: No, Your Honor.

16   THE COURT: Thank you. You may step down, Officer

17 Junkins. You're excused as a witness

18   THE WITNESS: Thank you, ma'am.

19   THE COURT: Free to go.

20   The Government may call its next witness.

21   MS. WESLEY: Your Honor, we call Chief Corkrean. And

22 may I retrieve the evidence?

23   THE COURT: You may. And Chief Corkrean is the next

24 witness.

25 (Chief Corkrean enters the courtroom.)

This is page 232 line 25 and page 233 line 1 of my trial transcripts where it shows when prosecutor Zelda Wesley called special agent Mat Bassett to the witness stand it does not show that the court reporter placed on the record Mr. Bassett "enters the courtroom" as the court reporter placed on the record when the prosecutor called every other witness to the witness stand at my trial.

```
 1   was on August 2, 2017.

 2          MS. WESLEY:  May I have a moment, Your Honor?

 3          THE COURT:  Yes.

 4          MS. WESLEY:  I have no further questions of this

 5   witness, Your Honor.

 6          THE COURT:  All right.

 7      Cross-examination.

 8          MR. WALKER:  No questions, Your Honor.

 9          THE COURT:  Is the witness subject to recall?

10          MR. WALKER:  No, Your Honor.

11          THE COURT:  Thank you.

12      Chief Corkrean, you are excused as a witness and free to

13   go.  You're not subject to recall.

14          THE WITNESS:  Thank you.

15          MS. WESLEY:  Your Honor, we have one last witness who

16   is lengthy.

17          THE COURT:  All right. Can we get him started before

18   lunch?

19          MS. WESLEY:  Yes, Your Honor.

20          THE COURT:  Okay.  Thank you.

21          MS. WESLEY:  May we retrieve?

22          THE COURT:  We can retrieve the exhibits of the

23   witness who, I think, has them in his hand, can give them to

24   you.

25          MS. WESLEY:  Your Honor, we would call Special Agent
```

Page 233 line 1:

1 Matt Bassett.

2 THE COURT: All right.

3 Special Agent Bassett, if you'll approach the clerk,

4 she'll administer the oath to you before you take the witness

5 stand.

6 (MATT BASSETT WAS SWORN.)

7 THE CLERK: The witness is Special Agent Matt

8 Bassett. B-a-s-s-e-t-t.

9 DIRECT EXAMINATION

10 BY MS. WESLEY:

11 Q. Where do you presently work?

12 A. I am a Special Agent with the Bureau of Alcohol, Tobacco,

13 Firearms, and Explosives, commonly called ATF.

14 Q. And how long have you worked for the ATF?

15 A. Since July 2014.

16 Q. And what are your duties with the ATF?

17 A. I investigate violations of the federal firearms,

18 explosives, and narcotics laws.

19 Q. And in reference to Mr. Amanze Antoine, do you have any

20 information regarding whether or not he's a prohibited person?

21 A. I do.

22 Q. Okay. And did you obtain a copy of a conviction?

23 A. Yes, I did. Two of them.

24 Q. Okay. Only in reference to the conviction for firearms, a

25 weapons possession charge, sir. Is that a conviction you

This is page 275 lines 11-16 of my trial transcripts showing you judge Keeley asked prosecutor Zelda Wesley at the ending of Ms. Wesley questioning Special agent Bassett on the witness stands "Is there anything further for witness special agent Bassett" and Ms. Wesley stated "no your honor," then judge Keeley stating to special agent Bassett "You may return to your seat" proving, special agent Bassett was called to the witness stand by the prosecutor from inside of the courtroom and this is the reason why the court reporter never stated on the record in my transcripts that he enters the courtroom when he was called to the witness stand like of all of the rest of the witnesses who were called to the witness stand by prosecutor Zelda Wesley.

(Next Page)

```
1   Q.   Agent, the firearms were in a suitcase, correct.

2   A.   They were.

3   Q.   And the firearms were registered to Tommy Calhoun,

4   correct?

5   A.   The term -- an ATF agent, we try to stay away from the use

6   of the term "registry."  However, the -- there is no national

7   firearms registry; however, the 4473, which is the basis for us

8   being able to trace the original retail purchaser, said "Tommy

9   Calhoun" for two of the three firearms.

10            MR. WALKER:  Thank you.

11            THE COURT:  All right.

12        Is there anything further for the witness?

13            MS. WESLEY:  No, Your Honor.

14            THE COURT:  All right.

15        Mr. Bassett, you may return to your seat.

16        The Government may call its next witness.

17            MS. WESLEY:  The Government rests, Your Honor.  And

18   may I retrieve the exhibits?

19            THE COURT:  All right.

20        Subject to a check of the exhibits, I know you checked

21   them carefully before lunch, the Government has rested.

22        All right.  Ladies and gentlemen, because the Government

23   has rested, that means it's not going to kick up its heels, but

24   it has completed its case-in-chief. That's the phrase we use

25   for that.  It's now necessary for me to take up some matters
```

This is page 271 lines 14-16 of my trial transcripts showing you my attorney asked special agent Bassett when he was on the witness stand " was he in the courtroom when Ms. Parker testified" and special agent Bassett response was "I was ."

```
 1   A.   At Cashland?

 2   Q.   Yes.

 3   A.   In Morgantown?  Yes.

 4   Q.   So that would have been a third, correct.

 5   A.   Yes.  Yes, that would be the third attempt.

 6   Q.   One on May 27th, correct?

 7   A.   Yes.

 8   Q.   One on June 5th, correct?

 9   A.   Yes.

10   Q.   And an attempt on June 6th, correct?

11   A.   Yes.

12   Q.   And the one on June 6th was with another individual?

13   A.   Yes.

14   Q.   Now, you were in the courtroom when Ms. Parker testified,

15   correct?

16   A.   I was.

17   Q.   And you heard me ask her how many attempts she made,

18   correct?

19   A.   Yes.

20   Q.   You heard me ask that -- her response being she only made

21   two attempts, correct?

22   A.   I believe that's -- yes.

23   Q.   But as the case agent, you know there were actually three

24   attempts, correct?

25   A.   There were two successful purchases and a third
```

This is the fifth Amendment of the United States Constitution.

Amendment V [1791]

No person shall be held to answer for a capital, or otherwise infamous crime, unless on a presentment or indictment of a Grand Jury, except in cases arising in the land or naval forces, or in the Militia, when in actual service in time of War or public danger; nor shall any person be subject for the same offence to be twice put in jeopardy of life or limb; nor shall be compelled in any criminal case to be a witness against himself, nor be deprived of life, liberty, or property, without due process of law; nor shall private property be taken for public use, without just compensation.

CHAPTER 38

BASTON CLAIM

The next issue on our Court's calendar is a "Baston Claim". I know most of you reading this book have no idea or clue what the legal term "Baston claim" means, so let me break it down to you so you will have a clear understanding what it means:

For starters, a Baston claim is an issue a person convicted of a crime after trial can raise to the Court of Appeals in the district they were convicted in. Again, the Court of Appeals is the Court that decides on a person's appeal after a person submits an appeal to this Court after he or she has been convicted. The Court of Appeals takes a Baston Claim very seriously and normally grants a person a new trial if that person can successfully prove to the court that a Baston claim occurred.

All Court of Appeals in every single district in the United States are "supposed to take a Baston Claim very serious because it's a serious issue. However the 4th Circuit Court of Appeal who heard and ruled on my appeal neglected to take this issue seriously when I raised it on my appeal and told me they could not review my Baston Claim because I was the one who raised the issue and not my attorney. **I SWEAR TO GOD THAT WAS THE REASON THE 4TH CIRCUIT COURT OF APPEALS GAVE ME FOR NOT REVIEWING MY BASTON CLAIM. NORMALLY THE COURT OF APPEAL IN ANY DISTRICT ARE SUPPOSED TO GRANT A PERSON A NEW TRIAL ACCORDING TO IF A PERSON SUCCESSFULLY PROVE TO THEM THAT A BASTON CLAIM OCCURRED. WHAT YOU WILL READ BELOW IS THE SAME EXACT THING I WROTE TO THE 4TH CIRCUIT COURT**

OF APPEALS ABOUT MY BASTON CLAIM ISSUE. AFTER READING IT PLEASE ASK YOURSELF DID I SUCCESSFULLY PROVE A BASTON CLAIM AND WAS THE COURT OF APPEAL FAIR OR BIAS FOR DENYING MY BASTON CLAIM.

WHAT EXACTLY IS A BASTON CLAIM?

A Baston claim is a claim stating that the prosecutor or an lawyer used a peremptory challenge (excluding a potential juror from becoming a juror for a trial) to exclude a juror from being a juror for a trial on the basis of their race, religion, disability, age, or any other discriminatory factors. My Baston Claim is not based on a person's race, religion, disability, or age. My Baston Claim falls under another discriminatory factors." Let me explain:

During my jury selection proceedings the prosecutor used a peremptory challenge to exclude a person from becoming a juror for my trial on the basis of "that person being unemployed and because that person was unemployed the prosecutor felt he was conducive for drug use." Excluding a person from becoming a juror for a trial because that person was unemployed is very discriminating and therefore is a "discriminatory factor" to exclude someone from becoming a juror for a trial. Do you agree? The second unfair thing the prosecutor said in this situation was to make an assumption because this person was unemployed it made him conducive for drug use. That was also a discriminating reason to exclude a person from becoming a juror for a trial. Do you agree? The prosecutor did not know or have any proof whether or not this person did drugs in his life nor did the prosecutor know the reason why this person was unemployed. Maybe this person got laid off from work which is something out of his control or may be this person got in a very bad car accident that prevented him from working. The point I am getting at is it was very unfair for the prosecutor to use a peremptory challenge to exclude a person from becoming a juror for my trial based on that person being unemployed. That is a very "discriminatory factor" to exclude a person from becoming a juror in a trial and should be applied under a "Baston Claim" because a Baston Claim in general has to do with the prosecutor or an attorney using a peremptory challenge to exclude a person from becoming a juror for a trial involving a "discriminatory factor."

THE PROOF:

I have included at the end of this section page 111 lines 2-22 of my jury selection transcripts on **page 236** in this book to show you that the prosecutor stated she excluded a person from becoming a juror for my trial because he was unemployed, and because he was unemployed she thought he was conducive for drug use.

1. Do you feel I have a Baston claim under "a discriminatory factor"?
2. I did not know because a person who is unemployed makes that person conducive for drug use, and it also makes that person disqualified to become an impartial Juror for a trial according to prosecutor Zelda Wesley. Do you agree with prosecutor Zelda Wesley?

YOU BE THE JUDGE!!

Court Is in Session....

Legal terms you will see in my jury selection transcripts I will give you the meaning to:

1. The Court - means the judge
2. Ms. Wesley is the prosecutor
3. Strike - means peremptory challenge or excluding a potential juror from becoming an actual juror in a trial.

TRANSCRIPTS OR OTHER DOCUMENTS YOU TO IN I REFFERRED THIS SECTION

PAGE 111 lines 2-22 of MY TRIAL TRANSCRIPTS which shows the reason why the prosecutor excluded a person for becoming a juror for my trial.

```
                                                                111

 1   Green.  David Mitchell.  Anastasia Shaffer.
 2         THE COURT:  All right.  Before we go further, may I
 3   see counsel and the defendant up here at the bench, please.
 4   (Sidebar.)
 5         THE COURT:  The government has struck Mr. Saunders.
 6   Is there any challenge to the strike?
 7         MR. WALKER:  No, Your Honor.
 8         THE COURT:  Okay.  I want to know what the mutual
 9   reason is for the strike.
10         MS. WESLEY:  Because he's unemployed.  There were two
11   jury -- two potential jurors who are unemployed, and I struck
12   them both.
13         THE COURT:  Okay.  Why is that a strike in this case?
14         MS. WESLEY:  Well, I typically strike people who are
15   not employed.  Sometimes I strike people who are unemployed and
16   who I think are conducive for drug use.  That's my reasons.
17         THE COURT:  Okay.  Does it have anything to do with
18   his race?
19         MS. WESLEY:  Oh, absolutely not.
20         THE COURT:  Okay.
21       Is there any challenge to the strike --
22         MR. WALKER:  No, Your Honor.
23         THE COURT:  -- based on what you've heard?
24         MR. WALKER:  No, Your Honor.
25         THE COURT:  Okay.  Thank you.

              Stacy Harlow, CVR-M/CM/RVR-M/RCP/RBC
       Post Office Box 969  Clarksburg, WV 26302-0969  (304)623-7154
```

The next issue on our Court's calendar today is a violation of Rule 24 of the Federal Rules of Criminal Procedures.

Rule 24 Trial juror (b) Peremptory challenges (2) of the Federal Rules Criminal Procedures states:

"During Jury selection the prosecutor has "6" peremptory challenges and (me) the defendant or defendants jointly have "10" peremptory challenges when the defendant is charged with a crime punishable by imprisonment of more than one year." I have included a copy of rule 24 at the end of this section on **page 242** in this book that was copied out of the Federal Rules of Criminal Procedures handbook itself.

Again, I know a lot of you may not understand the law or the meaning of legal terms used in law books and courtroom so I will breakdown the meaning of the law above so you can get a clear understanding of it before I move on to explain how this rule was violated by the judge, the prosecutor, and my attorney. What Rule 24 means is the prosecutor gets 6 peremptory challenges and my attorney, and I get 10 peremptory challenges during jury selection. As I explained in this book peremptory challenges means the judge gives the prosecutor and my attorney the opportunity to remove a potential juror from becoming a juror for a trial without having to express any reason for it. The only exception with using a peremptory challenge is it cannot be used to exclude a person from becoming a juror for a trial based on a person's race, religion, age, disability, or any other discriminatory factors.

THE VIOLATION OF RULE 24 of the Federal Rule Criminal Procedures:

Rule 24 was violated because the judge gave the prosecutor 10 peremptory challenges and not the 6 that the law "only" allows the prosecutor to receive. Because of this I feel the jury selection process was tainted therefore declaring my entire trial unfair. How did this violation of rule 24 make my trial unfair? Here's how, some of the extra peremptory challenges the prosecutor received that she was not supposed to receive according to rule 24 was used to exclude people from becoming jurors in my trial who I wanted to be selected to become jurors in my trial. I felt for whatever reason after hearing them talk during "voir dire" that they were fair people and would be fair jurors to me if selected to be jurors in my trial, and base their verdict solely on the evidence being shown to them at my trial and not just find me guilty just because they could. The bottom line is the prosecutor was not supposed to get 10 peremptory challenges "ACCORDING TO THE LAW," and the judge was not supposed to allow that to happen in a courtroom. A judge is supposed to be the enforcer of all laws and rules in a courtroom, and not be blind to certain things that goes on inside of their courtroom like judge Irene Keeley did by giving the prosecutor more peremptory challenges than the law allows the prosecutor to receive. Do you agree?

THE PROOF:

Please look at page 109 lines 12-25, page 110 lines 12-25 and page 111 line 1 of my jury selection transcripts that I have included at the end of this section about this issue on **pages 243-245** in this book. These pages of my jury selection transcripts show the start and end of the peremptory challenge process done by my attorney and I along with the prosecutor. If you count all the names in total after all peremptory challenges were done by all parties which are on page 110 lines 18-25 and page 111 line 1 you will see it's a total of "20 names." It clearly shows "on the record" that more peremptory challenges were allowed that Rule 24 of the Federal Rules of Criminal Procedures permits. Again rule 24 of the federal rules of criminal procedures states the prosecutor gets 6 peremptory challenges and my attorney and I get 10 peremptory challenges during jury selection which is a total of "16 peremptory challenges that rule 24 allows. So why do you see in my jury selection transcripts 20 names were picked in total at the conclusion of the peremptory challenge process? The answer to that is because the prosecutor received 4 extra peremptory challenges that she was not supposed to receive according to Rule 24 of the Federal Rule of Criminal and Procedures. I remember as if it was yesterday me saying to my attorney during jury selection, "why is the judge giving the prosecutor more peremptory challenges than rule 24 permits?" Because believe you me I was counting them. My attorney's answer to me was "Shhhhhhhhhhhhhhhh, shut the fuck up in a low tone like he normally did when he did not want others to hear him in the courtroom." I remember that shit like it happened yesterday and I am still angry like that shit happened yesterday because I know in so many angles I did not get the justice I was supposed to receive in judge Keeley's courtroom according to law.

The worst part about this situation is the judge who is supposed to be fair to both sides allowed this to happen in her courtroom. Even though the judge knew what rule 24 states she still did not follow it. That shows you what type of person the judge is which is not a fair one. By the judge allowing this to happen in her courtroom she broke "**MANY CANON JUDICIAL ETHIC RULES**" that all judges in the United States are "obligated" to follow. And these "**CANON JUDICIAL ETHIC RULES**" the judge violated are the 3rd, 4th, and 5th "**CANON JUDICIAL RULES**" that are in the Canon Judicial Ethic Rulebook that I have included in the back of this section on **page 246** in this book. One by one I will give you each of the Ethic rules the judge violated and tell you what it states.

The 3rd Canon Judicial Ethic Rule titled "Constitutional Obligations" states:

"It is the duty of all judges in the United States to support the federal constitution and that the state whose laws they administer; in so doing they should fearlessly observe and apply fundamental limitation and guarantees.

The 4th Canon Judicial Ethic Rule titled "Avoidance of Impropriety" states:

"A judge's official conduct should be free from impropriety and the appearance of impropriety; he should avoid infractions of law; and his personal behavior, not only upon the bench and in the performance of Judicial duties but also in his everyday life should be beyond reproach."

And lastly 5th Canon Judicial Ethic Rule titled "Essential Conduct" states:

" A judge should be temperate, attentive, patient impartial and since he is to administer the law and apply it to the facts, he should be studious of the principles of the law and diligent in endeavoring to ascertain facts."

QUESTIONS FOR THE READERS:

1. Do you feel the judge violated any of the three Canon Judicial Ethic Rules I listed above that all judges throughout the United States are "obligated" to follow? If so which ones? And how?

2. Do you feel by the prosecutor receiving four extra peremptory challenges made my jury selection proceedings and trial unfair? If so, how?

3. Do you think my attorney should have spoken up for me and ask the judge why is she giving the prosecutor more peremptory challenges that Rule 24 allows when I brought it to my attorney's attention?

4. Do you feel prosecutors and judges should face consequences when they do not follow laws and rules out of the Federal Rules of Criminal Procedures Rulebook? If so, what should their consequence be?

5. Did you see anything wrong with the judge allowing the prosecutor to receive 4 extra peremptory challenges? Why?

YOU BE THE JUDGE!!

Court Is in Session...

Legal terms you may need to understand in this section:

1. Government - means prosecutor

2. Voir dire – means when a potential Juror is asked questions by either the judge, prosecutor, or an attorney to figure out if the person would be an impartial Juror if selected to be a Juror in a trial. Also during the Voir dire process all questions asked to the person must be answered truthfully.

3. While reading page 109 of my Jury selection transcripts you will see the word "strikes." Strikes is just another way of saying "peremptory challenges."

TRANSCRIPTS OR OTHER DOCUMENTS I REFFERRED YOU TO IN THIS SECTION

This is a copy of Rule 24 out of the Federal Rules of Criminal Procedures Handbook that all lawyers, prosecutors and judges are "obligated" to follow. This rule is showing you the prosecutor has 6 peremptory challenges during jury selection and my attorney and I have 10 peremptory challenges during jury selection.

Rule 24. Trial Jurors

(a) Examination.

(1) *In General.* The court may examine prospective jurors or may permit the attorneys for the parties to do so.

(2) *Court Examination.* If the court examines the jurors, it must permit the attorneys for the parties to:

(A) ask further questions that the court considers proper; or

(B) submit further questions that the court may ask if it considers them proper.

(b) **Peremptory Challenges.** Each side is entitled to the number of peremptory challenges to prospective jurors specified below. The court may allow additional peremptory challenges to multiple defendants, and may allow the defendants to exercise those challenges separately or jointly.

(1) *Capital Case.* Each side has 20 peremptory challenges when the government seeks the death penalty.

(2) *Other Felony Case.* The government has 6 peremptory challenges and the defendant or defendants jointly have 10 peremptory challenges when the defendant is charged with a crime punishable by imprisonment of more than one year.

(3) *Misdemeanor Case.* Each side has 3 peremptory challenges when the defendant is charged with a crime punishable by fine, imprisonment of one year or less, or both.

USCSRULE   1

These are pages 109 lines 12-25, page 110 lines 12-25 and page 111 line 1 of my jury selection transcript showing you the prosecutor was given more peremptory challenges than Rule 24 of the Federal Rules of Criminal Procedures allows.

1   THE COURT: Thank you. You can be seated.

2   Does the Government have any objection to the seating of

3   either of the jurors?

4   MS. WESLEY: No, Your Honor.

5   THE COURT: Does the defendant?

6   MR. WALKER: None, Your Honor.

7   THE COURT: All right.

8   Any final objections before I declare the panel qualified?

9   MS. WESLEY: Not from the Government.

10   MR. WALKER: None, Your Honor.

11   THE COURT: Thank you.

(12) Ladies and gentlemen, I declare the panel qualified and

(13) the counsel may take their strikes.

(14) Now, ladies and gentlemen, let me explain to you what is

(15) going to happen. Some of you may have -- be familiar with this

(16) from prior jury service, but the attorneys are now going to use

(17) a very low-tech version to take strikes. They have -- there's

(18) a board and there are cards with your names and your juror

(19) numbers on them, and the attorneys are going to review that and

(20) strike down from the jurors we currently have to a panel of 12

(21) main jurors and two alternates. So the -- you have 14 seats in

(22) the jury box and we're going to fill those seats.

(23) The Government and the defendant will go back and forth

(24) taking their strikes. This does take a few minutes, but I

(25) would expect that we will be finished, have the jury in place,

Stacy Harlow, CVR-M/CM/RVR-M/RCP/RBC
Post Office Box 969 Clarksburg, WV 26302-0969 (304)623-7154

Page 110 lines 12-25:

1 and those jurors who not have been selected free to go by noon.

2 Okay? So I appreciate your patience and, as I said, you're

3 sitting longer for this this morning than any juror will sit

4 during trial.

5 (Parties exercising strikes.)

6   THE COURT: Now ladies and gentlemen, just so long as

7 it's quietly and not about the case, you're free to discuss --

8 introduce yourself to your neighbors or to discuss any matter

9 you want to. No objection to you -- this isn't church. You

10 don't have to be absolutely quiet.

11 (Parties continuing to exercise strikes.)

12   THE COURT: Ladies and gentlemen, we're getting

13 close.

14 (Parties conclude exercising strikes.)

15   THE COURT: All right, ladies and gentlemen, please

16 attend to the clerk. As she calls your name, please leave your

17 seat and take a seat in the back of the courtroom.

18   THE CLERK: Kelly Sanders. Briana Rodriguez.

19 Raymond Hudson. John Roberts. Christy Thomas. Jonathan

20 Saunders. Joseph Kurczak. Pamela Lambert. James Allen.

21 Michelle Muckleroy. Cindy Hutton. Daniel Brown. William Hays.

22 Christina Minor. Amy Edmond.

23   THE COURT: You-all can fill in the other side of the

24 courtroom as well.

25   THE CLERK: Cory Oleska. Anthony Nastasi. James

Page 111 line 1:

1 Green. David Mitchell. Anastasia Shaffer.

2   THE COURT: All right. Before we go further, may I

3 see counsel and the defendant up here at the bench, please.

4 (Sidebar.)

5   THE COURT: The government has struck Mr. Saunders.

6 Is there any challenge to the strike?

7   MR. WALKER: No, Your Honor.

8   THE COURT: Okay. I want to know what the mutual

9 reason is for the strike.

10   MS. WESLEY: Because he's unemployed. There were two

11 jury -- two potential jurors who are unemployed, and I struck

12 them both.

13   THE COURT: Okay. Why is that a strike in this case?

14   MS. WESLEY: Well, I typically strike people who are

15 not employed. Sometimes I strike people who are unemployed and

16 who I think are conducive for drug use. That's my reasons.

17   THE COURT: Okay. Does it have anything to do with

18 his race?

19   MS. WESLEY: Oh, absolutely not.

20   THE COURT: Okay.

21   Is there any challenge to the strike --

22   MR. WALKER: No, Your Honor.

23   THE COURT: -- based on what you've heard?

24   MR. WALKER. No, Your Honor.

25   THE COURT: Okay. Thank you.

These are a copy of the 3rd, 4th and 5th Canon Judicial Ethic rules copied out of the Canon Judicial Ethic rulebook pinpointing 3 ethical rules all judges in every single courtroom in the United States are "obligated" to follow.

CANONS OF JUDICIAL ETHICS *
With Amendments to January 1, 1968

Ancient Precedents

"And I charged your judges at that time, saying Hear the causes between your brethren. and judge righteously between every man and his brother, and the stranger that is with him.

"Ye shall not respect persons in judgment; but ye shall hear the small as well as the great; ye shall not be afraid of the face of man; for the judgment is God's; and the cause that is too hard for you, bring it unto me, and I wil hear it."—*Deuteronomy*, I, 16–17.

"Thou shalt not wrest judgment; thou sha't not respect persons, neither take a gift; for a gift doth blind the eyes of the wise, and pervert the words of the righteous."—*Deuteronomy*, XVI, 19.

"We will not make any justiciaries, constables, sheriffs or bailiffs, but from those who understand the law of the realm and are well disposed to observe it."—*Magna Charta*, XLV.

"Judges ought to remember that their office is *jus dicere* not *jus dare*; to interpret law, and not to make law, or give law." . . .

"Judges ought to be more learned than witty; more reverend than plausible; and more advised than confident. Above all things, integrity is their portion and proper virtue." . . .

"Patience and gravity of hearing is an essential part of justice; and an over speaking judge is no well-tuned cymbal. It is no grace to a judge first to find that which he might have heard in due time from the Bar, or to show quickness of conceit in cutting off evidence or counsel too short; or to prevent information by questions though pertinent."

"The place of justice is a hallowed place; and therefore not only the Bench, but the foot pace and precincts and purprise thereof ought to be preserved without scandal and corruption." . . —*Bacon's Essay "Of Judicature."*

Preamble.

In addition to the Canons for Professional Conduct of Lawyers which it has formulated and adopted, the American Bar Association, mindful

* These Canons, to and including Canon 34, were adopted by the American Bar Association at its Forty-Seventh Annual Meeting, at Philadelphia, Pennsylvania, on July 9, 1924. The Committee of the Association which prepared the Canons was appointed in 1922, and composed of the following: William H. Taft, District of Columbia, Chairman; Leslie C. Cornish, Maine; Robert von Moschzisker Pennsylvania; Charles A Bosun, New York; and Garret W. McEnerney, California. George Sutherland, of Utah, originally a member of the Committee, retired and was succeeded by Mr. McEnerney. In 1923, Frank M. Angellotti, of California, took the place of Mr. McEnerney.
Canons 28 and 30 were amended at the Fifty-Sixth Annual Meeting, Grand Rapids, Michigan, August 30–September 1, 1933. Canon 28 was further amended at the Seventy-Third Annual Meeting, Washington, D. C., September 20, 1950. Canons 35 and 36 were adopted at the Sixtieth Annual Meeting, at Kansas City, Missouri, September 30, 1937. Canon 35 was amended at San Francisco, Calif., Sept. 1952.

that the character and conduct of a judge should never be objects of indifference, and that declared ethical standards tend to become habits of life, deems it desirable to set forth its views respecting those principles which should govern the personal practice of members of the judiciary in the administration of their office. The Association accordingly adopts the following Canons, the spirit of which it suggests as a proper guide and reminder for judges, and as indicating what the people have a right to expect from them.

1. Relations of the Judiciary.

The assumption of the office of judge casts upon the incumbent duties in respect to his personal conduct which concern his relation to the state and its inhabitants, the litigants before him, the principles of law, the practitioners of law in his court, and the witnesses, jurors and attendants who aid him in the administration of its functions.

2. The Public Interest.

Courts exist to promote justice, and thus to serve the public interest. Their administration should be speedy and careful. Every judge should at all times be alert in his rulings and in the conduct of the business of the court, so far as he can, to make it useful to litigants and to the community. He should avoid unconsciously falling into the attitude of mind that the litigants are made for the courts instead of the courts for the litigants.

3. Constitutional Obligations.

It is the duty of all judges in the United States to support the federal Constitution and that of the state whose laws they administer; in so doing, they should fearlessly observe and apply fundamental limitations and guarantees.

4. Avoidance of Impropriety.

A judge's official conduct should be free from impropriety and the appearance of impropriety; he should avoid infractions of law; and his personal behavior, not only upon the Bench and in the performance of judicial duties, but also in his everyday life, should be beyond reproach.

5. Essential Conduct.

A judge should be temperate, attentive, patient, impartial, and, since he is to administer the law and apply it to the facts, he should be studious of the principles of the law and diligent in endeavoring to ascertain the facts.

6. Industry.

A judge should exhibit an industry and application commensurate with the duties imposed upon him.

CHAPTER 39

TODAY'S ISSUE

Today's issue on our Court's calendar is whether or not there was enough evidence to convict me after trial for receiving firearms from individuals unlawfully in West Virginia, trafficking those firearms to New York from West Virginia, and distributing crack cocaine in the Northern District of West Virginia.

Let us first talk about the distributing crack cocaine charge, AKA 21 U.S.C Section 846 and 841 (b) (1) (c) which is the statute of this charge and how it looks in law books. According to the judge's instruction to the jury of my trial for them to find me guilty of this charge the prosecutor must prove the following elements beyond a reasonable doubt:

1. One, two, or more people agreed to possess cocaine base, also known as "Crack" with the intent to distribute. Two, the person charged with this crime had to know of the conspiracy, and three the person charged with this crime knowingly and voluntarily became part of the conspiracy.

2. The phrase "to distribute" means to deliver or to transfer possession or control of something from one person to another. The phrase "to distribute" includes the sale of some thing by one person to another.

3. The term "knowingly" means voluntarily and intentionally. A person acts knowingly when he or she is conscious and aware of his or her actions and does not act because of mistake or accident. Knowledge may be proven by the defendant's conduct and words, and by all the facts and circumstances surrounding the case.

THE PROOF:

I have included page 326 of my trial transcripts in this section on **page 254** speaking about this issue. This page of my trial transcripts shows "exactly what judge Keeley told the jury of my trial what the prosecutor needed to prove beyond a reasonable doubt in order for them to find me guilty of conspiracy to distribute crack cocaine in the Northern District of West Virginia. Now that you understand what the prosecutor needed to prove beyond a reasonable doubt to prove I was guilty of this crime let us move forward.

WHAT ABOUT ME BEING FOUND GUILTY ON THIS CHARGE DOES NOT MAKE SENSE OR ADD UP:

I was never found with crack cocaine. I was never caught selling any crack cocaine nor were the people I allegedly distributed crack cocaine to ever found in possession of crack cocaine. So I do not understand how I was even charged with distributing crack cocaine never mind being convicted of it after trial. I want you to completely understand this so I am going to break it down in a way so you can fully comprehend what I am trying to convey to you. If someone is being charged for distributing crack cocaine that person should have been caught distributing it, correct? Yes, that is correct. That is the only thing that makes sense. You get charged with what you were caught doing.

Also for a person to get charged with distributing crack cocaine, actual crack cocaine should be "actually" found on either the person allegedly selling it or on the person allegedly buying it to prove that crack cocaine was "actually" intended to be sold or distributed. Does that make sense? It does to me!

Distributing crack cocaine can also be proven by text messages or if your phone is being tapped into, and agents or police officers are listening to your conversation and hear you discussing the distribution of crack cocaine. Distributing crack cocaine can also be proven through a video recording showing you actually distributing crack cocaine. Correct? Definitely correct!!

If no crack cocaine was ever found or seen in my possession EVER or in the possession of the alleged person the prosecutor claims I sold or distributed crack cocaine to I do not understand how could the prosecutor Zelda Wesley even charge me with distributing crack cocaine in the first place. There were no recorded phone conversations or phone texts of me discussing the distribution of crack cocaine nor was there any video recordings showing me distributing crack cocaine. So again I do not understand how Zelda Wesley (the prosecutor) could even charge me with the crime of distributing crack cocaine.

For starters **"WHERE IS THE ACTUAL EVIDENCE OF DISTRIBUTING CRACK COCAINE WHICH IS THE "ACTUAL" CRACK COCAINE ITSELF!!!"** Does that make sense? It damn sure does!! Why does it make sense? It makes sense because how would a prosecutor know what type of distributing drug charge to give a person if no drugs were ever found? In order for a prosecutor to charge a person for distributing a certain type of drug would it be safe to say that certain type of drug needs to actually be found on the allege distributor of that drug or on the person this drug was allegedly distributed to? Would it?

I did not hear your answer, so I am going to ask you again. Would it be safe to say in order for a prosecutor to charge a person with distributing crack cocaine, there must have been crack cocaine found on either the alleged seller or buyer of the crack cocaine? But not only found!! Once found it must be sent to a scientific laboratory in order for it to get tested to know exactly what drug it is which is the proper procedure that is supposed to be taken in order for a prosecutor to charge a person for distributing a certain type of drug. How else would a prosecutor know what type of drug to charge a person for distributing if what is found they claim is a drug is not tested to see what drug it actually is.

For those of you who still do not get the point I am trying to make let me break it down to you this way. For a doctor to diagnose a person with **COVID**-19 that doctor must test that person for it. True or not true? True! How else would a doctor know if a person has **COVID**-19 if that person did not actually go into the doctor's office and get tested for it and the results of that test was positive. There is no other way a doctor could find out if his or her client has **COVID**-19 or not. The only way is through a laboratory test. Besides that a doctor would never "actually" know if a client has **COVID**-19 or not. True or not true? True! So with that being said how could a prosecutor charge a person for distributing crack cocaine if no drugs were ever found let alone brought to a scientific laboratory to be tested to see if what this person was allegedly selling was actually crack cocaine in order to charge that person for distributing crack cocaine? Rather the question I should have asked you was how could a West Virginia Federal Prosecutor charge me with distributing crack cocaine if no crack cocaine or nothing that looks like crack cocaine was ever found on me or on the alleged people I allegedly distributed crack cocaine to even take to a laboratory to get tested, let alone to even get charged with distributing crack cocaine? What the fuck is the prosecutor a fucking psychic or something? I think the prosecutor is a psychic. I think her name is Ms. Cleo because her psychic reading is off as fuck!! I am not even trying to be funny. I am being extremely serious because I do not understand how the prosecutor could charge me with the crime of distributing crack cocaine when crack cocaine was never actually found on me or the allege people I supposedly distributed it to.

Everything I just explained above is **"EXACTLY"** what happened to me. I was charged and convicted after trial for distributing crack cocaine and I never "not once" was found in possession of crack cocaine or the people I allegedly distributed it to. So how and why was I even charged for distributing crack cocaine in the first place is the question I have been trying to find the answer to for years. What prosecutor Zelda Wesley calls me being guilty of distributing crack cocaine is calling 3 witnesses to the witness stand at my trial and had them lie and tell the Jury of my trial I distributed crack cocaine to them despite the fact crack cocaine was never found ever!! There was no actual proof of me distributing crack cocaine and I was still convicted at trial. This makes me frustrated and very very very upset!! In order for me to be found guilty and convicted of this charge at trial according to the judge's instructions to the jury of my trial as you read it on page 326 of my trial transcripts the prosecutor had to prove "beyond a reasonable doubt" I possessed crack cocaine and made a sale of it to another person. If no crack cocaine was ever found in my possession or on the alleged people I distributed it to nor was I ever caught making a sale of crack cocaine to another person how could that be proven beyond a reasonable doubt by prosecutor Zelda Wesley of West Virginia? **IT CAN'T!!!!!!** That is the bottom-line point-blank period!! Do you agree? If you don't agree, what you are saying is anyone could go to federal agents or other law enforcement and tell them can someone distributed drugs to them and without any proof of this happening the person who allegedly distributed this drug to them get charged for it, and get convicted at trial of it based on someone saying that person distributed drugs to them without any proof of any drugs being distributed or without there being drugs found on the alleged seller or buyer which is exactly what happened to me. **THAT IS NOT JUSTICE!! THAT IS INJUSTICE!!** Please look at page 274 lines 1-4 of my trial transcripts that I have included at the end of this section about this issue on **page 255.** That page of my trial transcripts shows when my attorney asked special agent Bassett when he was on the witness stand were there any drugs recovered on any of the people involved in this case and special agent Bassett response was no. There goes your proof right there that no drugs were ever recovered in my case from anyone which includes me or the allege people the prosecutor claims I distributed crack cocaine to.

Now let's move on to the charges of me allegedly receiving firearms from individuals in West Virginia unlawfully and allegedly trafficking those firearms to New York then, selling them according to prosecutor Zelda Wesley. Please review pages 59 lines 13-25 and page 60 line 1 of my trial transcripts I have included in the back of this section on **pages 256 and 257** showing you the above statement is exactly what prosecutor Zelda Wesley told the jury of my trial I did.

WHAT DOES NOT MAKE SENSE OR ADD UP ABOUT THESE CHARGES:

I was never seen or caught receiving any firearms from anyone in the state of West Virginia, and I was never found in possession of or caught with any of the firearms the prosecutor claims were given to me by individuals in West Virginia. I was also never caught trafficking any firearms to New York from West Virginia and I was never caught selling any firearms to individuals nor were any of the firearms the prosecutor claims I trafficked to New York was ever found or recovered in New York on anyone so I do not understand how could the prosecutor even charge me with these firearm charges if none of what I just explained above happened.

Like the same as the crack distribution charge, what the prosecutor calls proving I was guilty of these firearm charges was by putting 3 individuals on the witness stand at my trial and have them lie to the jury of my trial stating they bought and gave me firearms that I trafficked to New York and sold to individuals once they made its way into the New York area. There was no actual proof proving I did these crimes, just individuals coming on the witness stand at my trial stating I did all and that was enough to get me convicted at trial. **THAT IS NOT JUSTICE!! THAT IS NOT FAIR!! THAT IS EXTREMELY UNJUST!!** Actual proof of someone committing a crime is the only way a person should be initially charged with a crime and convicted at trial, not just because of what someone said a person did, who agrees? If you do agree with me you will learn the ACTION you can take further on in the book to help change this unfair court system in every state in the United States. It would be very appreciated not just by me but by so many people who went through or going through some type of injustice in the court system.

QUESTIONS FOR THE READERS:

1. Do you feel a person should be initially charged for distributing drugs just because someone said that person distributed drugs to them, when no drugs were found or recovered on the allege distributor or buyer?

2. Do you think it was fair for me to get convicted at trial for distributing crack cocaine when I was not found in possession of crack cocaine or caught selling crack cocaine to anyone?

3. Do you feel it was fair for me to get charged and convicted after trial for one, receiving firearms from individuals in West Virginia, for two, trafficking those allege firearms to New York if I was never seen or caught receiving firearms from anyone from West Virginia nor caught or seen trafficking any firearms to New York?

4. Do you think it was fair for me to get charged with being in possession of firearms when no firearms were ever found in my possession?

YOU BE THE JUDGE!!

Court Is in Session...

TRANSCRIPTS OR OTHER DOCUMENTS I REFFERRED TO YOU TO IN THIS SECTION

This is page 326 lines 6-19 of my trial transcripts showing you exactly what the judge said the prosecutor had to prove beyond a reasonable doubt in order for them to be able to find me guilty of distributing CRACK COCAINE

```
 1   pertinent part, that any person who attempts or conspires to
 2   commit any offense defined in this subchapter shall be subject
 3   to the same penalties as those prescribed for the offense, the
 4   commission of which was the object of the attempt or
 5   conspiracy.
 6       To find the defendant guilty of a conspiracy to possess
 7   cocaine base with the intent to distribute, as charged in Count
 8   Two of the Superseding Indictment, the Government must prove
 9   each of the following essential -- three elements, excuse me,
10   beyond a reasonable doubt:
11       One, two or more people agreed to possess cocaine base,
12   also known as "crack," with the intent to distribute.
13   Two, the defendant, Amanze Antoine, knew of the conspiracy;
14   and, three, defendant, Amanze Antoine, knowingly and
15   voluntarily became part of the conspiracy.
16       The phrase "to distribute" means to deliver or to transfer
17   possession or control of something from one person to another.
18   The phrase "to distribute" includes the sale of something by
19   one person to another.
20       As defined earlier, the term "knowingly" means voluntarily
21   and intentionally.  A person acts knowingly when he or she is
22   conscious and aware of his or her actions, and does not act
23   because of mistake or accident.  Knowledge may be proved by the
24   defendant's conduct and words, and by all the facts and
25   circumstances surrounding the case.
```

Stacy Harlow, CVR-M/CM/RVR-M/RCP/RBC
Post Office Box 969 Clarksburg, WV 26302-0969 (304)623-7154

This is page 274 lines 1-4 of my trial transcripts showing you my attorney Mr. Walker asking special agent Bassett were there any drugs found on anyone involved in this case and Mr. Bassett's response to that question was no.

1   Q.   You were asked about drugs being recovered from Mr.

2   Antoine. Were there drugs recovered from any of the defendants

3   who were charged in this case?

4   A.   No.

5   Q.   And that would include Margaret Parker, Tommy Calhoun, and

6   Chris Anderson; is that correct?

7   A.   My -- correct. My understanding is each one of them was

8   either arrested or served with a summons for court. And, to my

9   knowledge, I don't know of anyone having been found in

10 possession of controlled substances at the time of their arrest

11 or service.

12 Q.   Is that unusual if individuals are using controlled

13 substances?

14 A.   That is not unusual.

15 Q.   And in reference to Mr. Antoine being found in possession

16 of firearms, were their firearms in the vehicle that he was in?

17 A.   Yes.

18 Q.   Okay. And did he flee from that vehicle?

19 A.   He did.

20   MS. WESLEY: I have nothing further, Your Honor.

21   THE COURT: All right.

22 Further cross-examination.

23   MR. WALKER: Yes.

24   RECROSS EXAMINATION

25 BY MR. WALKER:

This is page 59 lines 13-25 and page 60 line 1 of my trial transcripts showing you prosecutor Zelda Wesley telling the jury of my trial I received firearms from individuals in the state of West Virginia and trafficked those firearms to the state of New York then sold them.

59

1   focal point of the investigation, because the focal point of

2   this investigation and the defendant's criminal enterprise is

3   firearms. The state of New York, and places in big cities in

4   New York, is a source of drug supply for West Virginia, meaning

5   that that's one of the locations where drugs are transported so

6   that they are distributed and used by users in West Virginia.

7   And, unfortunately for West Virginia, firearms is a source

8   location. And West Virginia guns is a source of supply in New

9   York. And basically what that means is that there's this thing

10 called a straw purchase, and you will hear about it. And that

11 is when people will purchase firearms not for themselves, but

12 for others, and that was what the defendant did.

13   The defendant deliberately, consciously made the choice to

14 find individuals in West Virginia who were addicted to

15 controlled substances. They had to be addicted and they could

16 not have a felony record. Therefore, they could purchase

17 firearms for him. And how did he get them to purchase these

18 firearms? Drugs, because of their addiction. He preyed upon

19 individuals who had drug addictions. And you will hear from

20 these people who he used. Although the Government will call

21 them as witnesses, they're his witnesses because they were the

22 people who he brings before you. They're the people who he

23 chose. They were the people who had drug addictions. They

24 were the people who did not have convictions so that they could

25 buy firearms for him that he can traffic back to New York and

Stacy Harlow, CVR-M/CM/RVR-M/RCP/RBC
Post Office Box 969 Clarksburg, WV 26302-0969 (304)623-7154

60

1 sell.

2   There were two individuals who trafficked in firearms with

3 him, and that is Margaret Parker and Tommy Calhoun. And you

4 will hear from them both. And just as important, you will see

5 the videos. You will see the videos from the businesses that

6 sold the firearms, and you will see Margaret Parker and Tommy

7 Calhoun purchase these firearms with the defendant coming in

8 and out of those stores making certain they did exactly what he

9 wanted them to do.

10   You will also hear the testimony of law enforcement

11 officers, in particular, Officer Junkins, because on one day in

12 particular, on June the 19th of 2017, the defendant went to

13 West Virginia Jewelry and Pawn Shop, which is in Westover, West

14 Virginia, with Tommy Calhoun, and purchased several firearms.

15 It was the defendant's intention, after purchasing those

16 firearms, to travel back to New York so that he could sell

17 those guns, but he was stopped with Tommy Calhoun in Tommy

18 Calhoun's truck in Star City, West Virginia. And as a result

19 of that traffic stop, the defendant fled, left, ran away from

20 the vehicle, got away from that scene, because in that vehicle

21 were the three firearms that he had, intending to take back to

22 New York to sell.

23   Tommy Calhoun will tell you that those were the firearms

24 that he had purchased that day for the defendant. The officer

25 will tell you that it was the defendant who fled. Most

257

CHAPTER 40

THE PROSECUTOR'S PROSECUTION!!

oday's issue on the Court's calendar is whether or not federal prosecutor Zelda Wesley violated certain ethical rules she is obligated to follow.

The prosecutor is responsible for achieving a "fair, efficient and effective enforcement of criminal law." Because the role of a prosecutor is so crucial to a fair system of Justice and because inevitable conflicts arise, the American Bar Association for Criminal Justice set Model Rules that address the conduct that all prosecutors are obligated to follow. These are not all the ethical rules a prosecutor is obligated to follow but the following ethical rules are the ethical rules I feel prosecutor Zelda Wesley violated. These rules paraphrased from the American Bar Association Rules of Professional Conduct, and related to the American Bar Association Standards for Criminal Justice that all prosecutors throughout the United State in all courtrooms whether state or federal are "obligated" to follow.

1. "It is unethical to bring charges the prosecutor knows are without sufficient admissible evidence or to seek charges greater in number or degree evidence will not reasonably support" (standard 3-3.9, Model Rule 3.8 (a)

2. "It is unethical intentionally to misrepresent facts or mislead the Court" (standard 3-2.9, Model Rule 3.3)

3. "It is unethical when addressing a jury to express opinion on the truth or falsity of evidence or guilt of a defendant." (standard 3-5.8, Model Rule 3.4)

HOW DID FEDERAL PROSECUTOR ZELDA WESLEY VIOLATE THE FIRST ETHICAL RULE ABOVE?

The first ethical rule above is basically saying it is unethical for a prosecutor to bring up charges on someone that the evidence does not reasonably support. With that being said the evidence did not reasonably support the prosecutor charging me with distributing crack cocaine because for one I was never found in possession of crack cocaine, for two I was never caught selling or distributing crack cocaine, and for three the people who the prosecutor claims I allegedly distributed crack cocaine to were never caught or found in possession with the crack cocaine the prosecutor alleged I distributed to them in order to show proof of crack cocaine being actually distributed to them. Not just being distributed to them but being distributed to them by me. The prosecutor did not have any video recordings of me distributing crack cocaine to these people she claimed I distributed crack cocaine to nor did the prosecutor have any other form of evidence of me distributing crack cocaine to "anyone" such as text messages or a recorded phone conversation of me discussing distributing crack cocaine. Therefore, there was no reasonable evidence to support the prosecutor charging me with distributing crack cocaine which the first ethical rule I stated on the prior page prohibits.

A QUESTION FOR THE READERS:

1. Do you think the prosecutor violated the first ethical rule by charging me with distributing crack cocaine when there is no reasonable evidence proving I did?

YOU BE THE JUDGE!!

Court Is In Session...

PART 2 OF THE CASE INVOLVING FEDERAL PROSECUTOR ZELDA WESLEY VIOLATING THE FIRST ETHICAL RULE:

I was charged with receiving firearms unlawfully from individuals from the state of West Virginia, and also charged with trafficking those firearms allegedly given to me in West Virginia to the State of New York. However, I was never seen or caught receiving any firearms from "anyone" in the state of West Virginia nor was I ever caught trafficking these allege firearms to New York allegedly given to me by individuals in West Virginia. None of these allege firearms the prosecutor claims were given to me by individuals in West Virginia were found or recovered in the state of New York where the prosecutor claims I trafficked and sold them too. in no time was I ever found in possession of this firearms the prosecutor claims individuals from West Virginia gave me.

A QUESTION FOR THE READERS:

1. Based on all the things I said above said do you feel federal prosecutor Zelda Wesley is in violation of the first ethical rule by her charging me with receiving firearms from individuals unlawfully and trafficking firearms to the state of New York when the evidence does not reasonable support her charging me with these charges? As a reminder the first ethical rule is below.

    "It is unethical to bring charges the prosecutor knows are without sufficient admissible evidence or to seek charges greater in number or degree evidence will not reasonably support" (standard 3-3.9, Model Rule 3.8 (a)

YOU BE THE JUDGE!!

Court Is in Session....

HOW DID THE PROSECUTOR VIOLATE THE 2ND ETHICAL RULE ABOVE?

During federal prosecutor Zelda Wesley's closing arguments at my trial which is a chance for the prosecutor to highlight key evidence and assist the jury in weighing and drawing inferences from that evidence before the jury decides their verdict. The prosecutor when addressing the jury during her closing arguments made two opinionated statements to the jury and these 2 opinionated statements made to the jury misrepresented the facts in my case, and mislead them which is not allowed in the second ethical rule I listed on a previous page that all prosecutors in the United States are "obligated" to follow.

The statements made by the prosecutor to the Jury of my trial that misrepresented the facts in my case and mislead the jury was, "I trafficked crack cocaine to West Virginia and distributed that crack cocaine in the Northern District of West Virginia." Also said out of the prosecutor's mouth during opening statements was " I received firearms from individuals from West Virginia and trafficked those firearms to New York, then sold them in New York." I have also included page 338 lines 3-5, page 59 lines 13-25 and page 60 line 1 of my trial transcripts at the end of this section on **pages 268 -270** in order for you to read yourself the prosecutor stating all of the above to the jury of my trial during her opening and closing statements to them. These two statements made by prosecutor Zelda Wesley were intentionally done to misrepresent the facts of my case and to mislead the jury which is again not allowed in the 2nd ethical rule I listed on a previous page. It was never proven to be a fact that I trafficked crack cocaine to West Virginia and distributed it in the Northern District of West Virginia because I was never caught doing such a thing and the same goes for me receiving firearms from individuals in West Virginia unlawfully and trafficking those alleged firearms to New York then selling them to individuals in New York. This was never proven because I was never seen or caught receiving any firearms from anyone in West Virginia nor caught trafficking any firearms from West Virginia to New York or was I caught selling any firearms to individuals in New York nor is anyone in New York claiming I sold them a firearm. None of these crimes I am being charged with were never actually proven to be a fact that I committed them based on the evidence not supporting the crime and the prosecutor knew that but still made those statements to the jury of my trial while addressing them during her closing statements just to intentionally misrepresent the facts of my case and to mis lead the jury which is again prohibited in the 2nd ethical rule I listed on a previous page that all prosecutors in the United States are **"OBLIGATED"** to follow.

A QUESTION FOR THE READERS:

1. After reading the above do you feel that prosecutor Zelda Wesley violated the 2nd ethical rule which then again states:

    "It is unethical intentionally to misrepresent facts or mislead the court." (standard 3-2.9 Model Rule 3.3)

YOU BE THE JUDGE!!

Court Is in Session....

PART 2 OF THE CASE INVOLVING FEDERAL PROSECUTOR ZELDA WESLEY IN VIOLATION OF THE 2nd ETHICAL RULE ABOVE:

Also during the prosecutor's closing arguments which is again a chance for the prosecutor to highlight key evidence and assist the jury in weighing and drawing inferences from that evidence before the jury decides their verdict. the prosecutor intentionally made another opinionated statement that misrepresented those facts of my case, and mislead the jury which is again not allowed in the 2nd ethical rule on a previous page. The opinionated statement made by the prosecutor Zelda Wesley to the Jury of my trial this time during closing arguments was "I gave Chris crack cocaine to redistribute and sell, and after Chris was done selling the drugs I allegedly gave to him to redistribute he wired me the money to New York using Western Union. This statement was made by prosecutor Zelda Wesley because she had Chris come on the witness stand at my trial and lie to the jury claiming he wired me money he made using Western Union after he was done redistributing the drugs I allegedly gave him to sell for me. I have included page 339 lines 1-8 of my trial transcripts on **page 271** showing you the prosecutor stating the above to the Jury of my trial during her opening and closing arguments. This statement like the rest of the statements made by the prosecutor during her closing arguments to the jury of my trial was intentionally done to misrepresent the facts of my case and to mislead the Jury which again is not allowed in the 2nd ethical rule   because it was never actually proven to be a fact that Chris actually sent me money using Western Union, and this could have easily been proven if it really happened. Here's how, Western Union keeps in order to maintain a record of all transaction done through their company!! The prosecutor could have easily contacted whoever she had to contact in Western Union and get a printout or copy of this allege Western Union transaction sent by Chris from West Virginia to New York that was allegedly sent to me because Western Union keeps a paper trail of all transactions ever made in their company's personal records. That could have simply been obtained by the prosecutor to show to the jury of my trial that Chris "actually" sent money to me using Western Union to New York from West Virginia but the prosecutor neglected to do so. A person actually sending someone money through Western Union has to show identification before he or she is able to send money to someone using Western Union and their name is kept on western union's records as "the sender," and the person sending the money also must give the name of the person he or she is sending the money too which is also on Western Union's transactions records. Correct? Yes! And the person who picks up the money that was sent to him or her through Western Union "must" show identification to receive the money sent to him or her. Correct? Yes, correct! So why didn't prosecutor Zelda Wesley contact Western Union and tell them to send her an actual printout of this transaction allegedly made by Chris to me and show it to the jury of my trial which could have been easily obtained had the prosecutor contacted western Union and request it. But why was this not done by the prosecutor! I know the answer to that, **BECAUSE IT DID NOT**

HAPPEN, THAT'S WHY IT WAS NOT DONE BY THE PROSECUTOR!!

If Chris really did send me money through Western Union it's not a prosecutor breathing who would not have contacted Western Union before trial actual started to get a copy of this transaction on paper to show it to the jury of my trial to prove this transaction actually occurred. Does that sound like what any prosecutor alive would have done?

The statement made by the prosecutor during her closing arguments about Chris wiring me money to New York was clearly intentionally done to misrepresent the facts of my case and to mislead the jury (which again the 2nd ethical rule prohibits) because it was never proven to be a fact. In order for that statement to not misrepresent the facts of my case and mislead the jury it had to be proven that Chris actually sent me money through Western Union. That was never proven. Just because Chris and the prosecutor states it happened at my trial that does not "actually" prove that it happened. In order for it to have been "actually" proven Chris sent money to me through Western Union," all the prosecutors had to do was make a simple phone call to Western Union to obtain the actual physical printout of this transaction the prosecutor and Chris claims happened that Western Union I am sure would have records of, and show it to the jury of my trial. That would have proven that transaction to be an actual fact. Then and only if the prosecutor would have made that statement to the jury during her closing argument about Chris wiring me money that would it had not misrepresented the facts of my case and mislead the jury because it would had been proven a fact that he "actually did." There was no other way to prove that Chris actually wired money to me other than getting the actual paperwork from Western Union verifying that this transaction actually happened or by getting the video footage that was captured on the surveillance cameras that all Western Unions have in all their stores showing Chris sending me money through Western Union and the video footage of me picking the money up which easily could of been obtained by the prosecutor had she requested this from Western Union in order to show it in the jury of my trial but it was not. Why?

BECAUSE THIS WESTERN UNION TRANSACTION DID NOT HAPPEN, THAT'S WHY!!!!!!!

A QUESTION FOR THE READERS:

1. Do you think Federal Prosecutor Zelda Wesley violated the 2nd ethical rule above when she misrepresented the facts of my case and mislead the jury of my trial when she stated during closing arguments to them Chris wired me money even though that was never actually proven to be a fact?

YOU BE THE JUDGE!!

Court Is in Session...

HOW DID PROSECUTOR ZELDA WESLEY VIOLATE THE 3RD ETHICAL RULE? AS A REMINDER THE 3RD ETHICAL RULE ABOVE STATES:

"It is unethical when addressing a jury to express opinion on the truth or falsity of evidence or guilt of a defendant." (standard 3 -5.8, Model Rule 3.4).

I have explained, Prosecutor Zelda Wesley when addressing the jury during her closing arguments expressed opinions on what she wanted the jury to believe was the truth about my guilt on these charges. Again the prosecutor's statements to the jury of my trial during her closing arguments were I trafficked crack cocaine to West Virginia, and distributed it in the Northern District of West Virginia and I also received firearms from individuals, from West Virginia unlawfully then trafficked those firearms to New York then sold them to individuals along with Chris wiring me money to New York once he sold all the drugs I allegedly gave to him to redistribute. Again all of these statements said by the prosecutor during closing arguments was never proven to be a fact therefore, those statements made by the prosecutor was opinions on the truth that she expressed to the jury of my trial when addressing them during closing arguments which is not allowed in the 3rd ethical rule. Those statements made by the prosecutor during closing arguments were inaccurate and falsified the guilt of me breaking the law which is also prohibited in the 3rd ethical rule.

QUESTION FOR THE READERS:

1. Is Prosecutor Zelda Wesley guilty or not guilty for violating the 3rd ethical rule?

YOU BE THE JUDGE!!

Court Is in Session....

A Legal term you may need the meaning of in this section of **YOU BE THE JUDGE**:

1. Defendant - means the person being charged with a crime.

TRANSCRIPTS OR OTHER DOCUMENTS I REFFERRED YOU TO IN THIS SECTION

These are pages 338 lines 3-5, page 59 lines 13-25 and page 60 line 1 of my trial transcripts showing prosecutor Zelda Wesley intentionally misrepresenting the facts of my case which is not allowed in the 2nd ethical rule I listed in the section. These are also the same pages of my trial transcripts that shows prosecutor Zelda Wesley telling the Jury of my trial " I received firearms from individuals in the state of West Virginia, and then I trafficked those firearms to New York and sold them.

(Next Page)

1 it's his conspiracy. That means that Chris Anderson worked for
2 him. He was the one who brought the crack cocaine from New
3 York to West Virginia, with the exclusive purpose of having
4 that crack cocaine distributed in the Northern District of West
5 Virginia.
6   Let's talk about the bus depot. It's interesting because
7 sometimes people don't necessarily understand how things work
8 unless they're a part of it. And how you understand how that
9 whole scenario worked was Margaret Parker, who testified that
10 the bus depot, where it was located in Morgantown, was close to
11 the Rails Trails. So it was easy for people to get in and out;
12 it was easy to run away if cops showed up. It was a hub, a
13 central location at that time in Morgantown for distributing
14 crack cocaine. And what's also interesting about that location
15 is that is where the two first players met. That is where
16 Amanze Antoine first met Chris Anderson. It was at this bus
17 depot. Chris Anderson told you "I'd never known him before.
18 I'm there to get crack, and I need him." And from that very
19 first beginning, they created a relationship. That
20 relationship was that -- for him to provide him with crack
21 cocaine and he was going to provide him with a place to live.
22 That was how it started, and Chris Anderson would be paid in
23 crack cocaine for the privilege of giving him a place to live
24 while he was in West Virginia.
25   That is where it started but that's not, certainly, where

This is page 59 lines 13-25 and page 60 line 1 of my trial transcripts showing you Prosecutor Zelda Wesley telling the jury of my trial I received firearms from individuals in the state of West Virginia and trafficked those firearms to the state of New York, and then sold them.

1   focal point of the investigation, because the focal point of

2   this investigation and the defendant's criminal enterprise is

3   firearms. The state of New York, and places in big cities in

4   New York, is a source of drug supply for West Virginia, meaning

5   that that's one of the locations where drugs are transported so

6   that they are distributed and used by users in West Virginia.

7   And, unfortunately for West Virginia, firearms is a source

8   location. And West Virginia guns is a source of supply in New

9   York. And basically what that means is that there's this thing

10   called a straw purchase, and you will hear about it. And that

11   is when people will purchase firearms not for themselves, but

12   for others, and that was what the defendant did.

13   The defendant deliberately, consciously made the choice to

14   find individuals in West Virginia who were addicted to

15   controlled substances. They had to be addicted and they could

16   not have a felony record. Therefore, they could purchase

17   firearms for him. And how did he get them to purchase these

18   firearms? Drugs, because of their addiction. He preyed upon

19   individuals who had drug addictions. And you will hear from

20   these people who he used. Although the Government will call

21   them as witnesses, they're his witnesses because they were the

22   people who he brings before you. They're the people who he

23   chose. They were the people who had drug addictions. They

24   were the people who did not have convictions so that they could

25   buy firearms for him that he can traffic back to New York and

269

1 sell.

2   There were two individuals who trafficked in firearms with

3 him, and that is Margaret Parker and Tommy Calhoun. And you

4 will hear from them both. And just as important, you will see

5 the videos. You will see the videos from the businesses that

6 sold the firearms, and you will see Margaret Parker and Tommy

7 Calhoun purchase these firearms with the defendant coming in

8 and out of those stores making certain they did exactly what he

9 wanted them to do.

10   You will also hear the testimony of law enforcement

11 officers, in particular, Officer Junkins, because on one day in

12 particular, on June the 19th of 2017, the defendant went to

13 West Virginia Jewelry and Pawn Shop, which is in Westover, West

14 Virginia, with Tommy Calhoun, and purchased several firearms.

15 It was the defendant's intention, after purchasing those

16 firearms, to travel back to New York so that he could sell

17 those guns, but he was stopped with Tommy Calhoun in Tommy

18 Calhoun's truck in Star City, West Virginia. And as a result

19 of that traffic stop, the defendant fled, left, ran away from

20 the vehicle, got away from that scene, because in that vehicle

21 were the three firearms that he had, intending to take back to

22 New York to sell.

23   Tommy Calhoun will tell you that those were the firearms

24 that he had purchased that day for the defendant. The officer

25 will tell you that it was the defendant who fled. Most

This is page 339 lines 1-8 of my trial transcripts showing you Prosecutor Zelda Wesley telling the jury of my to trial Chris wired me money to New York using Wester Union even though there was never proven to be a fact that Chris did.

1 it ended because it went from there to Chris Anderson being a
2 middleman for him. That meant that he was dealing crack
3 cocaine for him. And then it went even further. It went from
4 him dealing his crack cocaine, to when this man was out of
5 town, to Chris Anderson being fronted. And he explains to you
6 that that meant that the defendant gave him crack cocaine for
7 him to redistribute and sell, and that he would wire the money
8 back to him while he was in New York.
9   And then we can bring in Tommy Calhoun, who testified that
10 what he did was he would drive Chris Anderson and Amanze
11 Antoine to various locations, usually at a bus depot, and he
12 would wait for them while they would distribute crack cocaine.
13 It wasn't something that was sporadic. It was a regular and
14 continuous business that happened all the time. They had
15 regular customers. They sold from the bus depot. In addition
16 to that, they would sell from Chris Anderson's residence, which
17 was T and S Rentals, somewhere in Morgantown. It is clear,
18 abundantly clear from the evidence, that Chris Anderson and the
19 defendant conspired to distribute crack cocaine.
20   The crack cocaine business does not end with just
21 distribution because crack cocaine is a currency. It's not
22 just something that Amanze Antoine was able to use to get
23 money, it was also something that he was able to use to obtain
24 firearms, and that's where this case grows.
25   It went from a crack cocaine conspiracy to a drug

CHAPTER 41

HOW THE HELL!!

I know after reading thus far in this book a lot of you are wondering how the hell could I have been charged with a crime in the first place due to the lack of evidence against me believe you me. I thought about that same question since the first day I was arrested on these charges. I will now break down the process on how criminal charges are initially given to a person by any prosecutor whether in a state or federal courtroom. After reading the process on how charges are initially given to someone by a prosecutor you will realize there is a **"COMPELLING NEED"** to change certain things about this process!!!

THE GRAND JURY PROCEEDINGS!

The first step for any prosecutor in the United States must do who wants to charge someone with a felony is present the evidence that they feel makes that person guilty of whatever crime to a grand jury. A "grand jury" is a body of citizens that hears evidence regarding possible criminal activity presented by the prosecutor then decides whether that evidence is sufficient to bring up charges against a person or persons the prosecutor feels committed a crime. This process is known as the **"GRAND JURY PROCEEDINGS."** The grand jury proceedings were supposed to be designed to protect people from unfounded and unnecessary prosecutor charges. After the prosecutor presents the evidence he or she feels makes a person guilty of a crime to the grand jury in order to seek criminal charges against that person or persons, the grand jury "supposed" to deliberate in secret and make a decision to bring up charges or not on that person or persons then communicate that decision to the prosecutor. The grand jury must consist of 16 to 23 people. At least 12 members of the grand jury must agree to bring up charges on someone after the prosecutor presents the evidence to them to initially seek criminal charges on a person or persons. If 12 or more members of the grand jury agrees to bring up criminal charges on a person or persons after the prosecutor presents the evidence it has on a person that the prosecutor feels makes a person or persons guilty of criminal charges an indictment is issued. The legal term indictment means a written accusation charging that a person therein named has done some act, or been guilty of some omission, which by law is a public offense that is punishable. The Fifth Amendment in the United States Constitution (which I have also included in the back of this section on **page 277** states:

"No person shall be held to answer for a capital or otherwise infamous crime, unless on a presentment or indictment of a grand jury."

What the Fifth Amendment is basically stating person is any charge with a possible sentence of a year or more that a prosecutor would like to charge someone with, in order for a prosecutor to charge that person with such of a crime a grand jury has to give the prosecutor the green light to do so after the prosecutor presents evidence to them that he or she feels makes that person guilty of a certain crime.

The grand jury has three functions: Charging, investigating, and supervising.

1. Charging is the issuing of an indictment which again means 12 or more people from the grand jury voted to bring up charges against someone after the prosecutor presented evidence to them about criminal activity the prosecutor felt this person was involved in.
2. Investigating entails inquiring into an entire area of suspicious activity to see if any wrongdoing has occurred and, if so, by whom.
3. Supervising involves the grand jury's authority to oversee and issue reports on the local jail and other offices and officials.

The powers of the grand jury make it an effective weapon for investigating crimes. Grand Juries can subpoena witnesses, data, and documents without showing probable cause, which neither the prosecution nor police may do on their own. This power is restricted by a somewhat vague and inconsistent standard that permits the quashing (voiding) of an unreasonable demand. The grand jury proceedings are a "potent and vital" part of the criminal justice system because this is where the choice of bringing up criminal charges against someone is decided on!!

WHAT'S THE PROBLEM ABOUT THE GRAND JURY PROCEEDINGS?

The problem about the grand jury proceedings is the only person who presents evidence to the grand jury members and the only person allowed to be in the same room as the grand jury when evidence is being presented to them "IS THE PROSECUTOR." "The prosecutor is the only adviser and facilitator to the grand jury." That is the problem with the grand jury proceedings and the reason why it is unfair and extremely easy for a prosecutor who works for a state of federal prosecution office to manipulate "the grand Jury proceedings." Judges and lawyers are not allowed to be in the same room with the prosecutor when the prosecutor is presenting evidence to a grand jury in order to get charges brought up on someone which means no one is in the room with the prosecutor during the grand jury proceedings to monitor what the prosecutor does and to make sure the prosecutor is not doing anything foul or unethical to bring up criminal charges against someone, such as lie on someone or present false evidence against someone just to secure an indictment by the grand jury. It is very simple for a prosecutor to bring up charges against someone even if the grand jury voted not to bring up charges against someone after the prosecutor presented evidence to them that he or she felt made a person guilty of a crime. That can very easily be done by a prosecutor 1000% of the times because when the grand jury as a whole decides to bring up charges against someone or not on a person after seeing and hearing all the evidence the prosecutor presents to them, "The only person who hears the grand jury decision to bring up charges on a person or not is THE PROSECUTOR." There is no record kept of the grand jury's decision. It is just a verbal statement made by the grand jury in totality to the prosecutor on whether the grand jury decides to bring up charges on someone or not. The grand jury can tell a prosecutor they decided not to file and charge a person or persons with a crime and as soon as the grand jury leaves to go home the prosecutor can still file an indictment against someone as if the grand Jury decided to bring up charges on that person. Who is in the room with the prosecutor to make sure this does not happen? **NOBODY!!** So this very possibly can happen!! All indictment "are suppose" to be signed by the person of the grand jury who was assigned to be the foreman, but 95% of the time the indictment is never signed by the Forman of the grand jury in order to truly verify 12 or more members of the grand jury voted to bring up charges on this person or persons. For those of you who knows someone right now who is incarcerated ask them the next time they call you or you go visit them was their indictment ever signed by the foreman of the grand jury and I bet my life 95% of all the answers from the person that you know who is incarcerated will say "No"! Who is to say the prosecutor still does not bring up charges on a person who the grand Jury voted not to bring up charges on? **NOBODY**!! Remember the prosecutor is the "ONLY" person in the room with the grand jury when the grand Jury gives their decision on whether or not to bring up charges on someone or not after the prosecutor shows them evidence he or she believes makes a person or persons guilty of a specific crime, so the prosecutor can truly do whatever the fuck he or she wants after the grand jury tells the prosecutor they all voted not to bring up charges on a person or persons. Again there is no one in the room with the prosecutor during the grand jury proceedings to monitor the prosecutor's behavior. So this very very very easily could be done by a prosecutor. Do you agree?

1. Do you think it is fair that the prosecutor is the only person in charge of the grand jury proceedings?

2. Do you think it is fair that the prosecutor is the only person to present evidence to a grand Jury that he or she feels makes a person or persons guilty of a crime?

3. Do you think anyone else should be in the same room with the prosecutor when the prosecutor is presenting evidence to the grand Jury during the grand Jury proceedings? If so who should be in the same room as the prosecutor and why?

YOU BE THE JUDGE!!

Court Is in Session...

TRANSCRIPTS OR OTHER DOCUMENTS I REFFERRED YOU TO IN THIS SECTION

This is a copy of the Fifth Amendment of the United States Constitution showing you an indictment must be made by a grand jury.

Amendment V (1791)

NO PERSON SHALL BE HELD TO ANSWER FOR A CAPITAL OR OTHERWISE INFAMOUS CRIME UNLESS ON A PRESENTMENT OR INDICTMENT OF A GRAND JURY EXCEPT IN CASES ARISING IN THE LAND OR NAVAL FORCES OR IN THE MILITIA WHEN IN ACTUAL SERVICE IN TIME OF WAR OR PUBLIC DANGER; NOR SHALL ANY PERSON BE SUBJECT FOR THE SAME OFFENCE TO BE TWICE PUT IN JEOPARDY OF LIFE OR LIMB; NOR SHALL BE COMPELLED IN ANY CRIMINAL CASE TO BE A WITNESS AGAINST HIMSELF NOR BE DEPRIVED OF LIFE LIBERTY OR PROPERTY WITHOUT DUE PROCESS OF LAW; NOR SHALL PRIVATE PROPERTY BE TAKEN FOR PUBLIC USE WITHOUT JUST COMPENSATION.

CHAPTER 42

THE INJUSTICE CONTINUES!!

Some may think the injustice stops after a person is sentenced to Jailtime in a courtroom and no longer has to go in front of a judge again. That is not the case for many!! For many of us a whole new set of injustices begins. Let me now laser focus you on what I faced and seen others face after being sentenced to Jailtime in a courtroom and no longer have to go in front of a judge again.

For those of you who saw the book cover and did not know what the letters F.B.O.P meant let me tell you what those letters stand for. F.B.O.P stands for "Federal Bureaus of Prisons" which is a fancy way for the government to say "all the Federal Prisons in the United States." They always have a fancy way to say something that has a simple meaning. Anyway, after the judge sentenced me to 120 months, I was sent to one of these federal prisons in the F.B.O.P to serve the remainder of my time. The federal prison I was sent to was F.C.I Raybrook which I am currently incarcerated in that is in the State of New York. I came to this prison sometime in April of 2019. The first week I came to this prison I made it clear to Ms. Denton who is the dental assistant that I needed dental work done in my mouth that entailed the cleaning of my mouth and a few fillings according to the dentist in the last Jail I was in before I was transferred to F.C.I Raybrook. I told Ms. Denton the dentist in the last jail I was in told me my dental records will follow me to whatever prison I am transferred to (which it did) and the dental service in that prison will take a look at my dental records and see the dental work I needed done and finish off where they left off at in terms of giving me the proper dental care I needed done that was not able to be completed due to me getting transferred. Just like the dentist said in the last jail I was in my dental records followed me to this prison. Ms. Denton received and reviewed my dental records from the last jail I was in and became fully aware of "all the dental work I need done" after reading my dental records. After Ms. Denton was aware of all the dental work I needed in my mouth and told me she placed me on the waiting list, and I will be seen by a dentist soon. Here it is almost 3 years later, and I have yet to receive the Dental Care I am still in desperate need of! Not only what I am in desperate need of but what the United States Department of Justice, Federal Bureau of prisons program statements states I am "obligated to receive, which are a set of policies that "all federal prisons in the United States are obligated to follow." According to the **U.S** Department of Justice Federal Bureau of Prisons Program statements one of those policies listed that you see below states I have the right to dental care as defined in Bureau of Prisons Policy to include preventative services, emergency care and routine care. Routine care consists of a yearly cleaning of the mouth and fillings if needed yearly.

```
10. You have the right to receive prescribed medications and
treatments   in   a   timely   manner,   consistent   with   the
recommendations of the prescribing health care provider.

11. You have the right to be provided healthy and nutritious food.
You have the right to instruction regarding a healthy diet.

12. You have the right to request a routine physical examination,
as defined by Bureau of Prisons' Policy. (If you are under the
age of 50, once every two

years; if over the age of 50, once a year and within one year of
your release).

13 You have the right to dental care as defined in Bureau of
Prisons' Policy to include preventative services, emergency care
and routine care.
```

Also in the **U.S** Department of Justice Federal Bureau of Prisons program statement is a section titled " Priority of Services," which is below that defines four priority levels on acuity that determine the imminence of treatment for inmates in a federal prison. It also discusses categories for priority dental care in all federal prisons in the United States.

Lastly the last policy in the **U.S** Department of Justice Federal Bureau of Prison's program statements I would like to bring to your attention is the part of the program statement that states the "Health Services Administrator (**HSA**) of each federal prison has a budget and procurement oversight for the Dental Clinic, and also in that section of the program statement as you see states," During periods when a dentist is not available (annual refresher training, Annual Leave, **CME,** etc.) the local **HSA** or designer will arrange one of the following in options:

Contracting (Amend Existing Contract). Incorporate a requirement for temporary Dentist back-up coverage in the comprehensive medical contract.

Now that you know a little bit about what some of the policies states in the **U.S** Department of Justice Federal Bureau of prison program statements that "all federal prisons are obligated to follow," now let me tell you what happened.

Like I said I have been in the prison since April 2019 and I have not received the proper dental care I am "obligated" to receive according to the **U.S** Department of Justice Federal Bureau of prison program statements you have read above. In fact, since I been in this prison no inmate has received the dental care they are "obligated" to receive according to the **U.S** Department of Justice Federal Bureau of Prisons program statements. Throughout my entire time being incarcerated at F.C.I Raybrook I have wrote over 20 complaints complaining about me not getting the proper dental care I need and also complaining about the pain I have in my mouth when I eat but I still have yet to receive the proper dental care I need. Last year I put in a complaint about the pain in my mouth to the Health Services because I was having pain in my mouth while eating. The dentist was not around so I was seen by Doctor Mark Zimmerman who is a **GREAT** caring doctor. He prescribed me 800mg of ibuprofen tablets to take two times a day for 14 days. I have included a copy of a page from my medical records showing this encounter which Doctor Zimmerman in the back of this section on **page 290**. This encounter happened with Doctor Zimmerman on "2-27-2020." A year and some change later on May 19, 2021 I went to see Ms. Denton the dental assistant and told her 3 of my back teeth broke due to this prison's dental service not giving me a simple filling in my mouth that they knew I needed from the first month I came into this prison which was again April of 2019. I told Ms. Denton if I would have received a simple filling that she knew I needed going on years, the breaking of my 3 back teeth could have been prevented. But since I didn't receive the fillings I needed in each tooth it greater my chances for the need to repair them in the future because the likelihood for them to break after not receiving a filling in so long increased enormously, thereafter causing the need for more repair of those teeth at a later date. After I brought up the breaking of 3 of my back teeth to Ms. Denton's attention she told me "She will only look at one broken tooth and not the 3 of them, so I needed to pick one for her to look at. She told me to pick the one that hurts the most for her to look at. I told her they all hurt equally and all three of my broken teeth needed to be attended too. Ms. Denton insisted in a very very very very rude manner to pick one of the 3 teeth for her to look at or I just will not get none of my broken teeth looked at by her at all. I knew I could not go back and forth with Ms. Denton because the energy she gives off she seems like the type to write up a disciplinary infraction against me and have me placed in the hole for a long time, so I just walked out of the dental room out of frustration and went to my cell and wrote a complaint against her to the administration in the prison which I have included in the back of this section on **pages 291 and 292**. In the complaint I wrote to the Administration in this prison back on May 19, 2021 you can clearly see I wrote exactly what I said happened above. And the crazy part is I have yet to receive the dental care I am obligated to have even after filing my complaint to the Administration of this prison. The Administration in this prison is fully aware of the dental care I need because I wrote so many complaints to them about the pain in my mouth besides the complaint I sent to them complaining about Ms. Denton rude and unprofessional ass. The administration in this prison condones everything Ms. Denton does in terms of not giving inmates the dental care they are "obligated" to receive according to the **U.S** Department of Justice Federal Bureau of prisons program statements that you have read in previous pages. Not only is Ms. Denton not making sure all inmates (I hate that inmate word) are receiving the dental care they are obligated to have, she is extremely rude and disrespectful. I cannot believe she has a job here!! She should not be working in this prison until she learns how to treat and talk to people with respect no matter if they are a prisoner or not. Ms. Denton reminds me of Maziarski (the recreation supervisor) and Dr. Nagle (the psychologist who works in this prison a few times a week per year) because they all have one thing in common which is they are all **SUPER RUDE AND DISRESPECTFUL** even when you show them the upmost respect. **ALL PRISONERS ARE HUMAN BEINGS FIRST**!! She needs to learn from fellow co-workers such a F. Riveria, G. Jenne, Mr. and Mrs. Rule, J. Bruce, LA forest, M. Russell, Kelly, both Ms. Martins, A.W Bridges, Mr. and Mrs. Ahern, Doctor Zimmerman, Nurse practitioner Sorrell, Mrs. Carpenter, J. Dukette, Mr. Carpenter LT. Columbe, Meeske, T. Goodman, J. Rockhill and Duprey, Barrett, Garner, Gunther, Gushea, Ms. Hall, Lt. McClean, Ms. Trombley and Kurtz on how to respect other people even if they are inmates. The staff members I just named above are some of the staff members I took notice to because of the way they carry themselves and the respect they give to others despite the fact they are inmates. As long as you give them their respect they will return it wholeheartedly. Ms. Denton on the other hand even if you give her the upmost respect, she disrespects you and talk down on you just because you are an innate in her eyes. So the best thing for me to have done after she spoke to me in a rude manner stating for me to pick one tooth for her to look at after I told her all 3 of my broken teeth hurt equally was to simply not say anything to her and walk out calmly and write a complaint against her to the administration of this jail because if I would had returned the same energy to her that she was giving to me, she would of had me sent to the hole for disrespecting her for God only knows how long, and maybe would have lied on the disciplinary infraction she would of had to write about me like my lazy lying ass case manager Mr. James Weldon.

Speaking about Mr. Weldon let's talk about this guy now. Mr. Weldon is my case manager definitely not by choice. His job description is supposed to entail performing correctional case work in this institution, setting, developing, evaluating, and analyze program needs and other data about all inmates on his caseload; evaluating progress of individuals on his caseload, coordinate and integrate inmate training programs, develop social histories, evaluate positive and negative aspect of each person in his caseload and develop a release plan for everyone on his case load who is soon to be released. Where do I start with this guy? Let's start with the story about what Mr. Weldon's lying ass did to a person named Shy. Shy was a dude from Jersey City who had one year left to go home. Because he had one year left he was eligible to go into a halfway house in order to help him make a smoother and positive transition to his community after doing so many years in prison, I believe Shy did 12 years in prison. Because Shy wanted to make a positive transition back into his community he asked Mr. Weldon to submit the paperwork to the halfway house he wanted to go to in New Jersey in order for him to be accepted into which 9 times out of 10 because he had a year left he would of been accepted in it right away. Let me rewind a little bit. I want you to get a full understanding about the purpose of a halfway house. The purpose of any halfway house in the United States is to help inmates who are being released to make a positive transition to their communities to decrease their chances of coming back to prison. Halfway houses help soon to be released inmates seek employment, help them get into vocational training, help get people into alcohol or drug rehabilitation programs if needed, and help with getting people into educational programs to increase their chances of not returning back to prison. The lack of education is the reason why many people come to prison in the first place and the halfway houses throughout the United State help increase a person's educational and vocational level in many ways to help newly released prisoners decrease the recidivism rate. Halfway houses do many more thing but above is the overview of what they do to help newly release inmates to make a positive transition back to their communities. Ok so now back to what case Manager Weldon did to Shy. After Shy asked Mr. Weldon to submit the paperwork to the halfway house he wanted to go to Mr. Weldon looked at him with a "sincere" face and told him he already submitted it. How I know Mr. Weldon said that with a sincere face? I was right there, that is how I know. Mr. Weldon also stated to Shy he was waiting for the halfway house to give him the date for Shy to get released to the halfway house. So Shy took Mr. Weldon's word for it. Now six months later Shy went back to Mr. Weldon's office and asked him did the halfway house people give him a date yet, for him to be released to the halfway house, and Mr. Weldon lied to Shy with a sincere face again and told him no they did not send him a date yet. When Shy told me what Mr. Weldon told him I told Shy that motherfucker is lying about something because from what I seen so far in this prison when a case manager submits paperwork to a halfway house for an inmate to get released to them it normally takes 45 to 60 days for them to give the case manager a date for the prison to release an inmate to them. After I told Shy that Shy had his girlfriend call the halfway house Mr. Weldon supposedly submitted this paper work to and asked them what was taking them so long for them to give Shy his date to be released to them and the person at the halfway house told Shy's girlfriend Mr. Weldon was lying and never submitted any paper work for them to release Shy. Shy's girlfriend told Shy what the halfway house told her and Shy told Mr. Weldon's boss about him lying to him about submitting paperwork to the halfway house in order for him to get released to them. This is when Mr. Weldon's boss had another case Manager Ms. G I believe her name is was to submit the paperwork to the halfway house for Shy. 45 days later Shy had a date to go to the halfway house and he been home for a few months now working and staying out of trouble. Good for you Shy, Keep up the good work! My whole point of bringing up Mr. Weldon's lying ass in this book is to show you how we prisoners are treated in here by some staff members, not all staff! Mr. Weldon would rather keep a person in prison longer than what he is supposed to be in prison than to fill out and submit paperwork to a halfway house in order to help that person make a positive transition back to his community to decrease his chances to return back to prison. Shy did an extra 9 months in prison just because lying ass Mr. Weldon did not do his job and submit paperwork to the halfway house so Shy could be released from prison early. That's fuck up!! Mr. Weldon is a piece of snake shit for that!! **FACTS!!**

Now let me tell you what Mr. Weldon did to me. Mr. Weldon wrote me up a disciplinary infraction because he said I started a conversation with him for the sole purpose for me to distract him so that another inmate by the last name of Hollis could go to a different housing unit which he was not supposed to do. Mr. Weldon assumed this because Mr. Hollis was from New York and I am from New York. So he made the assumption in his head because we both were from New York, I was assisting Mr. Hollis to go into a different housing unit. First and foremost, I did not even like Mr. Hollis to even put the thought in my head to assist him to do anything. That is the God's honest truth. Just because a person is from New York does not mean I like you!! That is a fact!! Mr. Hollis did the right thing however and told those people I did not assist him in doing anything and he acted on his own once he saw me talking to Mr. Weldon, which I respect he did. If Mr. Hollis would have never did that, I would have never beat the disciplinary infraction Mr. Weldon wrote about me saying I distracted him to help Mr. Hollis with his sneaking to a different unit mission. My point of bringing up this story to your attention is to show you what type of person Mr. Weldon is. **HE IS A LIAR** and he does not try to help no prisoners in a positive way which his job demands of him!! He only does things to set a person back and not help them move forward in a positive way which his job description tells him he must do!! That is his "obligation" to all inmates that is on his caseload. But he does not respect his obligation to us. In the words of Donnie Dixon, every time Mr. Weldon made his rounds in the SHU Mr. Dixon who's from my hometown of Mount Vernon use to yelled on the tier "Attention to everyone in the SHU, Case Manager Mr. Weldon is in the building!! He is the case manager who **GETS PAID TO DO NOTHING!!!!!!!!!!!!!!!!!!!!!!!! GOD** knows Mr. Dixon was telling the truth and so does Mr. Weldon and the rest of the inmates on his caseload!! Shout out to Mr. Donnie Dixon, I think he was transferred to F.C.I Berlin, keep your head up Mr. Dixon and stay out of trouble!! There is a rumor going on in this prison that Mr. Weldon is getting transferred to a different federal prison called F.C.I. Butner. If that rumor is true I wholeheartedly feel sorry for those prisoners who will have him as a case manager because he will do nothing to help them, I'll bet my last million dollars on that because I know that is a bet I will win without a doubt.

Now that is out my system about Mr. lying ass Weldon let me talk about the commissary in this prison. For those of you who do not know what the word "commissary" means, it is just another word that means the place where inmates buy their food from within the jail/prison they are incarcerated in. The prices on food items in this prison's commissary is higher than prices in Midtown Manhattan. This jail takes advantage of the inmate population. I say that because once they see a food item is being bought a lot by the inmates in the jail they go up on the prices. Let me give you some examples on things sold in commissary at this prison that is overpriced. Today date is 8-7-2022. As of today, the jail commissary sells Blue Plate Mayonnaise 18 FL.OZ that cost $6.75, that mayonnaise does not cost that much at your local supermarket. That shit cost more than gas in the streets right now and gas is at an all-time high everywhere. The person who sets the prices on food items (Mrs. Kerr) in this prison's commissary knows people buy Mayonnaise a lot and just for that reason she overpriced it, which is a form of **"OPPRESSION."** Along with the overpriced mayonnaise this prison's commissary sell Maruchan Ramen Noodle Soup 3 oz (85g) in size for 40 cents for one. In any supermarket in the United States you would see those same ramen noodle soups 10 for 1 dollar. That's a fact!! It's overpriced in here and in other jails in the United States because the inmates have no choice but to buy food from the prison's commissary, so by Mrs. Kerr knowing that as well she takes advantage of that and over price shit!! **VAN CAMP'S** by chicken of the sea whole Mackerel fillet in Brine 3.53 oz (100g) in size cost $1.50 in this prison's commissary. It does not cost that much in your local supermarket. They used to cost $1.00 three months ago but Mrs. Kerr sees how much it was selling so she went up 50 cents without warning. When I say without warning I mean exactly what I say. No one would not know mackerel fillet went up to $ 1.35 until after they bought it and looked at their receipt and saw they just bought a Mackerel for $1.50. You know how you go into a supermarket and there are prices on items to let you know the price of it before you decide to purchase it? Not here!! You will find out the price on items after you purchase it and look at your receipt. If that's not oppression I do not know what the hell is!! There are so many other items overpriced in this prison's commissary that it would take a lot more pages to list them all which I really do not feel like doing. I just wanted to bring to your attention the many different injustices many are faced with after being sentenced in a courtroom to prison time. The injustices do not stop just because a person no longer has to go back inside a courtroom. My second book will get into more detail about the injustices many faces in the prison system in general. It's not just the staff in the prison system who prisoners encounter injustices with. There's a lot of segregation in the prison system such as blacks only fuck with blacks, whites only fuck with whites, Spanish only fuck with Spanish, New York dudes only fuck with New York dudes, New Jersey dudes only fuck with New Jersey dudes, Philly dudes only fuck with Philly dudes, down south dudes only fuck with down south dudes, only people from New York can sit here, only people from the south can sit there, only whites can sit over there, only New Jersey dudes can sit here, and the fucking list goes on and fucking on. Not only do the courtroom oppress us, not only do the prison system in general oppress us, we come into the prison system and oppress each other!! **FUCK OUTTA HERE!! I HATE THIS SHIT!!!!**

QUESTIONS FOR THE READERS:

1. I still need dental work done to my teeth that the dental services at F.C.I Raybrook knew of since 2019. My teeth are slowly deteriorating on a daily basis due to me not getting the proper dental care this prison by policy is supposed to give me. Do you think the dental service at F.C.I Raybrook should pay a consequence for not giving me the dental care I am "obligated" to have according to the U.S Department of Justice Federal Bureau of prisons program statements I have shown you in previous pages in this section?

2. Do be you think Mr. James Weldon should be a manager in any prison?

3. Do you feel we as inmates are getting charged to much for food item in terms of food items going up in price just because most inmates are buying it?

YOU BE THE JUDGE!!

Court Is In Session...

288

This Is the Page of My Medical Records Showing My Encounter with Doctor Mark Zimmerman, that I mentioned in this Section

Bureau of Prisons
Health Services
Clinical Encounter

Inmate Name: ANTOINE, AMANZE
Date of Birth: 12/17/1980   Reg #:   85472-054
Encounter Date: 02/27/2020 13:20   Sex: M   Race: BLACK   Facility: RBK
                                          Provider: Zimmerman, Mark D.O/CD Unit: G01

Physician - Evaluation encounter performed at Health Services.

SUBJECTIVE:

    COMPLAINT 1   Provider: Zimmerman, Mark D.O/CD

    Chief Complaint: Pain

    Subjective: Inmate Antoine c/o diffuse oral pain in the teeth primarily of the R side of his mouth on both the uppers and lowers. Denies any fever or chills. Has some pain while eating on the R side also. No swelling or difficulty chewing. He states that he has had dental problems for some time and would like to be seen by the dentist.

    Pain: Yes

    Pain Assessment

Date:	02/27/2020 13:23
Location:	Mouth
Quality of Pain:	Aching
Pain Scale:	4
Intervention:	Medications and oral instructions.
Trauma Date/Year:	02/04/2018
Injury:	MVA
Mechanism:	
Onset:	1-2 Weeks
Duration:	1-2 Weeks
Exacerbating Factors:	NA
Relieving Factors:	NA
Reason Not Done:	
Comments:	

OBJECTIVE:

Exam Comments

On oral exam: there are no distinct areas of swelling, fracture or erythema around the teeth on both sides and on the uppers or lowers. Caries are noted. There is no surrounding lymphadenopathy.

ASSESSMENT:

Dental caries, K029 - Current - *Pain*

PLAN:

New Medication Orders:

Rx#	Medication	Order Date
	Ibuprofen Tablet	02/27/2020 13:20

Prescriber Order: 800mg Orally -   Two Times a Day x 14 day(s) -- 1/2 tab twice daily with food or water as needed for dental pain.

    Indication: Dental caries

    Start Now: Yes

    Night Stock Rx#: 20757-cn1

This Is the Complaint I Wrote to The Administration in This Prison about Dental Assistant Carrie Denton, that I have mentioned in this section

RBK 1330.18C
Page 6
Attachment A

FEDERAL CORRECTIONAL INSTITUTION
RAY BROOK, NEW YORK

INFORMAL RESOLUTION FORM

NOTICE TO INMATES: You are advised that prior to receiving and filing a Request for Administrative Remedy Form (BP-229[13]), you MUST attempt to informally resolve your complaint through your Correctional Counselor, or provide other documentary evidence of your attempt at informal resolution. Failing to attempt informal resolution may result in rejection of your request.

NAME: Amanze Antoine   REG. NO. 85472-054

PART A - INMATE REQUEST
(USE BACK IF NECESSARY - NO CONTINUATION SHEET ALLOWED)

On MAY 19, 2021 I went to a dental callout. When I went to dental I was seen by Carrie Denton, she asked me what was my problem and I told her I had 3 broken teeth in my mouth due to this prison not giving me a simple → turn page

Signature: [signature]   Date: MAY 19, 2021

PART B - RESPONSE
(EFFORTS MADE TO INFORMALLY RESOLVE / STAFF CONTACTED)

_____

_____

_____

_____

_____

Counselor: _____   Date: _____

Reviewed: _____, Unit Manager   Date: _____

		COUNSELOR'S TRACKING			
Tracking Number	Event Date	+ 20 Days	Form Issued	BP-9 Issued	BP-9 Returned

filling and my "entire" mouth is in pain. Ms Denton told me I had to "only" pick one tooth for her to look at and she will not look at all 3 teeth that are broken. I told her why can't you look at all 3 of my broken teeth because they all hurt equally. She then told me it's either I pick one tooth for her to look at or she will not see me at all. I then told her I can't pick one tooth because they all hurt equally. Ms Denton then told me to leave because I refuse to choose one tooth for her to look at. I am pleading with you to give me the proper dental care I am in need of which are fillings and partials because I can't properly eat or speak and my mouth is always in alot of pain. This prison does not give inmate routine dental care such as fillings, partials or just a yearly teeth cleaning. Dental Service tells all inmates they are on a waiting list to be seen by the dentist but no one never gets seen. The only time a inmate sees a dentist in this prison is when teeth needs to get pulled out but it's never for fillings, partials or routine dental care. Dental Care is more than pulling out teeth. I been here in this prison for over 2 years and still have not received the proper dental care that the dental service in this prison knows I need. This prison can't blame the COVID-19 pandemic for me not getting the proper dental care I need because they knew about the dental work I needed one year before the pandemic even started.

CHAPTER 43

QUESTIONS FOR THE READERS

I have two questions for all the readers who thought what the judge, the prosecutor and my attorney did to me was unfair:

1. Do you think the judge, the prosecutor and my attorney should receive consequences for what they did not me? If so, what do you feel their consequences should be?

My answer to those questions:

I feel the judge, the prosecutor, and my attorney should all be subject to consequences for each and every one of their unethical and deceitful acts. They should not be treated any differently than anyone else in any community who break the laws or rules for any type of structure I truly feel jailtime should be a part of their consequence in order for them to see how it feels to be in jail like all the people they have helped send to prison. The judge should get the most time because the judge is supposed to be the enforcer of all laws and rules are being followed in his or her courtroom, and make sure all proceedings held in his or her courtroom are conducted in a fair manner. A judge is not supposed to be breaking any laws or rules in his or her courtroom and once it is proven a judge broke a law or ethical rule they should pay for it to the fullest extent because they're supposed to know better than to do that!! The judge in my case judge Keeley and other judges are sending people to prison for breaking rules and laws so they too should be subject to the same exact thing when they break a rule or law. Once a judge shows any sign of deceitfulness or dishonesty he or she should be removed from the Bench and should not be able to be a judge. As well as these prosecutors and lawyers who break the law and rules in terms of the ethical rules, rules of criminal procedures and the laws that governs the Criminal Justice system. Just like a judge who displays the same deceitful and unethical behavior they too should be sent to prison and should not be able to be a lawyer or prosecutor anymore anywhere in the world!! why should a judge, prosecutor or lawyer not be subject to consequences when they break laws and rules? Anyone have an answer to that? Some judges, prosecutors and attorneys have received consequences for their misconduct, but it is not common enough and should regularly be done on a as need basis! Do you agree?

The unfairness you have read about what happened to me did not just happen to me. There are countless untold stories about people who have been treated unfairly in the Criminal Justice court system in the United States. Some of you may even know a few. while reading this book I am 1000% sure someone is going through some type of injustice in the court system in the United States. The court system is not designed to be fair in the United States, its designed to keep mostly anyone who enters it in jail for as long as it can!! I am not saying everyone that gets arrested is innocent!!!! That is for sure not true. However, a lot of people still get treated unfairly even though they are guilty of some type of crime. How? Let me give you some examples:

A friend of mine who used to be in this prison with me, but is no longer here because he was transferred to a different prison " received a sentence of 14 years for selling 7 grams of crack cocaine!!" Did he do it? Yes he did, he told me he did it and he took a plea deal because he did it according to what he told me. Ok he did it, but is sentencing someone to 14 years in prison for selling 7 grams of crack cocaine a fair sentence? To me it is not!! The reason why he was sentence to that much time was because he was sentenced in a federal court as a " Criminal Career Offender" which means because he had no prior drug offenses or one prior drug offense and 1 prior violent crime conviction he was mandated to be sentence to 14 year for selling 7 grams of crack cocaine. The judge could have not sentence him to 14 years because it up to the judge's discretion to sentence someone as a Criminal

294

Career offender even if they have 2 prior drug offenses or 1 prior drug offense and 1 prior violent offense. Unfortunately, the judge in his case use his minor drug offenses he had in order to sentence him as a "Criminal career offender" and sentence him to 14 years in prison for selling 7 grams of crack cocaine. Do you think that was fair for the judge to do that? The judge really sentenced that man to 14 years in prison for selling 7 grams of crack cocaine. **FUCK OUTTA HERE,** your honor. **THAT SHIT WAS NOT FAIR**!!! Sorry for the outburst but that is how I truly feel in the core of my heart!! That crime did not deserve a 14-year sentence!! For the crimes he already did time for in the past he is paying for again in the future. Is that double jeopardy or what?? That is just one example out of tens of thousands of people who received more time than they should have received for a crime he or she committed. What's crazy to me is that you have so many judges, prosecutors and attorneys who break all types of laws and ethical rules and nothing happens to them, but these are the same judges, prosecutors and lawyers who will quickly agree to sentence a man to 14 years for selling 7 grams of **CRACK COCAINE!!**

This Friday that just past the WNBA star Brittney Griner was sentenced to 9 years in prison in Russia for a petty drug offense which I feel was totally unfair!!!!!!!!!

I heard President Biden say on T.V that her sentence was not fair which again I totally agree with President Biden on that. I am respectfully telling Mr. Biden before you criticize the Court System in Russia you should correct the unfair laws that governs the Court System in the United States like the crack cocaine law you helped get into law many years ago that contributed to my friend getting 14 years for selling 7 grams of crack cocaine.

Remember earlier in the book I told you a lot of people get over charged with a crime, well here is a prime example. A person name Travis Davis from Louisiana who is currently incarcerated at F.C.I Raybrook with me was charged with possession of a weapon and distribution of crack cocaine. What is unfair about his situation is that the judge sentenced him under the mandatory sentence for someone who was caught Selling 3 Kilos of crack cocaine and more, but he was never caught selling 3 Kilos or more of crack cocaine. The only reason why he was sentenced under this mandatory sentence guideline for a person actually being caught selling 3 Kilos or more of crack cocaine is because during his trial the prosecutor had a witness come on the witness stand and say he used to buy 1 or 2 ounces of crack cocaine a week from Mr. Davis for a year straight. So just because this witness came on the witness stand and said that the judge took what the witness said to be the truth even though Mr. Davis was not caught selling this witness any crack at all. There was no proof Mr. Davis sold this witness 1 or 2 ounces of crack cocaine every week for a year straight, but the judge who sentenced Mr. Davis added up the ounces of crack cocaine each week for a year straight because the witness said this is what he used to buy from Mr. Davis weekly which added up to more than 3 Kilos of crack cocaine. The judge then sentenced Mr. Davis under the sentence guideline of a person "actually" getting caught red-handed selling 3 kilos or more of crack cocaine even though Mr. Davis was never caught selling 3 kilos or more of crack cocaine, or was never found in possession of 3 Kilos or more or crack cocaine. The only proof that was needed for the judge to sentence Mr. Davis under the sentence guideline for someone getting caught selling 3 Kilos of more of crack cocaine was someone just saying he did on the witness stand at Mr. Davis's trial. The legal term for that is called relevant conduct which means whatever someone comes on the witness stand and says you did at your trial you did even though there's no actual proof you did what they said, it's still considered to be a fact. So if a person comes on the witness stand at your trial and said you sold them 1 Kilo a day for a year straight the judge considers that to be true even if you were never caught with any drugs. How unfair is that? Super unfair!! The judge sentenced Mr. Davis to 15 years in prison for the drug count which is fucking insane because he was never caught selling drugs to the witness who came on the witness stand at his trial and said Mr. Davis sold him 1 to 2 ounces of crack cocaine every week for a year straight. This Criminal Court system must change because that is not fucking Justice! That's called sending someone to jail for something the evidence does not support!! There are so many people in the same situation as Mr. Davis in the federal prison system who are crying for justice!! There is a **"COMPELLING NEED"** for Criminal Justice Reform and it is in your power to get that need fulfilled!! You will learn after reading this book the things you can do to help contribute to changing this unfair Criminal Justice system in the United States!! You have no clue as to how many people are begging for justice because of the unfairness they were forced to deal with in the Criminal Court System.

Today I was reading an old newspaper article in the Philadelphia Inquirer Daily News dating back to August 12, 2021 which I have also included in the back of this section on **pages 305 - 306.** The article was about a man named Arthur "Cetewayo" Johnson who was released from prison after serving 50 years with 37 of those years done in solitary confinement!! Mr. Johnson was sent free from prison because judge Scott DiClaudio said the prosecution's case against Mr. Johnson was fraught with false and "highly suspect" statements. The district attorney wrote in a filing that those flaws "seriously undermine the integrity of Johnson's conviction for murder." Judge Di Claudio said the district attorney's filing made it clear that a 15-year-old witness was coerced during a 30-hour interrogation in which he gave multiple conflicting statements before finally implicating Johnson. The circumstances of that interrogation, some of it was withheld from Mr. Johnson's attorney when he went to trial in 1970. According to Mr. Johnson's court filings, his codefendant Gary Brame had given a statement that stated Mr. Johnson had no role in the murder who was sentenced his self to five to 15 years in prison. Mr. Johnson stated he was coerced to sign a statement saying he committed the murder through verbal and physical abuse he encountered by police officers while being in their custody for over 21 hours taking the abuse they were dishing out. I believe him because back then the police was getting away with murder more than they are getting away with it now so verbally and physically abusing someone until he or she was coerced to sign a statement saying they did something they really didn't do was nothing for police officers to get away with back in 1970. My whole point of bringing Mr. Arthur

297

"Cetewayo" Johnson's story to your attention in this book is to show the injustice he faced back then that many still face today in the criminal Justice system. Even though the prosecutor knew Mr. Johnson codefendant stated Mr. Johnson did not have a role in the murder and even the though the prosecutor knew after a 30-hour long interrogation of a 15 year old kid who gave police officers multiple conflicting statements then was coerced to implicate Mr. Johnson in a murder still had the fucking nerve to charge Mr. Johnson for murder and withheld from his attorney at the time of his trial the circumstance of that 15 year old kid's interrogation that lead him to being coerced by law enforcement to implicate Mr. Johnson in the murder again which his Mr. Johnson Codefendant stated he had no role in. This is just another prime example of a prosecutor's wrongdoing. The prosecutor withheld this 15 year old then kid circumstance from Mr. Johnson's lawyers at the time of his trial so it would not be known to the jury of his trial what this is 15 year old kid who implicated Mr. Johnson in a murder endured 30 hours of being interrogated by law enforcement before being coerced to implicate Mr. Johnson because the prosecutor knew it was very possible if the Jury of Mr. Johnson's trial knew that the chances of him winning at trial would of increased for him but to secure his murder conviction at trial the prosecutor withheld vital information from Mr. Johnson's attorney so that it could not be used at his trial to help prove Mr. Johnson's innocence!! I would like to exercise my first Amendment right to freedom of speech and tell the prosecutor who did that to Mr. Johnson, from the bottom of my heart **FUCK YOU, YOU PIECE OF SHIT!!!!!** Mr. Johnson lost out on a lot of years in life. As you read the article about him you will see he did 37 of those 50 years in solitary confinement. For those of you who do not know what solitary confinement is, it is when a person is locked in their cells 23 hours out the day for 7 days a week. He only came out of his cell for an hour of recreation every day and he only gets to take showers 3 days a week. You get no phones calls and your only form of communication to the streets is through mail. You cannot buy any food from the jail commissary; you have to just eat what the jail gives you to eat which is normally enough to keep you alive. The things Mr. Johnson and his family went through was hell!! He lost a lot of years out of his children's lives and the prosecution office who did all that underhanded shit to him should pay for that shit!! Why should they not? Including the police officers who coerced that 15-year-old kid to implicate Mr. Johnson in the murder. The prosecutor and law enforcement officers were caught doing some underhanded shit to Mr. Johnson and should pay for their unethical and unprofessional conduct just like the people who they arrest and send to jail who does under handed shit. Here it is prosecutors arrest people for robbing banks and other crimes having to do with theft and in Mr. Johnson's case it's in your face proof that the prosecutor and law enforcement involved with his case did some unethical and criminal shit that stole Mr. Johnson's life for fifty years and none of them paid a consequence for his or her actions that took Mr. Johnson's life for 50 years. I know all the people who were involved in doing Mr. Johnson wrong are not dead yet, so they should pay for what they did to Mr. Johnson no matter how old they are. Mr. Johnson spent 50 years of his life including the prime of his life in prison because the criminal justice system was not fair to him, and someone should pay for that shit! The way the court system gave back to Mr. Johnson was in a way coercing him to take a plea of 10 years in order to let him go home so he will not be able to sue their asses. They knew he was going to take the plea deal in order to go home. Who would not take a plea deal after doing fifty years in order to go home even if you are innocent? To this day Mr. Johnson maintain his innocence and I know he only took the plea deal because he knew if he took it, he would go home that day. I would of took that shit too.

Everyone is not so lucky as Mr. Arthur Johnson in terms of the Court system entertaining evidence that proves it's very possible they did not commit the crime and set them free after that evidence is taken into consideration. I have a friend who is currently incarcerated at F.C.I Raybrook with me named Gregory A. Milton. Mr. Milton was not as lucky as Mr. Arthur Johnson to regain his freedom after evidence was brought to the Court's attention proving it is very possible he did not commit the crime he is serving time for. Mr. Gregory A. Milton has been incarcerated for 28 years in this federal prison system and is currently serving a LIFE SENTENCE for a murder he did not commit!!!! He was convicted after a trial was held over 25 years ago and was also convicted of other charges that he has already served time for. However the only thing that is holding him back from going home is the murder charge he is serving a LIFE SENTENCE for I feel based on the evidence he has brought to my attention proves he was falsely charged for murder. This same evidence he brought to my attention he also brought it to a federal judge and federal prosecutor's attention in the state of Virginia. Despite him bringing this evidence to both the judge and prosecutor's attention they both did not entertain it or even look into it. They acted as if this evidence does not exist which is **EXTREMELY UNFAIR** to Mr. Milton because he is the one serving a LIFE SENTENCE IN PRISON for a crime he has evidence showing he did commit. That really gets me angry inside!! When I see Mr. Milton I could see the pain in his eyes, and I can tell he is dying to go home!!!! One thing he may not know is I really feel his pain as if it was my pain!!!! When I see him daily I really do not know what to say to him. What I can say to him, he is serving a LIFE SENTENCE for some shit he did not do!!!!!!! Through it all he still finds a way to laugh and to make others laugh which sometimes I do not know how he does based on his situation. I really wish a lawyer will come to his aid and represent him Pro-Se (for free) and fight to get him home based on the evidence he has proving he did not commit the crime he is serving a LIFE SENTENCE for!!!

I would like to exercise my 1st Amendment right again to freedom of speech:

America you have you some fucking nerve to arrest me and charge me with a crime that the evidence did not support I did! America you got some fucking nerve to sentence my friend to 14 years in prison for selling 7 grams of crack cocaine! America you get some fucking nerve to sentence Travis Davis under the sentence guidelines for selling 3 kilos or more of crack cocaine when he was never caught selling 3 kilos or more nor was there any prove of him doing that other than the prosecutor having a witness come on the stand at his trial stating he did which was a fucking lie! America you got some fucking nerve to charge Mr. Arthur Johnson with Murder when it was evidence showing he was innocent! America you got some fucking nerve to not let Mr. Gregory A. Milton out of prison because you do not want to entertain evidence that proves he did not commit the murder he is serving a LIFE SENTENCE for!! **YOU WANT TO KNOW WHY YOU GOT SOME FUCKING NERVE AMERICA!!** Because in 1707 if a slave master killed his slave, that slave master did not have a penalty for fucking **MURDER!!** America you really got some fucking nerve! **HERE'S THE PROOF:**

THE LEGAL FOUNDATIONS OF SLAVERY

While slavery did not officially begin in the Chesapeake Valley until the latter half of the 17th century, the region's courts distinguished between white and black indentured servants from the beginning. This chart of court cases illustrates the different punishments held for whites and blacks.

YEAR	CRIME COMMITTED	OFFENDER	PUNISHMENT
1630	Sleeping with a black maidservant	White servant	Whipped for "defiling his body by lying with a Negro"
1640	Conspiracy to escape	Four white servants and one black servant	White servants are sentenced to extra service; black servant is whipped, branded, and required to wear shackles for a year
1641	Running away	Two white servants, and John Punch, a black servant	An extra year of service for the whites, lifetime servitude for Punch
1661	Running away in the company of slaves	White servant	2 years of extra service
1660s	Maidservant becomes pregnant	White servant	2 years of extra service
1660s	Stealing a hog	White servant	1,000 pounds of tobacco or a year's extra service
1660s	22 days absent	White servant	3 months of extra service and the loss of one year's crop
1669	Disobeying the master	Black slave	Toes cut off
1707	Killing a slave	White master	No penalty

1. Do you think a 14-year sentence for selling 7 gram of crack cocaine was a fair sentence for my friend?

2. Do you think it was fair for the judge to sentence Travis Davis under the sentence guideline for selling 3 Kilos or more of crack cocaine when it was no prove he did?

3. Do you think prosecutors and law enforcement officers should face consequences for what they did to Mr. Arthur Johnson if they are still alive? If so, what consequence do you feel they deserve?

4. Do you think it was fair for a federal judge and federal prosecutor to not entertain the evidence Mr. Gregory A. Milton brought to their attention proving he was innocent of a murder charge he is serving a LIFE SENTENCE for?

If you do not think that is fair please write President Biden on behalf of Mr. Milton and respectfully ask him to review the evidence Mr. Milton has to prove he was falsely charged with a crime he is serving LIFE for. Then ask President Biden to pardon Mr. Milton based on that evidence if he feels the evidence shows it is very very very possible Mr. Milton was charged with a crime he did not commit, which I know he will feel that way once he reviews the evidence Mr. Milton has to prove his innocence. In the next chapter I will explain in detail what a Pardon is and give you an outline of one so that you know how to respectfully write to Mr. Biden requesting one for whom ever you want to request for.

YOU BE THE JUDGE!!

Court Is In Session...

Do you know what is so crazy? The federal government regulates and profits off of the distribution of the powerful drug we all call "tobacco." Because the federal government says tobacco is "LEGAL for THEM" to sell, it is ok for "THEM" to distribute that powerful drug throughout the entire United States despite the fact tobacco use is responsible for more than 480,000 deaths per year in the United States, including more than 41,000 deaths resulting from second hand smoke exposure, but it's still fine for the "FEDERAL GOVERNMENT" to "SELL" that powerful drug (tobacco) because the federal government states tobacco is legal for "THEM" to sell by regulating the distribution of tobacco.

More than 16 million Americans are living with a disease caused by smoking tobacco. These diseases include cancer, heart disease, lung disease, diabetes, emphysema, chronic bronchitis, and certain eye disease. Tobacco- use also causes strokes, problem of the immune system, erectile dysfunction in males and increases risk for tuberculosis. But despite all the harm and damage tobacco-use does to the American people the "FEDERAL GOVERNMENT" still made it "LEGAL" for "THEM" to control the distribution of it to the American people, just because "THEY" make a huge profit (27.2 billion per year) off of regulating the distribution of tobacco and receiving it's profits from "TAXING" each sale of tobacco products that retailers sell to consumers. The federal government face no consequences for regulating the distribution of this powerful drug called tobacco even though tobacco does "SO MUCH HARM" to the people in this country. But then the "FEDERAL GOVERNMENT" really has the "FUCKING NERVE" to sentence my friend to 14 years for selling 7 grams of crack cocaine when "THEY" (the federal government) is doing more harm to the United States people by selling tobacco products than my friend did by selling 7 grams of crack cocaine. I am not in anyway saying it's ok to sell crack cocaine, but you get the point I am making.

It is not hard to tell that the federal government in the United States motto is "Do not do what I do, do what I allow you to do, OR ELSE!!" This is the same exact motto a communism nation is ran by. So my question to you, is this country really a "DEMOCRACY" like the picture the federal government tries to paint to us or is the United States a "COMMUNISM" country? This country is really a communism country in a lot of ways. I am not just basing that statement on the tobacco example I just gave you about how the federal government in the United States is allowed to sell a powerful drug we all know as "tobacco" without receiving any consequeces for doing so, but simultaneously will punish a person extremely harshly for selling a different type of drug (crack, weed, etc.) that does not cause the same amount of damage or harm in the United States as the powerful drug (tobacco) the federal government distributes throughout the "ENTIRE" United States. This country has it's benefits but a lot of shit still needs to be destroyed and rebuilt in this country or not rebuilt at fucking all.

With the federal government knowing all the damage and harm tobacco does to it's people in the United States it still allows 8.2 billion or more dollars a year to be spent on advertising and promoting cigarettes and smokeless tobacco which includes dry snuff, moist snuff, plug/twist, loose-leaf chewing tobacco, snus, ,and dissolvable products. Now you tell me does the United States federal government really give a fuck about it's people!!??

YOU BE THE JUDGE!!

This Is the Newspaper Article from The Philadelphia Daily News about Mr. Arthur Johnson dated back August 12, 2021 that I have mentioned in this section.

Free after 50 years in jail . . . 37 in

By Samantha Melamed
STAFF WRITER

IN 2017, Arthur "Cetewayo" Johnson won the right to leave solitary confinement after a remarkable 37 years on "restricted release" status in the Pennsylvania Department of Corrections — an indefinite punishment for escape attempts dating back to the 1970s.

Now, the same legal team that advocated to move Johnson into the general population has won an even bigger victory: his release from prison after half a century of incarceration.

On Wednesday, the Philadelphia District Attorney's Office and Common Pleas Court Judge Scott DiClaudio agreed the prosecution's case against Johnson for the 1970 murder of Jerome Wakefield in North Philadelphia was fraught with false and "highly suspect" statements. The DA wrote in a filing that those flaws "seriously undermine the integrity of Johnson's conviction."

DiClaudio said the DA's filing made clear that a 15-year-old witness was coerced during a 10-hour interrogation in which he gave multiple conflicting statements before finally implicating Johnson. "The circumstances of that interrogation, some of it was withheld from your lawyer at the time of trial," he told Johnson.

Assistant District Attorney Lyndra Retacco, of the DA's Conviction Integrity Unit (CIU), said Wakefield's family told her they felt Johnson had served enough time. "They were just kids," she said they told her. Johnson was two months past his 18th birthday when prosecutors say he stabbed Wakefield, who had already been shot by Johnson's juvenile codefendant, Gary Brame. Brame was sentenced to five to 15 years.

On Wednesday, Johnson

Arthur Johnson (left) and son Kevin Brockington, during a visit at SCI Smithfield in Huntingdon, Pa.

agreed to a 10-to-20-year sentence — effectively time served — and pleaded guilty to a lesser charge. Before imposing the sentence, DiClaudio asked Retacco to provide the sentencing guidelines. "Guidelines didn't exist in 1970," she said. (Nor did the current third-degree murder statute, sending lawyers and court clerks scrambling to figure out how to correctly code Johnson's new conviction and sentence so he could be released.)

The Abolitionist Law Center, a Pittsburgh-based nonprofit represented Johnson in his pleas first to be released from solitary and then from prison. In 2017, a federal judge wrote in the first case that confining him "for at least 23 hours per day, to an area

smaller than the average horse stall," amounted to "an unconstitutional deprivation."

"I done forgot," he told The Inquirer in 2016, "how it feels to touch another person or to talk to another person without a [glass] screen or phone."

Along the way, lawyer Bret Grote came to believe a review of Johnson's criminal case was decades overdue.

"When he was convicted, Frank Rizzo was the police commissioner. Richard Nixon was president. The U.S. was in Vietnam. He was a teenager. He just turned 69 years old," said Grote, of the Abolitionist Law Center. "His strength of character has been an inspiration for countless people passing through Pennsyl-

305

nition of Johnson's strength and endurance.

Johnson has long maintained his innocence, Holbrook said. Though he signed a statement confessing to the stabbing, he said it was fabricated and his signature coerced through verbal and physical abuse over 21 hours in police custody.

According Johnson's court filings, his codefendant Brame also has given a statement that Johnson had no role in Wakefield's murder, instead implicating two other people who were questioned by police but not charged.

"We didn't get justice, because I believe that he is innocent," Holbrook said. "But we got freedom, and we are grateful to the CIU for agreeing to this."

Friends and family who have known Johnson for more than half a century piled into the courtroom Wednesday, crying as his release was approved and vowing to support him as he starts over as a senior citizen. He has two sons, babies when he was jailed and now in their early 50s.

Julie Burnett, who describes herself as Johnson's "cousin/sister" — his mother died when he was young, so he came to stay with her family — said she plans to take him into her home.

"I learned how to address envelopes shortly after he was taken to prison, and I've been corresponding with him ever since," said Burnett, 55. "I just want him to know we never forgot him."

She took off two weeks from work to help him get situated. "He can get up and go downstairs to the refrigerator when he wants to. He can go for a walk," she said. She referenced the prison term _____, meaning friends who walk the yard together. "I'm going to be his walkie on the outside."

vania prisons over the last half century."

One of those people was Robert "Saleem" Holbrook, a former inmate and now the Abolitionist Law Center's executive director, who met Johnson in "the hole" at State Correctional Institution Green, about 20 years into Johnson's time in solitary. "He was a very stabilizing force on us. He encouraged us to read, to stay away from the dog-eat-dog prison culture, and to focus on bettering ourselves. Even though we all had life-without-parole sentences, he never gave into that hopelessness, nor did he allow us to give into that hopelessness."

Another prisoner gave Johnson, who was perpetually working out, the nickname Cetewayo, after a Zulu leader, in recog-

✉ smelamed@inquirer.com
© 215-854-5053🐦 samanthamelamed

CHAPTER 44

WAYS YOU CAN HELP ME AND PREVENT FUTURE INJUSTICES TO OTHERS WHICH SHOULD BE YOUR MAIN OBJECTIVE!!

If after reading this book you feel I was treated unfairly, and you would like to take actions to help contribute to me getting the justice I need and deserve here is how:

Bringing as much awareness you can about what happened to me in the court system to the world, through word of mouth and social media will help so much to bring the proper attention to my situation. Writing a letter to President Biden respectfully asking him to give me a pardon due to the unfairness I have encountered in the court system is another way you can contribute to helping me get the justice I deserve.

For those of you who do not know what a pardon is, it is when the President can just release me from prison for whatever reason he feels like releasing me for. I will wholeheartedly appreciate you taking the time out of your day to write Mr. President Biden respectfully asking him to pardon me, the more willing he would be to consider your request to pardon me.

I am respectfully and humbly asking you all to please write a letter to Mr. President Biden on my behalf and to get as many people as you can to write him as well. I have included a sample letter on how to outline your letter to President Biden if you do decide to write a letter on my behalf. However please feel free to use your own outline if you would rather do that. Thank You in Advance!!!!

SAMPLE OUTLINE LETTER TO PRESIDENT BIDEN:

Dear Mr. President,

My name is (your name). I currently reside at (your address). After reading the book called **YOU BE THE JUDGE,** I feel this letter to you is very much needed and past overdue. I am now writing to you Mr. President respectfully asking you to please pardon Amanze Antoine, federal inmate #85472-054. I am respectfully asking you to pardon him for the following reasons:

EXAMPLES OF REASONS TO USE:

1. Amanze Antoine was treated extremely unfair by the judge, the prosecutor, his very own attorney, and he did not receive a fair trial because <u>(fill in the blank).</u>

2. Amanze Antoine was not supposed to get charged with a crime in the first place because (fill in the blank) so his release from prison is way overdue.

Thank you so much Mr. President for your time and I pray you give Amanze Antoine the pardon he deserves.

Sincerely,

Date: <u>Sign</u>

Print your name

Your mailing addresses

IT'S NOT JUST ABOUT HELPING ME GET A PARDON!!! The main purpose of this book is for me to help contribute to prevent the unfairness I and others have encountered in the Court System in the United States from happening to others in the future in this country. You have no idea about all the countless untold stories of people who have been treated in the Court System throughout the United States of America. Some people have been treated worse, the same or not as bad as I was treated in the Court system in the United States. But the bottom line is that, some type of injustice was done to them and it is about time things change in the Criminal Justice System in the United States. If you want to take actions to help contribute to the prevention of future injustices to others in the Criminal Justice system in the United States here is how:

The only way to truly change the court system in the United States is to I change the laws that governs the court system. In order to get the laws to change that governs the court system you have to write your Senators, your Congressmen or Congress women for the district you live in and "respectfully" express to them you're feeling about them changing certain laws and why. Also express to them why there is a **"COMPELLING NEED"** to change them.

If your Senators, Congressmen of Congress women get enough complaints about certain laws people want to change they have to act on it!!! Remember you put them in office by voting for them, so they really work for you!! If they are not doing what you want them to do, **YOU DON'T HAVE TO VOTE FOR THEM TO GET INTO OFFICE**!!! Senators, Congressmen and Congress women are the reason why laws become law. If you want a law to change or try to have them introduce a new law, they can make that happen. It's in all Senators, Congressmen, and women power to make any law come into effect that **"THE PEOPLE"** want to come into effect. This is why I feel writing to them is a great idea if you want to help contribute to changing laws (not just criminal law but any law about anything you feel is unfair) you feel are unfair and or to introduce your ideas for new laws.

It would be very appreciated by so many people if you took some time out of your day to write your Senators, Congressmen and Congresswomen of the district you reside in all the things you are respectfully demanding them to change about the unfair Criminal Justice system in the United States. I have included a sample outline letter on how to address your Senators, Congressmen, and women if you do decide to write to them. However, please feel free to use your own outline when writing to them.

I would like to say **THANK YOU** on behalf of everyone you would be helping if you took the time out of your day to write your Senators, Congressmen and women asking them to change this unfair Court system in the United States.

SAMPLE LETTER TO YOUR SENATORS, CONGRESSWOMEN OR MEN OF YOUR DISTRICT:

Dear (Name of your Senator, Congressmen, or women),

My name is (your name). I reside at (your address). Which is within the district you are the (Senator, Congressmen or Congresswomen) in. I am writing to you respectfully asking that you please change certain laws due to the unfairness of them. I feel the Criminal Justice System is extremely unfair and needs to be changed. There is a "COMPELLING" need for the Criminal Justice System in the United States to change and Criminal Justice Reform is mandatory in the United States. Below are the things I would like changed about the Criminal Justice System and also the things I would like to become law in order to make the Criminal Court system fair:

1. Judges, lawyers, and prosecutors should face criminal charges when it is proven they have broken any law or ethical rule that they are supposed to follow throughout Criminal Court proceedings.

2. A prosecutor should not be the only person conducting or allowed to be in the room with the Grand Jury when conducting the Grand Jury proceedings. Nor should the prosecutor be the only person presenting evidence to the

Grand Jury during the Grand Jury proceedings, when trying to convince a Grand Jury to indict a person or persons. A lawyer should also be able to present evidence to a Grand Jury to help prove his client is innocent. Why is the prosecutor the only person presenting evidence to a grand Jury to show how guilty he or she "thinks" a person is of committing a crime, that has to change!!

3. A prosecutor should not be able to attempt to bring up charges on someone unless there is concrete evidence proving a person committed a crime, and not just hearsay as evidence to bring up charges on someone.

4. A person should not be charged with distributing drugs if no drugs were ever found or there was no concrete proof other than hearsay to prove this person "actually" distributed drugs.

5. Sentencing a person as a Criminal Career offender in any courtroom is unfair because (fill in the blank).

Thank you for your time. I hope and pray you do the right thing and make all the above laws so that the Criminal Justice System is much more fair.

Sincerely, <u>Sign</u>

Print your name

Date:

CHAPTER 45

THERE'S STILL MORE INJUSTICE PLEASE KEEP READING!!

After I found out what the Judge in my case Irene Keeley did to me in her court room was unethical, and her conduct was in no way acceptable to the standards the American Bar Association sets for Criminal Justice in all court rooms throughout the United States that states all judges are "obligated" to follow. I wrote a complaint to the Judicial Investigation Commission of West Virginia, giving them a detailed complaint about all of the unethical things done to me by judge Irene Keeley. The purpose of the Judicial Investigation Commission in any state is to investigate any complaint received about a Judge and to penalize him or her if the complaint calls for that.

The Judicial Investigation Commission responded back to me after receiving my complaint and stated their office has no jurisdiction over judge Irene Keeley, which that is a fucking lie!! I didn't understand their response back to me because the sole purpose of their office is to investigate any and all complaints received in their state. The purpose of their office to also recommend sanctions for any Judge who committed an unethical act, including removal from the bench.

There is no other place to write a complaint against a judge in the state of West Virginia, so why would the Judicial Investigation Commission in West Virginia tell me they do not have Jurisdiction over judge Irene Keeley when they clearly do.

After I received their response from complaint telling me they have no jurisdiction over Irene Keeley, I asked my Mother to call their office and ask them since they claim they had no Jurisdiction over judge Keeley then who does? The person my Mom spoke to did not know who does and could not direct her to anyone or place. REALLY!! I have a question for the readers. Why would the Judicial Investigation Commission in West Virginia indirectly tell me they will not investigate my complaint against judge Irene Keeley, by telling me they do not have Jurisdiction over her when the sole purpose of their office is to investigate any and all complaints about any judge who is employed in their state?

My answer to that question is the judge has to know someone who works in that office who will simply not except any complaint against her and or the Judicial Investigation Commission in the state of West Virginia is full of shit and just do not care to investigate any complaint made against any judge who is employed in their state.

What are your thoughts on that?

YOU BE THE JUDGE!!

I have included on **pages 316-339** a copy of the actual complaint I sent to the Judicial Investigation Commission of West Virginia, along with a copy of the Judicial Investigation Commissions response back to me about my complaint on **page 315.**

1. Does anyone know where else I can file this complaint against the judge? If so, please write to me and let me know. In fact I would like to hear all your comments and answers to the **YOU BE THE JUDGE** section of the book. You can write to me and send me your email address so we can communicate through emails. Once I receive your email address, I will then send you an email request by sending it to your email address that you must accept in order for us to start communicating through emails. I look forward to hearing from all of you.

Please before sending your comments and your email address to me please go to the website **FBOP.GOV** and type in my name and inmate number that you see below in order to find out what prison I am in, so you can mail me your comments and email address to the correct prison I am incarcerated in. In the prison system a person at any given time can be moved or transferred to a different prison without notice. So it is important you find out first what prison I am in before mailing me anything. Below is my name and inmate number:

Amanze Antoine 85472-054

This is the response I received from the Judicial Investigation Commission about my complaint I sent them about judge Irene Keeley. **(NEXT PAGE)**

This is the response I received from the Judicial Investigation Commission about my complaint I sent them about judge Irene Keeley.

JUDICIAL INVESTIGATION COMMISSION
City Center East - Suite 1200 A
4700 MacCorkle Ave., SE
Charleston, West Virginia 25304
(304) 558-0169 • FAX (304) 558-0831

February 17, 2021

Amanze Antoine #85472-054
F.C.I. Ray Brook
P.O. Box 900
Ray Brook, NY 12977

Dear Mr. Antoine:

Your complaint was recently received by our office. The complaint is regarding Irene Keeley, the Senior United States District Judge of the United States District Court for the Northern District of West Virginia. Please be advised that our office has no jurisdiction over this person.

Should you have any other questions concerning this matter, please do not hesitate to contact this office.

Sincerely,

Pam Schafer
Executive Assistant

This is the entire complaint I sent to the Judicial Investigation Commission about judge Irene Keeley that includes my Jury Selection transcripts pertaining to my complaint against judge Keeley.

The next 24 pages is the complaint I sent to the Judicial Investigation Commission:

February 13,2021

Dear Judicial Investigation Commission,

My name is Amanze Antoine and I am currently incarcerated at a
federal prison in New York, F.C.I. Ray Brook. I am writing to
you because I would like to report the unethical conduct that
was committed to me by the honorable Irene Keeley of the
Northern District of West Virginia.

I have enclosed the complaint about the judge's unethical
conduct with my trial and jury selection transcripts to
effectively prove the unethical conduct that was done to me. I
am respectfully asking you to please hold the judge accountable
for her conduct because she must be deterred from doing this
type of conduct. My criminal number for my case in the Northern
District of West Virginia courtroom is 1:18-cr-00017.

Sincerely,

Amanze Antoine
#85472-054
F.C.I. Ray Brook
PO Box 900
Ray Brook, NY 12977

Impropriety Conduct By The Court Violated The Defendant's
Fundamental Right To Due Process And The Defendant's
Substantial And Constitutional Rights Were Violated.
Please Apply Plain-Error Review:

The Honorable Irene Keeley allowed a witness to stay inside
of the courtroom after she granted my attorney's motion of sequester and instructed all witnesses to leave the courtroom. Judge
Irene Keeley willfully, knowingly and voluntarily allowed this
witness to stay in the courtroom. This conduct is unethical, unprofessional, shows the Judge is not trustworthy, deceitful, dishonest
and not fit to be a Judge under the Constitution which demands an
impartial Judge that the Honorable Judge Irene Keeley clearly
proves she's not.

Special Agent Matt Bassett was a witness in my trial who was
allowed to stay inside the courtroom for my entire trial and listen
to every witness testimony before he was called to the witness stand.
Despite the Honorable Irene Keeley's instructions for all witnesses
to leave the courtroom after my attorney's motion of sequester was
granted Special Agent Bassett did not follow that instruction to
leave the courtroom but instead continued to stay seated next to
the U.S. Attorney Zelda Wesley. I feel this is unfair and denied
me a fair trial because Agent Bassett was not supposed to be in the
courtroom while other witnesses are testifying to prevent his testimony from getting influenced by what he was going to hear from
the other witnesses' testimonies during my entire trial. In other
words to prevent "let's get my story straight" syndrome. Special

3

317

Agent Bassett was the very last witness to get called to the witness stand by the government which means he was afforded the opportunity to hear every single witness testimony before he was called to the witness stand and had the chance to tailor his testimony based on all the other witnesses' testimonies he heard during my entire trial proceedings, which is not fair and violates my Constitutional and Absolute Right to a fair trial which is a trial by an impartial and disinterested tribunal in accordance with regular procedure and a trial in which my Constitutional and legal rights are respected.

Please take a look at page 62 lines 22-25 of my trial transcripts where the record reflects my attorney Mr. Walker put in an oral motion of sequester to the Court to remove all witnesses in my trial who was inside the courtroom before the government presented her case in chief to the jury of my trial. Now please take a look at pages 62 lines 24-25 and page 63 line 1 of my trial transcripts where the record reflects the Honorable Irene Keeley's reply to my attorney's motion of sequester to remove all witnesses from the courtroom. The Judge stated, "All right motion to sequester granted," and then stated, "if there are any witnesses in the courtroom, please leave." As you can see by reading those pages the Court reporter whose job is to put on the record everything that occurs in the courtroom "never made a record of anyone exiting the courtroom after the Honorable Irene Keeley instructed all witnesses who were involved in my case who was in the courtroom at that time to please leave the courtroom. Special Agent Matt Bassett never respected the Judge's instructions for all witnesses to leave the

4

courtroom even though he knew he was going to be called to the witness stand at my trial. The Honorable Irene Keeley also knew Special Agent Bassett was going to be a witness in my trial but still allowed him to stay inside the courtroom after she instructed all witnesses present to leave the courtroom. To quickly prove the Honorable Keeley knew Special Agent Bassett was going to be a witness in my trial please take a look at "page 76 lines 20-21 of my jury selection transcripts where the record reflects the Honorable Irene Keeley asked all prospective jurors did they know Special Agent Bassett because he was a witness for my trial." So that clearly proves the Judge knew Special Agent Matt Bassett was a witness to be called in my trial. When Special Agent Matt Bassett was instructed to leave the courtroom because he was a witness he refused to do so and continued to stay seated in his chair which was side by side by the U.S. Attorney Zelda Wesley at the government's table where the government sat during my entire trial with Special Agent Bassett. To prove Special Agent Matt Bassett was seated at the government's table with U.S. Attorney Zelda Wesley please take a look at page 57 lines 13-16 of my trial transcripts where the record reflects during the government's opening statement U.S. Attorney Zelda Wesley stated "her name to the jury and then introduced everyone seated at her table at the "start" of my trial" which you can see includes Special Agent Bassett. Please also take a look at page 275 lines 11-16 of my trial transcripts where the record reflects where the Honorable Irene Keeley asked U.S. Attorney Zelda Wesley at the end of Ms. Wesley's redirect examination of Special Agent Bassett "Is there anything further for witness

Special Agent Bassett" and Ms. Wesley stated "no Your Honor"
and then the Honorable Keeley said to Special Agent Bassett "You
may return to your seat" which was the seat he was seated at during
my entire trial at the government's table. The fact that the Judge
told Special Agent Bassett to return to his seat after he was done
on the witness stand clearly proves Special Agent Bassett was called
to the stand from the courtroom not from outside the courtroom like
all the rest of the witnesses called to the witness stand by the
government. When both parties didn't have anything further for a
witness on the stand the Honorable Keeley did not tell that witness
to return to your seat as she did to Special Agent Bassett, the
Honorable Keeley told those witnesses who were done "you are free
to go," as the record reflects for each witness that was done on
the witness stand. My point of bringing this up is just to clearly
prove the Honorable Keeley knew Special Agent Bassett was in the
courtroom after she granted my attorney's motion to sequester. To
further prove that Special Agent Bassett did not leave the courtroom when instructed to do so by the Honorable Keeley and stayed
in the courtroom during my entire trial and listened to every
single witness testimony before he was called to the witness stand
please take a look at page 256 lines 16-18 of my trial transcripts
where the record reflects during the government's direct examination
of Special Agent Bassett the government asked Mr. Bassett, "Okay.
And Ms. Parker when she testified today, she testified regarding
that exchange, did she not?" And Special Agent Bassett replied,
"She did." How would he know what Ms. Parker testified to if he was
not in the courtroom to hear her testimony? The fact of the manner

320

is that he was in the courtroom when Ms. Parker testified when he was not supposed to be because he was instructed by the Judge before trial started to leave the courtroom due to my attorney's motion to sequester, but Mr. Bassett made a willfully and knowingly choice not to respect the Honorable Keeley's instruction to leave the courtroom and should be held accountable for his actions. To even further prove what I am saying is a fact about Special Agent Bassett please take a look at page 232 line 25 and page 233 line 1 of my trial transcripts where the record reflects that U.S. Attorney Zelda Wesley calls Special Agent Matt Bassett to the witness stand in order for him to testify against me but it was no record made by the court reporter of Mr. Bassett "entering the courtroom" when he was called to the witness stand as the court reporter noted on the record about every other single witness who was called to the witness stand by U.S. Attorney Zelda Wesley. Special Agent Matt Bassett is the only witness who was called by U.S. Attorney Zelda Wesley to take the witness stand who the court reporter didn't place on the record "witness enters courtroom" as was done for every single other witness who was called to the stand. And the reason for that is Special Agent Bassett was already in the courtroom sitting at the same table with U.S. Attorney Zelda Wesley when he was called to the witness stand so it was no need for him to "enter" the courtroom when he was called to the witness stand because he was already in it. Again all the other witnesses U.S. Attorney Zelda Wesley called to the witness stand the court reporter made the record reflect they did by stating on the record "the witness entered the courtroom" except for Special Agent Matt Bassett's

7

appearance to the witness stand. Please see page 63 line 12, page
67 line 21, page 73 line 7, page 75 line 25, page 96 line 19, page
126 line 6, page 149 line 25, page 161 line 19, page 195 line 6,
page 184 line 3, page 188 line 14 and page 217 line 25 of my trial
transcripts where the witness enters the courtroom "on the record".
when the witness enters the courtroom after being called to the
witness stand by the government and also after a court officer is
told to get the witness by either the Judge or government who is
"outside the courtroom" after the government calls him or her to
the witness stand.

Please look at all the pages I mentioned above when the record
reflects when all the witnesses "enters the courtroom" after being
called to the witness stand by U.S. Attorney Zelda Wesley, see
page 63 line 12 record reflects Victor Perez "enters the courtroom," page 67 line 21 record reflects Dennie Smiddy "enters the
courtroom," page 73 line 7 record reflects Anthony Mahdaui "enters
the courtroom," page 75 line 25 record reflects Will Jackson "enters the courtroom," page 96 line 19 record reflects Christopher
Anderson "enters the courtroom," page 126 line 6 record reflects
Marget Parker "enters the courtroom," page 149 line 25 record
reflects Special Agent Matt Kocher "enters the courtroom," page
161 line 19 record reflects Tommy Calhoun "enters the courtroom,"
page 184 line 3 record reflects Dawn Tatar "enters the courtroom,"
page 188 line 14 record reflects Maria Lopez "enters the courtroom,"
page 195 line 6 record reflects Officer Nick Junkin "enters the
courtroom," and page 217 line 25 the record reflects Chief Corkrean
"enters the courtroom." When all of the witnesses were called to

8

the witness stand by the government the record reflects when that
witness "enters the courtroom" with the exception of Special Agent
Matt Bassett. Please see page 232 line 25 and page 233 lines 1-8
of my trial transcripts where the record reflects the government
has called Special Agent Matt Bassett to the stand. The record
does not reflect when Special Agent Bassett "enters the courtroom"
to take the witness stand as the record reflects for all the other
witnesses who were called to the witness stand by the government.
Again the reason why the record does not reflect that Special Agent
Bassett entered the courtroom after the government called him to
the witness stand is because he was already in the courtroom sitting
next to the U.S. Attorney (like he was for my entire trial) at the
government's table when he was called to the witness stand. Lastly
to prove without a doubt that Special Agent Bassett did not follow
the instructions to leave the courtroom when he was asked to please leave,
take a look at page 271 lines 14-16 of my trial transcripts where
the record reflects during my attorney Mr. Walker's cross examination of Special Agent Bassett Mr. Walker asked Mr. Bassett "was
he in the courtroom when Ms. Parker testified and Special Agent
Bassett replied, "I was."

I have clearly proven that Special Agent Bassett sat at the
U.S. Attorney's table with the government during my entire trial
proceedings. Special Agent Bassett had the opportunity to hear
every witness testimony of my trial before being the last witness
to be called on the witness stand. This gave Mr. Bassett the opportunity to tailor his testimony on the stand before he was called
to the witness stand to fit the story of other witnesses' testimony

9

he heard throughout my entire trial which is unfair and is a
denial of my constitutional right to a fair trial. I feel Special
Agent Bassett's testimony when he took the witness stand was influenced by what he heard other witnesses testify to during my
entire trial. I truly feel Special Agent Bassett got his story
straight before taking the stand by tailoring his testimony to
fit what he heard other witnesses say on the witness stand before
he was called to the witness stand. The fact that Special Agent
Bassett did not leave the courtroom when he was asked to by the
Judge when the Court instructed all witnesses to leave the courtroom before the government started to present her case in chief
to the jury shows he has no respect for fairness, is very untruthful, unprofessional and does not have any consideration for ethic
rules, law or the Constitution and he should be held accountable
for his actions. Again what makes this worse is the Honorable
Keeley allowed this to happen when she is supposed to make sure
any and all proceedings are conducted in a fair manner in her courtroom. The Honorable Irene Keeley said nothing to Special Agent Bassett
when she instructed all witnesses to leave the courtroom before the
government presented their case in chief and Mr. Bassett did not
leave. The Honorable Keeley condoned Special Agent Bassett's deceitful, untruthful, unethical, and unprofessional conduct. By
condoning Special Agent's conduct not only did the Honorable Keeley
deny me my right to a fair trial under the Constitution, she also
does not respect her obligation to the Model Rules of Professional
Conduct which sets forth ethical guidelines for lawyers and Judges
organized in the form of 59 rules. Just to name three ethical rules

10

the Judge violated of the Canon Judicial Ethic Rules are the
3rd rule of the Canon Judicial Ethic Rules which is "Constitutional
obligation" the 4th rule which is "Avoidance of Impropriety" and
the 5th rule which is "Essential Conduct of the Canon Judicial Ethic
rules." For starters the Constitutional obligation rule of Canon
Judicial Ethic rules states:

"It's the duty of all Judges in the United States to support
the Federal Constitution and that of the State whose laws they
administer; in doing so, they should fearlessly observe and apply
fundamental limitation and guarantee." By the Judge allowing Agent
Bassett to stay in the courtroom after she instructed all witnesses
to leave the courtroom shows she does not respect her obligation to
support the Federal Constitution as the 5th Canon Judicial Ethic
rule demands because she denied me my Constitutional right to a fair
trial by allowing him to stay in the courtroom. My Fifth and Four-
teenth Amendment fundamental right to due process and my substantial rights were violated by the Honorable Irene Keeley unethical
and unprofessional conduct by allowing Special Agent Bassett to
stay in the courtroom after she instructed all witnesses to leave
the courtroom before the government presented her case in chief
to the jury of my trial. The second Canon Judicial Ethic rule the
Court violated is Avoidance of Impropriety which states:

"A Judge official conduct should be free from impropriety
and the appearance of impropriety; he should avoid infractions
of law; and his personal behavior, not only upon the Bench and in
the performance of Judicial duties but also in his everyday life,
should be beyond reproach."

11

325

Again by the Judge allowing Special Agent Bassett to stay
in the courtroom after she instructed all witnesses to leave the
courtroom was very improper conduct and its a "compelling need"
for this Court to address this type of behavior.

Lastly the last known Canon Judicial Ethic rule the Honorable
Irene Keeley violated is Essential conduct which states:

"A Judge should be temperate, attentive, patient, impartial
and since he is an administer of the law and apply it to the facts
he should be studious of the principles of law and diligent in
endeavoring to ascertain the facts."

Clearly the Honorable Irene Keeley's actions were not impartial
and there's no reason that can excuse what she did to me. The
Court's conduct was very bias   towards me and this type of conduct is not what my Constitution grants me. My Constitution grants
me to be tried in front of an impartial Judge which I was denied.
The Honorable Keeley should be held accountable for her actions.
The Honorable Keeley was supposed to perform her duty without bias
or prejudice to any party. The defendant and public expects I be
tried by an impartial Judge that follows the law and the Constitution which Honorable Irene Keeley did not do. The Honorable Irene
Keeley knowingly conducted herself in a manner that indicates a
propensity to lie or involve some element of deceit or untruthful-
ness. She earned the right to be distrusted. Disciplinary and criminal actions should be taken up against the Honorable Irene Keeley because she knowingly, willfully, and voluntarily deprived me
of life and liberty without due process of law. She stole my life
from me and sent me to prison for years without following the

12

Constitution that states no person should be deprived of life or liberty without due process and that should be a crime. No one should be above the law and I am respectfully asking you to address this issue accordingly.

The Honorable Irene Keeley should not stand in any higher station in the community than any other person because she is a Judge. She should be held accountable for her actions as everyone else in this world who breaks the law. Please give me justice.

During my entire jury selection proceeding Special Agent Matt Bassett who was the head investigator in charge of investigating my federal case, who testified at the grand jury in order to get me indicted on my initial indictment and superseding indictment and who also was going to be called as a witness in my trial "was assisting U.S. Attorney Zelda Wesley with selecting jurors for my trial and the Honorable Irene Keeley allowed it." Special Agent Matt Bassett should not have been allowed to partake in assisting the U.S. Attorney with selecting a jury for my trial because Special Agent Bassett does not have a law degree nor did he pass the bar to become an attorney therefore he is not qualified to act as an attorney and assist with selecting a jury for a trial. He is a special agent and his job description or duties does not consist of partaking in selecting a jury for a trial. Only an attorney is qualified to partake in the jury selection process, not a Special Agent. Please see page 2 lines 8-9 of my jury selection proceedings where the record reflects the appearance of Special Agent Matt Bassett at my jury selection proceedings. The record clearly reflects Special Agent Matt Bassett of the Bureau of Alcohol,

13

Tobacco and Firearms was there.

Please see page 13 lines 22-25 of my jury selection transcripts where the record reflects U.S. Attorney Zelda Wesley introduced Special Agent Matt Bassett to the prospective jurors before the jury selection was to actually start. Special Agent Matt Bassett was seated at the same table as the U.S. Attorney which the record clearly reflects per U.S. Attorney Zelda Wesley's introduction to the prospective jurors. U.S. Attorney clearly stated on the record, "I'm Zelda Wesley and seated at counsel table with me is Timothy Helman, who's also an attorney for the government. And this is Matt Bassett who is a Special Agent with the Bureau of Alcohol, Tobacco, and Firearms." This clearly shows Special Agent Matt Bassett was sitting at the same table with the U.S. Attorney partaking in the jury selection process which is not fair. Now please see page 76 lines 20-21 of my jury selection transcripts where the Judge asked the prospective jurors did they know Special Agent Bassett because the Judge wanted to know did any of the prospective jurors know any witnesses who were going to be called to testify in my trial and the Judge knew Special Agent Matt Bassett was a witness going to be called on the witness stand. I have shown you page 76 lines 20-21 just to show you how unfair the Honorable Irene Keeley is/ was. The Honorable Irene Keeley knew Special Agent Bassett was a witness in my trial and knew he was sitting at the same table with U.S. Attorney Zelda Wesley during the jury selection and would be assisting the U.S. Attorney with selecting jurors but still made the choice to not tell Special Agent Bassett he could not partake in the jury selection process knowing that's not Special Agent Matt Bassett's job description. Instead the Judge

14

played a blind eye and let Special Agent Matt Bassett assist U.S. Attorney Zelda Wesley with selecting a jury for my trial. It's a Court's duty to safeguard a defendant's right but the Honorable Irene Keeley failed to do so. Special Agent Bassett is not an U.S. Attorney but was still able to assist the U.S. Attorney with selecting jurors for my trial. By Agent Bassett being able to assist in selecting jurors for my trial denied me my constitutional right to a fair trial along with my substantial rights because I feel Special Agent Matt Bassett tailored a jury of "his liking" who he thought was going to return a guilty verdict which they did. I was deprived of my due process right which is fundamental fairness throughout all Court proceedings due to the fact Special Agent Bassett who was in charge of investigating my case, who testified at the grand jury to get me indicted along with him being a witness in my trial helped assist in selecting jurors for my trial. That is not equity. The Judge allowed this to happen and by the Honorable Irene Keeley condoning this it was very unethical and unprofessional of her. Not only was my constitutional and substantial rights violated the Honorable Irene Keeley has violated rules set forth in the Canon Judicial Ethic rules which is rules number 4 and 5 of those ethic rules. Rule 4 states:

"Avoidance of Impropriety which further states a Judge's official conduct should be free from impropriety and the appearance of impropriety; he should avoid infractions of law; and his personal behavior, not only upon the Bench and in the performance of judicial duties but also in his everyday life, should be beyond reproach."
By the Judge allowing Special Agent Bassett to assist with jury

15

329

selection with the U.S. Attorney was extremely improper conduct and shows the Honorable Keeley does not respect her obligation set forth in Canon Judicial Ethic Rules. The Honorable Irene Keeley also violated the fifth rule of the Canon Judicial Ethic rules which is Essential conduct that states:

"A Judge should be temperate, attentive, patient, impartial and since he is an administer of the law and apply it to the facts he should be studious of the principles of law and diligent in endeavoring to ascertain the facts." The Court's conduct was clearly not impartial in this matter. This improper conduct infected the court proceedings with unfairness as to make the resulting conviction a denial of due process along with violating my substantial rights and my constitutional right to a fair trial. The Court's conduct in allowing Special Agent Matt Bassett to assist in the jury selection process also shows the Honorable Irene Keeley does not respect her obligation in rule five set forth in Canon Judicial Ethic rules. There's no way Special Agent Bassett who was the head investigator of my case, who testified at my grand jury and got me indicted, who was going to be a witness in my trial and who does not have a law degree assist in selecting jurors for my trial.

One of the foundations of judicial ethics is judicial independence, objective, impartial decision making free of political, personal opinions and corrupt influences including those of Special Interest groups. The Judge's role in criminal matters is essential for the system to work with proper dignity, fairness and efficiency. I feel the Court was corrupted and my entire trial was rigged for me to lose not only by the Court's improper and unethical conduct

16

I have proven above but also by prejudicial statements made by
the Judge, the fact so many potential jurors knew the Judge that
was called to my jury selection proceedings to potentially be
potential jurors in my trial, the unfairness of the Judge to force
me to proceed to trial with an attorney I reported to the State of
West Virginia Bar which violates rules set forth in Canons, Rules
of Ethics along with other underhanded actions conducted by the
Judge.

Please see page 19 lines 18-25 of my trial transcripts. The
record reflects the prejudicial statement the Judge made to me and
I strongly feel because of that statement it proves the guilty
verdicts in my trial were premeditated to be a guilty verdict.
As you read page 19 lines 18-25 you can see the record shows the
Judge stated, "Okay. I don't how many times I don't mean to interrupt you again Mr. Antoine, but I told you at the final pre-
trial conference, the ruling on the motion to supress involving
your phone is over and done as this trial is just a moment. If you
want to take that up on appeal because you don't like it, fine."
The statement made by the Judge "If you want to take that up on
appeal because you don't like it, fine" was made before the government presented her case in chief to the jury of my trial which
indicates the Judge already knew what the verdict of my trial
was going to be which was a guilty verdict. For the Judge to tell
me to take an issue up on appeal before my trial even started insinuates the Judge already knew it was going to be a guilty verdict and the only way to raise an issue I had a problem about was
on appeal. How can a Judge give an option to raise an issue on

17

appeal if a jury has yet to hear or see evidence in the government's case in chief to determine a verdict in my case? The only way a Judge could make a statement stating "take it up on appeal" is if and only if they knew I was going to lose trial beforehand because the trial was rigged. I am entitled to a fair trial which is a trial by an impartial and disinterested tribunal which I feel I was denied by the Judge's statement and other unethical and unprofessional conduct committed by the Judge.

Please see page 10 lines 5-10 of my jury selection transcripts. The record reflects the Judge asked prospective jurors before both parties started the jury selection process did any of the prospective jurors know her (the Judge) personally. Many prospective jurors stated they knew the Judge. Please see page 11 lines 3-18 of my jury selection transcripts where the record reflects James Allen stated he knew the Judge because "the Judge is an acquaintance of our family." Also on page 11 prospective juror Anastasia Shaffer states, "She knew the Judge because they attend the same parrish." Then please see page 12 lines 1-6 of my jury selection transcripts where the record reflects another prospective juror Dennis Burnworth stated, "He knew the Judge because the Judge was acquainted with his wife Jean Ann Lynch and they attend the same church." As big as West Virginia is in population the question is how were three people selected and summoned to the Honorable Irene Keeley's courtroom to be potential jurors in her courtroom who was acquainted with her in some form? I wholeheartedly feel the answer to that question is Judge Keeley tailored the venire with people she knew. Another question is how many other prospective jurors were there

18

who was not truthful by stating they know the Judge when asked? I feel there were prospective jurors who were not truthful and perhaps selected as a juror in my trial to render a guilty verdict. I feel this is what happened because the Honorable Keeley has already shown clear and convincing evidence that she is not trustworthy, deceitful and does not respect ethic rules so this is very possible that she did in fact tailor the venire to people she knew and influenced the verdict of my trial because people she personally knew was selected as jurors of my trial and she knew she can influence them to get a verdict of her liking which was a guilty verdict. Another great question is how do we know that the Judge did not expect those prospective jurors to be truthful and state on the record they knew the Judge when asked and just thought they were going to be untruthful as she and play as if they didn't know her but still knew deep down if they were in fact selected as jurors for my trial she can influence the verdict to her liking based on their relationship they have outside the courtroom? I feel this too happened and its very possible it happened because the judge has already shown us how unethical she is so nothing could be put pass her on what she won't do. Birds of the same feather flock together and I feel the honorable Irene Keeley has shown untruthful behavior and have shown she is not trustworthy so I feel she too is associated with people of the same caliber as she is which is untruthful,dishonest and decitful so its very possible a juror could had been selected to be a juror in my trial who was not truthful about stating he/she knew the Judge when asked. I can't and don't put anything past Judge Irene Keeley. I don't and did

19

not trust the entire jury selection process because I feel/felt the Honorable Judge Keeley rigged that entire proceeding. For the Judge to make the statement "take an issue up on appeal" before evidence was presented to the jury of my trial truly shows and prove the Judge knew what the verdict was going to be beforehand. As stated before due to the unethical conduct she has already done she has shown us that this type of conduct is very much capable to had happen in her courtroom. When a person shows you who they are believe it and I for sure believe Judge Keeley is capable of doing everything I am saying she did. The proper or just action Judge Keeley to have done to the jurors that stated on the record they knew her was to remove them from the jury panel using "challenge for cause" so that no parties would feel in anyway shape or form the jury selection proceedings were rigged but because that was not done it opens the door for speculation in all aspects of the jury selection process especially after the fact the Judge shown she is very capable of unethical behavior. The other proper, fair and ethical action the Judge should have taken was voluntarily remove the jurors that she knew she had known by using a "challenge for cause" to remove them so that no party would feel they were at a disadvantage because prospective jurors were acquainted with the Judge. I say the Judge knew she had known prospective jurors because all three prospective jurors said the Honorable Keeley was acquainted with their family and two prospective jurors said they went to the same church as the Honorable Keeley. I feel with passion if someone goes to the same church as you, you are going to know that person's face and notice that person in your courtroom so the fair

20

thing the Honorable Keeley should have done was voluntarily say

I know you, you and you and because I know you all I will remove

you guys using a "challenge for cause." Instead the Honorable Keeley

asked the prospective jurors did they know her. I feel in hopes that

they were not going to be truthful and say they knew her? I feel

the Honorable Irene Keeley expected the three people who was truth-

ful about knowing her to not be truthful and that's why the Honor-

able Keeley did not take the initiative to state she knew the pro-

spective jurors she knew was in her courtroom. I honestly feel there

were prospective jurors who the Honorable Keeley expected not to be

truthful who was not truthful when asked did they know the Judge

who were possibly selected to be jurors in my trial that the Honor-

able Keeley had influence over to render a guilty verdict in my

trial. I have every right to feel this way and I truly feel this

is what happened because the Honorable Irene Keeley has proven and

shown us she is not trustworthy, deceitful, dishonest and does not

respect ethic rules so it's very possible this occured.

The Judge also did not abide by Canon's Rules of Ethics be-

cause she knowingly let me still proceed to trial with an attorney

she knew I reported to the board/Bar Association of West Virginia

even though she knew Canon's Rules of Ethics typically states when

someone reports an attorney to the Board that attorney is unable

to proceed. The Judge knew this but still did not respect it or

the system of moral tenets or principles designed by the American

Bar Association for standards for criminal justice. The Court knew

I reported my attorney Mr. Walker to the Board since my final pre-

trial conference or days before trial but still forced me to pro-

21

ceed to trial with this attorney. Please see page 7 lines 12-16
of my trial transcripts where the record reflects before trial
was to initially start the judge placed a copy of the complaint
I sent to the board/Bar Association of West Virginia about my
attorney on my attorney's table so it can be discussed. " This
is the same complaint the judge knew about days before trial was
going to actually start." Please see pages 11 lines 1-25 of my
trial transcripts where the record reflects the judge read a
brief part of my complaint on the record. Now please take a look
at page 9 lines 23-25 of my trial transcripts where the record
reflects the judge asked me is this complaint something I intend
to pursue and my reply to the judge was "Yeah,Yes, Your Honor."
Instead of the judge respecting the ethic rule of Canon that states typically when someone reports an attorney to the board that
attorney is unable to proceed the judge instead said to me in a
threaten tone "are you going to represnt yourself today. Is that
what you want? Do you want me to fire Mr. Walker and have you represent yourself." Please see page 14 lines 23-25 of my trial
transcripts where the record reflects that the judge told me that.
The judge then stated in a threaten tone " I'm saying your choice
now is Mr. Walker or yourself." Please see page 15 lines 12-13 of trial tra-
cripts where the record reflects this was also said by the Judge. I highly
doubt an attorney will be effective at trial after he was reported
to the Board by his client. The Honorable Irene Keeley actions proves she does not respect ethic rules or the law and does what she
wants which is prohibited by the Constitution and she should be
held accountable for her actions. The Court's unprofessional and

22

unethical conduct throughout my entire case needs to be addressed and it's a compelling need for it to be addressed. There's no telling what other unprofessional and unethical conduct the Honorable Irene Keeley committed in my case or to other defendant's in the past who never made a complaint against her because they did not know how to or who just didn't know their rights were getting violated by the Court due to their ignorance to the law and their ignorance to the Judge's obligation to rules set forth in Canons Rules of Ethics or standards set by the ABA for Criminal Justice.

Lastly I can't help but to bring this up. I feel I was treated so unfairly in Judge Keeley's courtroom. It's no telling what unethical conduct she won't commit so everything is suspect in my eyes. The judge told the jury of my trial they will receive a notebook in order for them to take notes about my trial throughout my trial and she instructed the jury they are to leave their notebooks facedown in their chairs whenever they leave the courtroom which included going to lunch, a brief break or going home at the end of each trial date to come back the next day to continue trial. The Judge also said those notebooks may be retrieved and placed in a safe. Please see page 56 lines 1-8 of my trial transcripts where the record reflects the Judge said this. There was a total of five times the Court throughout my trial instructed the jurors to leave their notebooks facedown in their chair and leave the courtroom. These notebooks that were left unattended was full of the jurors' notes they may have taken during the course of my trial and perhaps even notes of their personal feelings about my innocence of charges they felt about me based on the evidence presented at my trial or was not

23

presented at my trial. Please see page 158 lines 9-13, page 194 line 1-4, page 249 lines 9-11, page 276 lines 5-6 and page 287 lines 23-24 of my trial transcripts where the record reflects the Judge told the jury of my trial to exit the courtroom but before leaving they were instructed to leave their notebooks face down in their chairs. These notebooks were left in the jurors' chairs sometimes for minutes, hours or an entire day until trial was to continue the next morning unattended and "anyone" had access to these notebooks including the "government and Judge." There is no record of the notebooks being put in a safe as the Judge stated may happen to them when everyone supposedly leaves the courtroom including myself, my attorney, the government and the Honorable Irene Keeley. I say supposedly because who's to say the government or Judge or both at the same time did not read the jurors' notes that they wrote in their notebooks throughout my trial and perhaps notes about their personal feelings about my innocence that was written in their notebooks when no one was in the courtroom and it was only them in the courtroom. With every cell in my body I believed that happened. I also believe the government tailored her case in chief presentation to the jury of my trial to fit any notes she may have read in the jurors' notebooks of their personal feeling of my innocence based on the evidence presented at my trial or per- haps what the Judge may have read in the jurors' notebook and then informed the government of such notes she have read or what they read together in the jurors' notebooks. This is very possible because they condoned each other's unethical conduct. "The prime example" is when Special Agent Bassett was instructed to leave the courtroom

24

by the Judge because he was a witness but did not leave the Honorable Irene Keeley condoned U.S. Attorney Zelda Wesley's actions by Ms. Wesley not telling Special Agent Bassett to leave the courtroom who was sitting at the same table as she. And U.S. Attorney Zelda Wesley condoned the Honorable Irene Keeley's actions when the Honorable Irene Keeley did not tell Special Agent Bassett herself to leave the courtroom after she instructed all witnesses to leave the courtroom and the Honorable Keeley knew herself Special Agent Bassett was going to be a witness in my trial. The evidence clearly shows they condoned each other's unprofessional and unethical conduct so it's very possible that they both condoned each other's unethical conduct reading the jurors' notes in their notebooks either together or separate. I strongly feel this is what happened in the courtroom by the government and or Judge when no one was in the courtroom monitoring their actions. I truly feel I did not have a fair trial due to the Judge having already shown the unethical conduct she is capable of doing with the mere speculation of what I am claiming could have really happened due to the unethical conduct both the government and the honorable Keeley has shown they are capable of doing. The other thing I can't help but to view as suspect is that the Honorable Keeley brought the jury of my trial lunch while they were to deliberate my case to come up with a verdict. Please see page 335 lines 21-25 of my trial transcripts where the record reflects this. What was that a bribe of some sort? I don't think that's normal for a Judge to buy a jury of a trial lunch. Maybe it is normal or maybe it's not. I just never seen or heard that before so my antennas goes up especially after all the unprofessional and unethical conduct the judge has done to me.

25

The next 32 pages are trial transcripts pertaining to my complaint I wrote about the judge to the Judicial Investigation Commission

---

```
 1                    P R O C E E D I N G S
 2           (12-11-18 at 9:42 A.M., defendant present)
 3           THE COURT:  Is there any objection to the selection
 4   of the jury this morning?
 5       From the Government.
 6           MS. WESLEY:  No, Your Honor.
 7           THE COURT:  From the defendant?
 8           MR. WALKER:  No, Your Honor.
 9           THE COURT:  All right.  Are there any other matters
10   to take up prior to recessing for lunch?
11           MS. WESLEY:  Not...
12           MR. WALKER:  Your Honor, this morning I received a
13   letter from the clerk.
14           THE COURT:  Yes, I had -- I directed actually my law
15   clerk to leave a copy of that on your table so that you would
16   be aware that I had received another letter from your client.
17           MR. WALKER:  Your Honor, I spoke with Mr. Antoine at
18   -- should we address that now?
19           THE COURT:  Yes.
20           MR. WALKER:  I spoke with Mr. Antoine last night and
21   actually into this morning at the jail.  And I --
22           THE COURT:  Do you want to do this on an ex parte
23   basis?
24           MR. WALKER:  Yes, Your Honor.
25           THE COURT:  Would you prefer?  Okay.  I'll excuse --
```

Stacy Harlow, CVR-M/CM/RVR-M/RCP/RBC
Post Office Box 969 Clarksburg, WV 26302-0969 (304)623-7154

1 do at this point. Typically when someone reports you to the

2 board, you're unable to proceed. I'm willing to proceed.

3 We're here; we have a jury panel sworn. I'm ready to go, but I

4 have to abide by cannons, rules of ethics. I believe we've

5 spoken and resolved many of the conflicts. There's no issues

6 this morning, other than the minor disagreements. But, again,

7 I don't want to provide a path back from the court of appeals

8 to this courtroom at a later date because I didn't make a phone

9 call and follow up on something and seek --

10   THE COURT: All right. I have observed Mr. Antoine

11 actively participating in jury selection with you and that it

12 appeared to -- that you were consulting him. He was -- he had

13 quite a voice and was prepared to speak with regard to that

14 selection and participated actively in it, correct?

15   MR. WALKER: Yes, Your Honor.

16   THE COURT: Okay. All right. You'll let me know at

17 your earliest opportunity.

18   MR. WALKER: I will, Your Honor.

19   THE COURT: All right. Thank you, very much.

20 Mr. Antoine, did -- do you have a copy of whatever you

21 filed with the bar in Charleston?

22   THE DEFENDANT: Yes, Your Honor, I do.

23   THE COURT: Okay. Is that something that you intend

24 to pursue?

25   THE DEFENDANT: Yeah. Yes, Your Honor.

341

think -- yeah. Okay. This is a document dated November 11th
and it's addressed -- it appears to be addressed --

THE DEFENDANT: Yeah. That's it right -- sorry.

THE COURT: Pardon me?

THE DEFENDANT: Yeah. But that's it right there.

THE COURT: November 11th.

THE DEFENDANT: Yes, ma'am.

THE COURT: Okay. It says "To office of disciplinary
counsel/Honorable Michael Aloi, and the Bar Association of West
Virginia." And then it starts out with "First I would like to
address Mr. Honorable Aloi. I need a new attorney, sir, for
the following reasons. I wrote up my attorney, Mr. Walker, for
which is attached, sir." Nothing attached, I would add.

"I truly feel it's going to be a conflict of interest
between my attorney and I due to this write up. Can you please
give me new counsel? I no longer want to proceed forward with
Mr. Walker as my attorney. I can't move forward with him as my
attorney."

And then it says "To the office of disciplinary counsel
and the Bar Association, attached is a copy of a complaint I
would like to bring up against my attorney." But there was
nothing attached.

So I never saw a complaint.

THE DEFENDANT: Yes, there was.

THE COURT: Well, I'm just saying nothing was

1   THE COURT: So anything that you said to the bar

2   about please replace my attorney doesn't matter because they

3   don't have the power to do that. That's only before me or

4   Judge Aloi. You get that.

5   THE DEFENDANT: Yes, Your Honor.

6   THE COURT: Okay. So what did you specifically

7   report to the bar as a violation of attorney-client privilege?

8   THE DEFENDANT: I feel that -- that...

9   THE COURT: I'm not asking what you feel, Mr.

10 Antoine; I'm asking what you reported to the State Bar. Is it

11 paragraph one?

12   THE DEFENDANT: Yes, paragraph one, two.

13   THE COURT: Now, I took care of paragraph two, which

14 had to do with all the discovery.

15   THE DEFENDANT: And -- but it's more there, Your

16 Honor. It's more than just discovery there though.

17   THE COURT: I took care of your claims that he was

18 neglecting your criminal case and didn't care about you.

19 That's all on the record from the final pretrial conference.

20   THE DEFENDANT: There's more there where I had...

21   THE COURT: Okay. Go ahead.

22   THE DEFENDANT: The --

23   THE COURT: Are you going to represent yourself

24 today? Is that what you want? Do you want me to fire Mr.

25 Walker and have you represent yourself? Is that what you want?

```
 1  You're -- jeopardy is attached; we've got the jury.  You're
 2  going to trial.  You need to make up your mind what you're
 3  doing.
 4           THE DEFENDANT:  I want a lawyer that --
 5           THE COURT:  I already ruled on all of that.
 6           THE DEFENDANT:  That will --
 7           THE COURT:  I ruled on all of that, Mr. Antoine.
 8  Just because you want doesn't mean you're going to get.  I made
 9  those rulings.  They are final and I was very clear with you
10  about that at the final pretrial conference.
11           THE DEFENDANT:  All right.  So you saying that...
12           THE COURT:  I'm saying your choice now is Mr. Walker
13  or yourself.
14           THE DEFENDANT:  So, Judge Keeley, right?
15           THE COURT:  That's my name.
16           THE DEFENDANT:  When -- on November the -- no, on
17  December the 3rd when I came in here, we had left the courtroom
18  and Mr. Walker came to speak to me.
19           THE COURT:  I read your letter.
20           THE DEFENDANT:  Yeah.  Right?  I told Mr. Walker, all
21  right.  So let's speak about my defense.  He said...
22           THE COURT:  You don't have one.
23           THE DEFENDANT:  Yeah.  At all.  Then he had cut off
24  the light and he just left me in the dark about 20 minutes.
25  Then I feel that no lawyer should treat a client like that.
```

Stacy Harlow, CVR-M/CM/RVR-M/RCP/RBC
Post Office Box 969 Clarksburg, WV 26302-0969 (304)623-7154

344

1   need to change attorneys, because the facts aren't changing.

2   We're not changing attorneys. Okay? And this case is going to

3   be tried.

4   THE DEFENDANT: So, Your Honor, so was you like aware

5   that Mr. Walker told my mom and that -- that the prosecutor

6   does -- she does have the rest of the case? I mean the tape

7   that they just saying that they don't have.

8   THE COURT: If the prosecutor has anymore tape than

9   we saw at the final pretrial conference, you'll get to play it

10 at this trial. Okay? I told you that.

11   THE DEFENDANT: No, Your Honor. All right. Then on

12 the top of that, yesterday I told Mr. Walker that certain

13 things are not in my discovery that should be that the

14 Government should have gave over. So --

15   THE COURT: Like what?

16   THE DEFENDANT: My -- the -- the court ordered for

17 the phones. And there's only certain things that's --

18   THE COURT: Okay. I don't how many times -- I don't

19 mean to interrupt you again, Mr. Antoine, but I told you at the

20 final pretrial conference, the ruling on the motion to suppress

21 involving your phone is over and done as far as this trial is -

22 - just a moment.

23   THE DEFENDANT: All right, Your Honor.

24   THE COURT: If you want to take that up on appeal

25 because you don't like it, fine. That is not any evidence that

1 have moved on and you don't know what they said. When you

2 leave the courtroom during the trial, you'll leave your

3 notebook face down on the chairs. You'll notice there's a

4 number on the back of them. There should be at this point.

5 That is so that Debbie and Joyce may retrieve those notebooks.

6 They put them in our safe. We don't read them; we don't look

7 at them. They're taken up face down and they're put back

8 facing down. But I want you to be aware that notes are not

9 entitled to any greater weight than the memory or impression of

10 each juror as to what the testimony may have been. So whether

11 you take notes or not, each of you must form and express your

12 own opinion as to what the facts of the case are. If you do

13 not take notes, rely on your own memory of what was said and

14 don't be overly influenced of the notes of your fellow jurors.

15   In conclusion, I have a few key principles that sum all

16 this up. Your job is to decide all the factual questions in a

17 case, like who should be believed, who should not be believed.

18 I will decide all the legal questions like what testimony or

19 exhibits are received into evidence and which ones are not.

20 Please don't concern yourselves with the legal questions.

21   Mr. Antoine, the defendant, has pleaded not guilty. He is

22 presumed to be innocent. As such, he is not required to

23 produce any evidence whatsoever. By bringing the superseding

24 indictment, moreover, the Government has accepted the

25 responsibility of proving his guilt to the charges unanimously

1   beyond a reasonable doubt.

2   Don't discuss the case with anyone and keep an open mind

3   until all the evidence has been received. At that time, I will

4   give you your complete and final instructions, both orally and

5   in writing, and then and only then will you be fully prepared

6   to begin your deliberations and reach your verdict.

7   That concludes the preliminary instructions of the Court,

8   ladies and gentlemen. We'll now hear from the attorneys in

9   opening statement. The Government will begin.

10   Ms. Wesley.

11   MS. WESLEY: Thank you.

12   GOVERNMENT'S OPENING STATEMENT

13   May please the Court, and ladies and gentlemen of the

14   jury. Again, my name is Zelda Wesley and I'm the Assistant

15   United States Attorney. Seated at counsel table with me is

16   Special Agent Matt Bassett from the ATF, Tim Helman, who is an

17   AUSA from our Martinsburg's office, and Laurel Jones, who's a

18   paralegal in our office, and we're here today on behalf of the

19   Government.

20   Now, the Court has already advised you that this portion

21   of the trial is called opening statements, and it's an

22   opportunity for the parties to give you a preview of what we

23   expect the evidence in this case to be, and also to give you an

24   expectation of what we think the evidence in this case will

25   show.

1 expect. Why? We're not going to hear about DNA evidence.

2 We're not going to hear about fingerprints. All we're going to

3 hear is from individuals who are co-conspirators and have an

4 interest in the outcome, based on their testimony.

5   Now, as you're well aware, the defendant sits in this

6 chair clothed in the presumption of innocence, and he shall

7 remain clothed in that presumption unless and until the

8 Government, through Ms. Wesley, can prove him guilty beyond a

9 reasonable doubt. I don't believe they'll be able to do it.

10 Why? No DNA evidence, no fingerprint evidence, testimony from

11 co-defendants who are supremely interested in the outcome of

12 the case.

13   So at the conclusion of this case, I'll stand right here

14 before you and I'll ask you to return a verdict worthy of the

15 evidence you've heard, but also worthy of the evidence you

16 expected to hear and didn't hear. And I'm confident at the

17 conclusion, your verdict will be not guilty. Thank you.

18   THE COURT: All right.

19   Ladies and gentlemen, that concludes the opening

20 statements. The Government bears the burden of proof and may

21 begin its case-in-chief.

22   MR. WALKER: Your Honor, I move to sequester all

23 witnesses, if it hasn't been done.

24   THE COURT: All right.

25   Motion to sequester granted. If there are any witnesses

1   in the courtroom, please leave.

2   MS. WESLEY: Your Honor, the Government calls Victor

3   Perez.

4   THE COURT: All right.

5   The first witness is Victor Perez. Do you have someone

6   whose getting them?

7   MS. WESLEY: Yes, Your Honor.

8   THE COURT: Okay.

9   Ladies and gentlemen, since witnesses have been

10   sequestered, that means somebody has to get them and bring them

11   in. So there's always just a brief delay.

12   (Mr. Perez enters the courtroom.)

13   Mr. Perez, would you approach the clerk at the front of

14   the courtroom. She'll administer the oath to you before you

15   take the witness stand, sir.

16   THE WITNESS: Yes, ma'am.

17   (VICTOR PEREZ WAS SWORN.)

18   THE CLERK: The witness is Victor Perez. P-e-r-e-z.

19   THE COURT: You may proceed.

20   DIRECT EXAMINATION

21   BY MS. WESLEY:

22   Q.   Where do you work?

23   A.   I work for the New York State Department of Corrections

24   and Community Supervision, formerly known as The Division of

25   Parole of New York State. I'm a senior parole officer.

1   (DENNINE SMIDDY WAS SWORN.)

2   THE CLERK: The witness is --

3   MS. WESLEY: Your Honor, --

4   THE CLERK: -- Detective --

5   THE COURT: Oh, sorry.

6   MS. WESLEY: I'm sorry. She has an exhibit.

7   THE COURT: Yes, I see.

8 (Ms. Smiddy exits the courtroom.)

9   Ladies and gentlemen, we'll re-administer that oath when

10 she gets back with the exhibit.

11 (Ms. Smiddy enters the courtroom.)

12   All right. Please raise your right hand.

13   (DENNINE SMIDDY WAS SWORN.)

14   THE CLERK: The witness is Detective Dennine -- D-e-

15 n-n-i-n-e -- Smiddy. S-m-i-d-d-y.

16   THE WITNESS: Good afternoon.

17   THE COURT: All right. Ms. Smiddy, if you'll speak

18 in a loud, clear voice into the microphone so that the jurors

19 may all hear you.

20   You may proceed.

21   DIRECT EXAMINATION

22 BY MS. WESLEY:

23 Q. Where do you work?

24 A. Yonkers Police Department, New York.

25 Q. And how long have you worked there?

1   Before the witness leaves, she's got the envelope in which

2 the exhibit was contained. Is there any reason to hold that?

3 It was not admitted into evidence. I just want to make sure

4 before she leaves that she can take that with her.

5   MR. WALKER: Oh, no.

6   THE COURT: Okay. Thank you.

7 (Mr. Mahdavi enters the courtroom.)

8   Mr. Mahdavi, good afternoon, sir. Would you please

9 approach the clerk standing at the front of the courtroom in

10 the black jack and she'll administer the oath to you before you

11 take the witness stand.

12   (ANTHONY MAHDAVI WAS SWORN.)

13   THE CLERK: The witness is Anthony Mahdavi. M-a-h-d-

14 a-v-i.

15   THE COURT: All right. Mr. Mahdavi, please speak in

16 a loud, clear voice into the microphone so that all the jurors

17 may hear you.

18   You may proceed.

19   DIRECT EXAMINATION

20 BY MS. WESLEY:

21 Q.   Where do you work?

22 A.   Tony's Street Dreamz.

23 Q.   And how long have you worked there?

24 A.   My dad owns it, I've been here forever.

25 Q.   Okay. And in what capacity are you employed there?

1 Special Agent Matt Bassett of the ATF and provide him with a

2 recording of the surveillance footage that was captured on June

3 the 19th of 2017?

4 A.   Yes, ma'am.

5 Q.   And the surveillance recording that you provided to Mr.

6 Bassett, it was an accurate depiction of what was captured on

7 those video recordings?

8 A.   Yes.

9 Q.   Okay.

10   MS. WESLEY: I have nothing further to this witness,

11 Your Honor.

12   THE COURT: All right. Thank you.

13 Is there any cross-examination, Mr. Walker?

14   MR. WALKER: None, Your Honor.

15   THE COURT: All right.

16 Is the witness subject to recall?

17   MS. WESLEY: Not from the Government, Your Honor.

18   MR. WALKER: No, Your Honor.

19   THE COURT: All right. Thank you.

20 You may step down, Mr. Mahdavi, and you're free to go.

21   THE WITNESS: Thank you.

22   THE COURT: The Government may call its next witness.

23   MS. WESLEY: Will Jackson.

24   THE COURT: Will Jackson.

25 (Mr. Jackson enters the courtroom.)

1   MR. WALKER: Yes, Your Honor.

2   THE COURT: All right. Thank you very much. And the

3   same with the exhibits, right.

4   MS. WESLEY: Yes, Your Honor.

5   THE COURT: Okay. Thank you. You may call your next

6   witness.

7   Oh, sorry. We need to bring the jury in. I apologize for

8   that. I was trying to track the -- this is your fifth witness,

9   right?

10   MS. WESLEY: Chris Anderson, Your Honor.

11   THE COURT: Yeah, fifth witness is

12   Chris Anderson. Thank you.

13   (Jurors entering courtroom.)

14   THE COURT: Welcome back, ladies and gentlemen. The

15   Government's case-in-chief will continue.

16   Ms. Wesley, you may call your next witness.

17   MS. WESLEY: Your Honor, we call Chris Anderson.

18   THE COURT: Chris Anderson.

19   (Mr. Anderson enters the courtroom.)

20   THE COURT: All right. Mr. Anderson, would you

21   please approach the front of the courtroom. Do you see the

22   lady standing here in the black jacket with the blonde hair?

23   She's going to administer the oath to you before you take the

24. witness stand.

25   (CHRIS ANDERSON WAS SWORN.)

1   You may step down, Mr. Anderson. You're excused as a

2 witness and free to go.

3   The Government may call its next witness.

4   MS. WESLEY: Margaret Parker.

5   THE COURT: All right.

6 (Ms. Parkers enters the courtroom.)

7   THE COURT: Good afternoon, Ms. Parker. Would you

8 please approach the clerk here in the front of the courtroom?

9 She's standing in the black jacket. Please approach. She will

10 administer·the oath to you, if you come forward. Please raise

11 your right hand.

12   (MARGARET PARKER WAS SWORN.)

13   THE CLERK: The witness is Margaret Parker. P-a-r-k-

14 e-r.

15   THE COURT: Ms. Parker, I'm going to ask that you

16 speak in a loud, clear voice.

17   Ms. Parker, I'm over here. Would you speak in a loud,

18 clear voice into the microphone so that all jurors may hear

19 you, please?

20   THE WITNESS: Yes.

21   THE COURT: Thank you.

22   DIRECT EXAMINATION

23 BY MS. WESLEY:

24 Q. would you tell us how old you are?

25 A. 34.

1 Q.   Okay.

2   MR. WALKER: No further questions, Your Honor.

3   THE COURT: All right.

4   Is there any redirect?

5   MS. WESLEY: No, Your Honor.

6   THE COURT: Is the witness subject to recall?

7   MR. WALKER: No, Your Honor.

8   THE COURT: All right.

9   Ms. Parker, you may step down. You're excused as a

10 witness. You may leave.

11   THE WITNESS: Thanks.

12   THE COURT: You're free to go.

13   THE WITNESS: Thank you.

14   THE COURT: Ms. Wesley, I don't if -- how long your

15 next witness will be, but it's 20 till 5:00.

16   MS. WESLEY: We have an interstate nexus witness.

17 That should be short.

18   THE COURT: Okay. We'll call one more witness, then.

19   MS. WESLEY: We call Special Agent Matt Kocher. And

20 he's already getting the agent.

21   THE COURT: All right. Fine.

22   Ladies and gentlemen, I'm aware this has been a long day

23 for you. This will be the last witness for the day. Thank you

24 for your patience.

25 (Special Agent Kocher enters the courtroom.)

1   courtroom?

2   JURORS: (No verbal response.)

3   THE COURT: I'm glad, because we can't change the

4   temperature. It's not within my power. I can do a lot of

5   things as a judge, but I cannot change the temperature in this

6   courtroom. So you might be freezing tomorrow. We never know.

7   Just bring whatever you need and be prepared, and you can leave

8   what you don't need in the jury room.

9   We thank you for your attention and your patience today.

10 I know you were up early to get here, and I wish you safe

11 travels home. Thank you. You're free to go. Please leave

12 your notebooks face down on your chairs. We'll begin at 9:00

13 o'clock.

14 (Jurors exiting courtroom.)

15   THE COURT: We're going to print copies of the first

16 draft of the charge so that you can have it. Realistic

17 estimate, will the case go to the jury tomorrow or are we going

18 to need an extra afternoon to finish up --

19   MS. WESLEY: No, I --

20   THE COURT: -- the charge?

21   MS. WESLEY: I'm sorry. I provided him the list for

22 tomorrow. Tomorrow we're going to start with Dawn Tatar, Maria

23 Lopez. They're both from West Virginia Jewelry and Loan. They

24 will both be quick, although we will play the video with Maria.

25 Then Tommy Calhoun, Nick Junkins, and, of course, he's got the

```
 1                    P R O C E E D I N G S

 2           (12-12-18 at 9:08 A.M., defendant present)

 3           THE COURT:  Good morning.  All jurors are now here.

 4   The computer on the bench is fixed; we're ready to proceed

 5   unless there is any -- there are any matters that the parties

 6   would like to take up before I bring the jury in.

 7           MS. WESLEY:  Not from the Government, Your Honor.

 8           MR. WALKER:  Not from the defense.

 9           THE COURT:  All right.  Thank you.

10      We can bring the jury in.

11   (Jurors entering courtroom.)

12           THE COURT:  Good morning, ladies and gentlemen.

13   Welcome back.  Thank you for being here on a timely basis this

14   morning.  We're ready to resume the Government's case-in-chief.

15      Ms. Wesley, your next witness.

16           MS. WESLEY:  Your Honor, the Government calls Tommy

17   Calhoun.

18           THE COURT:  Tommy Calhoun.

19   (Mr. Calhoun enters the courtroom.)

20           THE COURT:  Mr. Calhoun.

21           THE WITNESS:  Yes.

22           THE COURT:  Good morning.  Would you please come

23   forward to the front of the courtroom where the clerk is

24   standing?  If you'll raise your right hand, she'll administer

25   the oath to you before you take the witness stand.
```

```
1   retrieve the exhibit?

2           THE COURT:  You may retrieve the exhibit.

3   (Ms. Tatar enters the courtroom.)

4           THE COURT:  Good morning, Ms. Tatar.  Would you

5   please approach the clerk?  She will administer the oath to you

6   before you take the witness stand.

7                   (DAWN TATAR WAS SWORN.)

8           THE CLERK:  The witness is Dawn Tatar.  T-a-t-a-r.

9           THE COURT:  All right.  Ms. Tatar, if you'll please

10  speak in a loud, clear voice into the microphone.

11      You may proceed.

12                  DIRECT EXAMINATION

13  BY MS. WESLEY:

14  Q.   Where do you work?

15  A.   WV Jewelry and Loan, LLC.

16  Q.   And in what capacity are you involved in that business?

17  A.   I am the owner/member.

18  Q.   Okay.  And how long have you owned that business?

19  A.   Eleven years.

20  Q.   And where is the business located?

21  A.   188 Highland Avenue, Westover, West Virginia.

22  Q.   And is that a business that will sell firearms?

23  A.   Yes.

24  Q.   And are you a federal firearms licensee?

25  A.   I am.
```

```
 1            MR. WALKER:  No.
 2            THE COURT:  You're excused as a witness and free to
 3   go.
 4            THE WITNESS:  Thank you.
 5            THE COURT:  Thank you.
 6            MS. WESLEY:  Your Honor, we would call Maria Lopez.
 7   And may I retrieve the exhibits?
 8            THE COURT:  You may call -- you may retrieve the
 9   exhibits and Ms. Lopez is the next witness.
10       Ms. Tatar, you are free -- it's a little congested in here
11   this morning, but you're free to go if you can wind your way
12   through there.
13            THE WITNESS:  Thank you.
14   (Ms. Lopez enters the courtroom.)
15            THE COURT:  Good morning, Ms. Lopez.  Please approach
16   to the front of the courtroom.  The clerk is standing there and
17   will administer the oath before you take the witness stand.
18                 (MARIA LOPEZ WAS SWORN.)
19            THE CLERK:  The witness is Maria Lopez.  L-o-p-e-z.
20            THE COURT:  Ms. Lopez.
21            THE WITNESS:  Yes.
22            THE COURT:  I'm here to your left.  This -- I'm Judge
23   Keeley.  I just wanted to instruct you to please speak in a
24   loud, clear voice into the microphone.  You can move it down
25   closer to your mouth.  I want to make sure all the jurors can
```

1 courtroom, at 10:15. Please leave your notebooks face down on

2 your chairs, and do not discuss the case among yourselves

3 during this recess. Thank you for attention.

4 (Jurors exiting courtroom.)

5   THE COURT: All right. Any matters to take up before

6 the recess?

7 (No verbal response.)

8   THE COURT: All right. Counsel, I wanted to let you

9 know, we should have another draft for you that's more in line

10 with what we're going to be looking at in the charge by noon.

11 Okay. Thank you.

12   MS. WESLEY: And we talked about it -- I'm sorry. I

13 just saw one little thing or two little things and so they

14 were...

15   THE COURT: I had a few more.

16   MS. WESLEY: Okay. All right.

17   THE COURT: Thank you. Court stands in recess until

18 10:15.

19 (Off the record at 10:02 A.M.)

20 (On the record at 10:21 A.M.)

21   THE COURT: Any matters to bring up before I bring

22 the jury back in?

23   MS. WESLEY: None, Your Honor.

24   MR. WALKER: None, Your Honor.

25   THE COURT: We can bring the jury in. Thank you.

1 (Jurors entering the courtroom.)

2   THE COURT: Welcome back, ladies and gentlemen. We

3 are ready to resume the Government's case-in-chief.

4   MS. WESLEY: We call Officer Nick Junkins.

5   THE COURT: Officer Nick Junkins.

6 (Officer Junkins enters the courtroom.)

7   THE COURT: Good morning, Officer Junkins. Please

8 approach the clerk in the front of the courtroom, who will

9 administer the oath to you before you take the witness stand.

10   (NICK JUNKINS WAS SWORN.)

11   THE CLERK: The witness is Officer Nick Junkins. J-

12 u-n-k-i-n-s.

13   THE COURT: Officer Junkins, will you please speak in

14 a loud, clear voice into the microphone so that all jurors may

15 hear you.

16   You may proceed.

17   MS. WESLEY: Okay.

18   DIRECT EXAMINATION

19 BY MS. WESLEY:

20 Q. Where do you presently work?

21 A. The Marion County Sheriff's Office.

22 Q. And how long have you held that employment?

23 A. Approximately eight months.

24 Q. Okay. And at some point in time did you work for Star

25 City Police Department?

1   Q.   Okay. Did you try to -- attempt to reconcile this

2   discrepancy with Mr. Calhoun?

3   A.   I did not.

4   Q.   Now, were any pictures taken of the suitcase and the

5   contents?

6   A.   No, I don't believe so.

7   Q.   Was a citation issued for the broken taillight?

8   A.   No.

9   MR. WALKER: Thank you, Your Honor. No further

10   questions.

11   THE COURT: All right.

12   Is there redirect?

13   MS. WESLEY: No, Your Honor.

14   THE COURT: Is the witness subject to recall?

15   MR. WALKER: No, Your Honor.

16   THE COURT: Thank you. You may step down, Officer

17   Junkins. You're excused as a witness

18   THE WITNESS: Thank you, ma'am.

19   THE COURT: Free to go.

20   The Government may call its next witness.

21   MS. WESLEY: Your Honor, we call Chief Corkrean. And

22   may I retrieve the evidence?

23   THE COURT: You may. And Chief Corkrean is the next

24   witness.

25   (Chief Corkrean enters the courtroom.)

Stacy Harlow, CVR-M/CM/RVR-M/RCP/RBC
Post Office Box 969 Clarksburg, WV 26302-0969 (304)623-7154

1   was on August 2, 2017.

2   MS. WESLEY: May I have a moment, Your Honor?

3   THE COURT: Yes.

4   MS. WESLEY: I have no further questions of this

5   witness, Your Honor.

6   THE COURT: All right.

7   Cross-examination.

8   MR. WALKER: No questions, Your Honor.

9   THE COURT: Is the witness subject to recall?

10   MR. WALKER: No, Your Honor.

11   THE COURT: Thank you.

12   Chief Corkrean, you are excused as a witness and free to

13 go. You're not subject to recall.

14   THE WITNESS: Thank you.

15   MS. WESLEY: Your Honor, we have one last witness who

16 is lengthy.

17   THE COURT: All right. Can we get him started before

18 lunch?

19   MS. WESLEY: Yes, Your Honor.

20   THE COURT: Okay. Thank you.

21   MS. WESLEY: May we retrieve?

22   THE COURT: We can retrieve the exhibits of the

23 witness who, I think, has them in his hand, can give them to

24 you.

25   MS. WESLEY: Your Honor, we would call Special Agent

1 Matt Bassett.

2   THE COURT: All right.

3   Special Agent Bassett, if you'll approach the clerk,

4 she'll administer the oath to you before you take the witness

5 stand.

6   (MATT BASSETT WAS SWORN.)

7   THE CLERK: The witness is Special Agent Matt

8 Bassett. B-a-s-s-e-t-t.

9   DIRECT EXAMINATION

10 BY MS. WESLEY:

11 Q.   Where do you presently work?

12 A.   I am a Special Agent with the Bureau of Alcohol, Tobacco,

13 Firearms, and Explosives, commonly called ATF.

14 Q.   And how long have you worked for the ATF?

15 A.   Since July 2014.

16 Q.   And what are your duties with the ATF?

17 A.   I investigate violations of the federal firearms,

18 explosives, and narcotics laws.

19 Q.   And in reference to Mr. Amanze Antoine, do you have any

20 information regarding whether or not he's a prohibited person?

21 A.   I do.

22 Q.   Okay. And did you obtain a copy of a conviction?

23 A.   Yes, I did. Two of them.

24 Q.   Okay. Only in reference to the conviction for firearms, a

25 weapons possession charge, sir. Is that a conviction you

1   MS. WESLEY: Your Honor, may I approach this witness?

2   THE COURT: You may.

3   MS. WESLEY: Your Honor, I have Exhibit 5G for

4   identification.

5   (Government Exhibit Number 5G was introduced into

6   evidence.)

7   THE COURT: All right.

8   BY MS. WESLEY:

9   Q.   Have you reviewed that text message before?

10 A.   Yes.

11 Q.   And where did you review it, sir?

12 A.   I reviewed it at my -- at the ATF field office, as well as

13 in other locations in the course of my work.

14 Q.   And it was extracted from the ZTE telephone?

15 A.   Yes.

16 Q.   Okay. And Ms. Parker, when she testified today, she

17 testified regarding that exchange, did she not?

18 A.   She did.

19 Q.   And, of course, already admitted into evidence is Exhibit

20 20C, is it not, sir?

21 A.   Yes.

22 Q.   Is that the picture of the phone that she took while she

23 was exchanging that text message?

24 A.   Exhibit 20C is the photograph of the German Sports Firefly

25 .22 caliber pistol, the one on the green.

Stacy Harlow, CVR-M/CM/RVR-M/RCP/RBC
Post Office Box 969 Clarksburg, WV 26302-0969 (304)623-7154

1   or the radio. Don't attempt any independent research at the
2   library, on your cell phone, or through any other medium. And
3   should a third person approach you and attempt to discuss the
4   case with you, please advise them that you've been directed not
5   to do so. If they persistent in trying to talk to you, you can
6   walk away from them and let me know through the court security
7   or Debbie that that contact has occurred.
8   We all appreciate your attention and your patience this
9   morning. You stand in recess until 1:15. Please leave your
10   notebooks face down on your chairs and follow court security
11   back to the jury room.
12   (Jurors exiting courtroom.)
13   THE COURT: All right. Mr. Bassett, you will be on
14   direct examination when you return. Please step down and be
15   prepared to resume the stand at 1:15. Thank you. If you have
16   any exhibits up there, would you please give them to -- either
17   to Ms. Wesley or the clerk? At this point, I think they're all
18   admitted, so you can give them directly to the clerk.
19   And just to make sure before we recess for lunch, could I
20   ask the clerk to check and make sure that all exhibits that
21   have been admitted are at the clerk's desk.
22   THE CLERK: Yes, Your Honor.
23   THE COURT: Thank you.
24   Ms. Wesley, do you have anything at your table?
25   MS. WESLEY: I do not, Your Honor.

```
 1   A.   At Cashland?

 2   Q.   Yes.

 3   A.   In Morgantown?  Yes.

 4   Q.   So that would have been a third, correct.

 5   A.   Yes.  Yes, that would be the third attempt.

 6   Q.   One on May 27th, correct?

 7   A.   Yes.

 8   Q.   One on June 5th, correct?

 9   A.   Yes.

10   Q.   And an attempt on June 6th, correct?

11   A.   Yes.

12   Q.   And the one on June 6th was with another individual?

13   A.   Yes.

14   Q.   Now, you were in the courtroom when Ms. Parker testified,

15   correct?

16   A.   I was.

17   Q.   And you heard me ask her how many attempts she made,

18   correct?

19   A.   Yes.

20   Q.   You heard me ask that -- her response being she only made

21   two attempts, correct?

22   A.   I believe that's -- yes.

23   Q.   But as the case agent, you know there were actually three

24   attempts, correct?

25   A.   There were two successful purchases and a third
```

1 Q. Agent, the firearms were in a suitcase, correct.

2 A. They were.

3 Q. And the firearms were registered to Tommy Calhoun,

4 correct?

5 A. The term -- an ATF agent, we try to stay away from the use

6 of the term "registry." However, the -- there is no national

7 firearms registry; however, the 4473, which is the basis for us

8 being able to trace the original retail purchaser, said "Tommy

9 Calhoun" for two of the three firearms.

10   MR. WALKER: Thank you.

11   THE COURT: All right.

12   Is there anything further for the witness?

13   MS. WESLEY: No, Your Honor.

14   THE COURT: All right.

15   Mr. Bassett, you may return to your seat.

16   The Government may call its next witness.

17   MS. WESLEY: The Government rests, Your Honor. And

18 may I retrieve the exhibits?

19   THE COURT: All right.

20   Subject to a check of the exhibits, I know you checked

21 them carefully before lunch, the Government has rested.

22   All right. Ladies and gentlemen, because the Government

23 has rested, that means it's not going to kick up its heels, but

24 it has completed its case-in-chief. That's the phrase we use

25 for that. It's now necessary for me to take up some matters

    1 out of your hearing. So although you've just come back to the
    2 courtroom recently, I'm going to ask you to briefly go back to
    3 your jury room, but please recall that we'll be working while
    4 you're waiting, and I appreciate your patience. Don't discuss
    5 the case among yourselves. Leave your notebooks face down on
    6 your chairs. Thank you.
    7 (Jurors exiting courtroom.)
    8   THE COURT: I'm happy to hear any motions at this
    9 time, should there be any.
   10   MR. WALKER: Yes, Your Honor. Defense moves for
   11 judgment of acquittal, pursuant to Rule 29, as to Count Three
   12 and Count Four of the superseding indictment, illegal transport
   13 and unlawful possession. I don't believe we've heard any
   14 testimony regarding illegal transport. And as for unlawful
   15 possession, the indictment pleads a specific date of June 19,
   16 2017. My recollection is that the questions were asked of Mr.
   17 Tommy Calhoun that "Did Mr. Antoine possess a firearm? Did you
   18 ever see him with a firearm?" And his answer was "I saw him
   19 with a firearm," but there was never a specific date on which
   20 he states he saw him with a firearm. Now, granted, I don't
   21 believe -- I will obviously argue that that is insufficient
   22 later on for proof beyond a reasonable doubt, but even at this
   23 juncture, as you look at the indictment, how its pled in the
   24 indictment, I don't believe they've met their burden, even at
   25 this juncture, as to Count Three or Count Four of the

1   federal court; you don't leave because in case we need you if a

2   juror should be -- a main juror should become unable to

3   continue to serve, juror number one and then juror number two

4   would follow to replace those -- one or more jurors.

5   All right. With that said, ladies and gentlemen, as you

6   leave tonight, remember, you don't have the case yet. Please

7   do not discuss the case among yourselves or with anyone else,

8   and do not read any media coverage of the case, whether on the

9   radio, TV, or in the newspaper. Don't attempt any independent

10   research on the Internet. Don't communicate about this on

11   Facebook, Instagram, or any other electronic means. And if a

12   third person approaches you and attempts to discuss the case

13   with you, you must walk away and tell them you're not allowed

14   to. If they persist, just report that contact me through court

15   security or Debbie. And, of course, don't do any independent

16   research the old-fashioned way by going to the library or, if

17   you're in the Morgantown area, driving around. You have to

18   take this case based on the evidence as it has been presented

19   here in court and the law as I give it to you, and nothing

20   else.

21   I want to thank you for your attention, your patience, and

22   wish you safe travels home. We'll resume at 9:00 o'clock

23   tomorrow morning. Thank you. Please leave your notebooks face

24   down on your chairs.

25   (Jurors exiting courtroom.)

1 attorney shall communicate or attempt to communicate concerning

2 the jury's deliberations or verdict with any member of the jury

3 before which the case was tried, without first obtaining an

4 order of the Court granting permission to do so. This rule

5 does not prevent you, the jury, from communicating with anyone

6 concerning your deliberations or verdict, but merely governs

7 the contact of you by other persons involved in the trial.

8   All right. Ladies and gentlemen, that concludes the

9 instructions, except for one final part of the charge which I

10. will read to you after the lawyers argue the case.

11   Now we have been at this for about 50 minutes. The

12 lawyers are going to argue the case to you after a recess.

13 They don't want to break it up with a recess, and I don't --

14 and I doubt you do, as well. So we'll take the recess now and

15 be back in here at 10 after 10:00, at which time you will hear

16 the arguments of the attorneys without a recess. I will

17 conclude the charge and then you will have the case to

18 deliberate. But you don't have it yet. Leave your charge face

19 down on your chair and then do not discuss the case among

20 yourselves during this brief recess. We'll be back in here to

21 continue with the closing argument at 10 after 10:00. Thank

22 you. Debbie is going to bring menus back to you so that we can

23 be ordering lunch for you while they're arguing the case to

24 you, and then you'll have your lunch while you're deliberating.

25 That's something we pay for.

Jury selection transcripts pertaining to my complaint about judge Keeley to the Judicial Investigation Commission.

```
 1                    APPEARANCES CONTINUED:

 2    FOR THE DEFENDANT:

 3         FRANKIE CARLE WALKER, II

 4         Frank Walker Law

 5         3000 Lewis Run Road

 6         Clairton, Pennsylvania  15025

 7

 8    SPECIAL AGENT MATT BASSETT

 9         Bureau of Alcohol, Tobacco, and Firearms.

10

11    The defendant was present in person.

12

13    Proceedings recorded utilizing digital recording, transcript

14    produced by computer-aided transcription.
15

16

17

18

19

20

21

22

23

24

25
```

1 microphones.

2   Does anyone have any question about the process? I'll

3 remind you as we go through it. Okay?

4   PROSPECTIVE JURORS: (No verbal response.)

5   THE COURT: Now, let me begin this process by

6 introducing you to the parties in the case. First, I should go

7 back. I've introduced you to myself. The lawyers and the

8 parties will want to know do any of you know me. So if you

9 know me personally or you've been involved in some kind of

10 professional capacity with me, please raise your hand.

11   PROSPECTIVE JUROR: (Raising hand.)

12   THE COURT: All right. In the front row of the

13 courtroom. Sir, would you stand and tell me your name.

14   PROSPECTIVE JUROR: James Green.

15   THE COURT: And, Mr. Green, how do you know me?

16   PROSPECTIVE JUROR: I had a court case before you in

17 2003. Julie Green v Monongalia County. A public education

18 case.

19   THE COURT: All right. As a consequence of your

20 involvement in that case, would that prevent you from being

21 fair to both sides in this case and trying the case solely on

22 the issues presented and the law as I will give it to you?

23   PROSPECTIVE JUROR: No, it would not.

24   THE COURT: Thank you, very much.

25   PROSPECTIVE JUROR: (Raising hand.)

1   THE COURT: Yes, sir. Would you please stand and
2 tell us your name?
3   PROSPECTIVE JUROR: James Allen.
4   THE COURT: And, Mr. Allen, how do you know me?
5   PROSPECTIVE JUROR: Acquaintance of our family.
6   THE COURT: All right. Would that that acquaintance,
7 in any way, affect your ability to serve as a juror in this
8 case and to be fair to both sides and make your decision based
9 solely on the evidence presented and the law as I will give it
10 in my charge?
11   PROSPECTIVE JUROR: No.
12   THE COURT: No. Thank you. You can be seated.
13   PROSPECTIVE JUROR: (Raising hand.)
14   THE COURT: Yes, ma'am. Your name? I'm sorry; I
15 didn't see your hand.
16   PROSPECTIVE JUROR: Anastasia Shaffer.
17   THE COURT: And, Ms. Shaffer, how do you know me?
18   PROSPECTIVE JUROR: We attend the same Parrish.
19   THE COURT: All right. Does the fact that we attend
20 the same Parrish church in any way affect your ability to serve
21 as a juror in this case and to be fair to both sides?
22   PROSPECTIVE JUROR: No, it would not.
23   THE COURT: Thank you.
24   PROSPECTIVE JUROR. (Raising hand.)
25   THE COURT: Yes, sir. Your name?

1   PROSPECTIVE JUROR: Dennis Burnworth.

2   THE COURT: And how do you know me?

3   PROSPECTIVE JUROR: You're acquainted with my wife

4 and her family, Jean Ann Lynch.

5   THE COURT: All right. Would --

6   PROSPECTIVE JUROR: We attend the same church.

7   THE COURT: Would the church and family acquaintance

8 in any way affect your ability to serve as a juror in this case

9 and to be fair to both sides?

10   PROSPECTIVE JUROR: No, it would not.

11   THE COURT: Thank you.

12   Anyone else?

13   PROSPECTIVE JURORS: (No verbal response.)

14   THE COURT: Thank you. Now, in this case, the

15 defendant, as you've heard, is Amanze Antoine. Mr. Antoine is

16 represented by his attorney, Mr. Frank Carle Walker, II. I'm

17 going to ask Mr. Walter to please stand to introduce himself to

18 you and to introduce his client.

19   MR. WALKER: Good morning. My name is Frank Walker

20 and I represent Mr. Antoine.

21   THE COURT: And, Mr. Antoine, if you'll please stand.

22   THE DEFENDANT: (Complies.)

23   THE COURT: Okay. Thank you. You can both be

24 seated.

25   THE DEFENDANT: (Complies.)

1   MR. WALKER: (Complies.)

2   THE COURT: Now, do any of the jurors know Mr.

3 Walker?

4   PROSPECTIVE JURORS: (No verbal response.)

5   THE COURT: Are you related to Mr. Walker?

6   PROSPECTIVE JURORS: (No verbal response.)

7   THE COURT: Have you had any professional dealings

8 with Mr. Walker, who is an attorney in Morgantown, West

9 Virginia?

10   PROSPECTIVE JURORS: (No verbal response.)

11   THE COURT: All right. Are any of you familiar, are

12 you related to or know Mr. -- familiar with, related to, or

13 know Mr. Antoine, the defendant in this case?

14   PROSPECTIVE JURORS: (No verbal response.)

15   THE COURT: Thank you.

16   Now, the government is represented by Assistant United

17 States Attorney Zelda Wesley and Assistant United States

18 Attorney Timothy Helman. I'm going to ask Ms. Wesley to stand,

19 introduce herself to you, and your fellow attorney, and also I

20 believe it's the Government representative or agent at the

21 table.

22   MS. WESLEY: Good morning. I'm Zelda Wesley and

23 seated at counsel table with me is Timothy Helman, who's also

24 an attorney for the Government. And this is Matt Bassett, who

25 is a Special Agent with the Bureau of Alcohol, Tobacco, and

1   PROSPECTIVE JUROR: Michelle Muckleroy, and he has

2   been at our facility to work with some of our staff.

3   THE COURT: All right. Is there anything about that

4   relationship with your employer and the staff of your company

5   that would affect your ability to serve as a juror in this case

6   and to be fair to both sides?

7   PROSPECTIVE JUROR: No.

8   THE COURT: You'll weigh his testimony just as you

9   would, for credibility, as you would any other witness?

10   PROSPECTIVE JUROR: Yes, I would.

11   THE COURT: Thank you.

12   Ruth Hunt.

13   No? Ms. Hunt is not being called.

14   Victor Propst, who is the chief of the Star City Police

15   Department.

16   Not called. Donald Fries.

17   No?

18   Shonda Joseph.

19   PROSPECTIVE JURORS: (No verbal response.)

20   THE COURT: Matthew Bassett is the case agent and

21   you-all have been introduced to Mr. Bassett.

22   PROSPECTIVE JURORS: (No verbal response.)

23   THE COURT: And as I understand it, none of you knows

24   Mr. Bassett, correct?

25   PROSPECTIVE JURORS: (No verbal response.)

CHAPTER 46

THE INJUSTICE KENNETH SADLER IS FACING:

December 21, 2021

Today I received some extremely bad news from a friend of mine from Detroit who is concurrently incarcerated with me at F.C.I Raybrook named Kenneth Sadler that seriously bothered me. Mr. Sadler told me today the warden of this prison denied his compassionate release request to be released from prison even though he fell under the guidelines for his compassionate release request to be granted by the warden.

For those of you who have no idea what a compassionate release request is let me explain to you what it is very briefly. A compassionate release request is a written request made by an inmate in a federal prison to the warden of the prison the inmate is incarcerated in asking the warden to release him or her from prison because of an "extraordinary and compelling" reason. Congress described to all wardens who work in a federal prison in the United States what should be considered an "extraordinary and compelling" reason to grant a prisoner's release when a prisoner submits a compassionate release request to him or her in the Bureau of Prisons Program Statement No. 5050.50.

The Bureau of Prisons Program Statement is another way of saying "all of the rules that all staff members who work in a federal prison including the warden of each prison are obligated to follow". The following reasons are the "extraordinary and compelling" reasons Congress told each and every warden who works in a federal prison in the United States were reasons for them to grant an inmate's compassionate release request that is submitted to them. These reasons below were placed in the Bureau of Prisons Program Statement by Congress which is again another way of saying a rulebook of all the rules that all wardens and staff members who work in a federal prison are "obligated" to follow:

See below:

1. Extraordinary and Compelling Reasons.-Provided the defendant meets the requirements of subdivision (2), extraordinary and compelling reasons exist under any of the circumstances set forth below:

(A) Medical Condition of the Defendant.-

(i) The defendant is suffering from a terminal illness (i.e., a serious and advanced illness with an end of life trajectory). A specific prognosis of life expectancy (i.e., a probability of **death** within a specific time period) is not required. Examples include metastatic solid-tumor cancer, amyotrophic lateral sclerosis (ALS), end-stage organ{**2021 U.S. Dist. LEXIS 7**} disease, and advanced dementia.

(ii) The defendant is-

(I) suffering from a serious physical or medical condition, (II) suffering from a serious functional or cognitive impairment, or (III) experiencing deteriorating physical or mental health because of the aging process,

that substantially diminishes the ability of the defendant to provide self-care within the environment of a correctional facility and from which he or she is not expected to recover.

(B) Age of the Defendant.-The defendant (i) is at least 65 years old; (ii) is experiencing a serious deterioration in physical or mental health because of the aging process; and (iii) has served at least 10 years or 75 percent of his or her term of imprisonment, whichever is less.

(C) Family Circumstances.-

(i) The **death** or incapacitation of the **caregiver** of the **defendant's** minor child or minor **children**. (ii) The incapacitation of the **defendant's** spouse or registered partner when the defendant would be the only available **caregiver** for the spouse or registered partner.

HOW DID WARDEN CHRISTENSEN OF F.C.I RAYBROOK NOT FOLLOW THE RULES CONGRESS TOLD HIM HE WAS "OBLIGATED" TO FOLLOW?
THE ANSWER:

Mr. Kenneth Sadler's compassionate release request to warden Christensen (which I have included on **pages 386-389**) was based on a reason congress told all wardens who work in a federal prison to consider an "extraordinary and compelling" reason to grant an inmate's compassionate release request submitted to them. And even though Congress made that clear to all wardens, warden Christensen disregarded t what Congress told him he was "obligated" to follow when making a decision to grant a prisoner's compassionate release request because he denied Mr. Sadler's compassionate release request even though it was solely based on a reason Congress told him was a reason to grant Mr. Sadler's compassionate release request that was submitted to him. Mr. Sadler's compassionate release request to warden Christensen was based on the death of the caregiver (his children's mother) of his 2 minor children. The Mother of Mr. Sadler's 2 minor children Renee Crutcher passed away from COVID-19 hours after giving birth to her sixth child.

In Mr. Sadler's written request for compassionate release to warden Christensen he explained to the warden that the mother of his 2 children Taelin Sadler and Jalin Crutcher (both who's picture I have included on **page 392**) passed away from COVID-19. Mr. Sadler also explained to the warden in his compassionate release request that his children's mother was their only support system (caregiver) other than him, and he badly needed to get home in order to care for his children who desperately need him right now. Mr. Sadler did all the necessary things to also prove to the warden his children's mother did in fact pass away, and he also proved he was the only available caregiver to care for his dependent children.

Mr. Sadler first proved to the warden that Renee Crutcher, the mother of his 2 minor children died by providing the warden with a copy of her death certificate which I have included on **page 393**. Mr. Sadler also then provided warden Christensen with a copy of Renee Crutcher's obituary which I have also included in this book on **pages 394-401.**

Mr. Sadler's mother, sister, cousin and friend also took the time out to write warden Christensen when Mr. Sadler's children's mother first died pleading with him to please grant Mr. Sadler's compassionate release request because Mr. Sadler is the only available caregiver for his children since their mother passed away. In each of their letters to warden Christensen they explained to him how badly Mr. Sadler's children needed him home to take care of them and how much their mother's death affected his children.

In Mr. Sadler's written compassionate release request he brought to warden Christensen's attention that he falls under one of the "extraordinary and compelling" reasons Congress told all wardens who work in a federal prison to consider an "extraordinary and compelling" reason for his compassionate release to be granted by warden Christensen's was "the death or incapacitation of the caregiver of his minor children." Even though on a previous page in this book I gave you a list of all the "extraordinary and compelling" reasons for a warden to grant a prisoner's compassionate release request, I have still included them on **page 402** so you can look and read for yourself. And to also see that Mr. Sadler did fall under one of the reasons Congress directed all wardens who work in a federal prison to consider an "extraordinary and compelling" release request to grant a prisoner's compassionate release request that has been submitted to them.

As you read all the reasons Congress states are reasons for a warden to grant a prisoner's compassionate release motion, you will see that one of the reasons is "the death or incapacitation of the caregiver of the defendant's minor child or minor children". This was the same reason Mr. Sadler based his compassionate release request he submitted to warden Christensen as you can see when you read Mr. Sadler's actual written compassionate release request he submitted to the warden which is again on **pages 386- 389**

Despite Mr. Sadler "clearly" proving to warden Christensen in his compassionate release request he submitted to him that he falls under the "same exact" reason Congress "obligated" warden Christensen to consider an "extraordinary and compelling" reason to grant Mr. Sadler's compassionate release request, warden Christensen still denied Mr. Sadler's compassionate release request.

Warden Christensen totally disregarded his "obligation" to follow the reasons Congress stated were reasons for him to grant Mr. Sadler's compassionate release request that was submitted to him. In the warden's denial letter he gave to Mr. Sadler denying him his compassionate release request, (which I have included on **page 403**) warden Christensen stated his reason for denying Mr. Sadler's compassionate release request was "due to the availability of other family members to care for his dependent children". That reason does not make any sense at all!!! What does not make any sense about the reason warden Christensen gave to Mr. Sadler for denying his compassionate release request is because "no family member of Mr. Sadler's or Mr. Sadler himself ever communicate to warden Christensen that a family member was available to care for Mr. Sadler's dependent children".

All of the letters written to warden Christensen by Mr. Sadler's family and friends repeated how badly Mr. Sadler's children needed him home and the effect of the sudden death his children's mother had on his children. The letters warden Christensen received from Mr. Sadler's family and friends also specified to the warden the took in Mr. Sadler's children "by force" due to the situation of their mother suddenly passing away and not wanting to leave them for the state to take.

They also specified in their letters to warden Christensen that the children's father (Mr. Sadler) is needed badly not just to care for his children but because them their selves could not properly nurture and care for his children due to their own serious health issues and also due to their personal responsibilities they already have on their plate before Mr. Sadler's children were forced onto them because of the sudden and shocking death of their mother. The letters written to warden Christensen by Mr. Sadler's family and friends undeniably expressed to the warden the importance of granting Mr. Sadler's compassionate release request because the children have altered their lives and it is too much for the bare.

Mr. Sadler and his entire family have no clue as to how warden Christensen came to the conclusion that Mr. Sadler has "other family members to care for his dependent children," and using that as the reason for denying Mr. Sadler's compassionate release request, when no one has ever communicated to warden Christensen that Mr. Sadler has other family to care for his dependent children. You can tell by reading the warden's denial letter he gave to Mr. Sadler denying him his compassionate release request that I have again included on **page 403**, that the warden is FULL OF SHIT and used any reason just to deny Mr. Sadler's compassionate release request.

I say this because in warden Christensen's denial letter he gave to Mr. Sadler he showed no evidence supporting his reason for Denying Mr. Sadler's compassionate release request as you can see. Congress has made it very difficult for prisoners to fit the criteria in order for their compassionate release request to be granted. So when a prisoner fits the criteria that Congress states is the criteria for prisoner's compassionate release request to be granted, a warden should not be allowed to give an unsupported denial letter to a prisoner denying his or her compassionate release request without showing factual evidence that supports their reason or reasons for denying a person's compassionate release request that has been submitted to them. In warden Christensen's denial letter to Mr. Sadler he never explained to Mr. Sadler how he came to the conclusion that Mr. Sadler has other family to care for his children, such as him stating "I received a letter or phone call from such and such who is family member of Mr. Sadler and they told me they would care for Mr. Sadler's dependent children." Warden Christensen's denial letter to Mr. Sadler did not include any of this type of information which shows he is an unfair and coldhearted person who did not follow the rules that Congress told him he was "obligated" to follow, which was to grant Mr. Sadler's compassionate release request, because it was based on " the death of the caregiver of his minor children" which is one of the reasons Congress states is a reason for a warden to grant a compassionate release request that is submitted to him or her.

Even after Mr. Sadler proved to warden Christensen that his children's mother passed away and explained to him how badly his children needed him home, including his mother, sister, cousin, and friends writing letters to the warden he still denied Mr. Sadler's compassionate release request That truly and effectively shows what type of person warden Christensen is!! He is uncaring, unsympathetic, cruel, merciless, tyrannous, lacks empathy and all of the other words that have the same meanings I used to describe what type of person he is. Not to forget Mr. Sadler "clearly" is qualified "according to Congress" for warden Christensen to grant his compassionate release request but warden Christensen still denied his request. Where is warden Christensen's heart at? I do not think he has one!!

How could he deny Mr. Sadler's compassionate release request knowing his situation and knowing Mr. Sadler's reason for his compassionate release request was based on a reason Congress "obligated" him to consider a reason to grant Mr. Sadler's compassionate release request. I feel warden Christensen denied Mr. Sadler's request because he is not facing any consequences for not following the rules and regulations Congress states he is "obligated" to follow. Had there been some type of consequence for warden Christensen not following the rules Congress directed him to follow, I think that would have motived him to follow the rules. There should be a consequence he has to deal with for not following the rules Congress states he is "obligated" to follow. Do you agree?

Mr. Sadler is a non-violent offender and has a low recidivism risk level, according to the case manager's written assessment about Mr. Sadler's recidivism risk level that was also included is his compassionate release request he gave to warden Christensen that I have also included **on pages 390-391**. That too should have been taken into consideration by warden Christensen when rendering a decision on Mr. Sadler's compassionate release request.

The injustice Mr. Sadler faced by warden Christensen denying his compassionate release request is NOTHING compared to the injustice he faced in a Michigan federal courtroom that got him in prison in the first place. His entire story will be included in my next book I write to prove yet again how unethical, unfair, underhanded, and deceitful "some" judges, prosecutors, lawyers, and law enforcement officers are.

QUESTIONS FOR THE READERS:

1. Do you feel warden Christensen was unfair to Mr. Sadler by denying his compassionate release request?

2. Do you feel Mr. Sadler's Compassionate release request should have been granted by warden Christensen?

3. Do you think warden Christensen should be subject to consequences for not following the rules Congress "obligated" him to follow?

YOU BE THE JUDGE!!

Court Is in Session...

If you feel Kenneth Sadler inmate number 54738-039 was treated unfairly by warden Christensen denying his compassionate release request and would like to help him get the justice he deserves, please write to President Biden respectfully expressing how you feel about Mr. Sadler's situation. Then respectfully and humbly ask him to please pardon Mr. Sadler so that he can go home and care for his children that truly need him right now.

A copy of Mr. Sadler's actual compassionate Release Request he gave to warden Christensen.

TO Warden
FROM: Kenneth Sadler
Inmate # 54738-039
Date: 9-15-2021
Reason: Request for Compassionate Release

I recently had a death in my family. The mother of my children has passed away and my children are left without a parent. The mother of my children was their only support system other than me. I am respectfully and humbly asking you to please find it in your heart to grant this Compassionate release request so I can be there for my children. Renee Crutcher who was the mother of my 2 children who are now 8 and 4 years old is no longer here to fulfill her obligation as a parent to love and our children. I ask of you sir to not let the system to take Control of my children and please give me a chance to be released to provide for my family, my children in many ways. Please my children need me emotionally, financially, for security and amongst other ways if you are a parent yourself. I currently fall under the Catergory of an extraordinary and Compelling reason why you can grant the compassionate release request which is a family circumstance (c) under U.S.S.G 1B1.13. U.S.S.G 1B1.13 states all the reasons a warden can grant an inmates request for compassionate release and one of the reasons is "the death or incapacitation of the care giver of the defendants minor child or children. Both of my children by Renee Crutcher are minor, they are 8 and 4 years old.

I have included with this request the obituary of the mother of my children to prove to you she did actually die. Also I have included page 15 of my presentence report showing I do have children by Renee Crutcher. In my presentence report the probation officer who completed it only added that I had one child from Renee but in fact its 2 children I have by her. If needed I can get additional information faxed to you to prove I have another child by Renee Crutcher

I have also included paperwork completed by staff at another facility that I am First Step Act Eligible and my recidivism risk level is low. This is my first time in prison. I have been convicted of non-violent crimes. I have only one criminal history point and was in Category one on the sentencing chart. I'm not a risk to the community and will not return if you grant my request for compassionate release. Sir please give me a chance to be the father and man I'm supposed to be for them and for me. My children need me and I need them before the system gets ahold on them. If I'm released I have a job waiting for me. This same job will assist me with our living. I have my own house which I own so a place a place to stay is not an issue. Sir, please give me a chance. Thank you for your understanding, your time and I am respectfully and humbly asking you to please give me a chance. In this manner all I need from you is to have a conscious heart and treat me the way you would want to be treated if you were in my shoes.

Lastly Sir U.S.S.G 1B1.13 that gives the reason why a compassionate release request can be granted does not state the amount of time a person has left remaining on his or her sentence should be considered when the Warden is considering granting a request for Compassionate release so I am respectfully asking you to not render your ruling on this request for Compassionate release.

Mr. Sadler's case manager's assessment and recidivism risk level:

his mother and grandparents. The defendant advised his maternal grandfather was instrumental in his upbringing and taught him work-ethic and structure.

61. The defendant has a biological sister, Keisha Frill, age 35. She resides in Detroit, Michigan and is employed at a cemetery in the maintenance department. The defendant's maternal half-brother, Demarco Tempo, age 30, is a codefendant in the instant offense and currently incarcerated; the defendant's paternal half-brother Kevin Sadler, Jr, age 30, resides in Detroit, Michigan, and is employed by a factory. The defendant's maternal half-brother William Dennis was shot and killed at age 20 in 2013.

62. The defendant recalled having a good childhood, free from abuse or neglect. The defendant advised he feels he was "spoiled" and had everything he needed as a child. He recalled having good paternal influences in his life and learned to work with his hands, whether it be on houses, vehicles, maintenance work, etc. He advised despite his current situation, he was raised with good morals and values.

63. The probation department spoke to the defendant's mother, Shelia Frill. She confirmed personal information about the defendant, advised the defendant has a good work ethic and she is confident he is capable of being successful. The defendant's mother declined to communicate further with the probation department and advised she will provide a letter to the Court directly.

64. The defendant has been in a relationship with Meion Melvin, age 30, for approximately 11 years. Together they have three children: twins Keyshion and Keyion Sadler, age 11, and Mekahi, age 6. Ms. Melvin is a licensed beautician and they reside in Detroit, Michigan. The defendant also has a son, Tallen Sadler, age 5, with Renee Crutcher. The defendant has been ordered to pay child support by Wayne County Friend of the Court and has been in contact with them in the past to address arrearages.

65. The defendant advised he is a lifelong resident of Detroit, Michigan. The defendant was living on Eastburn Street at the time of the instant offense, and moved onto Spencer Street in Detroit, Michigan, into a home he owned. The defendant advised a cousin of his is currently residing in the home. The defendant plans to return to Detroit, Michigan in the future.

Physical Condition

66. SADLER is 5'10" and weighs 165 pounds. He has brown eyes and black hair. The defendant has tattoos on both of his arms. His tattoos include his kids' names, his brother's name, the phrase "against all odds" "BO$$" and "RML."

67. The defendant advised he is healthy and has no history of health problems. He has no allergies to food or medication.

Mental and Emotional Health

68. The defendant has no history of mental or emotional problems and no history of treatment for such problems.

15

390

DATE REVIEWED: 12/3/19

INSTITUTION: FCI Hazleton   UNIT: M-1
INMATE NAME: Sadler, Kenneth   REG NO: 54738-039

FIRST STEP ACT (Circle One):   (ELIGIBLE) / INELIGIBLE

RECIDIVISM RISK LEVEL (Circle One):   MINIMUM (LOW) MEDIUM   HIGH

A picture of Mr. Sadler's 2 children Taelin Sadler (his son) and Jalin Crutcher (his daughter).

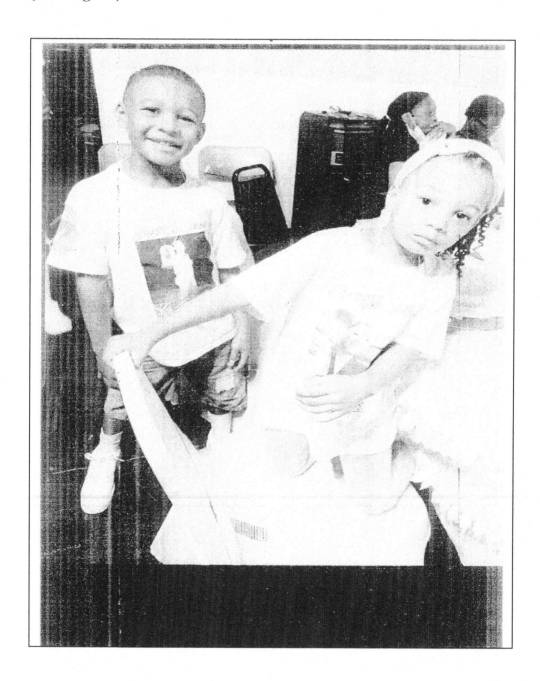

This is a copy of Mr. Sadler's children mother death certificate he gave to the warden of this prison to prove that the Mother (caregiver) of his children did in fact died.

STATE OF MICHIGAN
CERTIFICATION OF VITAL RECORD

COUNTY OF WASHTENAW
STATE OF MICHIGAN

D2021-02591
Pages: 1 of 1   DCT

STATE OF MICHIGAN
DEPARTMENT OF HEALTH AND HUMAN SERVICES
CERTIFICATE OF DEATH

STATE FILE NUMBER
069600

1. DECEDENT'S NAME (First, Middle, Last) Renee Reneyl Crutcher	2. DATE OF BIRTH February 01, 1990	3. SEX Female	4. DATE OF DEATH August 24, 2021
5. NAME AT BIRTH OR OTHER NAME USED FOR PERSONAL BUSINESS	6a. AGE- Last Birthday (Years) 31	6b. UNDER 1 YEAR MON 05 DAYS	6c. UNDER 1 DAY HOURS MINUTES

7a. LOCATION OF DEATH Michigan Medicine	7b. CITY, VILLAGE OR TOWNSHIP OF DEATH Ann Arbor	7c. COUNTY OF DEATH Washtenaw

8a. CURRENT RESIDENCE - STATE Michigan	8b. COUNTY Wayne	8c. LOCALITY Detroit	8d. STREET AND NUMBER 8357 Bliss

8e. ZIP CODE 48205	9. BIRTH PLACE Detroit, Michigan	10. SOCIAL SECURITY NUMBER	11. DECEDENT'S EDUCATION 11th Grade

12. RACE Black	13c. ANCESTRY African American		13b. HISPANIC ORIGIN No	14. EVER IN THE U.S. ARMED FORCES? No

15. USUAL OCCUPATION Homemaker	16. KIND OF BUSINESS OR INDUSTRY Domestic	17. MARITAL STATUS Never married	18. NAME OF SURVIVING SPOUSE (If wife, give name before first married)

19. FATHER'S NAME (First, Middle, Last) John Cructher	20. MOTHER'S NAME BEFORE FIRST MARRIED (First, Middle, Last) Mia Perry

21a. INFORMANT'S NAME John Crutcher	21b. RELATIONSHIP TO DECEDENT Father	21c. MAILING ADDRESS 19619 Fairport, Detroit, Michigan 48205

22. METHOD OF DISPOSITION Burial	23a. PLACE OF DISPOSITION Trinity Cemetery	23b. LOCATION City or Village, State Detroit, Michigan

24. SIGNATURE OF MORTUARY SCIENCE LICENSEE Quanika Cantrell	25. LICENSE NUMBER 4501007641	26. NAME AND ADDRESS OF FUNERAL FACILITY QA Cantrell Funeral Services, LLC, 22121 Kelly Road, Eastpointe, Michigan 48021

27a. CERTIFIER □ Certifying Physician ☒ Medical Examiner Signature and Title Allecia M Wilson, MD	28a. ACTUAL OR PRESUMED TIME OF DEATH 2010 Military Time	28b. PRONOUNCED DEAD ON August 24, 2021	28c. TIME PRONOUNCED DEAD 2010 Military Time
	29. MEDICAL EXAMINER CONTACTED Yes	30. PLACE OF DEATH Hospital	31. IF HOSPITAL Inpatient

27b. DATE SIGNED August 25, 2021	27c. LICENSE NUMBER 4301083538	32. MEDICAL EXAMINER'S CASE NUMBER 21-0979	33. NAME OF ATTENDING PHYSICIAN IF OTHER THAN CERTIFIER

34. NAME AND ADDRESS OF CERTIFYING PHYSICIAN
Allecia M Wilson, MD, Washtenaw County ME, 2800 Plymouth Road Building 35, Ann Arbor, Michigan 48109

35a. REGISTRAR'S SIGNATURE	35b. DATE FILED August 30, 2021

36. PART I ENTER the chain of events- diseases, injuries or complications- that directly caused the death. DO NOT enter terminal events such as cardiac arrest, respiratory arrest or ventricular fibrillation without showing the etiology. Enter only one cause on a line.		Approximate Interval Between Onset and Death
If distinct- may be underlying or contributing cause of death be sure to report deafness at either Part I or Part II of the cause of death portion on COVID-19	DUE TO (OR AS A CONSEQUENCE OF):	Months
IMMEDIATE CAUSE (Final disease or condition resulting in death)	DUE TO (OR AS A CONSEQUENCE OF):	
Sequentially list conditions, if ANY, leading to the cause on line 1 on a line for the UNDERLYING CAUSE (disease or injury that caused the events resulting in death) LAST	DUE TO (OR AS A CONSEQUENCE OF):	

PART II OTHER SIGNIFICANT CONDITIONS contributing to death but not resulting in the underlying cause given in Part I	37. DID TOBACCO USE CONTRIBUTE TO DEATH? □ Yes □ Probably □ No ☒ Unknown	38. IF FEMALE □ Not pregnant within past year □ Pregnant at time of death □ Not pregnant, but pregnant within 42 days of death □ Unknown if pregnant within the past year ☒ Not pregnant, but pregnant 43 days to 1 year before death

39. MANNER OF DEATH Natural	40a. WAS AN AUTOPSY PERFORMED? No	40b. WERE AUTOPSY FINDINGS AVAILABLE PRIOR TO COMPLETION OF CAUSE OF DEATH? Not Applicable	

41a. DATE OF INJURY	41b. TIME OF INJURY	41c. DESCRIBE HOW INJURY OCCURRED

41e. INJURY AT WORK	41d. PLACE OF INJURY	41f. IF TRANSPORTATION INJURY	41g. LOCATION

A1113202

I, LAWRENCE KESTENBAUM, CLERK/REGISTER OF SAID COUNTY OF WASHTENAW DO HEREBY CERTIFY that the foregoing is a true and exact copy of the original document on file in my office.

DATED: 10/04/2021

LAWRENCE KESTENBAUM
WASHTENAW COUNTY CLERK/REGISTER

ANY ALTERATION OR ERASURE VOIDS THIS CERTIFICATE

393

This is a copy of the obituary of Mr. Sadler 's children Mr. Sadler gave to warden Christensen when he handed him his compassionate release request back in September of 2021

RENEE RENYL CRUTCHER

My name is Renee Crútcher, I was born on February 1st 1990 to the union of John and Mia Crutcher. I grew up on the east side of Detroit Michigan and attended Southeastern high school. While in school I was an exceptional honor student. I had dreams of starting my own cleaning business before God called me home. He needed me sooner than later. I leave behind my Fiancé Barry Smith and six children Demaria, Demario, Tae'lin, Jaelin, Cameron and Camry whom I loved dearly. My Siblings Jasmine (Earnest), Jenee, John Crutcher III (Teika), Donsha, Shante, Dontae, Ronnea, Sirr and Vanessa. Remember there's nothing like a siblings' love we are each other's first best friends. I had ten nieces and nine nephews, which to me was an extension of my children. And a host of family and friends that I appreciated dearly and love.

People knew me for my contagious laugh, my jokes, dancing, selfless love and my love for tacos. Although I was always late when I showed up I showed out. You can say I was the life of the party. I enjoyed life to the fullest while I was here. I could get you anywhere in Detroit on the side streets because you couldn't pay me to get on the freeway. My siblings say I had jokes for days and I played around a lot, I just loved to see them happy and smiling. I always made sure everyone around me was okay even at my lowest time. Most of all I enjoyed spending time with my fiancé and kids.

To my fiancé, BJ I loved you so much! I know we planned to spend forever together, I'm sorry our forever was cut short. I appreciate the man you became for me and our children we are a family. I enjoyed our life together and wish we had more time. But don't worry I am still there with you through our kids and in spirit. I love you and will see you in the next life time.

To my children Demaria, Fatman, Tae, Jae, Cam and Camry, I loved y'all with all of my heart. My life revolved around you and I loved every moment of it. I'm sorry I couldn't be here in the physical form to watch you all grow up. Just know I'll be watching over you. Keep your grades up and continue to be yourselves. Please always stick together and remember the things I did teach you all. I know times will get hard and if I'm right you all will have a great support system and a lot of love. Take it easy on BJ and remember to take your vitamins.

To all of my loved ones this is not a "goodbye" it's an "I'll see you later". Don't worry about me I have plenty of support up here to protect and guide me. I'm with my Granddad Bobby, Uncle Glen, Grandma Gloria and with Mama S.P and many other loved ones. Don't cry celebrate my life, remember life is short so don't hold grudges.

ORDER OF SERVICE

Musical Prelude. . . . . .Pastor Kenneth Johnson

Musial Selection. . . . . Candice Hodges

Prayer. . . . . .Tamika Lindsey

Scripture. . . . . .Tamika Lindsey

Obituary. . . . . .Ter'ri Davidson

Solo. . . . . Candice Hodges

Eulogy. . . . . Tamika Lindsey

Remarks. . . . . .Friends and Family

Closing Remarks. . . . . .Pastor Kenneth Johnson

Musical Postlude. . . . . .Pastor Kenneth Johnson

Recessional. . . . .

Psalm 147:3

"He heals the broken hearted and binds up their wounds." God heals our
broken hearts, even when we lose someone we love.

398

Yellow, Daddy is so lost for words, its so many beautiful things I can say about you but it's not enough time or paper I was so not ready for this ever! – *Rest baby Daddy loves you*

Hey Renee why you had to leave so soon. I remember when you were a baby now your gone never would think I will see this day. Dang, I'm going miss you so much we laugh, talk and dance we was going out to eat we had so much fun I'm going to miss the fun we had together you're a wonderful mother you took really good care of your kids they are going miss you so much I'm going miss you so much we were so close I love you My Sexy Model Renee. – *Love Your Mother*

I love you mama and I wish you and me had more time together. I'm going to miss you so much and I will never forget you. – *Love Fatman*

Hey ma, I really miss and love you so much and I would've never thought you would've died so early and young. I feel like you worked so hard for nothing, I will continue to make you the happy mother you always was. – *Love Demaria*

Twin I miss you so much, I'm so mad at life right now. I will never understand why he took you so soon we still had so much to do. We literally lived together most of our life, so how am I supposed to live without you Renee? I did my first hot girl stuff with you lol I love you so much man I'm going to miss you calling me telling me to go look at stuff on Facebook, checking on me and Dell he was like your son. I got your kids forever I promise .Save me a spot right next to you please! I love you babygirl and I will still tell you all the latest gossip like I been doing. My partner& crime forever, you really hurt my heart with this one bro. – *Love your twin Shant'e*

I love you so much ReRe you made my life better in so many ways you are one of the best mothers I know you were so lovable and I enjoyed every minute with you. You were my best friend the love of my life the woman that made me a real man ah father and soon to be husband I miss you so much continue to watch over our babies we still need you and will always love you 💜💜💜 – *Love BJ*

DEAR RENEE: Only an Aunt can give hugs like a mother and share secrets like a sister, and share love like a friend. During your short period of time here we were brought together by blood and kept together by love. I can never bring you back but I can always cherish your smile, love and memories in my heart. Only God knows why he took you home so soon. Just know I will always and forever be your auntie also known as your second mother. In my heart you will always be LONG LIVE RENEE – *Love Auntie Joy Rest in Heaven my Child*

 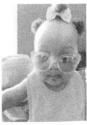  

LOVING SENTIMENTS

We've shared so much laughter, shared so many tears. Your life was a blessing, your memory a treasure. You are loved beyond words and missed beyond measure. Our hearts have grown closer with each passing of time. Through the ups and downs of life, we've come to understand what it means to have each other. I said a prayer for you to thank the Lord above for blessing me with a lifetime of your tender-heart love. And so I thank you from the heart for all you've done for me and the kids and I bless the Lord for giving me the best sister. – *Love always, Big Nose*

I never thought in a million years I will be writing this I don't even know where to start but the day I seen you take your last breath was the day you broke my heart. You always had my back I always had your front right wrong good or bad you always did your part It still feel like a dream I just wish I can see your smile hear your voice telling me you love me one last time this pain hurt deep I'm full of tears writing this I will never forget the times we had every single one was priceless life will never be the same without you your love ran deep every time I feel down you helped me back on my feet made sure I was fed when it came down to my music you was my number 1 fan I can go one for days about how much of an impact you had on my life. Just know I got you and your 6 kids back after death and for life. Until we meet again. – *Love lil bro aka turkey neck*

TO MY SISTER: Where do I begin? I have been lost spaced out angry don't want to be around nobody just mad at the world with so many questions as to why this happened to you I can't even begin where to start at when someone as pure as you spiritual as you are gone now. All I can say is I'm so sorry that this happened to you. When you left a part of me left. I wonder if you okay up there I was so worried when you were here on a regular now I'm wondering are you okay up there. We only know what they teach us so I really don't know but what I can say is that I was one lucky sister to have you on earth now I have to share you with someone else which is god. So I'm gone let you fly high baby girl I love you so much – *Love always Sis Donsha AKA Shay Shay*

MOM: Thank you for loving us and giving us the best that life has to offer...... You. We are sad that you are gone but we will celebrate your life together for eternity. You will always live in our hearts, minds and spirits. We are grateful to have been given love in the purest form....The Love of our Mother. – *Your babies*

Renee I love you with all my heart. I can't believe I'm writing this. I'm going to miss our conversations and hearing you laugh. I don't have much to say because I'm still in disbelief you're gone. Just know we got your kids always. Til next time little sis. – *Love Jasmine*

MY BEAUTIFUL SISTER: Never in a million years did I ever think I would be saying goodbye to my life size Barbie gone so soon. It feels so unreal. I keep thinking to myself why you? Why would god do this? What was his purpose? I wish we could've had more time to talk and make more memories. Your beautiful smile I will miss. I love you so much and I will forever miss you. I know you're at peace now. So fly high my angel until we meet again - *Love your big sister, Vanessa*

White girl....what's up Lil sis.. I miss you like crazy already. They say you don't know how much you miss or love someone until their gone, and one thing we can't get back is time that we missed out on....and it hurts. So keep me a spot open up there in heaven. Make us some tacos and kool-aid and Imma bring the drink so we can sit back and kick it like old times! Until then rest in paradise baby and be our white angel from above! – *Love always, your midget big bro, John*

PALLBEARERS

John Crutcher III   Dontae Crutcher   Shante Crutcher
Donsha Crutcher   Jenee Smith   Jasmine Mays

HONORARY PALLBEARERS

Alonzo Davis   Cornelius Knight   Willis Ellison
Anthony Daniels   Bobby Perry Jr   Jerome Brown

ARRANGEMENTS ENTRUSTED TO

QA Cantrell Funeral Services
22121 Kelly Road, Eastpointe, MI 48021

INTERMENT

Trinity Cemetery
5210 Mt Elliott St, Detroit, MI 48211

REPAST

Immediately after the interment
Legacy Hall
10820 Whittier, Detroit, MI 48224

ACKNOWLEDGEMENT OF APPRECIATION

The Family would like to thank you for the support, sympathy and
kindness in this difficult time.

This is a copy of what congress put in the federal prisons of bureau's policy that "obligates" all wardens who work in a federal prison to consider as an extraordinary and compelling reason to release an inmate on a compassionate release request.

1. Extraordinary and Compelling Reasons.-Provided the defendant meets the requirements **of** subdivision (2), extraordinary and compelling reasons exist under any **of** the circumstances set forth below:

(A) Medical Condition **of** the Defendant.-

(i) The defendant is suffering from a terminal illness (i.e., a serious and advanced illness with an end **of** life trajectory). A specific prognosis **of** life expectancy (i.e., a probability **of death** within a specific time period) is not required. Examples include metastatic solid-tumor cancer, amyotrophic lateral sclerosis (ALS), end-stage organ{2021 U.S. Dist. LEXIS 7} disease, and advanced dementia.

(ii) The defendant is-

(I) suffering from a serious physical or medical condition, (II) suffering from a serious functional or cognitive impairment, or (III) experiencing deteriorating physical or mental health because **of** the aging process,

that substantially diminishes the ability **of** the defendant to provide self-care within the environment **of** a correctional facility and from which he or she is not expected to recover.

(B) Age **of** the Defendant.-The defendant (i) is at least 65 years old; (ii) is experiencing a serious deterioration in physical or mental health because **of** the aging process; and (iii) has served at least 10 years or 75 percent **of** his or her term **of** imprisonment, whichever is less.

(C) Family Circumstances.-

(i) The **death** or incapacitation **of** the **caregiver of** the **defendant's** minor child or minor **children**. (ii) The incapacitation **of** the **defendant's** spouse or registered partner when the defendant would be the only available **caregiver** for the spouse or registered partner.

Warden Christensen's denial letter to Mr. Sadler denying him his compassionate release request.

INMATE REQUEST TO A STAFF MEMBER
Warden's Response

Name: Sadler, Kenneth

Reg. No.: 54738-039   Unit: Genesee A

You requested a reduction in sentence (RIS) based on the Death or Incapacitation of the Family member Caregiver. Specifically, you stated that Renee Crutcher was the caregiver for your two dependent children, Jalin Crutcher and Taelin Sadler.

Title 18 of the United States Code, section 3582(c)(1)(A), allows a sentencing court, on motion of the Director of the BOP, to reduce a term of imprisonment for extraordinary or compelling reasons. BOP Program Statement No. 5050.50, Compassionate Release/Reduction in Sentence: Procedures for Implementation of 18 U.S.C. §§ 3582(c)(1)(A) and 4205(g), provides guidance on the types of circumstances that present extraordinary or compelling reasons, such as the inmate's terminal medical condition; debilitated medical condition; status as a "new law" elderly inmate, an elderly inmate with medical conditions, or an "other elderly inmate"; the death or incapacitation of the family member caregiver of the inmate's child; or the incapacitation of the inmate's spouse or registered partner. Your request has been evaluated consistent with this general guidance.

Your request has been denied due to the availability of other family to care for your dependent children.

If you are not satisfied with this response to your request, you may commence an appeal of this decision via the administrative remedy process by submitting your concerns on the appropriate form (BP-9) within 20 days of the receipt of this response.

D. Christensen, Warden   12/10/2021
                                            Date

Given to i/m 12/14/21

CHAPTER 47

THE FIRST STEP ACT

In December of 2018, then President of the United States Donald Trump signed something into law called THE FIRST STEP ACT. I know most of you may not have a clue what the First Step Act is or what it consists of so let me do what I do best and break it down to you. The First Step Act consists of many things, but for now I would like to laser focus on the rules it consists of that warden Christensen and other wardens who work in a different federal prison are not following.

The First Step Act was designed by Congress to help reduce the federal prison recidivism and crime rate by providing meaningful employment and training opportunities to prisoners while they are incarcerated so it prepares them for a successful return to society. Along with providing them with other programs that are designed to reduce recidivism and lower the crime rate. I have included on **pages 409-416** a copy of the revised First Step Act of 2018 that Donald Trump signed into law, so you can read for yourself the Purpose of the First Step Act.

Congress also included in First Step Act that then President Donald Trump signed into law in 2018, an Approved Programs Guide list that included all the programs all wardens and other staff members who works in a federal prison, should consider a "evidence-based recidivism program or a productive activity," designed to ensure all prisoners who participate in them are equipped with the skills necessary to succeed upon being released.

These evidence-based recidivism reduction programs and productive activities are standardized across all federal prisons in the United States and are described in the Federal Prison Bureau's national policies. Congress listed all the "evidence-based recidivism reduction programs" in the Approved Program Guide list that was attached with the First Step Act when then President Donald Trump signed it into law. I have included this Approved Program Guide list with all programs and the purpose of these programs on **pages 417-464**.

Congress includes two different categories of programs in their Approved Program Guide list that they also gave to "all" wardens who works in a federal prison in the United States. The two categories of programs include "evidence-based recidivism reduction programs and productive activities."

The First Step Act requires all federal prisons to implement a "risk and needs" assessment on all prisoners. "Risk" refers to the likelihood that each individual prisoner will reoffend or recidivate after release. "Needs" refers to the specific areas a prisoner can address to lower his or her risk. In other words, need indicates "what" issues affect a prisoner's risk and what he or she should address by taking programs Congress placed in the Approved Program Guide list in order to reduce his or her risk of returning to prison.

The First Step Act "obligated" all wardens in federal prisons to have access in their prisons "needs" in 13 areas that directly impact one's ability to live a healthy and productive life. Specifically, these 13 areas are Anger/Hostility; Antisocial Peer; Cognitions; Dyslexia; Education; Family/Parenting; Finance/Poverty; Medical; Mental Health; Recreation/Leisure/Fitness; Substance Use; Trauma; and Work. Prisoners are supposed to be recommended to enroll in programs that are on the Approved Program Guide list that was designed to address their individual "needs" after a "risk and need assessment" is taken, but that "rarely" happens at F.C.I. Raybrook.

The First step act also provides incentives to prisoners who participate in the program or programs that address their needs. It also established the eligibility criteria for and incentivize participation in these programs by allowing a prisoner who participates in these programs to "earn time credit for prerelease custody defined as residential reentry center or for low-risk prisoners home confinement." For example a prisoner may earn 10 days of time credit for each 30 days of successful participation in a recidivism reduction program or productive activity that is in the Approved Program Guide list that Congress placed in The First Step Act that I have again included in this book. The First Step Act also states a prisoner that is classified as minimum or low risk for recidivating, and that has not increased their risk of recidivism over two assessments can earn an additional 5 day (for a total of 15 days' time credit for each 30 days of successful participation in a recidivism reduction program or activity that is in the Approved Program Guide list.)

Federal prisoners who are rendered violent and high-risk criminals after an assessment is done on them or have been convicted of certain serious offenses such as a dangerous sexual offenders, murderers and others are ineligible for anything the First Step Act has to offer in terms of the benefits it has such as being able to earn time credit off his or her sentence.

What is warden Christensen and other staff members who's job description includes making sure all prisoners who are eligible for what the First Step Act has to offer and reaps the benefits, not just in F.C.I Raybrook but also wardens and other staff members in different federal prisons across the United States not following about the First Step Act that Congress and then President Donald Trump "obligated" them to follow, and still under the Biden Administration are "obligated" to follow??

THE ANSWER:

MOSTLY EVERYTHING about the First Step Act is not being followed in so many federal prisons. However, I would like to focus on one prison (F.C.I Raybrook) where the warden is not following what Congress states he is "obligated" to follow in the First Step Act. I am putting this in my book in hopes to bring awareness to this and hopefully that will get things to change in this prison and in other prisons.

The rule I hear hundreds of prisoners complain about in this prison including myself is that warden Christensen and other staff members are not following that Congress states they are "obligated" to follow according to the First Step Act is "we are not receiving the incentive for successfully participating in a evidence-based recidivism reduction program or productive activities that are in the Approved Program Guide list that I have included in this book, which is again a list of all the programs and productive activities designed by Congress and provided to all federal prisoners to participate in to help reduce the recidivism and crime rate. Again the First Step Act "obligated" all wardens and staff members who's job entails handling a prisoner case load, to give federal prisoner 10 days of time credit towards his or her prerelease custody as an incentive for each 30 days of successful participation in each program that's on the Approved Program Guide list that he or she participates in, if after and only after an assessment is done on him or her, and the program he or she participated in is considered a need to lower his or her chances to return back to prison once released.

Warden Christensen and other staff members in this prison, just like many other federal prisons in the United States are not giving prisoner's their 10 days of time credit towards their prerelease custody, for every 30 days of successful participation in a program that is on the Approved Program Guide list that they are "obligated" to give us!!!! Even though it has been 4 years since the First Step Act was supposed to go into effect the federal prison system has yet to fulfill their "obligation" to give prisoners the incentives from the First Step Act. It is as if Donald Trump did not sign the First Step Act because a lot of prisons have yet to give the incentives to prisoners who qualify for them. There is nothing we prisoners can do about it because they do not respect us. Not all but a lot of staff members who works in a federal prison who have rank look down at prisoners as the scum of the earth just because we are in prison without even knowing your story. That's a damn shame because they are no better than us. But oh well that is their KARMA they have to deal with in the future!!

I would like to end this book on this note. Since I have been incarcerated in F.C.I Raybrook I have completed over 40 educational programs. I have included all of the certificates of completions for these programs on **pages 465-506.** 13 of these programs are programs that are on the Approved Program Guide list that is supposed to grant me 10 days of time credit towards my prerelease custody for every 30 days of successful participation. I have been in this prison for over 3 years and I have yet to receive the earned time credit towards my prerelease custody which is a total of one year. Do you think that's fair? Most importantly do you think it's fair to the other thousands of prisoners in all different federal prisons throughout the United States who are in the same boat as me? **YOU BE THE JUDGE!!**

This is the copy of the revised First Step Act showing you some rules all wardens case managers and unit teams who works in a federal prison are "obligated" to follow:

COMMITTEE *on the* JUDICIARY
CHAIRMAN CHUCK GRASSLEY   WWW.JUDICIARY.SENATE.GOV

The revised First Step Act of 2018 (S.3649)

Reducing Federal Recidivism and Crime

- Provides for increased programming designed to reduce recidivism and provides incentives for participation in those programs.

- Implements a post-sentencing dynamic risk assessment system to determine an inmate's risk of committing more crimes upon release from prison.

- Establishes eligibility criteria for and incentivizes participation in evidence-based recidivism reduction programs by allowing prisoners to earn time credits for prerelease custody (defined as residential reentry centers or, for low risk prisoners, home confinement). For example, a prisoner may earn 10 days of time credit for every 30 days of successful participation in a recidivism-reduction program or other eligible activity.

- Renders violent and high-risk criminals convicted of certain serious offenses ineligible for the pre-release custody program, including dangerous sexual offenders, murderers, and others.

Preparing Inmates for Successful Return to Society

- Provides more meaningful employment and training opportunities for inmates by expanding the federal prison industries program.

- Requires the Bureau of Prisons (BOP) to submit a report and evaluation of the current pilot program to treat heroin and opioid abuse through medication—assisted treatment.

- Extends the compassionate elderly release provision from the *Second Chance Act* that allows the prisoner to request for his or her compassionate release if he or she meets the requirements set out in the law.

- Codifies BOP's rules on using restraints on pregnant inmates, which generally prohibit the use of restraints on pregnant inmates except those who are an immediate and credible flight risk or threat of harm to herself, the baby or others.

- Mandates inmates be housed no more than 500 miles from the prisoner's primary residence and grants authority for prisoners to save earnings in an escrow account used for pre-release expenses, such as transportation and housing.

- Clarifies the formula by which the BOP calculates good time credit (time off for good behavior) in line with original Congressional intent. Under current law, prisoners can earn up to 54 days per year for good behavior in prison, but technicalities in the law keep prisoners on early release from utilizing those days.

Enhancing Prison Security and Officer Safety

- Requires the Director of BOP to provide a secure storage area outside the secure perimeter for employees to store firearms or to allow for vehicle lock boxes for firearms.

- Directs the Director of BOP to provide de-escalation training as part of the regular training requirements of correctional officers.

S.3649 - The First Step Act

Section-by-Section

Section. 1. Short Title; Table of Contents

Sets forth the short title for the entire Act as the "First Step Act" and sets forth the table of contents.

TITLE I: RECIDIVISM REDUCTION

Section 101. Risk and needs assessment system

Directs the Attorney General to conduct a review of the risk and needs assessment system used by the Bureau of Prisons and develop recommendations on evidence-based recidivism reduction programs and productive activities; to conduct ongoing research and data analysis on the programming and its effectiveness; to annually review and validate the risk and needs assessment system; to update and revise the risk and needs assessment system as determined appropriate; and to report to Congress.

Requires the Attorney General, in consultation with the Independent Review Committee created by this Act, to develop and release a risk and needs assessment system that will (1) determine the recidivism risk level (minimum, low, medium, or high) of each prisoner at intake, (2) assess and determine the risk of violent or serious misconduct of each prisoner, (3) determine the type and amount of programming for each prisoner and assign programming accordingly, (4) reassess each prisoner periodically and adjust programming assignments accordingly, (5) reassign the prisoner to appropriate programs, (6) determine when to provide incentives and rewards for successful participation in programming or productive activities, and (7) determine when a prisoner is ready to transfer into prerelease custody. In developing the risk and needs assessment system, the Attorney General may use existing tools as appropriate.

The risk and needs assessment system used by the Bureau of Prisons following enactment of this Act should provide that prisoners with similar risk levels are grouped together in housing and assignment decisions to the extent practicable.

Establishes incentives and rewards for prisoners to participate in programming and activities. This includes increased family phone and visitation privileges, transfer to an institution closer to the inmate's release residence, and earned time credits. Further, the Bureau of Prisons is instructed to develop additional policies to provide appropriate incentives for successful participation in programming which may include increased commissary spending limits and product offerings, extended opportunities to access the email system, and consideration of transfer to preferred housing units.

As an incentive for participation, prisoners shall earn 10 days of time credits for each 30 days of successful participation in recidivism risk reduction programming or activities. A prisoner that is

1

410

classified as minimum or low risk for recidivating and that has not increased their risk of recidivism over two reassessments can earn an additional 5 days (for a total of 15 days). Prisoners who have successfully participated in recidivism reduction programs or productive activities and who have been determined to be at minimum or low risk for recidivating at their last two reassessments may apply their time credits towards pre-release custody or supervised release. Similar reforms at the state level have closed prisons reduced crime.

A prisoner may not earn time credits for programming or activities participated in before enactment of this Act and before the prisoner's sentence commences. Makes prisoners ineligible to earn time credits if the prisoner is serving a sentence for conviction of certain offenses, including crimes relating to terrorism, murder, sexual exploitation of children, child pornography, espionage, or for the fentanyl drug trade if the offender was a leader, manager or supervisor of others in the offense.

Requires prisoners participating in the recidivism reduction programming or productive activities to be reassessed for recidivism risk not less than annually. Requires prisoners determined to be at medium or high risk and with an anticipated release date within 5 years to be reassessed more frequently. If a reassessment shows that a prisoner's risk of recidivating has changed, the Bureau of Prisons should update the prisoner's classification and reassign the prisoner to appropriate recidivism reduction programming based on the changes. Requires BOP to establish guidelines for reducing rewards and incentives for prisoners who violate prison, program, or activity rules, and for restoring those rewards and incentives based on individual progress.

Requires the Attorney General to develop training programs for BOP officials and employees related to the implementation and operation of the System and to conduct annual audits of the System.

Prior to releasing the risk and needs assessment system, in consultation with the Independent Review Committee created by this Act, the Attorney General shall review the effectiveness of evidence-based recidivism reduction programs that exist in prisons operated by the Bureau of Prisons, review such programs that exist in State-operated prisons throughout the U.S., identify the most effective evidence-based recidivism reduction programs, review policies for entering into evidence-based recidivism reduction partnerships, and direct the Bureau of Prisons on such programming and partnerships.

Directs the Attorney General to submit an annual report about the activities undertaken as a result of this Act.

Sets forth definitions used in this Act.

Section 102. Implementation of system and recommendations by Bureau of Prisons

Directs the Bureau of Prisons to: (1) implement the System and complete a risk and needs assessment for each prisoner; (2) begin to expand the effective programs it offers and add any new ones necessary to effectively implement the System; and (3) begin to implement the other risk and needs assessment tools necessary to effectively implement the risk and needs assessment system over time.

2

Requires the Attorney General to phase in such programs within 2 years and to develop and validate the risk and needs assessment tool.

Sets forth requirements for prerelease custody for risk and needs assessment system participants to include those who have earned time credits, have displayed and maintained a lower recidivism risk, and have been classified by the warden of the prison as qualified to be transferred into prerelease custody. Allows such prisoners to be placed in prerelease custody including home confinement, and residential reentry centers such as halfway homes. Requires the Attorney General to consult with the Assistant Director for the Office of Probation and Pretrial Services to issue guidelines for Bureau of Prisons' use to determine the appropriate prerelease custody for prisoners as well as consequences for violating prerelease custody conditions. Further requires the Director of the Bureau of Prisons to enter into agreements with the United States Probation and Pretrial Services to supervise prisoners place in home confinement or community supervision under this subsection.

Allows prisoners to receive mentoring services from a person that provided those services to the prisoner while incarcerated.

Section 103. GAO report

Requires the Comptroller General to conduct an audit on the BOP's use of the risk and needs assessment system, analyzing several factors of the risk and needs assessment system and its implementation in BOP facilities.

Section 104. Authorization of appropriations

Authorizes $75 million from 2019 to 2023 to carry out the activities described in the Act.

Section 105. Rule of construction

Sets forth that nothing in this Act may be construed to provide authority to place a prisoner on prerelease custody who is serving a term of imprisonment for a non-federal crime.

Section 106. Faith-Based considerations

Faith based programs will not be discriminated against.

Section 107. Independent Review Committee.

Establishes an Independent Review Committee, with members selected by the National Institute of Justice. The Committee shall assist the Attorney General in the development of the risk and needs assessment system and terminate after its enactment.

TITLE II: BUREAU OF PRISONS SECURE FIREARMS STORAGE

3

Section 201. Short Title

Sets forth the short title for Title II as the "Lieutenant Osvaldo Albarati Correction Officer Self-Protection Act of 2016."

Section 202. Secure firearms storage

Requires the Director of BOP to ensure that employees are allowed to store firearms in a vehicle lockbox approved by the Director of the BOP. Where storage in vehicles isn't possible, the BOP should provide alternative opportunities to store weapons.

TITLE III: RESTRAINTS ON PREGNANT PRISONERS PROHIBITED

Section 301. Use of restraints on prisoners during the period of pregnancy and postpartum recovery prohibited

Prohibits the use of restraints on prisoners during the period of pregnancy and postpartum recovery. The prohibition shall not apply if the prisoner is determined to be an immediate and credible flight risk or poses an immediate and serious threat of harm to herself, the fetus or others. In such a case, the least restrictive means will be used. Requires a report to be filed with the Director of BOP and prisoner's healthcare professional when restraints are used. Requires BOP to provide information to Congress annually. Requires appropriate training and the development of guidelines.

TITLE IV: SENTENCING REFORM

Section 401. Reduce and restrict enhanced sentencing for drug felonies

The enhanced mandatory minimums for prior drug felons are reduced: the three-strike penalty is reduced from life imprisonment to 25 years, and the 20-year minimum is reduced to 15 years. The offenses that trigger these enhanced minimum sentences are also reformed. Currently, those offenses could be any prior drug felony. This bill would both limit them to serious drug felonies and expand them to include serious violent felonies. The bill excludes from the definition of "serious drug felony," and therefore offers relief to, non-violent drug felonies for which the sentence was completed more than 15 years prior to the commission of the current offense. This provision is not retroactive and will not apply to any person sentenced before enactment of the Act.

Section 402. Broadening of existing safety valve

The safety valve is provision that authorizes a sentence below the statutory minimum for certain non-violent, non-managerial drug offenders with little or no criminal history. The existing safety valve is expanded to include offenders with up to four criminal history points, excluding 1-point offenses, such as minor misdemeanors. However, offenders with prior "3 point" felony convictions or prior "2 point" violent offenses will not be eligible for the safety valve. This

4

provision is not retroactive and will only apply where a conviction is entered on or after the date of enactment.

Section 403. Clarification of section 924(c) of title 18, United States Code

This section clarifies that the enhanced mandatory minimum sentence for using a firearm during a crime of violence or drug crime is limited to offenders who have previously been convicted and served a sentence for such an offense – the so-called 924(c) stacking problem. This provision does not apply retroactively, and will not apply to any person sentenced before enactment of the Act.

Section 404. Application of Fair Sentencing Act

The Fair Sentencing Act of 2010 reduced the disparity in sentencing between crack and powder cocaine. This provision ensures the retroactive application to offenders sentenced under those provisions before they were modified, who will already have served eight years of their sentence. The section expressly prohibits successive requests for relief and double relief under the Fair Sentencing Act and the First Step Act.

TITLE V: MISCELLANEOUS CRIMINAL JUSTICE

Section 501. Placement of prisoners close to families

Provides that prisoners should be, subject to bed availability and the prisoner's security designation and other considerations such as mental and medical health needs, placed in a facility as close as practicable to the prisoner's primary residence, but not more than 500 driving miles from the prisoner's primary residence. A prisoner with a security designation higher than the facilities closest to its release will not be transferred to a lower-security prison as a result of this provision.

Section 502. Home confinement for low-risk prisoners

Requires the Bureau of Prisons to place prisoners with lower risk levels and needs on home confinement for the maximum amount of time permitted.

Section 503. Federal prisoner reentry initiative reauthorization; modification of imposed term of imprisonment

Expands consideration of compassionate release to home detention of elderly and terminally ill offenders.

Requires the Director of the Bureau of Prisons to provide an annual report describing requests and releases made under this subsection, as well as additional information.

Section 504. Identification for returning citizens

5

Requires that, prior to release from a Federal prison, an individual should be provided with his or her birth certificate and photo identification.

Section 505. Expanding inmate employment through federal prison industries

Authorizes new markets for Federal prison industries products, including to public entities for use in penal or correctional institutions or disaster relief, to the government of the District of Columbia, and (anything but office furniture) to any 501(c)(3), (c)(4), or (d) tax-exempt organization.

Section 506. De-escalation training

Requires the BOP to provide de-escalation training as part of the regular training requirements of correctional officers to assist them in managing encounters with prisoners, including prisoners who possess a mental illness or cognitive defect, to ensure the officers' and prisoners' safety.

Section 507. Evidence-Based treatment for opioid and heroin abuse

Requires BOP to submit a report and evaluation of the current pilot program to treat heroin and opioid abuse through medication-assisted treatment to Congress.

Section 508. Pilot programs

Requires BOP to establish two pilot programs for 2 years in 10 facilities. The first is a mentorship program for youth and the second is for the training and therapy of abandoned, rescued, or otherwise vulnerable animals.

Section 509. Ensuring supervision of released sexually dangerous persons

Provides U.S. Probation and Pretrial Services authority to supervise sexually dangerous persons who have been conditionally released from civil commitment.

Section 510. Data collection

Establishes for BOP a statistical and demographic data reporting requirement. This data must be provided to Congress annually for 7 years and as part of the National Prisoner Statistics Program.

Section 511. Healthcare products

Requires BOP to provide feminine hygiene products to female inmates at no cost.

Section 512. Adult and juvenile collaboration programs

Increases funding available for state and county adult and juvenile collaboration programs.

Section 513: Juvenile solitary confinement
The bill would impose limitations on the use of solitary confinement for juveniles housed in federal prison. The use of solitary confinement for juveniles is prohibited unless it is a temporary

6

response to a juvenile's behavior that poses a serious and immediate risk of physical harm to any individual including the juvenile.

_____   _____

7

This is a copy of the Approved Program Guide list of all the program congress designed and provided to federal prisoners in order to help reduce the recidivism and crime rate. These are also the programs as an incentive for participation prisoners earn 10 days of time credit towards their prerelease custody for every 30 days of successful participation in them.

U.S. Department of Justice
Federal Bureau of Prisons
Washington, DC

Reentry Services Division   **July 2021**

FIRST STEP ACT
Approved Programs Guide

The Federal Bureau of Prisons (Bureau) protects public safety by ensuring federal inmates receive relevant and meaningful reentry programming to support their return to the community as law-abiding citizens. Reentry efforts increase opportunities, reduce recidivism, promote public safety, and reduce institution misconduct. To this end, the Bureau is committed to provide a robust menu of programs to address thirteen need areas for a diverse inmate population, located in 122 institutions of varying security levels across the nation.

417

TABLE OF CONTENTS

EVIDENCE BASED RECIDIVISM REDUCTION (EBRR) PROGRAMS   #

ANGER MANAGEMENT   4

APPRENTICESHIP TRAINING   5

ASSERT YOURSELF FOR FEMALE OFFENDERS   6

BASIC COGNITIVE SKILLS   7

BRAVE*   8

BUREAU LITERACY PROGRAM   9

CERTIFICATION COURSE TRAINING   10

CHALLENGE PROGRAM*   11

COGNITIVE PROCESSING THERAPY   12

CRIMINAL THINKING   13

DIALECTICAL BEHAVIOR THERAPY   14

EMOTIONAL SELF-REGULATION   15

FEDERAL PRISON INDUSTRIES   16

FEMALE INTEGRATED TREATMENT (FIT)*   17

FOUNDATION   18

ILLNESS MANAGEMENT & RECOVERY   19

LIFE CONNECTIONS PROGRAM   20

MENTAL HEALTH STEP DOWN PROGRAM*   21

MONEY SMART FOR ADULTS   22

NATIONAL PARENTING FROM PRISON PROGRAM   23

NON-RESIDENTIAL DRUG ABUSE PROGRAM   24

POST-SECONDARY EDUCATION   25

RESIDENTIAL DRUG ABUSE PROGRAM (RDAP)*   26

RESOLVE PROGRAM   27

SEEKING SAFETY   28

SEX OFFENDER TREATMENT PROGRAM NON-RESIDENTIAL   29

SEX OFFENDER TREATMENT PROGRAM*   30

SKILLS PROGRAM*   31

SOCIAL SKILLS TRAINING   32

STAGES PROGRAM*   33

THRESHOLD PROGRAM   34

VOCATIONAL TRAINING   35

PRODUCTIVE ACTIVITIES   36-46

BOP INSTITUTION INDEX   47-48

RDAP LOCATIONS   49

*RESIDENTIAL (MODIFIED THERAPEUTIC COMMUNITY)

418

ANGER

MANAGEMENT

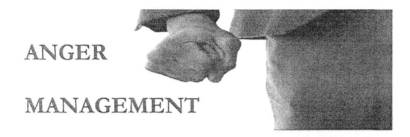

Anger Management for Substance Abuse and Mental Health Clients is a cognitive-behavioral curriculum designed to help individuals better manage their anger. The protocol can be used in a 12-session group or in an individual format. The curriculum and workbook are available in English and Spanish.

The workbook is designed to be used in group treatment by individuals with substance use or mental health issues. It provides participants with a summary of core concepts, worksheets for completing between-session challenges, and space to take notes for each of the sessions. The concepts and skills presented in this anger management treatment protocol are best learned by interactive practice, review, and by completing the between-session homework.

HOURS

18 hours of EBRR program credit.

LOCATIONS

Available at all BOP institutions.

NEEDS

Anger/Hostility and Cognitions

PROGRAM DELIVERY

To ensure program fidelity and proper credit, **Anger Management** must be delivered by Psychology Services staff.

419

APPRENTICESHIP TRAINING

The Bureau's Career Technical Education (CTE) program falls under three broad categories:
1) Apprenticeship Training, 2) Certification Course Training, and 3) Vocational Training.

Apprenticeship Training: Apprenticeship training prepares the student for employment in various trades through structured programs underneath a journeyman in that trade, approved at the state and national levels by the Bureau of Apprenticeship and Training, U.S. Department of Labor.

Generally, these programs require inmates to have completed the high school equivalency, but concurrent enrollment is sometimes possible. Each individual program is designed to enhance post-release employment opportunities by providing inmates with the ability to obtain marketable, in-demand employment skills. Programs follow standardized work processes with related trade instruction, which teaches specific job skills and leads to a Department of Labor apprenticeship certificate.

A large variety of standardized Department of Labor apprenticeships are offered throughout the Bureau and are highly encouraged; inmates may participate in 2,000 to 8,000 hour programs, which are supervised by local journeymen.

HOURS
500 hours of EBRR program credits.

LOCATIONS
Available at all BOP institutions.

NEEDS
Work

PROGAM DELIVERY

To ensure program fidelity and proper credit, **Apprenticeship Training** must be delivered by a qualified journeyman in the specific trade.

ASSERT YOURSELF FOR FEMALE OFFENDERS

DESCRIPTION

This program for incarcerated women promotes interpersonal effectiveness and targets behavior that can lead women to feel helpless about their lives. The majority of female offenders are survivors of abuse and struggle with low self-esteem. In this program, women learn to be assertive while respecting the boundaries of others. Through homework assignments and role-play, women practice skills learned throughout the program.

HOURS

8 hours of EBRR program credit.

LOCATIONS

FPC Alderson	FCI Aliceville	MDC Brooklyn	FPC Bryan
FMC Carswell	MCC Chicago	SCP Coleman	FSL/SPC Danbury
FCI Dublin	SCP Greenville	MDC Guaynabo	SFF Hazelton
FDC Honolulu	FDC Houston	SCP Lexington	MDC Los Angeles
SCP Marianna	FDC Miami	MCC New York	FTC Oklahoma City
SCP Pekin	FDC Philadelphia	SCP Phoenix	MCC San Diego
FDC SeaTac	FCI Tallahassee	FCC Tucson	SCP Victorville
FCI Waseca			

NEEDS

Cognitions and Family/Parenting

PROGRAM DELIVERY

To ensure program fidelity and proper credit, **Assert Yourself for Female Offenders** is to be delivered by a Social Worker, Special Populations Program Coordinator, or Unit Team Staff.

421

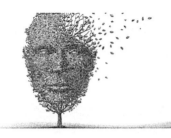

BASIC COGNITIVE SKILLS

Basic Cognitive Skills is a cognitive behavioral therapy (CBT) protocol that is used primarily for group treatment but may be used for individual treatment, in some cases. Through the use of this protocol, participants are taught basic concepts of CBT, including the Five Rules for Rational Thinking and the use of Rational Self-Analysis (RSA). This resource is consistent with the cognitive skills modules utilized in the Bureau's Drug Abuse Treatment Programs, BRAVE Programs, Challenge Programs, FIT, Mental Health Step Down Programs, Sex Offender Treatment Program, Skills Programs, and STAGES Programs.

The Basic Cognitive Skills journal was designed as a lead-in to other CBT protocols, specifically *Emotional Self-Regulation* and *Criminal Thinking*.

24 Hours of EBRR program credit.

Available at all BOP institutions.

Cognitions

To ensure program fidelity and proper credit, **Basic Cognitive Skills** must be delivered by Psychology Services staff.

DESCRIPTION

The Bureau Rehabilitation and Values Enhancement (BRAVE) program is a cognitive behavioral, residential treatment program for young males serving their first federal sentence. Inmates participate in this program at the beginning of their sentence. Programming is delivered within a modified therapeutic community (MTC). Participants interact in groups and attend community meetings while living in a housing unit separate from the general population.

The BRAVE Program is designed to facilitate favorable institutional adjustment and reduce incidents of misconduct. In addition, the program encourages inmates to interact positively with staff members and take advantage of opportunities to engage in self-improvement throughout their incarceration. Inmates participate in treatment groups for four hours per day, Monday through Friday. Program content focuses on developing interpersonal skills, behaving prosocially in a prison environment, challenging antisocial attitudes and criminality, developing problem solving skills, and planning for release.

HOURS
500 hours of EBRR program credit.

LOCATIONS
FCI Beckley (Medium)   FCC Victorville (Medium)

NEEDS
Antisocial Peers and Cognitions

PROGRAM DELIVERY
To ensure program fidelity and proper credit, **BRAVE** is only delivered by Psychology Services staff.

BUREAU LITERACY PROGRAM

DESCRIPTION

The Bureau of Prison's literacy program is designed to assist every inmate who does not have a high school diploma or high school equivalency credential. The literacy curricula consists of an Adult Basic Education and General Educational Development (GED) to accommodate all academic levels. Upon arrival, each inmate is evaluated to determine their current level of education and academic needs. They are placed in a class based on their academic levels and an individualized plan is developed for them to assist with their knowledge and skill in reading, math, and written expression, and to prepare for the GED exam.

The GED curricula is comprehensive and was designed around College and Career Readiness (CCR) Standards that provide guidelines for what students should learn, and offers consistent expectations of students across all BOP institutions. The curriculum offers a "Teaching Notes" section to help teachers work across a number of content areas. Additionally, "Suggested Class Activities and Resources" sections include activities to use in the classroom to support specific objectives. Lastly, it identifies skills assessed on the GED test, which help instructors make a significant impact on increasing student performance on GED tests.

HOURS
240 hours of EBRR program credits.

LOCATIONS
Available at all BOP institutions.

NEEDS
Education

PROGRAM DELIVERY
To ensure program fidelity and proper credit, the **Bureau Literacy** program must be delivered by the appropriately credentialed contractors or Education staff.

424

CERTIFICATION COURSE TRAINING

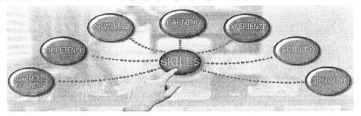

DESCRIPTION
The Bureau's Career Technical Education (CTE) program falls under three broad categories: 1) Apprenticeship Training, 2) Certification Course Training, and 3) Vocational Training.

Certification Course Training: Training programs that lead to an obtainment of an industry recognized certification and is comprised of 99 instructional hours or less.

Generally, these programs require inmates to have completed the high school equivalency, but concurrent enrollment is sometimes possible. Each individual program is designed to enhance post-release employment opportunities by providing inmates with the ability to obtain marketable, in-demand employment skills. Most programs follow a competency based curriculum, which teaches specific job skills and leads to a recognized credential, or certificate.

Some institutions offer inmates the opportunity to acquire college certificates and associates degrees through Advanced Occupational Education or local Pell Grant programs.

HOURS
50 hours of EBRR program credit.

LOCATIONS
Available at all BOP institutions.

NEEDS
Work

PROGAM DELIVERY
To ensure program fidelity and proper credit, **Certification Course Training** must be delivered by Education and Federal Prison Industries staff. This program may also be delivered by a qualified volunteer or contractor.

425

CHALLENGE PROGRAM

RESIDENTIAL

The Challenge Program is a cognitive behavioral, residential treatment program developed for male inmates in the United States Penitentiary (USP) settings. The Challenge Program provides treatment to high-security inmates with substance use problems and/or mental illnesses. Programming is delivered within a modified therapeutic community (MTC); inmates participate in interactive groups and attend community meetings while living in a housing unit separate from the general population. In addition to treating substance use disorders and mental illnesses, the program addresses criminality, via cognitive behavioral challenges to criminal thinking errors.

The Challenge Program is available in 13 high security institutions. Inmates may participate in the program at any point during their sentence; however, they must have at least 18 months remaining on their sentence. The duration of the program varies based on inmate need, with a minimum duration of nine months.

An inmate must meet one of the following criteria to be admitted into the Challenge Program:
- A history of drug use as evidenced by self-report, Presentence Investigation Report (PSI) documentation or incident reports for use of alcohol or drugs.
- A serious mental illness as evidenced by a current diagnosis of a psychotic disorder, mood disorder, anxiety disorder, or severe personality disorder.

HOURS
500 hours of EBRR program credit.

LOCATIONS

USP Allenwood	USP Atwater	USP Beaumont	USP Big Sandy
USP Canaan	USP Coleman I & II	USP Hazelton	USP Lee
USP McCreary	USP Pollock	USP Terre Haute	USP Tucson

NEEDS
Anger/Hostility, Antisocial Peers, Cognitions, Mental Health, and Substance Use

PROGRAM DELIVERY
To ensure program fidelity and proper credit, the **Challenge Program** must only be delivered by Psychology Services staff.

COGNITIVE PROCESSING THERAPY

Cognitive Processing Therapy is an evidence-based intervention for the treatment of Posttraumatic Stress Disorder. In a 12-session format, this intervention combines cognitive techniques with written exposure therapy to address negative affect, intrusive images, dysfunctional thoughts, and avoidance behavior.

HOURS

18 hours of EBRR program credit.

LOCATIONS

Available at all BOP institutions.

NEEDS

Cognitions, Mental Health, and Trauma

PROGRAM DELIVERY

To ensure program fidelity and proper credit, **Cognitive Processing Therapy** must be delivered by Psychology Services staff.

DESCRIPTION
The purpose of the Criminal Thinking group is to help the participant see how criminal thinking errors impact decisions in daily life. Techniques from cognitive behavioral therapy (CBT), especially the Rational Self Analysis (RSA), are used to identify the patterns of criminal thinking occurring in a wide range of situational contexts.

The Criminal Thinking treatment groups are based on CBT and use the same eight criminal thinking errors as other BOP programs. Participants learn to conduct an RSA to improve decision making about criminal behaviors exercise.

HOURS
27 hours of EBRR program credit.

LOCATIONS
Available at all BOP institutions.

NEEDS
Antisocial Peers and Cognitions

PROGRAM DELIVERY
To ensure program fidelity and proper credit, **Criminal Thinking** must be delivered by Psychology Services staff.

428

DIALECTICAL BEHAVIOR THERAPY

DESCRIPTION

Dialectical Behavior Therapy is a cognitive behavioral treatment teaching self-management of emotions and distress. This program is specifically for individuals who engage in self-directed violence, such as self-cutting, suicidal thoughts, urges, and suicide attempts. The types of skills discussed and practiced include, but are not limited to, mindfulness skills, distress tolerance skills, emotion regulation skills, and interpersonal effectiveness skills. This group is approximately 12-15 sessions, depending the participants.

HOURS

104 hours of EBRR program credit.

LOCATIONS

Available at all BOP institutions.

NEEDS

Cognitions, Mental Health, and Trauma

PROGRAM DELIVERY

To ensure program fidelity and proper credit, **Dialectical Behavior Therapy** must be delivered by Psychology Services staff.

429

DESCRIPTION

Emotional Self-Regulation is a cognitive behavioral therapy (CBT) protocol for mild to moderate depression, anxiety, or adjustment disorders. The Emotional Self-Regulation protocol is ideal for inmates presenting with mild to moderate symptoms of depression, anxiety, or stress. There is ample evidence that CBT approaches are as effective as medication in addressing these types of disorders. It may be used for either group or individual psychotherapy. Treatment in Emotional Self-Regulation group or individual therapy may be considered either an alternative to or an adjunct to treatment with medication.

HOURS

24 hours of EBRR program credit.

LOCATIONS

Available at all BOP institutions.

NEEDS

Cognitions and Mental Health

PROGRAM DELIVERY

To ensure program fidelity and proper credit, **Emotional Self-Regulation** must be delivered by Psychology Services staff.

DESCRIPTION

The mission of Federal Prison Industries, Inc. (FPI) is to protect society and reduce crime by preparing inmates for successful reentry through job training. FPI (also known by its trade name UNICOR) is a critical component of the Bureau's comprehensive efforts to improve inmate reentry. By providing inmates the skills needed to join the workforce upon release, FPI reduces recidivism and helps curb the rising costs of corrections.

FPI is, first and foremost, a correctional program. Its impetus is helping inmates acquire the skills necessary to successfully make the transition from prison to law-abiding, tax paying, productive members of society. The production of items and provision of services are necessary by-products of those efforts, as FPI does not receive any appropriated funds for operation. FPI is required by statute to diversify its product offerings as much as possible in order to minimize the program's impact on any one industry. FPI currently produces over 80 types of products and services and has six business groups: Clothing and Textiles; Electronics; Fleet; Office Furniture; Recycling; and Services.

Inmate workers are ordinarily hired through waiting lists. A renewed emphasis has been placed on the use of job sharing and half-time workers. This allows for an increase in the number of inmates who benefit from participating in the FPI program. FPI has placed emphasis on prioritizing inmates on the waiting list within three years of release for available FPI positions, with the aim of hiring inmates at least six months prior to release. FPI has also placed an emphasis on prioritizing inmates on the waiting list who are military veterans, as well as those with financial responsibilities.

HOURS

500 hours of EBRR program credits.

LOCATIONS

FCC Allenwood	FCC Beaumont	FCC Butner	FCC Coleman	FCC Forrest City	FCC Lompoc
FCC Oakdale	FCC Petersburg	FCC Pollock	FCC Terre Haute	FCC Victorville	FCC Yazoo City
FCI Ashland (L)	FCI Bastrop (L)	FCI Beckley (M)	FCI Cumberland (M)	FCI Dublin (L)(F)	FCI Edgefield (M)
FCI El Reno (M)	FCI Elkton (L)	FCI Englewood (L)	FCI Estill (M)	FCI Fairton (M)	FCI Fort Dix (L)
FCI Gilmer (M)	FCI Greenville (M)	FCI Jesup (M)	FCI La Tuna (L)	FCI Manchester (M)	FCI Marianna (M)
FCI Memphis (M)	FCI Miami (L)	FCI Milan (L)	FCI Phoenix (M)	FCI Safford (L)	FCI Sandstone (L)
FCI Schuylkill (M)	FCI Seagoville (L)	FCI Sheridan (M)	FCI Talladega (L)	FCI Tallahassee (L)(F)	FCI Texarkana (L)
FCI Waseca (L)(F)	FMC Lexington	FPC Bryan (F)	FPC Montgomery	FPC Pensacola	USP Atlanta (M)
USP Atwater (H)	USP Leavenworth (M)	USP Marion (M)	FCI Terminal Island (M)		

Key: FCC = Complex; FPC = Federal Prison Camp; SCP = Minimum; (L) = Low; (M) = Medium; (H) = High; (F) = Female

NEEDS

Work

PROGRAM DELIVERY

To ensure program fidelity and proper credit, **Federal Prison Industries** must be delivered by UNICOR.

431

DESCRIPTION

The Female Integrated Treatment (FIT) Program functions as an institution-wide, residential treatment program that offers integrated cognitive behavioral therapy (CBT) for substance use disorders, mental illness, and trauma-related disorders, as well as vocational training, to female inmates. Inmates who would otherwise qualify for the Residential Drug Abuse Program (RDAP) and whose treatment plans address substance use in this residential program may qualify for the early release benefit associated with RDAP.

FIT operates as a modified therapeutic community (MTC) utilizing cognitive behavioral treatments in a trauma-informed, gender-responsive environment. Criminal thinking is addressed through the identification of criminal thinking errors and the promotion of prosocial interactions with staff and peers. There is a special emphasis on vocational training to prepare women with the skills they will need to support themselves and their families upon release. For example, some women are trained as peer companions and have the opportunity to complete an apprenticeship that prepares them for work in the community as a Peer Specialist. The program works closely with Psychology Services, Recreation, Unit Management, Education, and Correctional Services to promote a multidisciplinary approach to treatment and skill building. Program content is designed to promote successful reentry into society at the conclusion of incarceration. Program staff further support reentry by collaborating with community partners prior to release.

HOURS
500 hours of EBRR program credit.

LOCATIONS
FSL Danbury (Low)   SFF Hazelton (Low)

NEEDS
Antisocial Peers, Cognitions, Mental Health,
Substance Use, Trauma, and Work

PROGRAM DELIVERY
To ensure program fidelity and proper credit, the **Female Integrated Treatment** program must be delivered by Psychology Services and Education staff.

432

FOUNDATION

DESCRIPTION

Foundation is a program designed to assist women in assessing and advocating for their individual needs and translating the results of that assessment into the selection of programs and plans to meet their reentry goals. The Foundation Program was designed to help newly incarcerated women chart a healthy path for themselves during their time of incarceration. Throughout the program, participants learn about a number of issues facing women. They have the opportunity to identify positive changes that will lead to a successful reentry, and consider programs and services within the facility that can help them make these changes.

The Change Plan, a Productive Activity, is a follow up to the Foundation Program that focuses on the goals established in Foundation.

HOURS

15 Hours of EBRR program credits.

LOCATIONS

FPC Alderson	FCI Aliceville	MDC Brooklyn	FPC Bryan
FMC Carswell	MCC Chicago	SCP Coleman	FSL/SCP Danbury
FCI Dublin	MDC Guaynabo	SCP Greenville	SFF Hazelton
FDC Honolulu	FDC Houston	SCP Lexington	MDC Los Angeles
SCP Marianna	FDC Miami	MCC New York	FTC Oklahoma City
SCP Pekin	SCP Phoenix	FDC Philadelphia	MCC San Diego
FDC SeaTac	FCI Tallahassee	FCC Tucson	SCP Victorville
FCI Waseca			

NEEDS

Cognitions, Education, Mental Health, and Work

PROGRAM DELIVERY

To ensure program fidelity and proper credit, **Foundation** must be delivered by a Special Population Program Coordinator or Social Worker. At facilities housing pretrial women the Reentry Affairs Coordinator can also deliver the Foundation program.

433

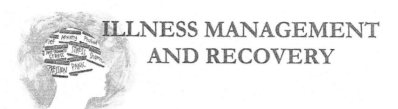

ILLNESS MANAGEMENT AND RECOVERY

Illness Management and Recovery (IMR) is a psychoeducational intervention for individuals suffering from serious mental illness. It is composed of ten modules and can be completed through weekly sessions over the course of a year. Topics include recovery strategies, practical facts about mental illness, the stress-vulnerability model, building social support, using medication effectively, reducing relapses and coping with stress, problems and symptoms. IMR is considered a front line intervention for the treatment of serious mental illness.

HOURS

60 hours of EBRR program credit.

LOCATIONS

Available at all BOP institutions.

NEEDS

Mental Health

PROGRAM DELIVERY

To ensure program fidelity and proper credit, **Illness Management and Recovery** must be delivered by Psychology Services staff.

434

LIFE CONNECTIONS PROGRAM
Residential

The Life Connections Program (LCP) is a faith-based reentry program designed to address religious beliefs and value systems. Participants are connected with a community mentor at the institution or with a faith-based or community organization at their release destination. The LCP is an 18 month residential program aimed at strengthening participants' understanding of what it means to live and work effectively in the community. The LCP is open to inmates of all faiths and those who have no religious background. Participants approach the program from their own faith teachings or values-based background. The program uses standardized curricula including interactive journaling in a therapeutic group setting. It seeks to engage participants in community service projects, victim impact, mentoring, healthy living skill development, and release preparation.

The LCP uses agency chaplains and mentor coordinators as well as contracted spiritual guides, community mentors, and volunteers to work in small groups and one on one with program participants. This gives participants the opportunity to learn from others. Upon release, the LCP provides continued community mentoring and faith group support for these returning citizens.

HOURS
500 hours of EBRR program credits.

LOCATIONS
FCC Petersburg (L)   FCI Milan (L)   FMC Carswell (F)   USP Leavenworth (M)   USP Terre Haute (H)
FCI Aliceville (F)

Key: (L) = Low; (M) = Medium; (H) = High; (F) = Female

NEEDS
Family/Parenting

PROGRAM DELIVERY
To ensure program fidelity and proper credit, the **Life Connections Program** must be delivered by Chaplaincy staff or appropriately credentialed volunteers or contractors.

MENTAL HEALTH STEP DOWN
(Residential)

DESCRIPTION

Mental Health Step Down (Step Down) is a unit-based, residential program offering intermediate level of care for inmates with serious mental illness who do not require inpatient treatment but lack the skills to function in general population. The goal of Step Down is to provide evidence-based treatment that maximizes the participants' ability to function while minimizing relapse and the need for inpatient hospitalization.

Step Down operates as a modified therapeutic community (MTC) using cognitive behavioral treatments, peer support, and skills training. Staff work closely with psychiatry to ensure participants receive appropriate medication and have the opportunity to build a positive relationship with the psychiatrist. Criminal thinking is addressed through the identification of criminal thinking errors and engagement in prosocial interactions with staff and peers. When inmates are preparing for release, intense coordination is done with social workers, Community Treatment Services (CTS), Residential Reentry Centers (RRC), Court Services and Offender Supervision Agency (CSOSA), and United States Probation Officers (USPOs) to facilitate continuity of care for reentry.

HOURS

500 hours of EBRR program credit.

LOCATIONS

USP Allenwood (H)   USP Atlanta (H)   FCC Butner (M)   FMC Fort Worth (L)

Key: (L) = Low; (M) = Medium; (H) = High

NEEDS

Antisocial Peers, Cognitions, and Mental Health

PROGRAM DELIVERY

To ensure program fidelity and proper credit, the **Mental Health Step Down** program must be delivered by Psychology Services staff.

MONEY SMART FOR ADULTS

DESCRIPTION

Money Smart for Adults is an instructor-led course consisting of eleven training modules that cover basic financial topics. Topics include a description of deposit and credit services offered by financial institutions, choosing and maintaining a checking account, spending plans, the importance of saving, how to obtain and use credit effectively, and the basics of building or repairing credit.

HOURS

32 hours of EBRR program credits.

LOCATIONS

Available at all BOP institutions.

NEEDS

Finance/Poverty

PROGRAM DELIVERY

To ensure program fidelity and proper credit, **Money Smart for Adults** must be delivered by Business Office Staff or Unit Team. This program may also be delivered by a qualified volunteer or contractor.

437

DESCRIPTION

The Bureau's National Parenting from Prison Program is a two-phase model, focusing on services for incarcerated parents.

PHASE I: National Parenting Program Workshop. Phase I is a dynamic, psychoeducational course focused on parenting basics. This phase covers topics such as appropriate discipline and developmental milestones supplemented with discussion and practical exercises. An interactive DVD series is used for a portion of the Phase I program, to ensure standardization across facilities. The DVDs include discussion clips from national experts and incarcerated persons. Inmates engage in discussion and complete significant homework assignments as part of this program.

PHASE II: National Parenting Specialty Programs. Phase II focuses on specific parenting needs such as parenting as an incarcerated mother, father, grandparent or parenting a child with a disability. Phase II programming includes the following courses: Inside Out Dad, Mothers of Adolescents, Preparing for Motherhood, Parenting Inside Out, Parenting a Second Time Around (PASTA), Partners in Parenting, Parenting Children with Special Needs (available in Spanish), and To Parent or Not to Parent (available in Spanish).

HOURS
40 hours of EBRR program credits.

LOCATIONS
Available at all BOP institutions.

NEEDS
Family/Parenting

PROGAM DELIVERY

To ensure program fidelity and proper credit, the **National Parenting from Prison** program is to be delivered by a Teacher, Social Worker, Special Population Program Coordinator, or Unit Team staff.

NON-RESIDENTIAL DRUG ABUSE PROGRAM

The Non-Residential Drug Abuse Treatment Program (NRDAP) is a psychoeducational, therapeutic group designed for general population inmates who report a history of problematic substance use. NRDAP is available to inmates at every institution. The purpose of NRDAP is to afford all inmates with a substance use problem the opportunity to receive treatment.

NRDAP groups are conducted 90 – 120 minutes per week for a minimum of 12 weeks and a maximum of 24 weeks. The content addresses criminal lifestyles and provides skill-building opportunities in the areas of rational thinking, communication skills, and institution/community adjustment.

24 hours of EBRR program credit.

Available at all BOP institutions.

Cognitions and Substance Use

To ensure program fidelity and proper credit, the **Non-Residential Drug Abuse Program** must be delivered by Psychology Services staff.

DESCRIPTION

The post-secondary education program includes courses offered to inmates who have completed high school equivalency requirements and are seeking to enhance their marketable skills. College level classes are provided by credentialed instructors from the community who deliver coursework leading to either the Associates or Bachelor's degree. Specific prerequisites for each program are determined by the school providing the service.

HOURS

Up to 500 hours of EBRR program credits.

Credits will vary depending on the college program requirements leading to a Certificate, Associates, or Bachelor's degree awarded by the college.

LOCATIONS

FCI Bennettsville	FCI Beaumont (Low/Medium)	MDC Brooklyn
FPC Bryan	FCI Cumberland	FCI Dublin
FCI Englewood	FCI Gilmer	FCC Lompoc
FCI Milan	FCI Ray Brook	FCI Williamsburg
FCI Waseca	FPC Yankton	FCI Yazoo City

NEEDS

Work

PROGRAM DELIVERY

To ensure program fidelity and proper credit, the **Post-Secondary Education** program must be delivered by Education staff or appropriately credentialed contractors.

RESIDENTIAL DRUG ABUSE PROGRAM

The Residential Drug Abuse Program (RDAP) is operated as a modified therapeutic community (MTC); the community is the catalyst for change and focuses on the inmate as a whole person with overall lifestyle change needs, not simply abstinence from drug use. RDAP encourages participants to examine their personal behavior to help them become more pro-social and to engage in "right living"— considered to be based on honesty, responsibility, hard work, and willingness to learn.

RDAP emphasizes social learning and mutual self-help. This aid to others is seen as an integral part of self-change. As program participants progress through the phases of the program, they assume greater personal and social responsibilities in the community. It is expected that program participants take on leadership and mentoring roles within the MTC as they progress in their program. Progress in treatment is based on the inmate's ability to demonstrate comprehension and internalization of treatment concepts by taking behaviorally observable action to change his or her maladaptive and unhealthy behaviors. It is important to note that successful completion of the Bureau's RDAP requires completion of all three components of the program:

- Unit Based Treatment, described above, occurs in prison.
- Follow-Up Treatment continues for inmates who complete the unit-based component of the RDAP and return to general population. An inmate must remain in Follow-Up Treatment for 12 months or until he/she is transferred to a Residential Reentry Center.
- Community Treatment is provided while the inmate transitions to the community through an RRC.

HOURS

500 hours of EBRR program credit.

LOCATIONS

Please refer to page 44 for institutions.

NEEDS

Antisocial Peers, Cognitions, Substance Use, and
Mental Health (Dual Diagnosis Programs)

PROGRAM DELIVERY

To ensure program fidelity and proper credit, the **Residential Drug Abuse** program must be delivered by Psychology Services staff.

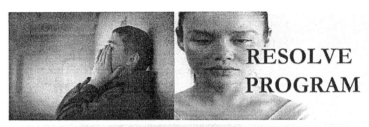

RESOLVE PROGRAM

DESCRIPTION

The Resolve Program is a cognitive behavioral therapy (CBT) program designed to address the trauma-related mental health needs of inmates. Specifically, the program seeks to decrease the incidence of trauma-related psychological disorders and improve level of functioning. In addition, the program aims to increase the effectiveness of other treatments, such as drug treatment and healthcare. The program uses a standardized treatment protocol consisting of three components: 1) initial educational workshop (Trauma in Life/Traumatic Stress & Resilience); 2) a skills based treatment group (Seeking Safety) and; 3) Dialectical Behavioral Therapy (DBT), Cognitive Processing Therapy (CPT), and/or a Skills Maintenance Group.

The purposes of the program include the following:
- Improving the inmate's functioning by decreasing mental health symptoms that result from trauma;
- Increasing the effectiveness of other treatment programs available to the inmate;
- Reducing misconduct that results from mental health and trauma related difficulties; and
- Reducing recidivism.

HOURS
80 hours of EBRR program credit.

LOCATIONS

FPC Alderson (F)	FCI Aliceville (L)(F)	FCI Ashland (M)	FPC Bryan (F)
FMC Carswell (F)	SCP Coleman	USP Coleman (H)	FCI Cumberland (M)
FCI Danbury (L)	FCI Dublin (L)(F)	FCI Edgefield (M)	ADX Florence
SCP Greenville (F)	SFF Hazelton (L)(F)	USP Leavenworth (M)	SCP Lexington (F)
SCP Marianna (F)	FCI Otisville (M)	FCI Oxford (M)	FPC Pekin (F)
FPC Phoenix (F)	FCI Sheridan (M)	FCI Tallahassee (L)(F)	USP Terre Haute (H)
FCI Victorville (M)	SCP Victorville (F)	FCI Waseca (L)(F)	

Key: ADX = Administrative; SCP = Minimum; (L) = Low; (M) = Medium; (H) = High; (F) = Female

NEEDS
Cognitions, Mental Health, and Trauma

PROGRAM DELIVERY

To ensure program fidelity and proper credit, the **Resolve** program must be delivered by Psychology Services staff.

DESCRIPTION

Seeking Safety is a present-focused, evidence-based approach to treat trauma symptoms and substance use concurrently. It is based on the premise that healing from each disorder requires attention to both disorders. This intervention teaches inmates to manage and decrease symptoms and gain control over both disorders by addressing current life problems. The Seeking Safety curriculum is called Seeking Strength at male institutions to encourage participation among male inmates.

HOURS

12 – 16 hours of EBRR program credit.

LOCATIONS

Available at all BOP institutions.

NEEDS

Antisocial Peers, Cognitions, Mental Health, Substance Use, and Trauma

PROGRAM DELIVERY

To ensure program fidelity and proper credit, **Seeking Safety** must be delivered by Psychology Services staff.

443

SEX OFFENDER PROGRAM NON-RESIDENTIAL

The Non-Residential Sex Offender Treatment Program (SOTP-NR) is designed to target dynamic risk factors associated with re-offense in sexual offenders, as demonstrated by empirical research. These factors include sexual self-regulation deficits and sexual deviancy; criminal thinking and behavior patterns; intimacy skills deficits; and emotional self-regulation deficits. The SOTP-NR uses cognitive-behavioral techniques, with a primary emphasis on skills acquisition and practice. Inmates participate in interactive psychotherapy groups multiple times per week.

The SOTP-NR is available in eight institutions with varying security levels. Inmates ordinarily participate in the program during the remaining 36-48 months of their sentence. The duration of the program is 9-12 months.

Most participants in the SOTP-NR have a history of a single sexual offense and many may be first-time offenders serving a sentence for an Internet-based sexual crime. Programming is voluntary. Prior to placement in the SOTP-NR, potential participants are screened with a risk assessment tool to ensure their offense history matches with moderate intensity sexual offender specific treatment.

HOURS
500 hours of EBRR program credit.

LOCATIONS

FMC Carswell (females only)	FCI Elkton (program at the FSL)
FCI Englewood	FCI Marianna
USP Marion	FCI Petersburg
FCI Seagoville	USP Tucson

NEEDS
Cognitions

PROGRAM DELIVERY
To ensure program fidelity and proper credit, the **Non-Residential Sex Offender Treatment** program must only be delivered by Psychology Services staff.

SEX OFFENDER PROGRAM RESIDENTIAL

The Residential Sex Offender Treatment Program (SOTP-R) is designed to target dynamic risk factors associated with re-offense in sexual offenders, as demonstrated by empirical research. These factors include sexual self-regulation deficits and sexual deviancy; criminal thinking and behavior patterns; intimacy skills deficits; and emotional self-regulation deficits. The SOTP-R uses cognitive behavioral techniques, with a primary emphasis on skills acquisition and practice. The modified therapeutic community (MTC) model is used to address criminal attitudes and values.

The SOTP-R is available at two institutions. Inmates ordinarily participate in the program during the remaining 36 to 48 months of their sentence. The duration of the program is 12-18 months.

Participants in the SOTP-R have a history of multiple sexual offenses, extensive non-sexual criminal histories, and/or a high level of sexual deviancy or hypersexuality. The program is voluntary. Prior to placement in the SOTP-R, potential participants are screened with a risk assessment tool to ensure their offense history matches with high intensity sexual offender specific treatment.

HOURS

500 hours of EBRR program credit.

LOCATIONS

FMC Devens   USP Marion

NEEDS

Antisocial Peers and Cognitions

PROGRAM DELIVERY

To ensure program fidelity and proper credit, the **Residential Sex Offender Treatment Program** must only be delivered by Psychology Services staff.

445

DESCRIPTION

The Skills Program is a unit-based, residential treatment program designed to improve the institutional adjustment of inmates who have intellectual and social impairments. Inmates with lower IQs, neurological deficits from acquired brain damage, fetal alcohol syndrome, autism spectrum disorder, and/or remarkable social skills deficits are more likely to be victimized and/or manipulated by more sophisticated inmates. As a result, they may be placed in the Special Housing Unit for their protection or may have frequent misconduct reports because of their limited decision making skills. Only inmates who have a demonstrated need for the Skills Program and who are appropriate for housing in a medium or low security facility will be considered for participation.

Through using a modified therapeutic community (MTC), the Skills Program employs a multi-disciplinary treatment approach aimed at teaching participants basic educational and social skills over a 12-month period. The goal of the program is to increase the academic achievement and adaptive behavior of this group of inmates, thereby improving their institutional adjustment and likelihood for successful community reentry. Some participants may become Mental Health Companions; inmates who are carefully screened and serve as supports and role models for Skills Program participants.

HOURS
500 hours of EBRR program credit.

LOCATIONS
FCI Coleman (M)   FCI Danbury (L)

Note: (L) = Low; (M) = Medium

NEEDS
Antisocial Peers, Cognitions, and Mental Health

PROGRAM DELIVERY
To ensure program fidelity and proper credit, the **Skills Program** must be delivered by Psychology Services staff.

446

DESCRIPTION

Social Skills Training for Schizophrenia is a structured skills training intervention focused on improving social skills. Although designed for individuals suffering from schizophrenia, this resource is appropriate for any inmate with moderate social skills deficits. With this intervention, social skills are taught and practiced in a small group setting. Skills include basic social skills, conversation skills, assertiveness skills, conflict management skills, communal living skills, friendship and dating skills, health maintenance skills, vocational/work skills, and coping skills for drug and alcohol use.

HOURS

60 hours of EBRR program credit.

LOCATIONS

Available at all BOP institutions.

NEEDS

Antisocial Peers, Cognitions, and Mental Health

PROGRAM DELIVERY

To ensure program fidelity and proper credit, **Social Skills Training** must be delivered by Psychology Staff.

STAGES PROGRAM - Residential

**High-Intensity Cognitive Behavioral Therapy for
Serious Mental Illness and Personality Disorders**

Steps Toward Awareness, Growth, and Emotional Strength (STAGES) is a unit-based, residential Psychology Treatment Program for male inmates with a diagnosis of Borderline Personality Disorder. The program uses an integrative model that includes an emphasis on a modified therapeutic community (MTC), cognitive behavioral therapy, and skills training. It uses evidence-based treatments to increase the time between disruptive behaviors, fosters living within the general population or community setting, and increase prosocial skills. This program aims to prepare inmates for their transition to less-secure prison settings and promote successful reentry into society at the conclusion of their terms of incarceration.

The typical STAGES inmate has the following behavioral characteristics:
- A history of long-term restricted housing placements
- Multiple incident reports and/or suicide watches
- A long and intensifying pattern of behavior disruptive to the institution
- A demonstrated willingness to engage with treatment staff and change the way he deals with incarceration (although behavioral problems may continue)

HOURS

500 hours of EBRR program credit.

LOCATIONS

FCI Florence (H)   FCC Terre Haute (M)

Key: (M) = Medium; (H) = High

NEEDS

Antisocial Peers, Cognitions Mental Health, and Trauma

PROGRAM DELIVERY

To ensure program fidelity and proper credit, the **STAGES** program must be delivered by Psychology Services staff.

THRESHOLD PROGRAM

Faith-based program focused on values and life skills

The Threshold Program is a non-residential faith-based reentry program open to male and female federal offenders. Like the more intensive Life Connections Program, it is open to inmates across the agency seeking grounding in positive values and responsibility, regardless of the presence of a religious affiliation. Ordinarily, inmates should have less than 24 months from their proposed release dates to be considered for the program. Curriculum is also available for participants who desire to participate from a non-religious perspective. Typically, cohorts meet weekly in 90-minute sessions for six to nine months and include no more than 20 participants.

Threshold is offered throughout the Bureau utilizing the leadership of agency chaplains, religious contractors, community volunteers, and mentors.

HOURS

72 hours of EBRR program credits.

LOCATIONS

Available at all BOP institutions.

NEEDS

Family/Parenting

PROGRAM DELIVERY

To ensure program fidelity and proper credit, the **Threshold** program must be delivered by Chaplaincy staff, or the appropriately credentialed volunteers or contractors.

VOCATIONAL TRAINING

The Bureau's Career Technical Education (CTE) program falls under three broad categories:
1) Apprenticeship Training, 2) Certification Course Training, and 3) Vocational Training.

Vocational Training: Marketable training that provides specific entry level or advanced job skills and certification that is instructor led with hands on skill building, as well as, live work projects. A variety of skilled-trades are offered to include: building trades, welding, heating ventilation and refrigeration (HVAC), highway construction, and wind-turbine technology.

Generally, these programs require inmates to have completed the high school equivalency, but concurrent enrollment is sometimes possible. Each individual program is designed to enhance post-release employment opportunities by providing inmates with the ability to obtain marketable, in-demand employment skills. Most programs follow a competency based curriculum, which teaches specific job skills and leads to a recognized credential, certificate, or degree. It should be noted some programs offer "exploratory courses," which allow inmates to explore a possible program before making a long-term commitment.

HOURS
125 hours of EBRR program credit.

LOCATIONS
Available at all BOP institutions.

NEEDS
Work

PROGAM DELIVERY
To ensure program fidelity and proper credit, **Vocational Training** must be delivered by Education and Federal Prison Industries staff. This program may also be delivered by a qualified volunteer or contractor.

450

PRODUCTIVE ACTIVITIES

Productive Activities & Descriptions	Hours	Location(s)	Need(s) Addressed	Program Delivery
A Healthier Me The Healthier Me Program is designed to help incarcerated women build healthy lifestyles by considering what a healthy life means to them and practicing skills for stress management, healthy relationships, physical activity, and mindful eating.	10	All female sites	Recreation/Leisure/Fitness	Recreation Social Worker Special Population Program Coordinator Unit Team
A Matter of Balance Falling, or fear of falling, can negatively impact older adults by causing them to refrain from enjoyable or therapeutic activities. This program helps to build self-efficacy related to strength and mobility by decreasing fail-related fears. It teaches older inmates to problem-solve and improve their self-esteem.	16	All institutions	Recreation/Leisure/Fitness	Health Services Recreation
AARP Foundation Finances 50+ This program provides financial education and counseling for vulnerable households, particularly adults age 50+. Older adults face unique challenges in financial planning and weak job prospects. This program will assist the older adult in financial goal setting that translates into positive financial behaviors.	5	All institutions	Finance/Poverty	Reentry Affairs Coordinator Unit Team Volunteers
Access This program is designed for incarcerated women who are survivors of domestic violence. It assists women in identifying suitable career options to be economically independent upon reentry. An interactive computer component (which can be printed and used in class) is used to explore career options. Participants also complete testing to determine what career field is best for them.	10	All female sites	Cognitions Mental Health Trauma	Social Worker Special Population Program Coordinator
Alcoholics Anonymous (AA) Support Group This self-help approach to change reduces the likelihood of problematic drinking behaviors. AA can be guided by any Bureau staff member but is essentially a self-help program.	50	All institutions	Substance Use	Contractors Volunteers

451

Program				
Arthritis Foundation Walk with Ease The Arthritis Foundation's Walk with Ease six-week program teaches participants how to safely make physical activity part of everyday life. Backed by studies from the Institute on Aging and Thurston Arthritis Foundation's Research, after completing this program, participants will reduce the pain and discomfort of arthritis; increase balance, strength, and walking pace; build confidence in the ability to be physically active; and improve overall health.	6	All institutions	Medical Recreation/Leisure/Fitness	Contractors Health Services Recreation Unit Team Volunteers
Beyond Violence: Prevention Program for Criminal-Justice Involved Women Beyond Violence focuses on anger and utilizes a multi-level approach and evidence-based therapeutic strategies (i.e., psychoeducation, role playing, mindfulness activities, cognitive-behavioral restructuring, and grounding skills for trauma triggers). The program is designed to assist women in understanding trauma, the aspects of anger, and emotional regulation.	40	All female sites	Anger/Hostility Cognitions	Social Worker Special Population Program Coordinator
Brain Health as You Age: You can Make A Difference! Improve memory and decision-making This program fosters self-improvement by providing inmates with knowledge related to brain health and its impact on memory, judgment, decision-making, and overall physical health, as well as the contributory effect brain health has on society as a whole.	5	All institutions	Medical Recreation/Leisure/Fitness	Contractors Health Services Recreation Unit Team Volunteers
Brief CBT for Suicidal Individuals This treatment was developed for individuals who are at risk of suicide. Initial focus is crisis intervention such as the development of a safety plan. The protocol also focuses on the development of cognitive strategies to help modify negative thoughts that can lead to self-directed violent behaviors. This treatment can be offered individually or in a group setting.	20	All institutions	Mental Health	Psychology
CBT for Eating Disorders Cognitive Behavioral Therapy for Eating Disorders involves assessment, stabilization, and education for individuals who have been diagnosed with an eating disorder. The program focuses on behavioral monitoring, body image concerns, and the development of new skills. It can be offered in an individual or group therapy format over the course of 20 one-hour sessions.	20	All institutions	Mental Health	Psychology

452

CBT for Insomnia Cognitive Behavior Treatment for Insomnia helps to identify maladaptive thoughts and behaviors that can lead to persistent insomnia. The program combines aspects of sleep hygiene, stimulus control, sleep restriction, and cognitive therapy into an integrated approach. It can be offered individually or in a group format.	10	All institutions	Mental Health	Psychology
CBT for Prison Gambling This set of four self-guided cognitive-behavioral handouts is designed to help individuals assess their prison gambling behavior and to develop the commitment to quit.	20	All institutions	Antisocial Peers Cognitions	Psychology
Change Plan The Change Plan, a Productive Activity, is a follow up program and focuses on the goals established in Foundation. As part of the Foundation Program's Personal Priorities Plan, participants identified three positive changes they wanted to make during incarceration. Change Plan gives participants the opportunity to focus on one of these changes, guiding them through ten evidence-based strategies they can apply to this change.	15	All female sites	Cognitions Education Mental Health Work	Contractors Education Health Services Psychology Social Worker Special Population Program Coordinator Unit Team Volunteers
Circle of Strength Circle of Strength is a protocol designed specifically for women in Federal Detention Centers or other short-term settings. It uses a structured format to provide information and resources about topics important to women while encouraging social support among participants.	20	All female sites	Cognitions Mental Health Trauma	Psychology Social Worker Special Population Program Coordinator Unit Team
Disabilities Education Program (DEP) DEP is a support group designed specifically for inmates living with physical disabilities while in institutions of varying security levels and focusing on reentry concerns. It uses a structured format to provide information and resources about topics important to inmates with varying physical disabilities while encouraging social and peer support among participants.	10	All institutions	Antisocial Peers Cognitions Medical	Reentry Affairs Coordinator Special Population Program Coordinator Social Worker

453

Drug Education	15	All institutions	Substance Use	Psychology
This program is designed to encourage participants with a history of drug use to consider the consequences of their drug use and identify their drug treatment needs. Participants are connected with appropriate treatment programs such as the Residential Drug Abuse Program (RDAP) or the Non-Residential Drug Abuse Program (NRDAP).				
Embracing Interfaith Cooperation	10	All institutions	Cognitions	Chaplaincy Contractors Volunteers
Embracing Interfaith Cooperation fosters interfaith dialogue, discussion, and understanding. It breaks down stereotypes and barriers for people and communities to serve together toward meeting common civil rights and community goals. The goal of this program is to provide an effective strategy in countering religious discrimination and extremism.				
English-as-a-Second Language	500	All institutions	Education Work	Contractors Education Volunteers
English-as-a-Second Language (ESL) is an English language education study program for non-native speakers. Students receive individual attention from their teachers as a part of differentiated learning classroom models driven by individual learning needs. Students learn English in cultural and social contexts found in the community. Classes teach different English language skills according to the students' English ability, interests, and needs. The ESL program teaches the following skills: grammar, reading, comprehension, writing, and vocabulary.				
Federal Prison Industries (FPI) Lean Basic Training	16	(51) FPI facilities	Work	FPI
Lean Basics Training provides the foundation of Lean Six Sigma practice, methodology and experience with basic tools for process improvement. This includes information regarding the development and success of LSS practice as it has evolved in major corporations.				
Franklin Covey 7 Habits on the Inside	50	All institutions	Family/Parenting	Unit Team
This program addresses interpersonal skills impacting relationships. It emphasizes character, integrity, and becoming trustworthy. It helps individuals move from the dependent state to the independent state where they accept responsibility for their thoughts and actions. The ultimate goal of the course leads to improved relationships with family, work, and peers.				

454

Getting to Know Your Healthy Aging Body This program discusses changes in organs, physique, and other physiological processes as we age. It also helps the aging population understand how to maintain the health of major biological systems. These major biological systems include the cardiovascular, digestive, and renal systems. The program also gives you valuable information on skin, ear and eyes, weight management, and sexual health.	12	All institutions	Medical Recreation/Leisure/Fitness	Contractors Health Services Recreation Unit Team Volunteers
Health and Wellness Throughout the Lifespan This program addresses the psychological effects of stress and aging. It explores the developmental psychology of people changing throughout life from infancy, through childhood, adolescence, adulthood, and death with individual needs being met at every stage of growth and development. It stresses the importance of understanding the development and the psychological effects of aging that occurs throughout the human lifespan.	3	All institutions	Medical Recreation/Leisure/Fitness	Contractors Health Services Recreation Unit Team Volunteers
Healthy Steps for Older Adults Healthy Steps for Older Adults is an evidenced-based falls prevention program designed to raise participants' knowledge and awareness of steps to take to reduce falls and improve health and well-being. The goal of the program is to prevent falls, promote health, and ensure that older adults remain as independent as possible for as long as possible.	3	All institutions	Medical Recreation/Leisure/Fitness	Contractors Health Services Recreation Unit Team Volunteers
Hooked on Phonics Hooked on Phonics is a program that aides in combating Dyslexia as well as low level readers. Research has shown that combining phonics instruction and reading is the best way to develop a good reader. Reading that includes a high percentage of familiar patterns gives the student the opportunity to read for meaning. Hooked on Phonics includes books and stories woven into the program at the appropriate readability level to provide opportunities for someone to read for meaning and enjoyment.	500	All institutions	Dyslexia	Contractors Education Volunteers

House of Healing: A Prisoner's Guide to Inner Power and Freedom Houses of Healing is an intervention program that teaches emotional literacy skills. Emotional literacy is the ability to perceive, understand, and communicate emotions with self and to others. Emotional literacy is also consistent with the concept of emotional intelligence--the ability to monitor one's feelings and emotions, and to use that information to guide thinking and actions.	24	All institutions	Cognitions	Chaplaincy Contractors Volunteers
K2 Awareness Program This program is for individuals suspected of or known to have used K2. It is designed to educate them about the risks of drug use, motivate them to seek drug treatment during their incarceration, and increase their awareness of available treatment resources. The ultimate goal is to reduce K2 use among the inmate population, thereby increasing the safety and security of the institution for staff and inmates.	5	All institutions	Substance Use	Contractors Custody Education Health Services Reentry Affairs Coordinator Unit Team Volunteers
Living a Healthy Life with Chronic Conditions This program assists participants in improving mental and physical well-being. This program is designed for older adults impacted by chronic conditions. It includes 19 topics with flexibility to modify sessions based on group needs.	24	All institutions	Medical Recreation/Leisure/Fitness	Contractors Health Services Recreation Unit Team Volunteers
Managing Your Diabetes Managing Your Diabetes is designed to teach inmates to effectively manage their chronic disease.	12	All institutions	Medical	Medical Volunteers (with appropriate credentials Nurse/Dietician)
Mindfulness-Based Cognitive Therapy Mindfulness-Based Cognitive Therapy is a group intervention aimed at preventing symptom relapse in individuals who have a history of depression and anxiety. In this treatment program, participants learn to engage in daily practice mindfulness skills and cognitive behavioral techniques to treatment the symptoms of depression and anxiety.	16	All institutions	Mental Health	Psychology

456

Money Smart for Older Adults Money Smart for Older Adults (MSOA) provides awareness among older adults on how to prevent elder financial exploitation and to encourage advance planning and informed financial decision-making. There are seven segments covering the following topics: Common Types of Elder Financial Exploitation, Scams Targeting Veterans, Identity Theft, Medical Identity Theft, Scams that Target Homeowners, Planning for Unexpected Life Events, and How to Be Financially Prepared for Disasters.	28	All institutions	Finance/Poverty	Business Office Contractors Unit Team Volunteers
Narcotics Anonymous This self-help approach to change reduces the likelihood of future drug use. NA can be guided by any Bureau staff member but is essentially a self-help program.	50	All institutions	Substance Use	Volunteers
National Diabetes Prevention Program This is a preventative program to assist at-risk and older adults in living healthier lifestyles and increasing physical activity. Diabetes can affect persons at all ages, but this program is recommended by the developers for any person over 60, because risk increases with age.	16	All institutions	Medical Recreation/Leisure/Fitness	Contractors Medical Recreation Unit Team Volunteers
PEER The Personal Education & Enrichment Resources (PEER) support group is designed for inmates living with cognitive and physical disabilities while in institutions of varying security levels. This facilitator-led group provides information and resources about topics important to inmates with varying disabilities while encouraging social and peer support among participants.	10	All institutions	Antisocial Peers	Social Worker Special Population Program Coordinator Unit Team
Pu'a Foundation Reentry Program This is a trauma-informed care program for female inmates at FDC Honolulu grounded in Hawaiian culture. The program focuses on families affected by trauma and incarceration with a special emphasis on women, girls, and Native Hawaiian participants.	20	FDC Honolulu	Family/Parenting Trauma	Contractors Education Social Worker Unit Team Volunteers

Resilience Support Resilience Support is a support group designed specifically for veteran inmates living in institutions of varying security levels. It uses a structured format to provide resilience-building skills to veteran inmates of all uniformed services encouraging peer and social support among participants. It emphasizes positive interpersonal relationships, physical and mental wellness, discovery of life purpose and meaning, self-compassion, and personal growth. The support group provides strategies to improve an individual's ability to adapt to adversity.	8	All institutions	Antisocial Peers Cognitions	Reentry Affairs Coordinators Special Population Coordinators Unit Team Volunteers
Service Fit This program is an eight-week, uniformed service inspired program designed specifically for inmate veterans. It uses a structured format to provide physical activity supporting a healthy lifestyle while encouraging social and peer support among participants.	16	All institutions	Recreation/Leisure/Fitness	Contractors Medical Recreation Reentry Affairs Coordinators Unit Team Volunteers
Sexual Self-Regulation (SSR) The SSR treatment protocol is designed to teach the practice of a set of self-management skills to gain effective control over deviant sexual urges and behaviors. To accomplish this task, participants are required to understand deviant sexual fantasies or urges and the factors that exacerbate or escalate sexual arousal. With this understanding, participants construct a plan to manage recurrent deviant arousal.	100	All institutions	Cognitions	Psychology
Soldier On Soldier On is a support group designed specifically for veterans living in varying security levels. It uses a structured format to provide information and resources about topics important to veterans of all uniformed services encouraging social and peer support among participants.	15	All institutions	Antisocial Peers Trauma	Contractors Social Worker Special Population Program Coordinator Unit Team Volunteers

458

Square One: Essentials for Women Square One is a basic life skills program designed specifically for female offenders. Although any woman may participate, it is designed to meet the needs of lower functioning women or those who have not lived or worked independently. The program adheres to principles associated with cognitive-behavioral approaches.	12	All female sites	Finance/Poverty Mental Health Recreation/Leisure/Fitness	Business Office Contractors Education Medical Reentry Affairs Coordinators Social Worker Special Population Program Coordinator Unit Team Volunteers
START NOW This program is designed for use in correctional facilities to treat offenders with behavioral disorders and associated behavioral problems. Start Now is designed as a strengths-based approach, focusing on an accepting and collaborative clinical style. It places the primary responsibility for change on the individual. It includes a gender-responsive program that was developed specifically for female offenders.	32	All institutions (gendered curricula)	Anger/Hostility Cognitions	Contractors Education Health Services Psychology Reentry Affairs Coordinators Social Worker Special Population Program Coordinator Unit Team Volunteers
Supported Employment Supported Employment is designed to carefully match seriously mentally ill (SMI) individuals with competitive job opportunities suitable to their interests and abilities by incorporating therapeutic support through the process of job acquisition and daily performance.	20	All institutions	Education Mental Health Work	FPI Health Services Psychology
Talking with Your Doctor: Guide for Older Adults This program offers tips on how older adults can prepare for a medical appointment; effectively discuss health concerns; coordinate assistance from family and friends; make decisions with the doctor about treatment; identify appropriate assisted living; and much more.	5	All institutions	Medical Recreation/Leisure/Fitness	Education Health Services

459

Trauma Education Trauma in Life (for females) and Traumatic Stress and Resilience (for males) - The purpose of the Trauma Education workshop is to provide information about understanding traumatic experiences, the impact of traumatic experiences, building resilience, and resolving difficulties through treatment. This group is designed to be educational and does not discuss specific personal traumas during group sessions.	8	All institutions	Mental Health Trauma	Psychology
Ultra Key 6: The Ultimate Keyboarding Tutor Ultra Key 6 places a strong emphasis on learning proper typing technique and typing accuracy, as well as speed. It emphasizes mastery of correct typing posture and fluent keystroke memory results in improved typing speed with practice. The program is adaptive and allows users to progress at their own pace.	20	All institutions	Education Work	Contractors Education
Understanding Your Feelings: Shame and Low Self Esteem This program helps women evaluate the role of shame and low self-esteem in their lives. Risk factors are identified for each individual, and coping skills to improve self-worth are learned and practiced.	7	All female sites	Cognitions Mental Health Trauma	Education Health Services Social Worker Special Population Program Coordinator
Victim Impact: Listen and Learn A rehabilitative program that puts "victims first." Students who participate will be provided with a skillset to understand the impact crimes have on their victims.	26	All institutions	Cognitions	Health Services Unit Team
Wellness Recovery Action Plan The Wellness Recovery Action Plan (WRAP) is a recovery-oriented, evidence-based practice that teaches individuals with a serious mental illness to maintain their recovery through wellness activities and to identify desired treatment and supports prior to crises. It consists of 8 sessions of 2.5 hours each.	20	All institutions	Mental Health	Psychology
Women in the 21st Century Workplace This program addresses workforce and soft skills of women with longer sentences. It is based on a Department of Labor program and adapted for use with incarcerated women. The program identifies women's roles in the modern workforce and assists participants in understanding important job-related skills.	10	All female sites	Education Work	Contractors Education FPI Social Worker Special Population Program Coordinator Volunteers

460

Women's Aging: Aging Well The Aging Well Program is for incarcerated women ages 45 and up. Its goal is to help women learn valuable information on aging, learn helpful strategies for change, and access the support of positive peers. The program helps women age well in the areas of meaning and purpose, physical health, mental and emotional well-being, healthy relationships, and planning for the future.	10	All female sites	Medical Recreation/Leisure/Fitness	Social Worker Special Population Program Coordinator Volunteers
Women's Relationships This cognitive behavioral therapy group assists women in identifying and developing healthy, prosocial relationships with friends, family, and acquaintances.	5	All female sites	Antisocial Peers Cognitions Family/Parenting	Contractors Education Social Worker Special Population Program Coordinator Volunteers
Women's Relationships II This is a trauma-informed and gender-responsive program for women. It focuses on relationships and communications, setting healthy boundaries, relationship with self, relationships in prison, relationships outside of prison, and relationships in transition.	10	All female sites	Cognitions Trauma	Social Worker Special Population Program Coordinator

461

BOP Institution Index

Alabama
FCI Aliceville   FPC Montgomery   FCI Talladega

Arizona
FCI Phoenix   FCI Safford   FCC Tucson

Arkansas
FCC Forrest City

California
USP Atwater   MDC Los Angeles   FCI Herlong   FCC Lompoc
FCI Mendota   MCC San Diego   FCI Terminal Island FCC Victorville   FCI Dublin

Colorado
FCI Englewood   FCC Florence

Connecticut
FCI Danbury

Florida
FCC Coleman   FCI Marianna   FCI Miami   FDC Miami   FPC Pensacola
FCI Tallahassee

Georgia
USP Atlanta   FCI Jesup

Hawaii
FDC Honolulu

Illinois
MCC Chicago   FCI Greenville   USP Marion   FCI Pekin   USP Thomson

Indiana
FCC Terre Haute

Kansas
USP Leavenworth

Kentucky
FCI Ashland   USP Big Sandy   FCI Manchester   USP McCreary   FMC Lexington

Louisiana
FCC Oakdale   FCC Pollock

Maryland
FCI Cumberland

Massachusetts
FMC Devens

Michigan
FCI Milan

Minnesota
FPC Duluth   FMC Rochester   FCI Sandstone   FCI Waseca

Mississippi
FCC Yazoo City

Missouri
MCFP Springfield

New Hampshire
FCI Berlin

New Jersey
FCI Fairton   FCI Fort Dix

New York
MDC Brooklyn   MCC New York   FCI Otisville   FCI Ray Brook

North Carolina
FCC Butner

Ohio
FCI Elkton

Oklahoma
FCI El Reno   FTC Oklahoma City

Oregon
FCI Sheridan

Pennsylvania
FCC Allenwood   USP Canaan   USP Lewisburg   FCI Loreto   FCI McKean   FCI Schuylkill
FDC Philadelphia

Puerto Rico
MDC Guaynabo

South Carolina
FCI Bennettsville   FCI Edgefield   FCI Estill   FCI Williamsburg

South Dakota
FPC Yankton

Tennessee
FCI Memphis

Texas
FCI Bastrop   FCC Beaumont   FCI Big Spring   FPC Bryan   FMC Carswell
FMC Fort Worth FDC Houston   FCI La Tuna   FCI Seagoville FCI Texarkana
FCI Three Rivers

Virginia
USP Lee   FCC Petersburg

Washington
FDC Sea Tac

West Virginia
FPC Alderson   FCI Beckley   FCI Gilmer   FCC Hazelton FCI McDowell   FCI Morgantown

Wisconsin
FCI Oxford

Specific information for each location can be found: https://www.bop.gov/locations/list.jsp

463

RESIDENTIAL DRUG ABUSE PROGRAMS (RDAP) AND LOCATIONS

NORTHEAST REGION
FCI Allenwood – L (PA)
FCI Allenwood – M (PA)
USP Canaan (PA)
FCI Danbury (CT)
FCI Elkton (OH)
FCI Fairton (NJ)
FCI Fort Dix 1 (NJ)
FCI Fort Dix 2 (NJ)
SCP Lewisburg (PA)
SCP McKean (PA)
FCI Schuylkill (PA)

MID-ATLANTIC REGION
FPC Alderson 1 (WV) ✳
FPC Alderson 2 (WV) ✳
FCI Beckley (WV)
USP Big Sandy (KY)
FCI-I Butner (NC)
FCI-II Butner (NC)
FCI Cumberland (MD)
SCP Cumberland (MD)
FMC Lexington 1 (KY)
FMC Lexington 2 (KY) ★
FCI Memphis (TN)
FCI Morgantown 1 (WV)
FCI Morgantown 2 (WV)
FCI Petersburg – L (VA)
FCI Petersburg – M (VA)

SOUTHEAST REGION
FCI Coleman – L (FL)
USP-II Coleman (FL)
SCP Edgefield (SC)
FSL Jesup (GA)
FCI Marianna (FL)
FCI Miami 1 (FL) Ś
FCI Miami 2 (FL) Ś
SCP Miami (FL)
FPC Montgomery 1 (AL)
FPC Montgomery 2 (AL)
FPC Pensacola (FL)
FCI Tallahassee (FL) ✳
FCI Yazoo City – L (MS)

NORTH CENTRAL REGION
FPC Duluth (MN)
FCI Englewood (CO)
FCI Florence (CO)
SCP Florence (CO)
SCP Greenville (IL) ✳
USP Leavenworth (KS)
SCP Leavenworth (KS)
USP Marion (IL)
FCI Milan (MI)
FCI Oxford (WI)
FCI Sandstone (MN)
MCFP Springfield (MO) ★
FCI Terre Haute (IN)
FCI Waseca (MN) ✳
FPC Yankton 1 (SD)
FPC Yankton 2 (SD)

SOUTH CENTRAL REGION
FCI Bastrop (TX)
FCI Beaumont – L (TX)
FCI Beaumont – M (TX)
SCP Beaumont (TX)
USP Beaumont (TX)
FPC Bryan (TX) ✳
FMC Carswell 1 (TX) ✳ ★
FMC Carswell 2 (TX) ✳ Ś
FCI El Reno (OK)
FCI Forrest City – L (AR)
FCI Forrest City – M (AR)
FMC Fort Worth (TX)
FCI La Tuna (TX)
FCI Seagoville 1 (TX)
FCI Seagoville 2 (TX)
SCP Texarkana (TX)

WESTERN REGION
FCI Dublin 1 (CA) ✳
FCI Dublin 2 (CA) ✳
FCI Herlong (CA)
FCI Lompoc (CA)
FCI Phoenix (AZ)
SCP Phoenix (AZ) ✳
FCI Safford (AZ)
FCI Sheridan (OR)
SCP Sheridan 1 (OR)
SCP Sheridan 2 (OR)
FCI Terminal Island 1 (CA)
FCI Terminal Island 2 (CA) ★

KEY
FCI = Federal Correctional
Institution
FMC = Federal Medical Center
FPC = Federal Prison Camp
FSL = Federal Satellite Low
MCFP = Medical Center for
Federal Prisoners
SCP = Satellite Camp Prison
SFF = Secure Female Facility
USP = U.S. Penitentiary

✳ Female Facility
★ Co-occurring Disorder
Program
Ś Spanish Program

83 RDAPs at 71 Locations

RDAPs in Red are at the same facility

RDAP Location List Updated: 3/30/2021

464

This is a copy of all my certificates of completion of all the programs I completed while being incarcerated a F.C.I. Raybrook. Some of these programs I completed are programs that are in the Approved Program Guide list that I am not receiving my earned days' time credit towards my prerelease custody.

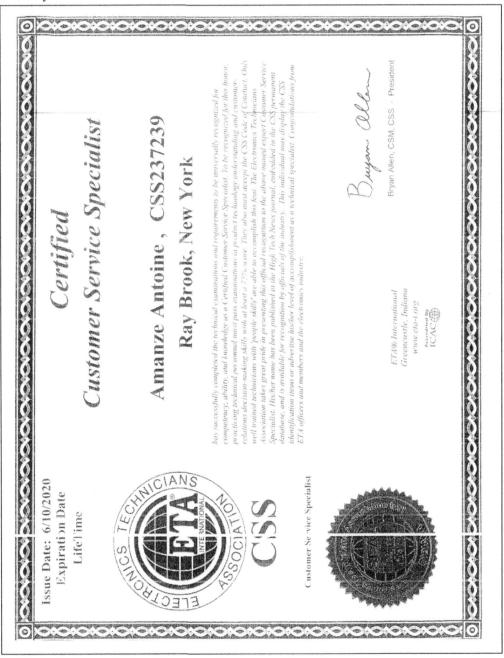

Certificate of Completion

Awarded to

Amanze Antoine

For successfully completing the

Non-Residential Drug Abuse Program

at FCI Ray Brook on November 27, 2019

D. Godfrey

FCI Ray Brook
Psychology Department

Presents this certificate of completion to:

Amanze Antoine

For the Successful Completion of the
Drug Abuse Education Course

The Drug Education Course is a minimum of 12 hours.

Presented February 2020

D. Godfrey – Drug Abuse
Treatment Specialist

467

ACT® WorkKeys® NCRC®

ACT certifies that

AMANZE ANTOINE

has earned the ACT WorkKeys National Career Readiness Certificate™ at the   level.

Registered Certificate # JT5979D7V27M
Issue Date: 6/5/20

468

Certificate of Completion

This Certificate hereby acknowledges

A. Antoine

For successfully completing the

National Parenting Program Phase 1 Course,

Demonstrating an ongoing commitment to personal

Growth and development through continuing education.

Awarded on this 2nd day of November, 2020

J. Rockhill, A.C.E. Coordinator

Certificate of Completion

This Certificate hereby acknowledges

A. Antoine

For successfully completing the

First Step Act Money Smart Course,

Demonstrating an ongoing commitment to personal

Growth and development through continuing education.

Awarded on this 7th day of December, 2020

J. Rockhill, A.C.E. Coordinator

470

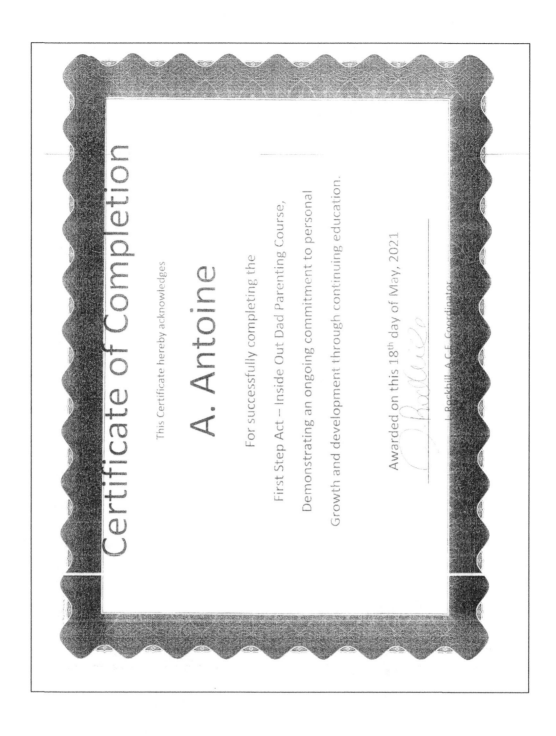

Certificate of Completion

This Certificate hereby acknowledges

A. Antoine

For successfully completing the

First Step Act – Inside Out Dad Parenting Course,

Demonstrating an ongoing commitment to personal

Growth and development through continuing education.

Awarded on this 18th day of May, 2021

L Rockhill A.C.E. Coordinator

Associate

Certified Electronics Technician

Amanze Antoine , AST247262

Ray Brook, New York

has successfully completed the technical examination and requirements to be adequately recognized to competency, ability, and knowledge as an Associate Certified Electronics Technician. To be recognized on the Senior, practicing technician with less than two (2) years of field work and electronics industry must pass examinations in 1X or more subcategories of basic electronics technology with 1+ Network. This well-earned and skilled crew-level technician provides a accomplished this test. The Electronics Technicians Association takes great pride in presenting this official recognition to the individual named electronics technician. His or name has been published in the High Tech News journal, entered into the ETI permanent database and knowledge for recognition by officials of the industry. The holder here may display this Associate CET to identification to meet advertise his/her level of accomplishment as a technician.

Certified Electronics Technician

ETA International
Greencastle, Indiana
www.eta-i.org

Issue Date: 4/22/2021
Expiration Date
April 22
2025

Bryan Allen CSM, CSS - President

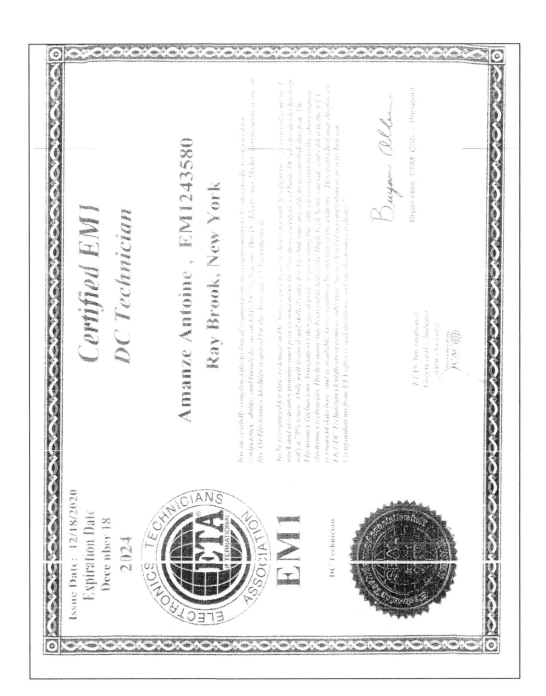

Certified EM1
DC Technician

Amanze Antoine , EM1243580
Ray Brook, New York

Issue Date : 12/18/2020
Expiration Date
December 18
2024

EM1

DC Technician

Bryan Allen CSTA CSS - President

473

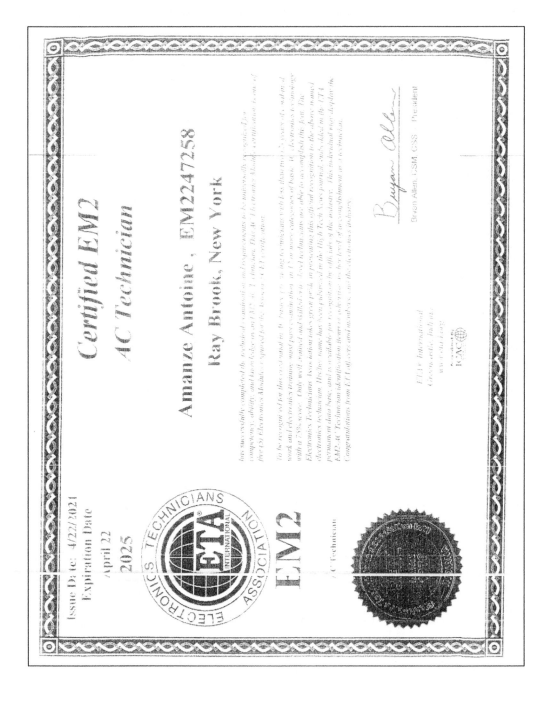

Certified EM2
AC Technician

Amanze Antoine , EM2247258
Ray Brook, New York

Issue Date: 4/22/2021
Expiration Date
April 22
2025

has successfully completed the technical, vocational, and requirements to be successfully recognized for competency, ability, and knowledge on an EM2 as a Technician, Basic Electronics Already a certification is one of five (5) Electronics Modules organized by Issue a of Certification.

To be recognized as this certificate as to be given (5) rating for technicians with levels than two (2) years development of work and electronics training, must pass examination then on two or more categories of these. All electronics technology with a 75% score. Only well-trained and skilled on level technicians are able to accomplish this feat. The Electronics Technicians Association takes great pride in presenting this official recognition to the above named electronics technician. His/her name has been endorsed in the High Tech News journal, included in the ETA premium data base, and is available for prospective employers at a level of accomplishment as a technician. EM2 AC Technician identification demonstrates the technician's ability, and knowledge, as well display on the Congratulations from ETA officers and members, on the electronics industry.

Bryan Allen
Bryan Allen, CSM, CSS   President

ETA International
Greencastle, Indiana
www.eta-i.org

Issue Date: 4/22/2021
Expiration Date
April 22
2025

Certified EM4
Digital Technician

Amanze Antoine , EM4247260

Ray Brook, New York

has successfully completed the technical examination and requirements to demonstrate his expertise, competence, ability and knowledge needed as an EM4 Digital Technician. This Digital Electronics Module certification is one of five ETA Electronics Modules required by the Associate CET certification.

To be recognized for this accomplishment in Digital Electronics, one had to demonstrate with test that two (2) years of combined work and electronic training must pass a minimum of 60 or more categories of a test Digital electronics technology with a 75 score. Only well-trained and skilled technicians are able to accomplish this test. The Electronics Technicians association takes great pride in presenting this official recognition to the above named electronics technician. His/her name has been published in the High Tech News journal, embedded in the ETA permanent data base, and is available, for recognition by officials of the industry. This individual may display the EM4 Digital Technician certification to its memberships or advertise his/her level of accomplishment as a technician. Congratulations to ETA officers and members, and he/she deserves industry.

Bryan Allen CSM CSS   President

ETA International
Greencastle, Indiana
www.eta-i.org
Accredited by
ICAC

ELECTRONICS TECHNICIANS ASSOCIATION
ETA INTERNATIONAL

EM4

Digital Technician

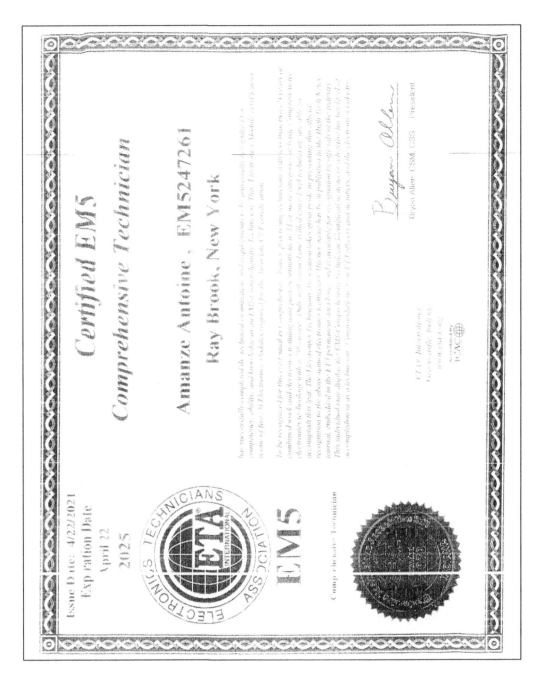

Issue Date: 4/22/2021
Expiration Date
April 22
2025

Certified EM5
Comprehensive Technician

Amanze Antoine , EM524261
Ray Brook, New York

has successfully completed the technical examination and requirements to successfully demonstrate competency, ability, and knowledge as an EM comprehensive Technician. This Technician should workbench on or all four of Electronic Modules requirements for the Associate CET Certification.

In being recognized for this credential as comprehensive Technician and as having technicians skills of over 3 years of comprehensive work and electronic technology and knowledge as a contribution to ECs in mid category in basic comprehensive electronic technology with over 98 score. This well demonstrates is required as a technician are able to accomplish this test. The Electronics Technician and is having technicians that specification is to workbench are able to recognition to the above named electronics technicians. His/her name has been published in the official help & Arts journal, concluded in the CET permanent archives and is available for examination by an application by officials of the industry. This individual may display his EM5 Comprehensive technician identification with honor and by acceptance as level of accomplishment in its field name. Congratulations to our CET officers and members and its achievement in its level.

ETA International
Greenville, Indiana
www.eta-i.org

Accredited by
ICAC

Bryan Allen
Bryan Allen CSM, CSS   President

EM5

Comp eheusive Technician

Certificate of Achievement

COMPLETION OF THE TRAUMA & RESILIENCY

WORKSHOP

awarded to

Antoine

#85472-054

A. Maxwell, PsyD
Staff Psychologist FCI Ray Brook

11/21/21
Date:

Certificate of Completion

This Certificate hereby acknowledges

A. Antoine

For successfully completing the

Self-Study "Crime and Punishment" Course,

Demonstrating an ongoing commitment to personal

Growth and development through continuing education.

Awarded on this 13th day of April, 2021

J. Rockhill, A.C.E. Coordinator

479

Certificate of Completion

This Certificate hereby acknowledges

A. Antoine

For successfully completing the

Self-Study "The Great Gatsby" Course,

Demonstrating an ongoing commitment to personal

Growth and development through continuing education.

Awarded on this 13th day of April, 2021

J. Rockhill, A.C.E. Coordinator

Certificate of Completion

This Certificate hereby acknowledges

A. Antoine

For successfully completing the

Self-Study "The Canterbury Tales" Course,

Demonstrating an ongoing commitment to personal

Growth and development through continuing education.

Awarded on this 13th day of April, 2021

J. Rockhill, A.C.E. Coordinator

Certificate of Achievement

COMPLETION OF 4 HOUR BIMONTHLY
SUICIDE COMPANION TRANING

awarded to

Amanze Antoine

A. Meinald Psy.D   9/10/2020

Staff Psychologist FCI Ray Brook   Date

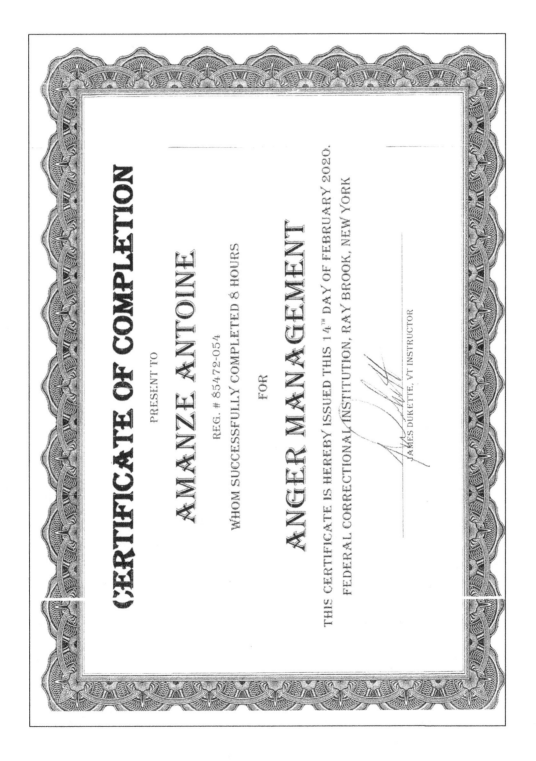

CERTIFICATE OF COMPLETION

PRESENT TO

AMANZE ANTOINE

REG. # 85472-054

WHOM SUCCESSFULLY COMPLETED 8 HOURS

FOR

ANGER MANAGEMENT

THIS CERTIFICATE IS HEREBY ISSUED THIS 14TH DAY OF FEBRUARY 2020.

FEDERAL CORRECTIONAL INSTITUTION, RAY BROOK, NEW YORK

JAMES DUKETTE, VT INSTRUCTOR

FEDERAL CORRECTIONAL INSTITUTION RAY BROOK, NEW YORK

CERTIFICATE OF COMPLETION

This certificate is awarded to

AMANZE ANTOINE

INITIAL SUICIDE WATCH COMPANION TRAINING

This certificate is hereby issued this 17TH day of January, 2020

Certificate of Completion

This certificate hereby acknowledges

Antoine Amanze

For Completing Part One of Five (12 of 60 hours)

The Great Courses: Science & Mathematics

Awarded on this day of October 1, 2019.

Ms. Rockhill, Adult Continuing Education Coordinator

Certificate of Completion

This certificate hereby acknowledges

Amanze Antoine

For successfully completing the
Resource Fair Course,

Demonstrating an ongoing commitment to personal
Growth and development through continuing education.

Awarded on this 14th day of November, 2019

J. Rockhill, A.C.E. Coordinator

486

FCI Ray Brook Recreation Department

Presents this certificate of completion to:

Amanze Antoine

For the Successful completion of the following First Step Act class: Getting To Know Your Healthy Aging Body

Presented March 29, 2021

B. Ojida – Sports Specialist

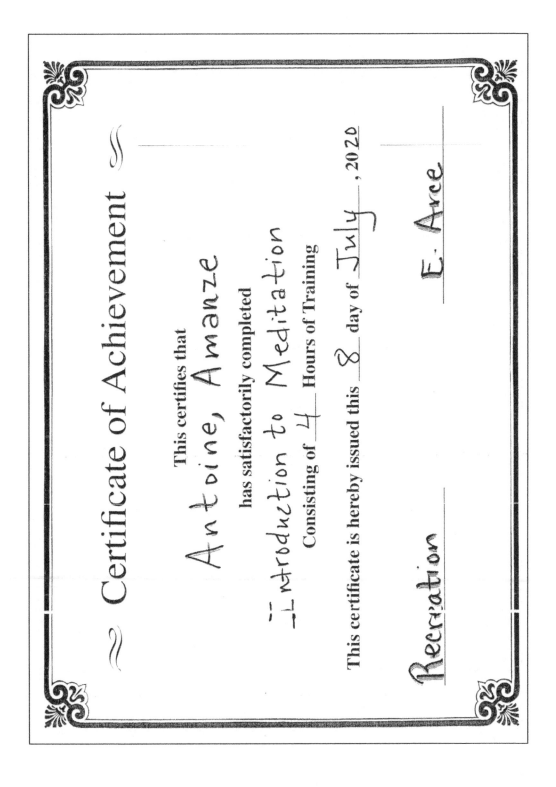

≈ Certificate of Achievement ≋

This certifies that

Antoine, Amanze

has satisfactorily completed

Introduction to Meditation

Consisting of 4 **Hours of Training**

This certificate is hereby issued this 8 **day of** July **, 2020**

E. Aree

Recreation

Certificate of Completion

This Certificate hereby acknowledges

A. Antoine

For successfully completing the

Self-Study "Diary of Anne Frank" Course,

Demonstrating an ongoing commitment to personal

Growth and development through continuing education.

Awarded on this 30th day of March, 2021

J. Rockhill, A.C.E. Coordinator

Certificate of Completion

This Certificate hereby acknowledges

A. Antoine

For successfully completing the

Self-Study WWI History Course,

Demonstrating an ongoing commitment to personal

Growth and development through continuing education.

Awarded on this 7th day of December, 2020

J. Rockhill, A.C.E. Coordinator

Certificate of Completion

This Certificate hereby acknowledges

A. Antoine

For successfully completing the

Self-Study Early American History Part 1 Course,

Demonstrating an ongoing commitment to personal

Growth and development through continuing education.

Awarded on this 7th day of December, 2020

J. Rockhill, A.C.E. Coordinator

491

Certificate of Completion

This Certificate hereby acknowledges

A. Antoine

For successfully completing the

Self-Study Early American History Part 2 Course,

Demonstrating an ongoing commitment to personal

Growth and development through continuing education.

Awarded on this 7th day of December, 2020

J. Rockhill, A.C.E. Coordinator

492

Certificate of Completion

This Certificate hereby acknowledges

A. Antoine

For successfully completing the

Self-Study WWII History Course,

Demonstrating an ongoing commitment to personal

Growth and development through continuing education.

Awarded on this 7th day of December, 2020

J. Rockhill, A.C.E. Coordinator

Certificate of Completion

This Certificate hereby acknowledges

A. Antoine

For successfully completing the

Self-Study African American History Course,

Demonstrating an ongoing commitment to personal

Growth and development through continuing education.

Awarded on this 7th day of December, 2020

J. Rockhill, A.C.E. Coordinator

Certificate of Completion

This Certificate hereby acknowledges

A. Antoine

For successfully completing the

Self-Study Famous Athletes History Course,

Demonstrating an ongoing commitment to personal

Growth and development through continuing education.

Awarded on this 23rd day of December, 2020

J. Rockhill, A.C.E. Coordinator

Certificate of Completion

This Certificate hereby acknowledges

A. Antoine

For successfully completing the

Self-Study Your Space Address Science Course,

Demonstrating an ongoing commitment to personal

Growth and development through continuing education.

Awarded on this 23rd day of December, 2020

J. Rockhill, A.C.E. Coordinator

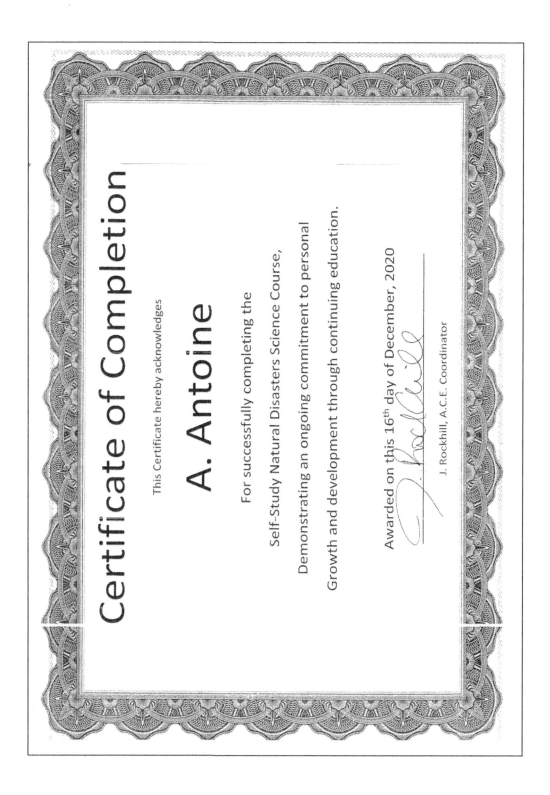

Certificate of Completion

This Certificate hereby acknowledges

A. Antoine

For successfully completing the

Self-Study Natural Disasters Science Course,

Demonstrating an ongoing commitment to personal

Growth and development through continuing education.

Awarded on this 16th day of December, 2020

J. Rockhill, A.C.E. Coordinator

Certificate of Completion

This Certificate hereby acknowledges

A. Antoine

For successfully completing the

Self-Study Continental Drift Science Course,

Demonstrating an ongoing commitment to personal

Growth and development through continuing education.

Awarded on this 16th day of December, 2020

J. Rockhill, A.C.E. Coordinator

Certificate of Completion

This Certificate hereby acknowledges

A. Amanze

For successfully completing the

Self-Study "Native Sun" Course,

Demonstrating an ongoing commitment to personal

Growth and development through continuing education.

Awarded on this 17th day of April, 2020

J. Rockhill, A.C.E. Coordinator

Certificate of Completion

This Certificate hereby acknowledges

A. Antoine

For successfully completing the

Self-Study "Catcher in the Rye" Course,

Demonstrating an ongoing commitment to personal

Growth and development through continuing education.

Awarded on this 8th day of February, 2021

J. Rockhill, A.C.E. Coordinator

Certificate of Completion

This Certificate hereby acknowledges

A. Antoine

For successfully completing the

Self-Study "To Kill A Mockingbird" Course,

Demonstrating an ongoing commitment to personal

Growth and development through continuing education.

Awarded on this 18th day of March, 2021

J. Rockhill, A.C.E. Coordinator .

Certificate of Completion

This Certificate hereby acknowledges

A. Antoine

For successfully completing the

Self-Study "Great Expectations" Course,

Demonstrating an ongoing commitment to personal

Growth and development through continuing education.

Awarded on this 18th day of March, 2021

J. Rockhill, A.C.E. Coordinator

Certificate of Completion

This Certificate hereby acknowledges

A. Antoine

For successfully completing the

Self-Study Solar System Science Course,

Demonstrating an ongoing commitment to personal

Growth and development through continuing education.

Awarded on this 18th day of March, 2021

J. Rockhill, A.C.E. Coordinator

Certificate of Completion

This Certificate hereby acknowledges

A. Antoine

For successfully completing the

Self-Study Ancient Egypt History Course,

Demonstrating an ongoing commitment to personal

Growth and development through continuing education.

Awarded on this 18th day of March, 2021

J. Rockhill, A.C.E. Coordinator

Certificate of Completion

This Certificate hereby acknowledges

A. Antoine

For successfully completing the

Self-Study Ancient Roman History Course,

Demonstrating an ongoing commitment to personal

Growth and development through continuing education.

Awarded on this 11th day of March, 2021

J. Rockhill

J. Rockhill, A.C.E. Coordinator

Issue Date: 4/22/2021
Expiration Date
April 22
2025

ELECTRONICS TECHNICIANS ASSOCIATION
ETA INTERNATIONAL

EM4

Digital Technician

Certified EM4
Digital Technician

Amanze Antoine , EM4247260
Ray Brook, New York

has successfully completed the technical examination and requirements to be universally recog_ized for competency, ability, and knowledge as an EM4-Digital Technician. This Digital Electronics M dule certification is one of five (5) Electronics Modules required for the Associate CET certification.

To be recognized for this credential in Digital basics, practicing technicians with less than two 2) years of combined work and electronics training must pass examinations in 6 or more categories of basi_ Digital electronics technology with a 75% score. Only well-trained and skilled entry-level technicians _re able to accomplish this feat. The Electronics Technicians Association takes great pride in presenting th s official recognition to the above-named electronics technician. His/her name has been published in the High Tech News journal, embedded in the ETA permanent data base, and is available for recognition by official of the industry. This individual may display the EM4-Digital Technician identification items or advertise his/he · level of accomplishment as a technician. Congratulations from ETA officers and members, and the elec ronics industry.

Bryan Allen, CSM, CS3 - President

ETA® International
Greencastle, Indiana
www.eta-i.org
Accredited By
ICAC

8iL

506

ABOUT THE AUTHOR

Amanze Antoine was born on December 17, 1980 in Mount Vernon New York. He is a first-time book writer and was inspired to write this book based on his own personal experience on how unfair the criminal court system is and based on how unfair he seen the criminal Court system treat so many others. Mr. Antoine has been through the criminal court system many times starting at the tender age of 16. However, that does not define the person Amanze has become today. All the bumps in the road he has endured throughout his entire life helped developed him into the great person he is today. His growth and development continue daily. Amanze knows that will not stop until he stops breathing. He has a huge heart and loves to give. He has no kids but loves kids (not the rude ones though) and plans on doing so much for children worldwide before his time is up on this earth!! Along with making sure the people he loves needs nor want for nothing in life ever again, the ones who deserve that!! Amanze is going to do so much to change the world. Just watch and see!!!!

GLORY TO UKRAINE

Do a good deed today and donate to Direct Relief (directrelief.org) to help the Ukraine people during the hard times they are going through!!!!! Direct Relief is working directly with Ukraine's Ministry of Health and other on -the-ground partners. Direct Relief is providing field medics with hundreds of emergency medical backpacks as well as a wide range of urgently requested supplies such as oxygen concentrators, antibiotics, Combat Application Tourniquets, and critical-care medicines. Direct Relief has been supporting hospitals in Ukraine since before the invasion began and has shipped more than 26 million in medical aid to the country in the past six months. However more supplies are still needed for the Ukrainian people!!!!!!!!!!!!!!!!!!!!!!!!!!!!!!!!!!!! If you were in the Ukrainian people's shoes would you want all the help you can receive from anywhere it comes? I think we all answered yes to that question so do a good deed today and donate whatever you can afford to help the people of Ukraine. Even if it is only one dollar!!!! It is not the amount that you donate, it is the thought and your intentions that "MATTERS MOST".

Made in the USA
Monee, IL
25 September 2022

14662619R00286